Continuity and Change in Brazil and the Southern Cone/ Continuidade e mudanças no Brasil e no Cone Sul

SALALM Secretariat
General Library
University of New Mexico

Continuity and Change in Brazil and the Southern Cone: Research Trends and Library Collections for the Year 2000

Continuidade e mudanças no Brasil e no Cone Sul: tendências de pesquisa e acervos bibliográficos para o ano 2000

Papers of the Thirty-Fifth Annual Meeting of the
SEMINAR ON THE ACQUISITION OF
LATIN AMERICAN LIBRARY MATERIALS

Fundação Getúlio Vargas, Rio de Janeiro
and The Library of Congress Office, Rio de Janeiro

Hotel Meridien Copacabana
Rio de Janeiro, Brazil

June 3-8, 1990

Ann Hartness
Editor

SALALM Secretariat
General Library, University of New Mexico

ISBN: 0-917617-30-4

Printed in the United States of America

Contents

Actualizaciones en bibliotecología en el Cono Sur

Coleções especiais brasileiras

Brazilian Non-Book Materials

Periodicals in the Southern Cone and Brazil

Preface

The location of the thirty-fifth annual meeting of SALALM—Rio de Janeiro, Brazil—suggested the theme for the program. It provided the opportunity not only to examine the changes taking place in that dynamic and beautiful country in the late twentieth century, and the traditions underlying them, but also to examine similar and divergent trends in its Southern Cone neighbors, Uruguay, Argentina, Chile, and Paraguay. Social, economic, political, and cultural trends and manifestations of change, and their implications for libraries responsible for collecting research materials from the region, were the focus of the meeting, as were recent developments in publishing, bookselling, libraries, and information technology.

Perhaps most importantly, it afforded a unique opportunity for many librarians, scholars, publishers, booksellers, and bibliophiles from those countries to join their colleagues from other places in discussing those trends in the thirteen substantive sessions of the meeting, and in the many informal occasions that marked the conference.

English, Portuguese, and Spanish were the official languages of the meeting, and simultaneous translation was provided at the sessions. Each paper is published here in the language in which it was written and presented. The title of each panel and round table is in the language chosen by its coordinator.

The papers published in this volume reflect the substance of the program but do not represent it in its entirety. Notes, rather than formal papers, were the basis of some theme panel presentations, and a discussion format characterized some of the round tables. The "Program of Substantive Panels, Round Tables and Field Trips" at the end of this volume lists all the sessions and their participants. Summaries of most presentations were published in the *SALALM Newsletter* (vol. 18, no. 5 [May 1991]), and cassette recordings of the sessions are available at the SALALM archive at the Benson Latin American Collection, The University of Texas at Austin.

Ann Hartness

Acknowledgments

We owe thanks and warm appreciation to the two institutions in Rio de Janeiro co-sponsoring SALALM XXXV: The Fundação Getúlio Vargas and The Library of Congress Office, and to their representatives and the other individuals who served so ably on the Local Arrangements Committee:

CHAIRPERSON: Lucy Rocha Souza, The Library of Congress Office
Lygia Ballantyne, The Library of Congress, Washington, DC
Esther Bertoletti, Biblioteca Nacional
Vera de Araújo, Susan Bach, Ltda.
Eugênio Decourt, Fundação Getúlio Vargas
Ann Hartness, The Library of Congress Office and The University of Texas at Austin
Carmen Meurer Muricy, The Library of Congress Office
Smith Richardson, The Library of Congress Office

Special thanks are also due IBM do Brasil, Metal Leve, and Susan Bach, Ltda. for their generous financial support. Their gifts were a major contribution to the international character of the meeting, through travel support for participants from several South American countries, and through underwriting simultaneous translation of the proceedings.

Carmen Meurer Muricy and Eugênio Decourt helped the editor of these proceedings to identify some acronyms and to complete some elusive bibliographic citations. Their gracious assistance is very much appreciated.

Opening Session

1. Keynote Address

José Mindlin

It is very gratifying that a meeting as important as this one should take place in Brazil. As a Brazilian, I feel proud about it, and it is with deep pleasure that I extend to all the foreign visitors a most cordial welcome, a welcome that of course includes all participants. To me personally, it is also very gratifying that I was invited to be the keynote speaker at this opening meeting, and I want to thank SALALM for this great distinction, which I duly appreciate.

Although it really is a great distinction, it also creates a problem, for it is not easy to determine what to say to such a diverse audience. I can see here, if you will pardon my irreverence, a very mixed fauna—librarians, booksellers, book lovers, scholars, collectors, and, I would imagine, participants who came out of pure curiosity. It is very mixed indeed, but we are all united by one common link—the book, the love for books, the interest in books. This in itself makes very strong ties. There is actually another strong link: Latin America, which brings up, or may bring up, an interesting discussion. Nobody can question the existence of books as such, but the existence of Latin America as an entity has been the object of many doubts and wonderings. You need not worry about the possible danger of my delving deeply into what could end up becoming a very polemical issue. I just wanted to mention that the doubt about Latin American unity exists, and, therefore, that we should explore this fluid and somewhat mysterious entity which, for lack of a more precise definition, came to be called Latin America.

Historically, we have not formed a unit. At most, we can divide the vast area with which we are dealing into two great categories: Spanish America and Portuguese America. But even this would certainly not be correct, because other cultures existed on this continent before the arrival of the Spaniards and the Portuguese, and still exist today. So much so that as we approach the Columbus quincentennial, there is talk less of discovery and more of encounter. Actually, our countries only recently began seriously to try to know each other. For centuries we looked more to Europe than to any other place, and there was very little cultural communication among us. This has been changing during the last few decades, very fortunately indeed.

If we consider these two entities, the book and Latin America—assuming they are entities—we may be faced with some very curious situations, both probable and improbable, all depending on our own personal opinions. I refer to their existence and to what their future can be or will be. As far as books are concerned, I said already that there can be no doubt about their existence—they have been here for centuries—but it can be argued that new technologies may bring about the obsolescence of books. Let me say outright that I do not share this opinion. My firm belief is that books will continue to exist. But the rather dreadful possibility of their disappearance cannot be ignored. To fight it successfully, we must admit it. With Latin America, quite the contrary is happening: it did not exist as an entity for the first four centuries since the continent was discovered or encountered, but it is beginning to shape up, and once unity is reached, it will most probably be here for good.

All this being said, by way of exploring the territory with which we are dealing, I believe we can turn to the theme of this meeting, in which I would like to stress the importance of Latin American books, or books on Latin America. I realize that this is a vast subject, but again you need not worry: I will try to be brief.

The interest in Latin American studies is consistently growing, both in and outside of Latin America. History, literature, art, politics, social problems, anthropology, environment, economic development, geography, natural resources, fauna, flora, scientific and technological development, all this and probably much more are awakening the interest of more and more people; and what could be a better instrument for the acquisition and diffusion of the desired knowledge than books? Existing libraries are growing, and new libraries are being formed, which accounts for the presence of so many participants in this meeting. Obviously, for good libraries to be formed, the participation of all the interests represented here today is indispensable. Librarians, booksellers, book lovers, scholars, collectors, all must bring together their knowledge and their experiences, and SALALM seems to be an ideal forum. We all form a masonry of joint and intertwining interests—I hope you will allow me to consider myself part of this world—and not only a vast group of common interests but also a group where a great and very special solidarity prevails. Critical outsiders go as far as to say that book people form a Mafia. I would say there is envy in that view, and I certainly prefer the designation of masonry. The envy is understandable, because people who live outside the book world miss a pleasure the nature of which is unknown to them, but looking at us, they cannot fail to realize that it exists. Well, let us hope, for their own good, that they will join us someday.

Personally I have enjoyed this pleasure since my childhood, for I began to build my library at the age of thirteen, and books gradually became one of the central interests of my life. I strongly recommend it to anyone whose philosophical wanderings are directed to finding a purpose in life. This requires some clarification. Books are obviously essential for any studies, so that what we explore in this meeting about Latin American studies can be applied universally. But books can and should be much more than an object of study, or an instrument of knowledge. They can afford intellectual, artistic, and physical pleasure. Besides the contents, and in some cases regardless of the contents, they can be meaningful for their typography, layout, illustrations, binding, and last but not least, rarity. Because rare books form a very special category, a very respectable, and, I might as well confess, a very attractive field of interest, I believe it deserves a special mention in this meeting. The book in Brazil is a latecomer, for printing began only in 1808, but in Spanish America it has existed since the sixteenth century, and there is no end to the search for rare books, which I assume is part of the interests of SALALM. The mention of rare books should only be, however, a brief one, because they can be a touchy matter when librarians and collectors get together. There is obviously a potential conflict of interests. . . .

You may be wondering why nothing was said until now about our theme "Continuity and Change in Brazil and the Southern Cone: Research Trends and Library Collections for the Year 2000." The reason is very simple: once my speech is delivered, that is exactly what you are going to talk about, and I did not deem it appropriate to anticipate your thoughts and opinions. Moreover, I hesitate to express a forecast of what the situation will be ten years from now. Personally, I believe research will be more and more intensive, and libraries will continue to grow for a few more years. There are, however, two important factors to be considered, possibly influencing the present trend of book accumulation. I refer to technological changes and the possibility of initiatives such as the revival of the Library of Alexandria, which would reduce the need to accumulate. When I talk of technological changes, I am thinking not only of the danger of obsolescence of the book, which I mentioned earlier, but also of the increasing ways of communication about books between libraries, which may spread knowledge without the physical presence of the books themselves. I am sorry that this may take some booksellers unhappy, but we cannot ignore this trend, namely, that in the future it will not be imperative that every library have all books, even if it were possible. I do not intend to discuss this subject, and wish only to point out that such a new phenomenon may have enormous multiplying effects and save much effort and cost to librarians and libraries. The same thing can make some people happy and others unhappy. . . . This trend will have, I daresay, more influence as far as Latin American materials are concerned, not only because of growing interest in the region but also because other areas are already better covered in North American and European libraries and archives. The number of new books is increasing. The availability of rare books is decreasing. Therefore it is very important, and to my mind beneficial, that the vast and largely unexplored holdings of Latin American materials in public and private libraries and archives of our countries should be accessible to foreign institutions and scholars through new technological devices.

I earnestly hope that this seminar will meet your expectations and that it will be fruitful and enjoyable as well.

Beyond Our Own Libraries: Standards, Trends, and Data Collection for Latin American Collections

2. National Trends in the Support of Latin American Studies

David Block

Support for area studies in general and Latin American studies in particular has reached a state of near crisis—AGAIN. A combination of foundation neglect and shrinking federal investments has forced universities to carry an increasing share of international studies costs at a time when these institutions are swamped with proposals for new programs and services, especially in the high tech areas. How did we get into this mess, and more important, how do we get out? Herein I offer a brief chronicle of the growth of area studies in the United States and a comment on the current crisis, and suggest what the future may hold.

Area studies, defined in the ethnocentric context of anything outside the United States and Western Europe, dates from the turn of the twentieth century when Harvard, Yale, and Columbia universities began systematic attempts to investigate Russia and the Far East. Shortly thereafter the University of California established itself as a center for Latin American scholarship, and in the 1920s the University of Chicago created its Oriental Institute for the study of the Middle East and South Asia. The 1930s saw further expansion in Latin America with the University of Texas's establishment of its Institute of Latin American Studies. World War II, however, found the country's expertise in areas that became theaters of the conflict, even Europe, woefully inadequate. There was a national shortage in language facility, cultural understanding, and holdings of basic source materials (maps are one area always cited) from much of the world. This realization led to the establishment of crash language programs and an attempt to bring to the United States printed materials deemed important in prosecuting the war effort. And even though these programs withered with the end of hostilities, they did not disappear. In the case of research libraries the realizations of the war created a climate, fueled by postwar prosperity, amenable to large-scale expansion.

The postwar period saw the first surveys of area studies in the country with reports by Robert Hall (1947) and Wendell C. Bennett (1951).[1] These studies fix the size of the enterprise at between fourteen and twenty-five programs with Latin America having the greatest representation followed by East Asia and Eastern Europe.

By the mid 1960s the number of area programs had grown to at least 300. These years of spectacular growth can be traced to two factors. The first was the entry of the Ford Foundation into the realm of area studies. Through its International Training and Research Program, Ford granted in excess of 270 million dollars to U.S. universities between 1953 and 1966. On a personal note, Cornell's Latin American Studies Program sprang from a Ford grant in 1961, an event replicated at many institutions. The second factor was the national reaction to a perceived knowledge gap between the United States and the Soviet Union in the late 1950s. The National Defense Education Act, passed less than a year after Sputnik's launch in 1957, was designed to meet the Soviet challenge through education. Though the lion's share of NDEA monies found their way into science and technology (so what else is new?), the law also defined programs to create a critical mass of experts in foreign area studies. The National Defense Foreign Languages (NDFL) and Foreign Language and Area Studies (FLAS) fellowship programs of this era provided many of us with the means for attending graduate school, and the acquisition of library materials was a priority in the NDEA effort.

It is important to point out the justification for this program: national security and a national insufficiency in key fields of knowledge. In the words of the bill, "the Congress hereby finds and declares that the security of the Nation requires the fullest development of the mental resources and technical skills of its young men and women."[2] These issues of national defense, very much a function of East-West tensions (and for Latin America difficulties with Cuba), and national needs have undergirded support for the NDEA and its successors for thirty years. As late as 1979 a President's commission on area studies would warn its readers that "nothing less is at issue than the nation's security. At a time when the resurgent forces of nationalism and of ethnic and linguistic consciousness so directly affect global realities, the United States requires far more reliable capacities to communicate with its allies, analyze the behavior of potential adversaries, and earn the trust and sympathies of the uncommitted."[3] This security posture created a rationale and a climate in Washington and among academic specialists that viewed area programs as unquestionably a part of the national interest and as essentially humanities and social sciences enterprises, views that have hampered responses to changing realities of policy.

The age of expansion ended in the early 1970s. Richard Nixon argued that while area expertise was very much in the national interest, national sufficiency had in fact been met. Nixon's arguments translated into action with the axing of 61 of the 107 federally designated area studies centers and the total abolition of teacher-training programs for elementary and secondary teachers in 1973. This change in federal spending coupled with the dramatically decreased availability of foundation support—Ford by this time had folded the rump of its area budget into the Social Science Research Council's fellowship programs— forced serious retrenchment at campuses across the United States and the beginning of serious readjustments in library acquisitions as well.

Only a brief flicker of enthusiasm for support of area studies during Jimmy Carter's presidency has interrupted a steady downward slide of federal support for area studies. This trend reached its nadir with Ronald Reagan's almost yearly proposals that Title VI of the Higher Education Act (the successor to the NDEA) be zero funded. I would contend that this threat to the remaining source of federal funds actually had a salutary effect in forcing the often divergent area studies community to work in concert and to force academics to organize a lobbying effort in the halls of Congress. As you know, Reagan's proposals for Title VI were ultimately defeated and we have a kinder, gentler President today.

As I speak to you, area studies finds itself largely confined to a university-based-and-supported locus. And in this setting, we are not doing well. First, area studies has lost out to the hardening of the social sciences and to the ascendancy of critical theory in literature. Undeservedly, area-focused scholars have taken a back seat to colleagues trained in abstract methodologies. And in times of retrenchment areas not on the cutting edge of a discipline are highly vulnerable. The dispersion of Latin Americanists across the university has also had serious consequences. In their infancy two models of organization for area studies presented themselves. The first, followed to a large degree by Asian studies, established separate departments alongside traditional disciplines. Latin America, like most other areas, took its place within existing structure, placing specialists in departments of history, literature, economics, and so on. This model was no doubt valuable for purposes of faculty development but ultimately destructive of political leverage. For now, with most universities in no more than stasis, area specialists consistently lose intradepartmental battles over replacement decisions as senior colleagues retire. Again, and I want to stress its importance, this tendency is one that afflicts not only Latin Americanists. But Latin Americanists have become increasing aware of their declining numbers on university faculties as they assess staffing needs for the coming decades, and here I would refer you to a very useful unpublished paper by Gilbert Merkx, "The National Need for Latin American and Caribbean Specialists," prepared for the National Council on Foreign Language and International Studies.

Large-scale federal support of area studies has not returned to universities despite a veritable ghost dance of writing designed to evoke it. Of the more than 26 billion dollars currently expended in education, writ large, the international component receives less than 0.01 percent, roughly 25 million dollars. Title VI centers now number in the eighties, but steady-state funding of the program near the 15 million dollar level has drastically reduced the impact of federal spending from its high watermark in 1970. Some scholars, including Merkx, continue to see federal dollars as the only escape from the current stagnation. However, as early as ten years ago, even Congressional supporters advised that Latin Americanists must look beyond the national government for support. In a curiously worded pronouncement, the chair of the House Subcommittee on International Operations warned that area studies "must rely less on the federal government for support while at the same time seeking more federal funds."[4] I interpret Dante Fascell's words as urging a more visible lobbying effort in Washington.

Current federal programs for area studies support have created an environment beset with contradictions and punctuated by intense competition. Potential allies are pitted against each other, dividing what might be an effective, unified voice. Postsecondary educators compete against representatives of elementary and secondary education; Title VI centers compete against all comers in the triennial predatory sweepstakes. In addition, the lack of a clear federal policy on international education and an absence of even a shared vision for potentially complementary programs in educational, diplomatic, and cultural aspects further diffuse our energies. The only substantive change in federal programs in the last decade has been the establishment of a Part B to Title VI, the Business and International Education Program with the rationale that "the future economic welfare of the United States will depend on increasing international skills in the business community and creating an awareness among the American public of the internationalization of our economy."[5] This change, despite its potential for adding money to the program, has caused misgivings in the area studies community. It is hard for core faculty in the humanities and social sciences to see how to effectively bend their efforts to take advantage of the current preoccupation with international competitiveness. But the darkest hour may have passed.

First, foundation support may be turning back toward area studies. The Luce Foundation—as in Henry Luce the publisher—has targeted Southeast Asia for grants totaling over 10 million dollars in the past two years alone. And both the Rockefeller and Mellon Foundations are asking for proposals from area studies centers. The best news I have heard from the foundation front is Mellon's decision to fund a joint Latin American center between Duke and the University of North Carolina. A grants coordinator has recently compared foundations to schooling fish. They all seem to be heading in one direction when for no discernible reason the whole school simultaneously changes course. I doubt that this anonymous administrator uses this analogy when he talks to foundation representatives, but let us hope that he is on to something and that the state of North Carolina's good fortune will signal a significant shift.

Signals from Washington are not as encouraging, but at least they are mixed. Title VI has apparently received a new lease on life. In fact, it has received its first significant increase in a decade, $10 million. However, these monies will be equally divided between Parts A and B, that is, between the traditional area studies component and the new international business one. The Library of Congress has proposed a program for expanding foreign area acquisitions. While a number of us have expressed reservations about the implications of this proposal, its potential for expanding the availability of research materials in the United States should not be lost on area librarians.

I do not believe these actions constitute a change in direction in federal programs. Some very attractive, dare I say innovative, proposals have been afoot in Washington. The most interesting, perhaps, is that designed by Rose Hayden, the creation of a National Defense Education Trust Fund.[6] This would be an independently chartered entity funded "off budget" by private donations and a 3 percent assessment from AID loans and foreign military sales—swords into plowshares if you will. But this proposal was made in 1983, and no one seems to be talking about it now. What is new in Washington is the higher profile of area studies advocates, grown no doubt out of desperation. Former adversaries have learned to cooperate in the struggle to save Title VI, and this augurs well for future action.

This new spirit of alliance has produced an organization with an ugly acronym all its own, CAFLIS, the Coalition for the Advancement of Foreign Language and International Studies. CAFLIS has picked up many of the proposals advanced over the past decade—postdoctoral research funding, international exchange of scholars, pilot programs for improved pedagogy, library development, and publications and other forms of dissemination of information in international education and research. All of this would be carried out through a counterpart of the National Endowment for the Humanities/National Endowment for the Arts (NEH/NEA), a National Endowment for International Education. In and of itself, CAFLIS represents only a new step in the ghost dance, a desire to bring Washington back into area studies. But as an organization supported by a broad coalition of area studies advocates, it may succeed in bringing its themes to a wider audience on the Hill.

So what *is* new? Well for starters, with the decrease in federal revenues, universities have become more forceful in working with their alumni, with private corporations, and with state legislatures. The *Chronicle of Higher Education* recently ran an article on state universities and their vigorous campaigns to curry private and alumni giving.[7] Ohio State University and the University of Michigan were mentioned as having been particularly successful in this regard. And I hear through the grapevine that a number of big city Latin American programs have been successful in attracting support from such major corporations as Shell Oil and Kaiser. Before we leave the theme of alumni involvement in area studies, I should point out that Cornell has begun to view area librarians as effective speakers for the university. The curator of our South East Asian collection recently completed a road show in the midwest, and I have been meeting with Brazilian and Venezuelan alumni trying to encourage them to make contributions in local currencies to defray book purchases in their countries.

The proceedings of the 1989 National Governors Conference specifically cite their support for programs with international emphases and promise to aid institutions of higher education develop programs to share expertise with school districts and the business community.[8] On the more tangible side, New York and California have grudgingly picked up some of the area studies slack left by the federal pullout. Even in this tight year, New York continues to provide foreign area fellowship support and a preservation program which area librarians at Cornell have used extensively.

Finally, and most exotically, there is the potential for using debt swaps for financing area studies. There is apparently a daunting amount of red tape, but as I understand the strategy, it is roughly this: find a bank willing to sell debt in small enough quantities for a program (or consortium) to afford it; receive license from the debtor nation to redeem the securities at their face value (or something near it) in domestic goods—everyone agrees that books would be a good candidate; cash the securities; buy the goods.

The year 1992 will find Latin American studies harking back to events of five hundred years before. And I think that Columbus's experience resonates through what I see as likely trends in area studies support for this decade. We will be chartered but not well supported by our governments; we must travel from capital to capital in search of funds; and we must try to hold together a crew with a variety of outlooks on the definitions and solutions to our problem. It looks like a long voyage.

NOTES

1. Robert B. Hall, *Area Studies: With Special Reference to Their Implications for Research in the Social Sciences* (New York, NY: Social Sciences Research Council, 1947); Wendell C. Bennett, *Area Studies in American Universities* (New York, NY: Social Sciences Research Council, 1951).

2. *The National Defense Education Act of 1958. A Summary and Analysis of the Act Prepared by the Staff of the Committee on Labor and Public Welfare United States Senate* (Washington, DC: Government Printing Officiate, 1958), p. 24.

3. *Strength through Wisdom: A Critique of U.S. Capability* (Washington, DC: GPO, 1979), p. 1.

4. *New Directions in Language and Area Studies Priorities for the 1980s* (Milwaukee, WI: CLASP, Center for Latin America, University of Wisconsin-Milwaukee, 1979), p. 119.

5. *Federal Support for International Education: Assessing the Options* (New York, NY: National Council on Foreign Languages and International Studies, 1985), p. 7.

6. Ibid.

7. "History Making Drive Expected to Raise 500-Million in Private Funds for Ohio State University Inspires Other Colleges," *Chronicle of Higher Education* 36, no. 17 (10 January 1990): A29-31.

8. *America in Transition, the International Frontier* (Washington, DC: National Governors Association, 1989), esp. p. 19.

3. The Development of Standards for Library Research Collections and SALALM's Task Force on Standards

Barbara J. Robinson

Definition and Types of Standards

Standards are often defined as authoritative models, measures, or patterns for guidance which when compared with other related things determine their quality and/or quantity. Library standards have been represented as approved goals, criteria, or minimal or ideal levels of excellence.

There are two commonly recognized types of standards: official or de jure and nonofficial or de facto standards. Adherence to either type of standard is voluntary and peer pressure is the only compliance mechanism.

De jure standards are exemplified by the numerous standards produced by the American Standards Institute (ASI) and the International Organization for Standardization. Thousands of standards have been approved internationally which impact libraries, particularly in technical areas, but which have little relevance to the development of library research collections.

De facto standards, the focus of this paper, include the familiar standards produced by the U.S. Library of Congress, the recommendations for libraries of the International Federation of Library Associations and Institutions (IFLA) and the United Nations Educational, Scientific and Cultural Organization (UNESCO), similar to standards, and those produced by the Association of Research Libraries, the Art Library Society of North America, the Association of College and Research Libraries, and various other national library associations.

Why Create Standards for Libraries?

Administrators and managers of libraries today demand greater accountability and justification for activities and services, both traditional and new ones. New technological capabilities and the use of automation in libraries, burgeoning collections and the resulting space crunch, diminishing budgets and erosion of buying power, and increasing costs of preservation and of everything else have influenced this demand for accountability.

Within academic communities librarians' roles generally are expanding to include new roles as managers, grant writers, fund raisers, instructors, and entrepreneurs. The subject specialist role in many fields has evolved from bibliographer, selector, and acquisitions librarian to the broader role of collection manager.

Overall the emphasis is shifting from collection building to services, access and sharing instead of ownership, usage of the collection and responsiveness to user demands. Concerns abound over the future of the research library and the traditional policy of collecting the universe of knowledge. Smaller more focused collections are recognized for their research quality.

These changes are forcing accommodation and responsiveness to even greater change ahead. Some of these changes can be anticipated and controlled but some cannot. These changes have led the library profession to tackle the issue of standards as one means of coming to grips with many of these issues.

Brief Background of Library Standards in the United States

A history of library standards has not been written. What exists are numerous articles and documents from the past thirty to forty years which describe the process of developing standards among libraries in the United States and other countries, and the various drafts, revisions, and approved standard documents published in library literature.

In the United States among the many de facto library standards are a few landmark efforts for college and research libraries. Additionally there are thousands of smaller standards that impact detailed operations of libraries and book publishing, but still a paucity of standards for library subject collections. None of them speaks specifically to the needs of area studies or Latin American research collections.

Existing library standards documents, developed collectively by library organizations and librarians, serve as instruments to evaluate progress and establish measures or goals for achieving excellence. These documents vary in content but are similar in intent, that is, their purpose is to evaluate designated libraries, or their collections and services, as educational instruments.

In the United States in 1959 the Association of College and Research Libraries (ACRL) developed and approved the first standards for American college libraries. The demonstrated effectiveness and success of these standards in improving college libraries motivated university libraries to begin work in 1967 on their standards. Twelve years and two major committees later (Downs and Smith committees), the Association of Research Libraries (ARL) with ACRL adopted the first university libraries standards document. It consists of a list of commonly agreed-upon principles with commentary. The approach differed from the college libraries standards and led to a firm rejection of quantitative measures.

Between 1986 and 1989 the University Library Standards were revised. The revision resulted in an outline of criteria, again without quantities, for library self-evaluation. These do not consist of comparative goals or measures as might be anticipated but a framework in which to measure each library against its own goals and expectations.

Soon after the approval of the first college and university library standards, library directors were surveyed. The surveys found that the majority of directors of university libraries were not as satisfied with their standards as the directors of college libraries who overwhelmingly found their standards to be very useful because of the specificity and inclusion of quantitative measures. Only time, or perhaps another survey, will demonstrate the usefulness of the 1989 revised university library standards.

Another landmark standard document, and one that might prove helpful to SALALM, is that of the Art Libraries Society of North America (ARLIS/NA). In 1983 this organization published its standards for staffing and collection development for art libraries, incorporating both quantitative and qualitative measures for various types and sizes of art collections, that is, small, medium, and large academic, museum, and public libraries.

The ARLIS/NA standards clearly and concisely combine qualitative commentary and correlations of ratios and quantitative measures for the various types of art collections allowing comparisons with similar types and sizes of collections. Quantitative criteria include the number of faculty supported, size of collection in volumes, the number of serial title subscriptions, annual growth rate in volumes, number of hours the collection is available to the public, circulation in volumes, and minimal levels of staffing and student assistance in full-time equivalents. A list of suggested staff positions and ranks is also included.

The major stumbling blocks in the struggle for standards of the past thirty years have been definitions and quantitative criteria. This apparent "squeamishness" over quantitative measures, as one writer puts it, has resulted in vague criteria and general principles rather than specific measures. For many librarians the resulting standards for university libraries are less useful for determining what is needed to achieve excellence, to justify budgets, and to upgrade collections, staffing levels, and services. On the other hand, ARLIS/NA standards do not sidestep these issues and, thus, I suggest they merit closer examination in the development of standards for area studies and subject collections of various sizes and for different types of institutions.

Several examples of standard documents for purposes of comparison are cited in the bibliography of this paper.

Why Use Both Statistics and Standards?

Statistics tell us what has been done, but standards (qualitative and quantitative) indicate what needs to be done. Statistics are measured by standards to determine if they are satisfactory or if there is need for improvement in certain areas. If so, standards reveal which areas and what is needed.

Statistics record quantities achieved, volumes of books and serials cataloged, the number of patrons served, monies allocated and spent on the collection, the number and levels of staff, the number of service transactions and information transfers. The list of what is or can be counted by libraries is extensive. Statistical data do not measure the quality of these activities nor the satisfaction of the library users. Standards, on the other hand, are designed as measurements or goals. They establish levels of excellence to work toward.

Statistics of our collections and activities should not be mistaken for standards, nor should we misuse standards to prove on the one hand how good our collection is to colleagues and how poor the collection is to administrators. Statistical data may assist in the process of determining realistic and achievable measures and goals but not necessarily the same for each type of library and collection. For this reason standards should recognize and relate to the various types and sizes of libraries or collections.

Trends Observed in Recent Standard Documents

New criteria in standard documents of recent years reflect the influence of new management theories and practices of the 1970s and 1980s. Elements in the recent standard documents not present in earlier ones, such as statements of purpose, planning and goal setting, description of the organization and management, criteria for staff training and development, are possible indications of the impact of the Association of Research Libraries, Office of Management Studies methodology on the library profession.

SALALM's Task Force on Standards

As President of SALALM in 1988-1989, I proposed the creation of the Task Force on Standards which began work on shaping the organization's response to some of the changes, trends, and challenges for Latin American research collections. The purpose of the new task force is to develop standards for Latin American research collections which will reach beyond the twentieth century. Participants represent various areas of specialization and diverse types and sizes of collections in the United States and Great Britain. The charge to the Task Force and the list of members are in Appendix A of this paper. Through collaboration and with input from the membership the task force hopes to develop a management tool to help each of our collections attain, improve, or sustain stronger institutional commitments for Latin American research.

Two events in the past three years have shaped the work of the Task Force on Standards. The first event took place at the University of Southern California. On March 20–21, 1987, the Boeckmann Center for Iberian and Latin American Studies hosted a colloquium on Latin American research collections, drawing on expertise of ten SALALM colleagues. This colloquium was an integral part of the library's planning process for USC's newly dedicated Boeckmann Center and collection and for the new initiatives at the University of Notre Dame in developing its Latin American collection.

The agenda for the colloquium incorporated the specific concerns of USC's and Notre Dame's emerging research collections as well as more universal problems associated with the definition of what constitutes a Latin American research collection and minimal levels of institutional support. Formal presentations and informal discussion covered philosophical and pragmatic issues: historical and current trends; existing criteria; acquisitions and collecting methods; selection of diverse types of materials; budget support; technical services support; preservation and binding; cooperation between libraries; and the relationship of the Library of Congress to major academic collections in the United States.

The second event was a panel at the 1988 SALALM meeting in Berkeley. Papers from the USC colloquium which focused primarily on collection development were read for the panel on "Building Latin American Research Collections" to share with the membership the concerns and questions that appropriately require SALALM's involvement and response: definitions of Latin American research collections; valid criteria and measures, in addition to the traditional measure of volume count or size; present trends that influence our collections; and present and future support required to maintain research quality collections.

Initial Tasks for the Task Force

The process of developing standards has various phases. There are questions that require answers, terminology that needs defining, and background information that needs to be explored before arriving at the goals and measures themselves.

Questions

The SALALM Task Force needs to determine and agree on: The audience, or who will use the standards? The purpose, or what will the standards be used for? What areas of performance to measure? What statistical data to collect? Which institutions will participate?

Measures of greatness of Latin American collections, especially in the United States, have been based predominantly on volume count or size of holdings, but there are other areas of performance on which we might base SALALM's standards. These are listed in Appendix B of this paper.

Terminology

Defining and clarifying terminology is another essential task. Some examples of undefined terms currently in use for describing Latin American collection are "significant," "comprehensive," "major," "research," and "ideal."

Sources

The SALALM *Papers*, other SALALM publications, and publications mentioned in the chapter "Library Resources on Latin America" in McNeil and Valk, *Latin American Studies: A Basic Guide to Sources*, contain many published sources from which to draw information about Latin American collections worldwide.

Suggested Guidelines for SALALM's Task Force on Standards

In approaching the development of standards for Latin American research collections, I suggest these guidelines for the task force:

1. Strive for uniform international, not national, standards for various sizes and types of collections, acknowledging differences to be preserved while simultaneously striving for the same qualities of excellence, yet not the same quantities.

2. Stimulate improvements in all Latin American studies collections, no matter the size, by setting attainable goals for each type or category. Standards arise from the possible not the impossible nor the unattainable. Our standards should not discourage smaller collections and yet should provide sufficient stimulation for the largest collections.

3. Aspire to produce a forward looking document, one that does not describe the present situation but builds on it. SALALM's standards should accommodate change and move with us into the next century.

4. Develop a vision of what we desire to attain. As part of this vision develop criteria for excellence not just adequacy. This vision should be based on research trends and patterns in Latin American area studies so that research collections are not working at cross purposes with the research in the field.

5. Learn as much as possible about existing collections, for example, collect, document, and share information widely, especially essential facts and statistics. Many of our present facts are ex cathedra. Some may have validity, other may require verification.

Statistical data collected are not to be confused with standards but are to assist in developing standards by providing a sound base on which to evaluate what has been accomplished before moving on to the next stage, that of establishing goals and criteria.

6. Finally, with the facts and data in hand, I urge that we incorporate both quantitative and qualitative measures in SALALM's standards. Concern for higher quality must be based on practical realities. It will provide a more rational management tool for the subject specialist and for library administrators.

In order to accomplish all this it will require cooperation, compromise, and consensus from SALALM's membership.

APPENDIX A

Charge to SALALM's Task Force on Standards: Developing and Maintaining Latin American Research Collections Beyond the 20th Century

The Task Force is charged with identifying criteria and developing standards with which to measure and chart the development and maintenance of Latin American research collections in meeting the needs of scholars beyond this century. The standards should assist in maximizing selection and acquisition activities by harmonizing the development of the collection with cataloging, other technical services, preservation, public services, and new methods of access and delivery of information and materials.

The project is not meant to describe the present but to set achievable goals. In carrying out the charge it may be necessary to survey the present development and maintenance of research collections and identify present and future trends in the field of library science and Latin American studies that impact our collections. It will be important to ascertain the impact of new technologies on the present and the future and to anticipate the needs of future scholars. It may also be necessary to document the unique constraints inherent in developing Latin American collections and predict changes and innovations in the coming decade.

The results of this project will be to strengthen our Latin American research collections in a concerted way through stronger institutional commitments, encourage unity of effort among Latin Americanists, and assist individual Latin American specialists in approaching administrators for support. Ultimately this will enhance SALALM's role in cooperative programs and activities.

The work of the Task Force will include a plan of operation, definition of terminology, a literature search, selection of methodology and criteria, and goal setting in order to arrive at qualitative and quantitative standards.

TASK FORCE MEMBERS

Barbara Robinson, *Chair*, University of Southern California
Lygia Ballantyne, Library of Congress
David Block, Cornell University
Walter Brem, University of California, Berkeley
Paula Covington, Vanderbilt University
Carl Deal, University of Illinois
Laurence Hallewell, University of Minnesota
William Ilgen, University of North Carolina
Deborah Jakubs, Duke University
Larry Lauerhass, University of California, Los Angeles
Shelley Miller, University of Kansas
Sharon Moynahan, University of New Mexico
Patricia Noble, University of London
Rafael Tarragó, University of Notre Dame
Ann Wade, British Library
Gayle Williams, University of Georgia

APPENDIX B

Potential Areas for SALALM's Standards

1. Collections: Written policy statement; size, growth rate, and scope; types of materials collected; evaluation or inventory methods; curricular and research support; selection and collection management methods.

2. Human Resources: Number and level of full-time equivalent staff and qualifications required; requirements for bibliographer or curator; support staff for collection development; technical services; public services; including languages and subject expertise; salaries; professional and staff training and development opportunities; internships.

3. Bibliographic Control: Choice of bibliographic utility, for example, OCLC, RLIN, or other; cataloging priorities and cataloging quotas; plan for eliminating uncataloged backlogs; reconversion projects; control for pamphlet collections; control and organization for other than book and serial collections.

4. Book and Materials Budget: Levels of support for new and retrospective acquisitions; for serials, continuations, and firm orders; for rare and unique materials; for nonbook materials; gifts received and solicited; methods of funding; percentages or ratios of budget support to other funding.

5. Acquisitions Methods: Approval and blanket plans; exchanges and gifts; catalog selection; buying trips; other creative methods; vendor performance evaluation methods.

6. Outreach and Networking: Faculty/library liaison network; advisory committee; friends group; newsletter or other methods of publicity; cultural programs; grants and exchanges for scholars.

7. Preservation/Conservation: Written policy; condition of collection survey; binding budget; binding methods: environmental controls; security and disaster preparedness.

8. National and International Cooperation: Institutional memberships in national or international organizations such as SALALM, LAMP, CRL, and others; joint projects in collection development, cataloging, reconversion, acquisitions and shared purchase programs, and preservation; participation in the North American Collections Inventory Project.

9. Public or User Services: Bibliographic instruction, reference service and information transfer services; course related instruction; instructional materials or guides to the collection and services; hours available; computer-based access to bibliographic information; document delivery; other indirect or direct information transfer or referral services.

10. Institutional Support: Number of faculty with Latin American interest; curriculum; graduate programs; Latin American research center; campus interest groups or international groups with Latin American focus; facilities and space requirements for housing the Latin American collection; delegation of authority and responsibility for the collection and services; consistency of financial support.

11. Responsiveness to Change: Creative implementation of new technology for collection development and other activities and services for the Latin American collection; creation of in-house access tools and databases; experimentation.

SELECTED BIBLIOGRAPHY ON STANDARDS FOR LIBRARIES AND LIBRARY COLLECTIONS

AECT-ACRL Joint Committee.* "Standards for Two-Year College Learning Resources Programs: A Draft," *College and Research Libraries News* 50 (May 1989), 496-505.

American Library Association. *Standards for College Libraries*. Chicago, IL: ALA, 1959.

Association of College and Research Libraries. *Quantitative Criteria for Adequacy of Academic Library Collections*. Chicago, IL: ALA, 1965.

Benson, Nettie Lee. "The Development of Comprehensive Latin American Collections." In *Latin American Collections*, W. V. Jackson, ed. Nashville, TN: The Editor, c1974. Pp. 7-14.

Brow, Ellen H. "Exploring the Third Bank of the River: Deciding What to Collect for a Research Library." In *Latin American Frontiers, Borders and Hinterlands: Research Needs and Resources*. Paula Covington, ed. Papers of SALALM XXXIII, Berkeley, California, June 6-10, 1988. Albuquerque, NM: SALALM, 1990. Pp. 175-182.

Brown, Helen M. "College Library Standards," *Library Trends* 21 (October 1972), 204-218.

Coale, Robert P. "Evaluation of a Research Library Collection: Latin American Colonial History at the Newberry," *Library Quarterly* 35 (July 1965), 173-184.

Deal, Carl W. "Latin American Collections: Criteria for Major Status." In *Latin American Frontiers, Borders and Hinterlands: Research Needs and Resources*. Paula Covington, ed. Papers of SALALM XXXIII, Berkeley, California, June 6-10, 1988. Albuquerque, NM: SALALM, 1990. Pp. 163-168.

Downs, Robert B. "Development of Research Collections in University Libraries," *University of Tennessee Library Lectures*, No. 4. Knoxville: University of Tennessee, 1954. 15 pp.

Downs, Robert B., and John W. Heussman. "Standards for University Libraries," *College and Research Libraries* 31 (January 1970), 28-35.

Frase, Robert W. "Procedures for Development and Access to Published Standards," *Library Trends* 31 (Fall 1982), 225-236.

Graham, Peter S. "Research Patterns and Research Libraries: What Should Change?," *College and Research Libraries* 50 (July 1989), 433-440.

Hall, Blaine H. *Collection Assessment Manual for College and University Libraries*. Phoenix, AZ: Oryx Press, 1985.

---

*Association for Educational Communications and Technology—Association of College and Research Libraries.

Havard-Williams, Peter. "International Standards," *Library Trends* 31 (Summer 1982), 173-185.

Heinritz, Fred J. "Quantitative Management in Libraries," *College and Research Libraries* 31 July 1970), 232-238.

Hirsch, Felix. "Introduction: Why Do We Need Standards?," *Library Trends* 21 (October 1972), 159-163.

Humphreys, K. W. "Standards for Libraries in Great Britain," *Library Trends* 21 (October 1972), 312-329.

Jackson, William Vernon, ed. *Latin American Collections.* Nashville, TN: The Editor, c1974. 142 pp.

Kania, Antoinette. "Academic Library Standards and Performance Measures," *College and Research Libraries* 49 (January 1988), 16-24.

Kantor, Paul B. *Objective Performance Measures for Academic and Research Libraries.* Washington, DC: Association of Research Libraries, 1984.

Kaser, David. "Standards for College Libraries," *Library Trends* 31 (Summer 1982), 7-20.

Lancaster, F. Wilfrid. *The Measurement and Evolution of Library Services.* Washington, DC: Information Resources Press, 1977.

Lohmann, Otto. "Efforts for International Standardization in Libraries," *Library Trends* 21 (October 1972), 330-353.

Lynch, Beverly P. "University Library Standards," *Library Trends* 31 (Summer 1982), 33-48.

_________. "Standards for University Libraries with Specific Reference to Developing Countries," *IFLA Journal* 2 (1987), 120-125.

McNeil, Robert A., and Barbara G. Valk, eds. *Latin American Studies: A Basic Guide to Sources.* 2d ed. rev. and enl. New York, NY: Scarecrow Press, 1990.

Moran, Barbara B. *Academic Libraries: The Changing Knowledge Center of Colleges and Universities.* Washington, DC: Association for the Study of Higher Education, 1984.

"Objectives and Standards for Special Libraries," *Special Libraries* 55 (December 1964), 672-680.

Robinson, Barbara J. "Summary Report of the Latin American Library Specialist Colloquium Held March 20-21, 1987, with Recommendations for USC's Collection." Unpublished report.

Shaughnessy, Thomas W. "The Search for Quality," *Journal of Library Administration* 8 (Spring 1987), 5-10.

Standards for Art Libraries and Fine Arts Slide Collections. Tucson, AZ: Art Libraries Society of North America, 1983.

"Standards for University Libraries," *College and Research Libraries News* 4 (April 1979), 101-110.

Stubbs, Kendon. *Quantitative Criteria for Academic Research Libraries.* Chicago, IL: ALA, 1984.

_________. "University Libraries: Standards and Statistics," *College and Research Libraries* 42 (September 1981), 527-538.

ULS, Association of College and Research Libraries, University Library Section, Committee on Guidelines for Branch Libraries. "Guidelines for Branch Libraries in Colleges and Universities: A Draft," *College and Research Libraries News* 50 (May 1989), 392-395.

__________. University Library Standards Review Committee. "Standards for University Libraries: Evaluation of Performance," *College and Research Libraries News* 50 (September 1989), 679-692.

Vaughan, Anthony. "Standards for British Libraries," *Library Trends* 31 (Summer 1982), 155-172.

Wallace, James O. "Two-Year College Learning Resource Standards," *Library Trends* 31 (Summer 1982), 21-32.

Watkins, David R. "Standards for University Libraries," *Library Trends* 21 (October 1972), 190-203.

4. Statistics for Latin American Collections: Preliminary Findings

Carl W. Deal

Introduction

This study reports on a survey that was prepared in response to a need expressed by the SALALM Task Force on Standards for Latin American Collections. As an experiment, this survey should continue only if those who have contributed will gain from the dissemination of the results. If it continues, the format will require alteration to assure that information which is not ephemeral, but which is viewed as the most essential, is preserved for comparison over time.

What is now needed is the kind of information that is useful to those in charge of Latin American collections in formulating arguments that are convincing to their administrations and to other funding agencies for both continuing and special support. I would argue that comparison with one's peer institutions is a time-honored method employed by academic institutions at all levels of administration to improve one's budgetary position. It is one with which all should be involved in the attempt to improve one's financial position.

There are other important purposes for which this information is useful. Among them are the benefits of providing a more complete national overview of Latin American funding vis à vis other world areas, of quantifying national strengths in the Latin American field, and of targeting problem areas like backlogs for special attention, to mention several.

The data for this survey will meet some of these needs. As an experiment, however, the survey will need refinement if it is to be continued. Two things should be decided. The first is whether an annual or periodic survey is required. The second is to begin to suggest changes for its improvement.

Models of Library Statistics

What models of library statistics provide useful guidance? The annually produced Association of Research Libraries (ARL) statistics have become a model of institutionalized statistics to which academic libraries constantly refer in the preparation of grant proposals and annual budget requests, as well as for providing a national view of the distribution of library resources. I believe these statistics have served the profession well. One could conceivably apply these areas of statistics exactly as they are to Latin American collections, although it is doubtful that the information could be provided by very many libraries.

The second statistical model, the listing of "Major Latin American Collections," was published by Marietta Daniels Shepard in the *List of Books Accessioned by the Columbus Memorial Library* [1] in December, 1956. It was reissued in 1960 as number 1 of the *Cuadernos Bibliotecológicos* [2] and was revised in 1970 by Kent E. Miller and Gilberto V. Fort. [3] While this survey asked many of the questions to which we needed to have answers, like the size of staff and collections, it was flawed somewhat by repeating information on the collections which was too general.

The third model is the one I have prepared since 1987 for the American Library Association/Association for Library Collection and Technical Services/Resources Section (ALA/ALCTS/RS) Collection Development Officers of Large Libraries Group. It incorporates some of the categories used by the annually published *ARL Statistics* [4] as well as areas of special concern to the group like cancellation statistics for serials and information on private funding. The survey has been kept at a level that requires only information that is largely available to the forty-seven libraries of this group. Members have come to depend upon it in preparation of annual budget requests.

A fourth survey is the familiar annual SALALM price survey that appears in the *SALALM Newsletter* [5] and later in Bowker's *Library and Book Trade Almanac.* [6] Its acceptance by Bowker is a credit to its usefulness.

Only one other area studies group, the East Asian group, prepares annual statistics for its libraries. The publication's title is "Current Status of East Asian Collections in American Libraries." Since 1988 it has appeared annually in *The Bulletin* [7] of the Committee on East Asian Libraries of the Association for Asian Studies, Inc. No other world area has such fine control of information resources, staff, collections, and annual expenditures for its major collections as the East Asian group.

Those are the five statistical examples consulted in constructing a SALALM survey questionnaire. The results of the questionnaire follow.

The SALALM Model

Questionnaire

The format of this survey concentrates on three areas. First is the library materials budget for Latin American materials, both allocations and expenditures. Information on methods of acquisition like blanket orders and approval plans, and on other sources of support, was also solicited. The funding of electronic information was also thought to be a significant development deserving attention. Serial cancellations, which have been an area of national disaster, were also an area of inquiry, as were the number of titles purchased and received as gifts. Uncataloged backlogs were also reviewed.

The second area of concentration is staffing, both professional and support staff, graduate assistants and students. An effort was made to learn about staffing of all departments in the library which contribute to the Latin American collections.

A final and third broad area surveyed within the category of "Other Information" attempts to compare the Latin American collection's level of support with other world areas, to determine its membership in the Center for Research Libraries (CRL) and the Latin American Microfilming Project (LAMP), and to provide information on cooperation and resource sharing.

Response to the Questionnaire

The questionnaire was sent to a single representative of each of the sixty-five libraries represented in the 1989/1990 SALALM membership list, although several libraries were overlooked in the mailing. The Library of Congress was not included, owing to the complicated nature of its operation, and the New York Public Library was also not sampled for the same reason. The Columbus Memorial Library, although not an academic library, was included because of the specialized strength and nature of its collection. The response of twenty-one libraries is sufficient for us to review the questionnaire and to determine what improvements and changes should be made if it is to be continued in the future.

For purposes of analysis the responding libraries have been divided into three groups based on total volume count. Table 1 displays the three groups with their total volume count and expenditures for library materials for fiscal year 1989.

The most interesting part of the survey is obviously the first part which deals with the collections and levels of funding. In Group I, three libraries had allocations in excess of $100,000, while four showed

Table 1. Volume Count and Expenditures for Fiscal Year 1989[a]

Library	Volume count	Expenditures
Group I		
Cornell University	265,000	$ 96,000
Duke University	200,800	64,000
Stanford University	230,000	252,000
University of California, Los Angeles	300,000	160,000
University of Illinois	343,000	106,000
University of New Mexico	287,000	157,200
University of Southern California	198,500	88,800
Columbus Memorial Library	764,000	39,200
Group II		
Arizona State University		
Brigham Young University		
San Diego State University		
University of California, San Diego	165,000	87,000
University of Massachusetts	109,000	83,000
University of Miami	121,000	34,500
University of Minnesota	102,000	48,800
Group III		
New York University	56,000	83,000
Ohio State University		
Pennsylvania State University		
Rutgers University	31,500	23,300
University of London	40,100	34,800
University of Notre Dame	27,500	96,100

[a] The figures for a number of libraries that reported are not included because they were not very complete or were so skewed by other factors as to render them not very compatible for comparison purposes. Amounts for Arizona State, Brigham Young, San Diego State, Pennsylvania State, and Ohio State, because they cannot be made public, are left blank. They are, however, included in averages reported in the text.

total expenditures below $100,000. Total library materials expenditures for four of the eight libraries were from 7.8 percent to 131 percent above the actual allocations, and this indicates that expenditures, not allocations, are a more important variable. This same pattern occurs for the Group II libraries. Figures for Group III are too incomplete to use.

The survey shows that blanket orders play a very large role in the collections at Group I libraries, with five institutions reporting from $35,000 to $81,000 expended, and one $8,000. For four of these libraries this is well over 50 percent of their allocations. Two libraries in Group II maintained blanket orders at $15,000 and $44,300 and one library maintained such a plan at $6,200. The implications of these figures on the one hand are that many of the major collections are dependent on blanket orders for current purchases. On the other hand, do they also imply that the major collections may well be putting together "look-alike collections?" The benefits from U.S. and foreign approval plans seem to be of minor importance to most of the libraries in all three groups, although they are significant for two libraries in both Groups I and II.

It is surprising that of the seven libraries supporting Title VI National Resource Centers, funds for library materials were received by only three libraries at amounts of $1,500, $4,200, and $14,100. Only one library reported any funding for preservation. This has implications for all of our collections which are very apparent, since so much of the material purchased in the first place is often already a preservation problem. None of our collections are charged for database searching yet, but that could occur in the future with the massive amount of electronic information now becoming available online.

With only four libraries reporting any serial cancellations, it appears this has not been a major problem for our Latin American collections. This is probably explained also because these collections are driven more by monographs than by serials. For example, serials are about 20 to 25 percent of the expenditures of the four reporting on serials expenditures in Group I libraries. This percentage is sustained by three of the four libraries from Group II.

Uncataloged backlogs are a significant problem for Group I libraries from which five reported over 10,000 backlogged volumes and one 98,500 volumes. The smaller collections in Group II also reported this to be a problem with one of the seven recording 9,100 volumes and two recording 15,000 volumes to be cataloged.

There is a better control of information on serial titles among Group III libraries than among the larger institutions. In Group III all libraries reported from 125 to 481 titles. Only four of the seven libraries reported from 328 to 650 titles in Group II, and only four of the largest eight libraries could record currently purchased serial subscriptions, including monographic series ranging from 467 to 3,000 titles.

Gifts play an important role for eleven of the twenty collections. The Columbus Memorial Library reported an outstanding number of 52,000 gift serial pieces.

In summarizing the first part of the survey, these statistics for this sample leave the following impressions about our collections. Total expenditures are a more important measure of funding support than are allocations, and blanket orders continue to play a major role in their development. With the strains from other funding pressures, Latin American studies programs, at least those that are National Resource Centers, are moving away from providing the past higher patterns of library support. While serial cancellations have not presented a great problem to date, uncataloged backlogs continue to plague many libraries.

The second category of the questionnaire was designed primarily to provide information on institutional support for Latin America and other world areas and formal and informal cooperative agreements with other library programs. Information on interlibrary loans was of secondary interest.

Eleven libraries in Groups I and II provided information comparing institutional support of the library materials funds among world areas.

In the six libraries that reported on Western European studies, the average expenditure was approximately double the expenditure for any other single world area. One is not surprised at such heavy resources, bearing in mind the number of language, humanistic, and social science scholars spread throughout university departments.

The eight larger academic libraries each reported expenditures for three areas: Latin America, East Asia, and the Slavic and East European area. Of the five reporting in the second group, three libraries also supported programs in these areas. One heavily supports South West Asia as well as these three areas, and one supports the Middle East as well as these three areas.

This tell us that our universities and libraries are providing the greatest area support for the Latin American, East Asian, and Slavic and East European programs. This excludes the Western European area which we must concede probably receives the heaviest support on most campuses.

One may look at the total expenditures of these eleven libraries in order to make a broad general assumption about how funding is distributed for library materials nationwide among world areas. It could be a dangerous assumption, however, since these libraries may not be representative of the nation's library allocations for area studies; but in the absence of additional data, one may assume that these data have a good chance of holding up as an accurate sample.

Of the twelve libraries in Groups I and II which reported on library materials allocations for eleven world areas, Latin America received the greatest support in four institutions, and was second highest in support in four libraries. The Slavic and East European area received the highest support in three libraries and was second highest in six. East Asia, the third major area, received the highest funding in three libraries, and the second highest in none.

We may conclude that Latin America may be the most strongly supported world area in U.S. access libraries. As one of the three big areas it is probably assured of a high priority among area studies programs in most libraries.

Information the survey yields on cooperation and interlibrary loans is not very impressive. Only four of the twenty-one libraries reported formal cooperative agreements with other libraries. Cooperation is much more heavily evident on an informal basis with nine institutions reporting.

The survey indicates that eleven of twenty-one libraries do not charge for interlibrary loans. However, among the remaining ten which do charge, three do not charge fellow Research Libraries Group (RLG) libraries. It may come as a surprise to learn that twenty of twenty-one reporting libraries engage in international library lending.

Responses to the third and final section of the questionnaire show that staffing has grown modestly in most institutions from 1985 to 1989 for librarians, for support staff and graduate assistants, and for student wages. An attempt was made to identify the amount of staff time in other units which was devoted to Latin American materials, but only eleven responded to this.

In summarizing this final section, Group I libraries have an average of 2.7 full-time equivalent librarians and 3.7 FTE support staff and graduate assistants. Only two libraries reported a decline in librarians, while seven reported modest increases. Reports on student hours were too inconclusive to measure.

The data in this survey, while they come from only twenty-one libraries, do suggest a profile of our collections might be possible as has been outlined in Table 2.

Table 2. Profile of Collections, Staff, and Expenditures

	Libraries		
Category	Group I[a]	Group II	Group III
Average expenditures			
FY1989	$126,000	$ 56,100	$ 52,833
Serial	$ 22,575	$ 11,633	No report
Volumes in collection	254,166	106,442	36,020
Uncataloged backlog	8,360[b]	7,516	2,900
Serial subscriptions	1,480	458	237
Percentage of area studies allocated[c]			
Latin America	23.9	36.2	No report
East Asia	23.4	11.3	No report
Slavic & East European	17.8	18.7	No report
FTE librarians FY1989	2.7	1.98	1
FTE support staff FY1989	3.7	2.64	1

[a] Excludes the Columbus Memorial Library.

[b] Excludes extraordinary backlog of 98,000 at Southern California resulting from a recent gift. Inclusion of Southern California's backlog drives the average up to 25,716.

[c] Excludes Western Europe. New Mexico's only area program is Latin America.

Upon reviewing the results of the survey, should SALALM make an effort to standardize a form of statistics for future annual reporting in the *SALALM Newsletter*? What form should the statistics take? I suggest that if this is continued in the future that the SALALM model might very much resemble the East Asian model which has been refined over a period of twenty-five years.

NOTES

1. Marietta Daniels Shepard, "Major Latin American Collections," *List of Books Accessioned by the Columbus Memorial Library* (December 1956), pp. 23-27.

2. Columbus Memorial Library, *Major Latin American Collections in Libraries of the United States*, Cuadernos bibliotecológicos, no. 1 (Washington, DC: Unión Panamericana, Secretaria General de la Organización de los Estados Americanos, 1960).

3. Kent E. Miller and Gilberto V. Fort, *Major Latin American Collections in Libraries of the United States*, 3d ed. (Washington, DC: Secretaria General, Organización de los Estados Americanos, 1970).

4. *ARL Statistics, 1974/1975–* (Washington, DC: Association of Research Libraries).

5. *SALALM Newsletter* 1– (January 1973–), Albuquerque, NM: etc.: SALALM Secretariat.

6. *Library and Book Trade Almanac, 1961–* (New York, NY: R. R. Bowker.)

7. *Bulletin* (New Haven, CT: Association for Asian Studies, Committee on East Asian Libraries).

Street and Study: Popular and Formal Expressions of Change

5. "Entre bueyes no hay cornadas" [Among Equals There Are No Disagreements]: The Argentine Popular Theater as a Source for the Historian

Donald S. Castro

Y él que atreve a decir
que no hay arte en un sainete,
no sabe dónde se mete
ni por dónde ha de salir.

[The person who is so bold as to say
that there is no art in the *sainete*
doesn't know what he is saying.]

Alberto Vacarezza

The *sainete porteño* (or the *sainete criollo*) is the short jocular play of Buenos Aires that evolved in the late nineteenth century. Its zenith of popularity was in the early part of this century. By the 1930s it was in decline, replaced by the tragicomedy play form of the *grotesco* (as exemplified by the works of Armando Discépolo, b. 1887) and by the *revista porteño* vaudeville form of popular theater. Inroads of the new electronic media—films and radio—also had their impacts. Notwithstanding these competitive forms of entertainment, the sainete probably died under its own weight because it lost its currency as a reflector of the attending audience, which had grown beyond the formula-driven (and possibly trite) plots of the sainete of the late 1920s.

When the sainete was a vibrant reflection of its audience, it was an excellent source for the study of Argentine or, better still, porteño, social history, given the themes and issues utilized by the writers of the sainete (*saineteros*). For the historian, the use of the sainete, as a nontraditional source for historical research, serves to humanize events in the history of Buenos Aires. It also provides insight into the living conditions and attitudes of the lower classes not necessarily available in

---

AUTHOR'S NOTE: Title for this paper is taken from the *sainete* written in 1908 by José González Castillo (1885-1937). Epigraph as quoted in Tulio Carella, ed., *El sainete criollo (antología)* (Buenos Aires: Librería Hachette, 1957), p. 7.

more traditional sources for social history. Statistical reports, journals, diaries, personal recollections, memoirs, and the like are better describers of the values and attitudes of the upper—or literate—classes toward the lower, or under classes, or do not deal with these classes at all. For example, the marvelous memoir of Julia Valentina Bunge, which is an excellent source on the social life of the elite, described the poor only in passing as a rationale for parties (cf. cotillions of the Sociedad de Beneficiaria para los Pobres).[1] The sainete, which in large part was written by members of the emerging middle class, who had not yet lost their ties with the lower classes, had a sense of immediacy with the problems of the lower or working classes of the expanding metropolis of Buenos Aires. This was true for its audiences as well.

In Argentina, the sainete fused elements from the Spanish light opera (*zarzuela*) and the comic popular theater of late nineteenth-century Spain (*género chico*, literally small genus or class, e.g., "small theater," or "lowbrow" versus "highbrow" theater). Another important source for the sainete was the gaucho theater element within the creole circus. By the 1880s it was customary to offer short sketches and comic arts as part of the circus program. One of the most popular was the short "play" which took its inspiration from the gaucho folk hero, Juan Moreira. This "play" introduced the first parody character of the immigrant which would become a standard part of many sainetes—*el cocoliche*.[2] The Argentine *saineteros*, or writers in the sainete genre, sought to create a hybrid cultural form from these sources that was inspired by the everyday life experiences of the common people, yet used the form of theatric productions that was acceptable to those who would be the paying audience—the emerging middle and lower middle classes, and in some instances the working class, of Buenos Aires.

Theater owners discovered that the sainete in its short one-hour format offered an opportunity for greater profits in that larger audiences could be accommodated at multiple performances. The ticket cost per performance in the early 1900s was about one peso. In contrast, tickets for comparable *platea* [orchestra] seats for productions in the elite porteño theaters, such as the Colón Opera House, cost more than four times that much.[3] Regardless of the relative inexpensiveness of the sainete performances, the profits were considerable for the theater owners, and writers in the genre could make a living out of production and writing of these plays. This economic incentive served to spur the writing of sainetes and their presentation to what appeared to be an insatiable audience hungry for the highly topical play form.

The most popular day for theater attendance was Sunday afternoon. Theater operators offered as many as seven performances on Sundays, starting at three in the afternoon. Weekday presentations were in the evening, starting at 8:30 P.M., and often included as many as four different sainete plays. This high exposure of the sainete placed a tremendous burden on the creative talents of the sainetero.[4] More than three hundred sainetes were written during the period from 1890 to 1930 and most show the strain felt by the writers in that very few have survived the passage of time. Many of those that have survived are valued as historical documents rather than as literary ones.

There were at least ten major theaters devoted to the sainete genre and numerous minor ones during the Golden Age of the sainete porteño (1915–1930). It is estimated by the author that these theaters represented a combined seating capacity of more than 3,000 seats, so that it is not difficult to say that the sainete was a "popular" cultural form. While it is true that most of these theaters were located "downtown," there were a number of functioning sainete theaters in the neighborhoods of Flores, Boedo, and Constitución that served as cultural centers of working class immigrant and creole populations in the growing city of Buenos Aires.[5] In many ways the jocular play during its heyday had the same impact on Buenos Aires nightlife that the Broadway musical had on New York in the early twentieth century. Further, theatrical companies went on tour on a regular schedule to La Plata (capital of the province of Buenos Aires) and to Rosario, which was the major city of the province of Santa Fe, carrying the sainete with them. Therefore the sainete had an impact on an area larger than just the city of Buenos Aires.

The locale of the sainete was Buenos Aires (with few exceptions such as "La gringa" by Florencio Sánchez, which took place in the countryside and was written in 1904) with its ethnic and cultural mix of immigrants and native Argentines—Afro-Argentines, mestizo creoles, and creoles—and the various social classes or strata of the city. The sainete themes are so thoroughly Argentine and current (most plays took place in *época actual* [present time]) that, unlike the works of "cultured" Argentine dramatists who aped European form and subject matter, the sainetero came to be *eminentemente nacional* (eminently native based).[6] Several saineteros were also newspapermen, and their biting satirical articles often got them into trouble with government officials. If they thought the use of the sainete for their social criticism made them immune to government control, they were wrong—at least in the early stages of the sainete's development. They were harassed by police agents who provoked demonstrations in the theaters and by the fire department for "infractions" of the municipal fire code. One of the most famous cases involved the sainetero and theater owner Emilio Onrubia in 1889. He was arrested for his satire and criticism of the Juárez-Celman government (1886–1890) and of some of its most notorious grafters (cf. "Lo que sobra y lo que pasa" [Things That Are Too Much and Things That Happen].[7] Other cases involved Carlos Mauricio Pacheco (1881–1924) and Nemesio Trejo (1862–1916). Onrubia also wrote for the popular magazine *Caras y Caretas* (Faces and Masques), which severely criticized the lack of governmental concern for the welfare of the urban poor. Harassment by the government declined as the sainete became a regular part of the porteño cultural scene. One contemporary theater critic, writing in the porteño daily newspaper *El Diario* in 1890, felt that the sainete was breaking new ground for press and literary freedom:

> La revista local, el sainete, la pieza breve . . . rompen hoy los lazos que la sujetaban, rehuyendo preocupaciones añejas que no tienen razón de ser y aparecen, vacilantes aún, pero preparando el terreno para que en el teatro pueda repetirse cuando se dice en la prensa sin temor a escándalo, persecuciones o multa. [The vaudeville theater, the sainete, the short play . . . are breaking today the ties of censorship which in the past have bound them, rejecting stale fears which no longer have any reason to exist and they, even though unsure at times, seem to be breaking new ground so that in the theater it is possible to say things which in the press might bring scandal, persecution, or fines.][8]

Therefore, the sainetero could portray on the stage issues that could embarrass political figures or governments; for example, graft and corruption in "Los políticos" (The Politicians) (1897); social problems of crime, prostitution, poverty, and alienation in "Los [e]scruchantes" (The Second-Story Men) (1911), in "Los disfrazados" (The Masqueraders) (1906), and in "Tu cuna fué un conventillo" (Your Cradle Was a Slum) (1920); and ethnic and labor conflicts such as in "Los devotos" (The Devout Ones) (1900), and in "Los inquilinos' (The Tenants) (1907). Florencio Sánchez (1875–1910) and Alberto Giroldo, author of "Alma gaucha" (Gaucho Soul) (1907), were known anarchists, and used most of their sainetes as vehicles for social criticism.

In its evolution from an Argentine version of a Spanish *zarzuela* to its fully developed form as an authentic Argentine genre, the sainete went through various stages. The first stage of the sainete (1890–1900) was characterized by a heavy reliance on the Spanish *zarzuela* and the *género chico* for the basic framework of the emerging sainete criollo. It was a period in which the Argentine authors imposed creole themes on Spanish theatrical forms and relied on Spanish touring companies to incorporate their works into the repertoire. This influence can be seen in the works of Miguel Ocampo, such as in his sainete "De paso por aqui" (Passing Through) (1890) and in the works of Ezequiel Soria, who has been called the creole "zarzuelist."[9]

The second stage of the evolution (1900–1915) is marked by the rise of a purely creole theatrical company (The Podestá Brothers), which evolved out of the Argentine-Uruguayan circus, and the increased use of Argentine actors, versus the earlier almost exclusive use of Spanish actors. The dedication of the Teatro Nacional (National Theater) to the exclusive production and presentation of the sainete (1915) clearly demonstrates the preeminence of this play form by World War I. Also during this period the sainete became completely creole (*acriollado*) in terms of authors, actors, content, and theater entrepreneurs. While other entertainment forms emerged during this time—such as the films and automobile racing (*automovilísmo*)—they could not compete with the sainete in terms of popularity based on attendance. Authors who were important during this period were Florencio Sánchez, Nemesio Trejo, Enrique De María, Alberto Novión, Enrique Garcia Velloso, and Carlos Mauricio Pacheco.

The third stage of the evolution of the sainete (1915–1930) has been called the Golden Age of this popular cultural form. It was during this period that the tango as a song form played an important part in the mass appeal of the sainete. For example, the first true tango as a song (*tango-canción* versus *tango-danza*, or tango as a dance) was written for the stage in 1917 by Pascual Contursi ("Mi noche triste" [My Sad Night]). Weekly magazines devoted to the sainete theater made their appearance at this time and these published complete texts of the more popular sainetes. The principal authors during this period were Alberto Mauricio Pacheco and Alberto Vacarezza. The impacts of the great depression (1929–1939), the coup d'état by General José F. Uriburu in September of 1930, and the spread of the electronic media of talking movies and the radio marked the end of this period.

The sainete also became too formula driven, too focused on life in the slum [*conventillo*], and perhaps too poorly written, to keep the attention of audiences, who had less money to spend on plays they already had seen (in terms of content) and found new pleasures in the escapist movies of the day. The sainete's overworked themes of poverty and despair did not provide the porteño audiences with the escape from the harsh realities that the military/conservative regimes and the depression brought into even sharper focus. It is reported that Carlos Gardel, the great tango interpreter, once complained that the sainetero (and the tango lyricist of the same period) knew only one theme—life of the poor in the *conventillo*—and that he was fed up with this overworked issue.[10] Gardel seemed to have captured, as he was so known to do, the sentiments of the porteño.

While relatively few saineteros were concerned with the rich and their lifestyle, there were a number of sainetes that described the elite. When this was done, it was more often to highlight the corruption of this class, as in the sainete by Nemesio Trejo, "Los políticos" (The Politicians) (1897), or in the play by Carlos Mauricio Pacheco, "La patota" (The Gang) (1922). Issues affecting the working class were also topics used by the sainetero: Among these are "El pan amargo" (Bitter Bread) (1911) by Pacheco and "A falta de pan" (Due to the Lack of Bread) (1918) by Pedro E. Pico. This is also a preeminent theme in many of Florencio Sánchez's works, such as "Moneda falsa" (Counterfeit Money) (1907) and "El desalojo" (The Eviction) (1906). Another major theme in the sainete was the relationship of the immigrant with the progressively displaced and marginalized urban creole. This took the form of the parody of the immigrant and his misuses of Argentine Spanish (*cocoliche*) or of violent (and deadly) conflict, such as the sainete by Carlos Mauricio Pacheco, "Los disfrazados" (The Masqueraders) (1906). For most of its history the sainete was able to capture the moment of events and provide audiences with a sense of immediacy of the issues portrayed on the stage. For example, in the play "Los inquilinos" (The Tenants) (1907), Nemesio Trejo presented his audience with a theatrical portrayal of an event going on outside the theater at the very moment of the play's presentation—the rent strike of 1907. The sainetero was an author of the "here and the now" and of subject matter that was of interest to his audience. As has been mentioned earlier, the typical sainete audience was composed of people who, if they did not actually live in the environment or conditions portrayed on the stage, could at least clearly understand and identify with the stage characters. These elements made the sainete truly a popular culture form of the porteño and gave it mass appeal.

The saineteros also had a great influence on the language spoken by the porteño. For example, in porteño popular speech, newsboys are called *canallitas*, from the sainete by Florencio Sánchez where the main character was called Canallita and the play described his struggle to make a living by selling newspapers ("Canallita," 1904). One modern Argentine author has stated that the playwrights of the popular theater had been created by World War I.

una especie de dialecto para escena breve, fugaz y humorística del sainete, que en virtud de su especialidad genérica, otorgaba libertad gramatical. Entre los términos del hampa, del caló bonarense, de aquellos herederos del gauchismo y criollismo rurales y al distorsión inmigratoria se compaginó la materia prima de una habla popular hasta entonces desconocida dentro del cuadro más o menos purista del contralismo idiomático español.[11] [a type of dialect for the brief, hurried and humorous staging of the sainete, which, given the writing needs of the genre, required the authors to take grammatical liberties. The terms used in crime, the street slang of Buenos Aires, the words from the gaucho and creole rural types, and the distortions of Spanish by the newly arrived immigrant all formed the base material for popular speech which until then was unknown within the framework of pure idiomatic Spanish.]

Since the sainete was not considered to be "true" theater by erudite authors contemporary to the period of its ascendancy and flowering, it was very often omitted from studies on the Argentine theater of that time. This is apparent in the monumental study by Ricardo Rojas on the history of Argentine literature (*Historia de la literatura argentina*, 8 vols., 1917–1922), which was written during the Golden Age of the sainete but which fails to mention the form.[12] It is mentioned in passing by Ernesto Quesada in 1902 only when he discusses the use of language in Argentina in his study *El criollismo en la literatura argentina* (Creole Language Influences in Argentine Literature) (1902). The only broad review of the theater in Buenos Aires that included the sainete was by Mariano G. Bosch, *Historia del teatro en Buenos Aires* (History of the Buenos Aires Theater) (1910), and it is incomplete, having been written during the early stage of the sainete's evolution.

Interest in the saineteros by writers on the Argentine theater of the time was primarily limited to collections of theater criticism, such as that by the theater critic for *La Nación*, Juan Pablo Echagüe, *Una época del teatro argentina, 1904–1918* (An Epoch of the Argentine Theater, 1904–1918) (1917–1918), or brief biographical sketches of authors and critical comments on their works such as *Puntos de vista (Crónica de bibliografía y teatro* [Bibliographical and Theatrical Chronicle] [1905]) also by Echagüe. Echagüe's writings evince a favorable bias toward Florencio Sánchez.

Even though Sánchez spent most of his short productive career in Buenos Aires, his Uruguayan origins inspired Uruguayan writers to claim him as one of their own and his great talent was recognized by Argentine authors who acknowledged him as a porteño in spirit. This is evident in the number of works that were written about him after his untimely death in 1910. Examples of these works are Juan José de Souza Reilly, *Hombres luminosos* (Men of Distinction) (1920) and the monumental study on Sánchez published in both Spain and in Argentina in 1917, *El teatro del uruguayo Florencio Sánchez* (The Theater Works by the Uruguayan Florencio Sánchez), 3 vols.

Argentine authors have only recently recognized the importance of the sainete in the development of Argentine literature. A major contributor to this recognition was Mariano G. Bosch (1865–1948), whose productive career coincided with the sainete era. Perhaps the most important of his studies to include the sainete in the context of general Argentine theater development are *Historia de los orígines del teatro nacional argentino y la época de Pablo Podestá* (History of the Origin of the Argentine National Theater and the Epoch of Pablo Podestá) (1929) and his earlier work on the history of the Buenos Aires theater, *Historia del teatro en Buenos Aires* (History of the Buenos Aires Theater) (1910). Luis Ordaz has also written extensively on the Argentine theater and the role the sainete has played in the development of a national theater. An example of his work in this area is his study, *El teatro en el Rio de la Plata desde sus orígenes hasta nuestros días* (The Theater in the Rio de la Plata from Its Origins until Today) (1946).

Notwithstanding the fact that Bosch and others have recognized the importance of the sainete, there is only one work that is devoted exclusively to the critical analysis of this genre of Argentine literature, that by Raúl Blas Gallo, *Historia del sainete nacional* (History of the National Sainete) (1958), who has also written on the tango and other topics related to the popular culture of the city of Buenos Aires. Other authors have written comments on the sainete as part of their introductions to anthologies: Among them are Tulio Carella in *El sainete criollo* (The Creole Sainete) (1957), Luis Ordaz in *Breve historia del teatro* (Brief History of the Theater), 7 vols. (1962–1965), and Abel Posadas in *El teatro argentino* (The Argentine Theater), vol. 6 (1980).

Sources from related areas of Argentine culture are also useful in the study of the sainete. Given the close relationship of the early sainete to the circus in Argentina, sources on the circus (while limited) are of great help in the understanding of the genre. These sources are almost exclusively the product of one Argentine scholar, Raúl H. Castagnino. His works date from 1958 when he wrote his first study, *Centurias del circo criollo* (Two Centuries of the Creole Circus), and include *El circo criollo* (The Creole Circus) (1967) and *Circo, teatro gauchesco y tango* (Circus, the Gauchoesque Theater, and the Tango) (1981). The study by Osvaldo Sosa Cordero on the vaudeville theater contemporary to the sainete is also essential to the understanding of the popular theater in Buenos Aires (*Historia de las varietes en Buenos Aires* [History of Vaudeville in Buenos Aires] [1978]). Domingo F. Casadevall's important research on the theme of criminality in the national theater is crucial to the understanding of the sainete and the role it played in highlighting social issues to its audiences (*El tema de la mala vida en el teatro nacional* [The Theme of Criminality in the National Theater]). Personal memoirs are also valuable sources such as the ones written by the sainetero Enrique Garcia Velloso (*Memoria de un hombre de teatro* [Memoirs of a Man of the Theater] [1938]), and by José J. Podestá, a pivotal member of the circus and theatrical Podestá family (*Medio siglo de farándula* [Half Century as a Comic Artist] [1930]).

Aside from those sources already mentioned—and Raúl Blas Gallo's book would be the most essential—the primary critical components are the sainetes themselves. More than two hundred individual authors wrote sainetes; many of them not of much artistic value (nor even historic value) and have been lost. Yet a number of the authors wrote sainetes of great merit and some were also important writers of tango lyrics. In many instances the best way to locate early tango lyrics is through the study of the sainete; thus, the tango cannot be understood without the sainete and the reverse is true as well. Of the three hundred sainetes that were written, fewer than one third have survived. Many appear in published collections. Unfortunately, the scholar is dependent on the judgment of the anthologist as to what is available for study and, given the concurrence among these collectors as to the importance of certain titles, this has led to a duplication of the sainetes that have been collected and published. A number of these collections exist: the most notable are those edited by Luis Ordaz, Tulio Carella, and Marta Speroni in collaboration with Griselda Vignolo. Nonetheless, these collections represent only some fifty plays.

In addition to these collections, there were a number of theater magazines (published by both theater owners and magazine companies) that reprinted the complete text of selected sainetes. The plays that were published in this form often were only the most popular ones and those that generated sufficient interest in the paying public to sell the magazine or, in the case of theater owners, such as the Apolo and the National theaters in Buenos Aires, theater tickets. During the Golden Age of the sainete, these magazines were published on a weekly basis at relatively low prices so that the runs of each edition were fairly large. Unfortunately for the scholar in the United States, however, the American library holdings of these publications are spotty and incomplete. The most important of the magazines that printed sainetes were *Bambalinas, Teatro Popular, El Teatro Argentino,* and *El Entreacto.* In essence, these magazines combined the features of the American monthly *Playbill Magazine* with comments on the authors, actors, theater runs, and so forth, in addition to the reprinting of selected sainetes.

Other sources also contain articles on saineteros and sainetes: They are in large part products of Argentine associations that are devoted to preserving the popular language and culture of Buenos Aires, such as the Academia Porteña del Lunfardo (The Porteño Lunfardo Academy) or to the study of the Argentine theater, such as the Instituto Nacional de Estudios del Teatro (The National Institute for the Study of Theater). These organizations have published focused studies on the theater or bulletins and journals on a more or less regular basis since the 1960s. Another important source for the study of the sainete—and for Argentine literature in general—is the Asociación General de Autores de la Argentina (The General Association of Authors of Argentina), which is better known for its acronym Argentores. This organization has served as a protective association to foster the rights of authors (copyrights, protection of artistic freedom, etc.) and has published a series of journals since the early 1930s. In addition to the journals published, these organizations also maintain libraries and archives of materials, which are available for use by scholars.

Very little has been written in English on the sainete as such, and what has been written concentrates on particular authors such as Florencio Sánchez. Perhaps this is due to the fact that lack of access to the sources has made the sainete an obscure topic to most American scholars, or that the sainete is viewed by language and literature "purists" as a genre of little literary merit (cf. Lawrence W. Levine, *Highbrow/Lowbrow: The Emergence of Cultural Hierarchy in America*, 1988). Herein lies a problem that impacts the study of the sainete and has significance for bibliographers in the United States: Is the topic obscure because it does not merit study due to its lack of literary credentials; or, is it not studied because of a lack of available resources?

This paper supports the argument that the sainete has merit—literary and historical—and is therefore a respectable source for scholarly activity. An argument needs to be made in defense of library acquisitions in this area of study. Popular culture generally is not an area of great academic import and less so for the focused study of Latin American popular culture. Therefore, the study of the sainete, which would be a very focused area of the subcategory of Latin American popular culture, is defined as obscure not because it is not important but because it is an area not well developed in the mind of the faculty. Unfortunately, this reinforces the "obscurity" of the topic because, if research materials are not readily available, research is often not carried out.

Clearly not all libraries need focused resources in every subject area. In the United States, the well-developed interlibrary loan program brings available research material to the scholar regardless of location. However, the resources must be located at one of the interlibrary loan affiliated libraries. What is needed is an expansion of the work being done by associations such as the Seminar on the Acquisition of Latin American Library Materials (SALALM) to foster cooperative acquisition and selective collection development programs in "marginalized" areas of research such as the one discussed here. All American university libraries should, however, subscribe to the basic periodical in the area of popular culture, *Journal of Popular Culture*, and for the study of popular culture in Latin America, *Studies in Latin American Popular Culture*, even if they do not plan to acquire more in-depth materials.

What also is needed is a cooperative program of reprinting of sources by Latin American and North American public and private entities. For example, the Instituto de la Literatura Argentina "Ricardo Rojas" of the University of Buenos Aires, or the Instituto Nacional de Estudios de Teatro of the Argentine Ministerio de Educación y Cultura, could be supported in their efforts by American and international agencies. Publishing houses such as Centro Editor de la América Latina and Ediciones Corregidor (both of which have published topics in the area of Argentine popular culture) could enter into joint publishing agreements with American academic presses. These joint efforts would serve as a means of preserving sources that then can be made available to the scholar in other countries.

Tulio Carella stated in 1957 that the sainete was virgin territory for the researcher. His words are still true today, and this modest attempt to highlight the significance of the sainete is done in an attempt to further research and to spur the creation of focused library collections as an aid to that research in the United States. As summed up by one sainetero, Carlos Mauricio Pacheco, the sainete "respira nuestra vitalidad, consulta nuestra necesidades y siente nuestras pasiones" (breathes our vitality, follows our needs, and feels our passions).[13]

NOTES

1. *Vida: época maravillosa, 1903–1911* (Buenos Aires: Emecé Editores, 1965).

2. For a discussion of the role of the play "Juan Moreira" and the introduction of the *cocoliche* character see José Podestá, *Medio siglo de farándula, memorias* (Córdoba: Talleres de la Imprenta Argentina, 1930), pp. 51 ff. and 62-63.

3. Raúl Blas Gallo, *Historia del sainete nacional* (Buenos Aires: Editorial Quetzal, 1958), p. 93.

4. Marta Speroni and Griselda Vignolo, eds., *El sainete*. Foreword by Abel Posadas, Vol. 6 of *El Teatro argentino*, 6 vols. (Buenos Aires: Centro Editor de la América Latina, 1978–1982), p. iii.

5. Gallo, *Historia del sainete nacional*, p. 95.

6. Tulio Carella, ed., *El sainete criollo* (Buenos Aires: Librería Hachette, 1957), p. 14.

7. Ibid., p. 15.

8. As quoted in Gallo, *Historia del sainete nacional*, p. 44.

9. Cf. Ismael Moya, *Ezequiel Soria: Zarzuelista criolla* (Buenos Aires: Instituto de la Literatura Argentina, Facultad de Filosofía y Letras, Universidad de Buenos Aires), 1938.

10. Interview between Gardel and the newspaperman Domingo Di Riscio as quoted in Gallo, *Historia del sainete nacional*, p. 163.

11. Ibid., pp. 161-162.

12. Complete citations for the works given in this paper are to be found below in "Works Cited." In addition, the section "Selected Bibliography" contains other references related to the topic of the sainete porteño.

13. As quoted in Carella, *El sainete criollo*, p. 35.

WORKS CITED

Argentores: Revista Teatral. Buenos Aires: Sociedad General de Autores de la Argentina. Vols. 1-5, Nos. 1-162 (1934-1938).

Bambalinas: Revista de Actualidades Teatrales y Artísticas. Nos. 1-726. Buenos Aires: March 1, 1918–August 18, 1934.

Boletín de la Academia Porteña del Lunfardo. Buenos Aires: Academia Porteña del Lunfardo, 1962—.

Boletín Social de la Sociedad General de Autores de la Argentina (Argentores). Buenos Aires: 1945—. Quarterly.

Bosch, Mariano G. *Historia de los orígenes del teatro nacional argentino y la época de Pablo Podestá*. Preliminary study by Edmundo Guinbourg. Buenos Aires: Editorial Solar/Hachette, 1969. First printed in 1929 by Talleres Gráficos L. Rosso in Buenos Aires.

______. *Historia del teatro en Buenos Aires*. Buenos Aires: Establecimiento Tipográfico "El Comercio," 1910.

Bunge, Julia Valentina. *Vida: época maravillosa, 1903–1911*. Buenos Aires: Emecé Editores, 1965.

Carella, Tulio, ed. *El sainete criollo (antología)*. Buenos Aires: Librería Hachette, 1957.

Casadevall, Domingo F. *Buenos Aires: Arrabal, sainete, tango*. Buenos Aires: Compañia General Fabril, Editora, 1968.

______. *El tema de la mala vida en el teatro nacional*. Buenos Aires: Editorial Guillermo Kraft, 19xx.

Castagnino, Raúl H. *Centurias del circo criollo.* Buenos Aires: Ediciones Perrot, 1959.

______. *El circo criollo: datos y documentos para su historia, 1757–1924.* Buenos Aires: Editorial Plus Ultra, 1969.

______. *Circo, teatro gauchesco y tango.* Buenos Aires: Instituto Nacional de Estudios de Teatro, 1981. Officially published by the Ministerio de Educación y Cultura.

Echagüe, Juan Pablo. *Una época del teatro argentino (1904–1918).* Buenos Aires: Editorial América Unida, 1926. First published in 1918.

______. *Puntos de vista (Crónica bibliografía y teatro).* Barcelona: Casa Editora Maucci, 1950. Also published in 1905 in Buenos Aires by Maucci Hermanos, Editores.

______. *Seis figuras del Plata.* Buenos Aires: Editorial Losada, 1938.

Gallo, Raúl Blas. *Historia del sainete nacional.* Buenos Aires: Editorial Quetzal, 1958.

García Velloso, Enrique. *En el barrio de las ranas.* Preliminary study by Raúl H. Castagnino. Buenos Aires: Instituto de la Literatura Argentina "Ricardo Rojas," Facultad de Filosofía y Letras, Universidad de Buenos Aires, 1985.

______. *"Gabino el Mayoral" y "Fuego fatuo."* Prologue by Roberto A. Tálice. Buenos Aires: Ediciones Culturales Argentinas, 1983. Officially published by the Secretaría de Cultura de la Presidencía de la Nación.

______. *Memorias de hombre de teatro.* Prologue by Ricardo Rojas. Buenos Aires: Editorial Guillermo Kraft, 1942.

Journal of Popular Culture. Bowling Green, OH: Bowling Green State University, 1967—.

Levine, Lawrence W. *Highbrow/Lowbrow: The Emergence of Cultural Hierarchy in America.* Cambridge, MA: Harvard University Press, 1988.

López de Gomara, Ezequiel Soria y Enrique García Velloso. *Tres sainetes criollos.* Preliminary study by Luis Ordaz. Buenos Aires: Centro Editor de la América Latina, 1981.

Moya, Ismael. *Ezequiel Soria: Zarzuelista criollo.* Buenos Aires: Instituto de la Literatura Argentina, Facultad de Filosofía y Letras, Universidad de Buenos Aires, 1938.

Ordaz, Luis, ed. *Breve historia del teatro argentino*, 7 Vols. Buenos Aires: Editorial Universitaria de Buenos Aires, 1962–1965.

______. *El teatro en el Río de la Plata desde sus orígenes hasta nuestras días.* Buenos Aires: Editorial Futuro, 1946.

Pacheco, Carlos M. *El diablo en el conventillo.* Buenos Aires: Ediciones del Carro de Tespis, "Ediciones Dintel," 1966. Part of Teatro breve argentino series.

______. *"Los disfrazados" y otros sainetes.* Ed. and prologue by Marta Elena Paz. Buenos Aires: Editorial Universitaria de Buenos Aires, 1964. Includes "Los disfrazados," "Las romerías," "La patota," "Tangos, tongos y tungos," and "La tierra del fuego."

______. "Don Quijano en la Pampa" and "Los fuertes." *Bambalinas* 5, 200 (Feb. 4, 1922), 1-18, 19-30.

______. "El otro mundo." *El Entreacto: Revista Teatral* 1, 4 (n.d.), 2-16.

______. "La ribera" and "Las romerías." *El Teatro Argentino: Revista Teatral* 3, 31 (July 16, 1920), 1-12, 13-24.

______. "Veinte años después" and "La quinta de los reyes." *El Teatro Popular: Revista Teatral* 3, 72 (March 29, 1929), 1-32.

Peña, David. *Próspero: Comedia en tres actos y prólogo.* Buenos Aires: Imprenta y Casa Editora de Adolfo Grau, 1903. Authorized by Teatro San Martín.

Playbill Magazine. Philadelphia, PA: Ira L. Kamens, Publisher. Monthly.

Podestá, José J. *Medio siglo de farándula (Memorias).* Córdoba: Imprenta Argentina, 1930.

Quesada, Ernesto. *El criollísmo en la literatura argentina.* Buenos Aires: Imprenta y Casa Editorial de Coni Hermanos, 1902.

Rojas, Ricardo. *Historia de la literatura argentina. Ensayo filosófico sobre la evolución de la cultura en el Plata.* 8 vols. Buenos Aires: Editorial Losada, 1948. First printed in 1917–1922.

Sánchez, Florencio. *"Canillita": sainete en un acto.* Buenos Aires: Librería Teatro Apolo, 1915.

______. "El desalojo." *El Teatro Nacional: Revista Teatral* 3, 110 (June 9, 1920), 6-14.

______. *El teatro del uruguayo Florencio Sánchez.* 3 vols. Madrid: Editorial Cervantes, 1917–1920. Volume 1 was also published in Buenos Aires in 1917 by Editorial Tor. Introduction to Volume 1 by Vicente A. Salaverri and to Volume 2 by José Soiza Reilly. Volume 3 carried no introduction.

Soiza Reilly, Juan José de. *Hombres luminosos.* Buenos Aires: Vicente Matera, Casa Editora, 1920.

Sosa Cordero, Osvaldo. *Historia de las varietes en Buenos Aires, 1905–1975.* Buenos Aires: Ediciones Corregidor, 1978.

Speroni, Marta, and Griselda Vignolo, eds. *El sainete.* Foreword by Abel Posadas. Vol. 6 (1980) of *El teatro argentino.* 6 vols. Buenos Aires: Centro Editor de la América Latina, 1978–1982.

Studies in Latin American Popular Culture. Tucson, AZ: University of Arizona, 1982—.

El Teatro Argentino. Buenos Aires: Nos. 1–159; October 1, 1910–1922(?).

Teatro Popular. Buenos Aires: Nos. 1–133. 1919–1922.

SAINETES CONSULTED

Date	Author	Title	Theme
1889	Emilo Onrubia	Lo que sobra y lo que pasa	Political and social critique of Júarez-Celman regime
1890	Miguel Ocampo	De paso por aqui	Buenos Aires in the 1890s
1897	Ezequiel Soria	Justicia criolla	Social conditions; life in conventillo
1897	Nemesio Trejo	Los políticos	Upper class political corruption
1898	Enrique Garcia-Velloso	Gabino El Mayoral	Sociopolitical conditions
1898	Enrique De Maria	Ensalada criolla	Social conditions/ street life
1900	Nemesio Trejo	Los devotos	Life of the poor cult of the Virgin of Lujan
1902	Enrique De Maria	Bohemia criolla	Life of the poor
1902	Enrique Buttaro	Fumadas	Illusion of love among the poor
1904	Florencio Sánchez	Canillita	Conditions of the poor, struggle to make a living

Date	Author	Title	Theme
1906	Carlos Mauricio Pacheco	Los disfrazados	Conflict between creole and immigrant/ life in conventillo
1906	Enrique Garcia-Velloso	Fuego fatuo	Social conditions/life of small shopkeeper
1906	Carlos Mauricio Pacheco and Pedro E. Pico	Música criolla	
1906	Florencio Sánchez	El desalojo	City's poor/slum life
1907	Nemesio Trejo	Los inquilinos	Rent strike of 1907/ life in conventillo
1907 (ca.)	Carlos Raúl de Paoli	El velorio del angelito	Life of the poor
1907	Florencio Sánchez	Moneda falsa	Criminal life/city's poor
1908	José González Castillo	Entre bueyes no hay cornadas	Life of the poor
1909	Carlos Mauricio Pacheco	La ribera	Port area of city/ immigrants/urban poor
1910	Alberto Novión	Los primerios frios	
1910	Enrique Garcia-Velloso	En el barrio de las ranas	Sociopolitical conditions/urban poor
1910	Florencio Sánchez	Los muertos	
1911	Carlos Mauricio Pacheco	El pan amargo	Condition of working class
1915	Carlos Mauricio Pacheco	El diablo en el conventillo	City's poor
1916	Carlos Mauricio	Veinte años después	
1916	Nemesio Trejo	Las mujeres lindas	Society life/parody of upper class
1916	Alberto Novión	La fonda del Pacarito	Sociopolitical conditions/life of immigrants
1916	Roberto Cayol	El debut de la piba	
1917	José Saldías	El candidato del pueblo	Political corruption/ working class conditions
1918	Pedro E. Pico	A falta de pan	Working conditions/ World War I/life of immigrants

Date	Author	Title	Theme
1918 (ca.)	Carlos Mauricio Pacheco	El otro mundo	Class conflicts
1918	Carlos Mauricio Pacheco	Tangos, tongos y tungos	
1920	Alberto Vacarezza	Tu cuna fué un conventillo	Life of the poor
1922	Carlos Mauricio Pacheco	La patota	The bohemian life/ upper class youth
1923	Carlos Mauricio Pacheco	La Tierra del Fuego	Prison life
1928	Alberto Vacarezza	Juancilo de la Ribera	Life of the poor

SELECTED BIBLIOGRAPHY

This bibliography does not pretend to be an exhaustive one on the subject of the sainete nor on the role of the circus in Argentine popular culture. It is given as a list of reference material essential to the study of the sainete in terms of its origins, development and impact on Argentine popular culture. All references mentioned in the text are listed in "Works Cited" above.

Anthologies

Carella, Tulio, ed. *El sainete criollo (antología).* Introduction by Tulio Carella. Buenos Aires: Librería Hachette, S.A., 1957.

López de Gomara, Justo S., Ezequiel Soria, and Enrique García Velloso. *Tres sainetes criollos*. Preliminary study by Luis Ordaz. Buenos Aires: Centro Editor de la América Latina, 1981.

Ordaz, Luis, ed. *Breve historia del teatro argentino.* 7 vols. Buenos Aires: Editorial Universitaria de Buenos Aires, 1962–1965.

______. *Historia de la literatura argentina*. 5 vols. Buenos Aires: Centro Editor de la América Latina, 1980–1982.

Paz, Marta Elena, ed. *"Los disfrazados" y otros sainetes*. Buenos Aires: Editorial Universitaria de Buenos Aires, 1964.

Speroni, Marta, and Griselda Vignolo, eds. *El teatro argentino.* 6 vols. Buenos Aires: Centro Editor de la América Latina, 1978–1982.

Individual Works

Garcia Velloso, Enrique. *En el barrio de las ranas*. Preliminary study by Raúl H. Castagnino. Buenos Aires: Instituto de la Literatura Argentina "Ricardo Rojas," Facultad de Filosofía y Letras, Universidad de Buenos Aires, 1985.

______. *"Gabino el Mayoral" y "Fuego fatuo."* Prologue by Roberto A. Tálice. Buenos Aires: Ediciones Culturales Argentinas, 1983. Part of a series commissioned by the Secretaría de Cultura de la Presidencia de la Nación.

Pacheco, Carlos M. *"El diablo en el conventillo."* Buenos Aires: Ediciones Dintel, 1966. Part of the series Teatro breve argentino.

______. *"Los disfrazados" y otros sainetes*. Prologue by Marta Elena Paz. Buenos Aires: Editorial Universitaria de Buenos Aires, 1964.

Peña, David. *Próspero: Comedia en tres actos y prólogo*. Buenos Aires: Imprenta y Casa Editora de Adolfo Grau, 1903.

Podestá, José J. *Medio siglo de farándula (Memorias)*. Córdoba: Imprenta Argentina [de Córdoba], 1930.

Sánchez, Florencio. *"Canillita": sainete en un acto*. Buenos Aires: Librería Teatro Apolo, 1915.

______. "El desalojo." *El Teatro Nacional* 3, 110 (June 9, 1920), 6-14.

______. *El teatro del uruguayo Florencio Sánchez*. 3 vols. Madrid: Editorial Cervantes, 1917–1920. Also published in Buenos Aires by Editorial Tor (Vol. 1 only), 1917. Introduction to Volume 1 by Vicente A. Salaverri; introduction to Volume 2 by José Soiza Reilly. No introduction to Volume 3.

Soiza Reilly, Juan José de. *Hombres luminosos*. Buenos Aires: Vicente Matera, Casa Editora, 1920. Contains a section on Florencio Sánchez who was a friend of author.

Contemporary Literary Criticism and Theater Magazines

Bambalinas. Buenos Aires: Nos. 1-762; March 1, 1918–August 18, 1934.

Echagüe, Juan Pablo. *Una época del teatro argentino (1904–1918)*. Buenos Aires: Editorial América Unida, 1926. 2d ed. First printed in 1917-1918. Reprints of his theater reviews as published in the Buenos Aires daily newspaper *La Nación* where author served as theater critic.

______. *Memorias de un hombre de teatro (selección)* Buenos Aires: Editorial Universitaria de Buenos Aires, 1962.

______. *Puntos de vista (Crónica bibliografía y teatro).* Barcelona: Casa Editora Maucci, 1950. Also published in Buenos Aires by Maucci Hermanos, Editores in 1905.

______. *Seis figuras del Plata.* Buenos Aires: Editorial Losada, 1938. Contains biographical sketches on Enrique Gárcia Vellos and Florencio Sánchez among others as well as a critique of their works.

_________. *Seis figuras do prata.* Translated by Eduardo Tourinho. Rio de Janeiro: Imprensa Nacional, 1946.

En Entreacto. Buenos Aires: Nos. 1–24; 1922–1923.

El Teatro Argentino. Buenos Aires: Nos. 1–159; October 1, 1910–1922(?).

Teatro Popular. Buenos Aires: Nos. 1-133; 1919-1922.

Secondary Sources

Artacho, Manuel. *Indice cronológico de datos contenidos en la Historia del teatro en Buenos Aires de Mariano G. Bosch.* Buenos Aires: Instituto de la Literatura Argentina, Facultad de Filosofía y Letras, Universidad de Buenos Aires, 1940. Part of the Trabajos de seminario series.

Bosch, Mariano G. *Historia de los orígenes del teatro nacional argentino y la época de Pablo Podestá.* Preliminary study by Edmundo Guinbourg. Buenos Aires: Editorial Solar/Hachette, 1969.

_______. *Historia del teatro en Buenos Aires.* Buenos Aires: Establecimiento Tipográfico "El Comercio," 1910.

Casadevall, Domingo F. *Buenos Aires: Arrabal, sainete, tango.* Buenos Aires: Compañia General Fabril Editora, 1968.

______. *El tema de la mala vida en el teatro nacional.* Buenos Aires: Editorial Guillermo Kraft, n.d.

Castagnino, Raúl H. *Centurias del circo criollo.* Buenos Aires: Ediciones Perrot, 1959.

_______. *El circo criollo: Datos y documentos para su historia 1757–1924.* Buenos Aires: Editorial Plus Ultra, 1969.

______. *Circo, teatro gauchesco y tango.* Buenos Aires: Instituto Nacional de Estudios de Teatro, 1981. Officially published by the Ministry of Education and Culture.

______. *Sociologia del teatro nacional.* Buenos Aires: Editorial Nova, 1963.

Corti, Dora. *Florencio Sánchez*. Buenos Aires: Instituto de Literatura Argentina, Facultad de Filosofía y Letras, Universidad de Buenos Aires, 1937.

Deleito y Piñuela, José. *Orígen y apogeo del género chico*. Madrid: Revista de Occidente, 1949. Discussion on the origins of the sainete and Golden Age in Spain (1868–1910).

Gallo, Raúl Blas. *Historia del sainete nacional.* Buenos Aires: Editorial Quetzal, 1958.

Moya, Ismael. *Ezequiel Soria: Zarzuelista criollo.* Buenos Aires: Instituto de la Literatura Argentina, Facultad de Filosofía y Letras, Universidad de Buenos Aires, 1938. Part of the Crítica series.

Ordaz, Luis, ed. *El teatro en el Río de la Plata desde sus orígenes hasta nuestras días.* Buenos Aires: Editorial Futuro, 1946.

Sosa Cordero, Osvaldo. *Historia de las varietes en Buenos Aires, 1905–1975.* Buenos Aires: Ediciones Corregidor, 1978.

Taullard, Alfredo. *Historia de nuestro viejos teatros.* Buenos Aires: Imprenta López, 1932.

Theater Journals

Argentores: Revista Teatral. Buenos Aires: 1934–1938.

Boletín Social de la Sociedad General de Autores de la Argentina (Argentores). Buenos Aires: 1945—.

6. Writing from the Front Line: An Overview of Brazilian Political Publications, Pamphlets, and Ephemera from the Period of the *Abertura*, 1978–1989

Cavan Michael McCarthy

Introduction

Rapid change, at least on a formal or governmental level, is characteristic of Latin American countries, and the recent history of Brazil offers a fascinating example of this process. Over a period of a decade a tightly controlled military government gave place to an extremely open style of government, where all currents of thought and opinion were tolerated. From a government of generals, chosen by senior officers in a closed process, Brazil evolved into a pluralist democracy which almost elected a working class candidate to the presidency.[1]

This transformation is generally referred to as the *abertura*, short for *abertura política* or political opening. The period covered is roughly from late 1978, when the draconian emergency legislation (Ato Institucional Número 5) was revoked and General João Baptista de Oliveira Figueredo chosen as president. He granted amnesty to political exiles and liberalized the country. Tancredo Neves was elected indirectly in 1985 as civilian president but fell ill, and his deputy, José Sarney, was sworn in. In the five years to 1989 the remaining emergency legislation was swept away and a wide range of candidates stood for fairly contested presidential elections at the end of 1989. In the run-off Fernando Collor, from a traditional political family, won by a small margin against a former factory worker, Lula (Luís Inácio Lula da Silva).[2] It would be incorrect to treat the abertura as a purely political phenomenon, fought out in legislative chambers over the heads of the people. It affected all sectors of Brazilian society and was a result of the activities of innumerable organizations and groups. Some were large, others small, some were limited to one neighborhood, others covered the entire country. Some organizations had purely political aims whereas others were dedicated to one social problem, such as land reform or housing, or specific groups, for instance blacks or women.

Whatever their type, these organizations produced a fascinating kaleidoscope of publications, ranging from newspapers and magazines, through political pamphlets, to purely ephemeral materials such as handouts and posters. The majority of their production was of printed materials, but significant quantities of audiovisual media were produced, as were visible signs of democratic electoral process, such as buttons, flags, and T-shirts.

This paper offers a brief overview of these materials, characterizing them first by physical type, for example, newspapers, pamphlets, films, and so on. The organizations responsible for their production are discussed and finally libraries and other institutions that have preserved significant collections are cited. As a professor of library science, I am interested in nonstandard or noncommercial publications such as *literatura de cordel*, regional imprints, or small press poetry. Resident in Brazil throughout this period, I examined numerous publications and retained samples of many. The abertura impacted upon a wide range of other activities that could not be covered in this brief paper; for instance, books by commercial publishers and popular music are discussed here only when they are of relevance to ephemeral publications.

Publications by Physical Type

Newspapers and Magazines

Newspaper format offers a familiar, popular means to communicate effectively and regularly with a wide audience; it was therefore frequently used for opposition publications of the period. The most famous newspaper publication was the long-lived *Pasquim*, which spanned and transcended this period, opposing and provoking the military in the blackest period of repression while managing to survive beyond the *abertura.*[3] It owed much of its flexibility to the fact that it published humor and comment instead of following a specific political line. The strident *Hora do Povo*, issued by the noisy MR8 splinter group, was probably the first hard-left publication to have national impact, coming out weekly from 1979 to 1980.[4] A more stable weekly newspaper was the Brazilian Communist Party's *Voz da Unidade*, legal from 1980 and still appearing regularly.[5] The appearance of a left-wing press met with a violent reaction from the still active Brazilian right in 1980; numerous threats were made and several newsstands were actually firebombed for selling political publications.[6] Newspaper format was also adopted when publishers wanted to get a message out to a wider audience; *Lampião*, Brazil's first homosexual publication, offered a clear example of this tendency.[7] *Beijo da Rua* (Kiss of the Street), a publication for prostitutes in Rio de Janeiro, owed much of its impact to a lively tabloid format with numerous photographs.[8]

Because of its familiarity newspaper format was frequently adopted even by relatively small organizations, for example, for *Tempos Novos*, the monthly newspaper for basic ecclesiastical communities of Maranhão.[9]

The newspapers discussed in this paper appeared weekly or monthly rather than daily; such frequencies were more suitable to the finances and organizational level of the institutions involved. For this reason the distinction between newspapers and magazines is not clearcut; a notable example here was offered by the major journal of the early part of the *abertura*, *Opinião*, a weekly magazine printed on newsprint from 1972 through 1979.[10] It frequently attracted the wrath of the authorities in those difficult times, often having half its articles censored. It was unable to survive to reap the benefits of the free press for which it had fought, although it can be considered the predecessor of glossier, middle-class-oriented weeklies such as *Isto É* and *Afinal*.

The traditional periodical format, with publication quarterly, semiannually, or irregularly, was frequently adopted by socially oriented groups and institutions of all types. These periodicals tended to be text oriented, printing articles of interest to people who already supported their policies. Of special interest were *Cadernos do CEAS*, issued every two months by the Centro de Estudos e Ação Social in Salvador.[11] More than 124 issues of this Jesuit-supported periodical have come out; it is an important information source for the study of ephemeral materials because its last few pages list publications of other organizations. Among periodicals of value for a study of this period can be noted *Lua Nova*,[12] *Novos Rumos*,[13] *Reforma Agrária*,[14] *Teoria e Política*,[15] *Novos Estudos CEBRAP*,[16] *Ensaio*,[17] and numerous others. Editorial standards are generally high in Brazil and political periodicals were usually well presented. Mimeographed periodicals had little impact at the time; one lively example, despite its simple production methods, was *Mulher-Libertação*, a periodical for prostitutes produced in São Paulo.[18] But the cruder productions methods were more frequently used for pamphlets than for periodicals.

On the one hand, the periodicals of the period of the abertura were generally of low circulation, not systematically found in bookshops, had erratic subscription arrangements, and were little known except to militants of their organizations. On the other hand, the increased financial resources available on the left in recent years permitted the existence of a few socially oriented magazines which have been able to reach a relatively high level of presentation, giving them a general appearance not far from that of the typical newsstand mass-production magazine. Here we can cite *Teoria e Debate*[19] of the Partido dos

Trabalhadores and *Tempo e Presença* of CEDI (Centro Ecumênico de Documentaçao e Informação).[20] Some of the better-organized periodicals, such as *Cadernos do CEAS* and *Presença da Mulher*,[21] even quoted a subscription price in dollars.

Labor union newspapers have recently become a major publishing area in Brazil. Union membership was compulsory for private-sector workers and unions received a regular, inflation-proof income, deducted from pay slips, equivalent to one day's pay each year for every worker. Numerous committed young journalists streamed annually from Brazil's fertile journalism faculties, so most labor unions were able to publish a newspaper or bulletin. This phenomenon was scarcely noted by the general public or by libraries, and the only systematic information I know of came from an article in the *Jornal do Brasil*.[22] It reported a total printing of 12 million copies per month and stated that four unions issued daily newspapers. The metalworkers in the industrial cities near São Paulo, where Lula first rose to prominence, were in the forefront of this process, printing 35,000 copies of a daily newspaper written by a team of twelve journalists.

The same article mentioned that the São Paulo bank workers newspaper, now printed daily in two colors, began by reprinting extracts from other newspapers. Clippings files constituted a major source of information in Brazil, in many organizations they were the only source of accurate recent information. This fact was reflected by the appearance of numerous bulletins which consisted basically of summaries, or even reprints, of news items taken from the daily press. The selection reflected committed points of view, and the editorial team wrote relevant supporting commentaries. Such publications were quite popular in Brazil, a geographically huge country without national newspapers. Here we can cite *Quinzena*,[23] *Boletim do AGEN*,[24] and *Aconteceu*,[25] all appearing regularly at the moment of writing. These publications were valuable on a day-to-day basis in Brazil but they constituted secondary, rather than primary, information sources; for this reason they may not be rated a high priority by research libraries overseas. A related publication, very useful at the grass-roots level in because but considered a secondary information source overseas, is the *dossiê*, a monographic collection of press clippings on a specific subject, reproduced by photocopy or by electronic stencil and mimeograph.

The use of press clippings as a source was taken a stage further by the Instituto Brasileiro de Análises Sociais e Econômicas (IBASE), a Rio de Janeiro organization that fed summaries of press reports into microcomputers and distributed the information nationally as a database for members of socially committed organizations. It was possible to subscribe to all information, or just to segments, such as popular movements, labor unions, or agrarian questions.[26] This was also the first socially committed organization in Brazil to use electronic mail.

Pamphlets

Pamphlets probably constituted the most fascinating ephemeral publications of the period. They were generally produced to communicate simplified messages to a wide audience of persons of relatively low educational level. For this reason they frequently had punchy titles, and the wrappers, within the limitations of their unsophisticated production methods, attempted to attract the attention of potential readers. The internal text frequently incorporated line drawings and was often spaced out and printed in large letters to facilitate reading by persons with little schooling. The vocabulary and constructions were also simplified. Most pamphlets were offset in black ink on cheap paper, although mimeographed and even photocopying were also used. A common size was 22 X 16 centimeters, roughly equivalent to an American legal-sized sheet, folded once; colored paper or card was frequently used for the wrapper. They were sold at low prices, made possible because they were frequently produced by religious or trade union organizations. It is notable that the basic objective of these groups was to modify social structures; the publication of pamphlets was seen as just one of many means of achieving that end.

It is difficult to communicate the flavor of these pamphlets in cold print, but it is worth trying to describe some typical examples. *Peasant Farmers: Production and Exploitation* was a 31-page pamphlet issued by Caritas from the Archbishop's Office in São Luís, Maranhão.[27] The tone was set on the front wrapper, a crude line drawing of a poorly dressed peasant, carrying a hoe, captioned "I work hard and have nothing. . . ." A comic strip occupied the first four pages, showing how landowners and wholesalers kept the riches produced by those who worked the land, "creating this situation so as to be able to dominate" the peasants. The text on the remaining pages was mostly in capital letters, double-spaced, broken into small paragraphs; it encouraged peasant communities to set up community warehouses to keep their produce for sale at a better price. This 22 X 16 centimeter pamphlet was cheaply offset on poor quality paper; most pages had simple line drawings.

From the industrial suburbs of São Paulo came *Constituent Assembly and Constitution: What the Shanty Towns Think.* This was a 24-page pamphlet from the Movement in Defense of the Rights of

Shanty Towns, with an address in the offices of the Roman Catholic parish of São Bernardo do Campo.[28] It suggested that meetings should be organized in shanty towns to inform the poor of the upcoming Constitutional Assembly and to collect proposals from the community. The document outlined agendas for a series of four meetings, covering subjects such as hunger, unemployment, minimum salary, medical care, sanitation, and urban services. The text was clear and simple, subdivided into small paragraphs with frequent use of capital letters. The numerous illustrations included both photographs and line drawings, showing roughly built shacks, poor people holding banners, and policemen throwing a man into jail.

As another typical example we can examine *Strike in Paradise*, a pamphlet describing a 1983 dispute involving forestry workers in Minas Gerais state.[29] This was published by the Commission for Rural Pastoral Activities of Minas Gerais State and was number two in the series The Story of the Struggle of the Rural Workers of Minas Gerais. The wrapper set the tone with a simple line drawing showing workers carrying placards saying "We want our rights!" and "Down with exploitation!" This pamphlet was also designed to be used at a series of nine meetings at which two person alternated the reading of brief paragraphs. Again, there were illustrations on most pages, for example, a determined-looking man with clenched fist saying "Our strength is in unity." Strike songs were included ("Bye, bye, boss, until we get our rights, we ain't gonna work no more"), and the owners of the pamphlets were encouraged to write down their own thoughts on the final page.

In general these pamphlets were difficult to obtain; they were normally produced in low print runs by small organizations, often in remote cities. The Centro de Pastoral Vergueiro (CPV) of São Paulo, was the major source for publications of this type, issuing catalogs and mailing materials on a COD basis.[30] A few items got into local bookshops, but it was difficult to find a bookstore with a wide range, and the pamphlets rarely appeared on the secondhand market. The organizations responsible normally had a small stock of recent examples, but no mechanism to send them out on a regular basis; the publication of pamphlets was not their major activity. Personal visits were difficult because offices were often located in far-flung suburbs. Living in Brazil, I wrote letters asking for them and enclosing a few stamps; most organizations sent something back. But both visits and individual letters were labor-intensive methods of obtaining materials.

At least one series of pamphlets was produced well enough to be taken up by Vozes, a major publisher; they were the catechism documents from the jungle diocese of São Félix do Araguaio, whose bishop Pedro Casaldáliga, an accomplished poet, was famous for defending the poor in the land wars that raged over that region. The series of booklets published by Vozes, based on documents of his diocese, were notable for the quality of their illustrations and for their combination of religious and political elements. For example, one pamphlet included line drawings of a priest baptizing chained slaves and of a policeman shooting a priest.[31] Catechism documents would rarely or never be acquired by research libraries, and their titles do not necessarily indicate the interest of their contents; the example described in the last sentence was from a pamphlet called "What Is the Church?"

Literatura de cordel is a specifically Brazilian phenomenon: small-format pamphlets of popular verse, sold to the masses in marketplaces, especially in the Northeast or in cities with a large number of people from that region. The abertura was fully commented on by popular poets in this format. Since I wrote a comprehensive paper on this subject for the 1989 SALALM conference,[32] I do not cover the subject in detail here. Political *cordel* shared many of the characteristics of pamphlets in general: snappy titles, simple cover illustrations, and popular language. Copies were available locally or via a few enthusiasts, but there was no systematic distribution postally or via bookshops. *Cordel* was, however, included among the numerous pamphlets and other materials distributed by the Centro de Pastoral Vergueiro. The CPV was responsible for printing one of the most interesting cordel items from this period, a collection of texts by the self-styled "factory gate poet," Crispiano Neto.[33] He versified everyday problems of the working class and proposed socialist solutions.

Comic books were extremely popular reading in Brazil, and it was natural to find socially oriented pamphlets that used that presentation. A humorous example was issued in 1986 by the Chemical Industry Workers' Union from the industrial suburbs of São Paulo.[34] This eight-page strip told the story of Skullman who did not join the union and did everything the boss asked, including cleaning a vat of corrosive liquid without protective clothing. He fell in, but his ghost came back to advise workers to unionize. "The Situation of the Working Class Minor" was a more complex thirteen-page strip, telling the story of César, a seventeen-year-old construction worker earning half the minimum salary.[35] When he finished his apprenticeship he was sacked because there were no vacancies for adult workers. Unable to get a job because he had not done his military service, he began to hang out with a group that minded parked cars and smoked marijuana. This comic strip depicted poor people in typical environments and the last page listed nine things that minors needed, such as fair wages, free education, and medical care.

The Brazilian press has a strong tradition of political cartoons which are generally beyond the scope of this paper.[36] No discussion of the abertura would be complete, however, without a mention of Henfil, a brilliant cartoonist who could be said to incorporate the spirit of the abertura and who published frequently in *Pasquim*. His stumpy, outlined figures with complex text influenced many other cartoonists, but unfortunately he did not live to the end of this period; he was a hemophiliac who got AIDS from a blood transfusion.[37]

Some posters were produced during the abertura but in general they had a relatively peripheral impact. The more interesting of the items I saw were printed for the land reform campaign. The cult items of the abertura were T-shirts and buttons.

Nonprint Materials and Ephemera

At the beginning of our period audiotapes, slides, tape-slide sets, or short films were frequently produced by committed groups. Slide sets were perhaps the most common; the "13 May—Nucleus for Popular Education" in São Paulo produced several, including one of no fewer than 314 items which told the history of the labor movement in Brazil.[38]

The period of the abertura coincided with major technological changes, especially in the field of audiovisual materials. By the end of the eighties the varied formats previously used were beginning to be replaced by the far simpler videotape. A CPV catalog of publications relevant to women published in 1988 gave as much space to videos as to tape-slide sets.[39] Videotapes listed in that guide included interviews with child prostitutes from the streets of Recife and discussions of contraception. As had happened with newspapers, committed groups adopted a familiar, popular medium to be able to communicate with the masses and it became possible to find organizations where the only audiovisual materials handled were in videotape. Although equipment was relatively expensive in Brazil as a whole, the existence of a free port in Manaus, the capital of Amazonas state, meant that inexpensive video cameras were readily available near the regions where land disputes were common. Activist-sponsored videos frequently showed mass meetings, people marching with banners, religious services, and so on. A São Paulo newspaper organized a festival of "militant video" in 1984.[40] One of the participants, a professor of journalism from Pará state, had produced 120 hours of tape documenting change and conflict in the Amazon region. He was careful always to return to the places that he had filmed to show the participants the tapes he had made. Television broadcasting, a monopoly of big companies in Brazil, is beyond the scope of this paper, but electoral law at the end of the abertura made lengthy TV slots available free of charge for all candidates and parties. It would not be possible to comprehend fully recent voting patterns without examining sample videotapes of programs and debates.

No activity of Brazil can take place without music, and the abertura was no exception: music was liberalized and released from censorship alongside newspapers and magazines. Paradoxically, singers who had been at the forefront of the struggle against the military regime, such as Chico Buarque and Caetano Veloso, tended to lose the attention of the public as the country became more relaxed. Activist groups rarely had the resources to make and distribute phonograph records, an area that continued to be dominated by major companies. A few activist records were sold via the highly efficient Paulinas chain of religious bookshops; a typical example was "The Path of the Martyrs," available as both an LP record and a cassette, launched by Bishop Pedro Casaldáliga for a national conference of basic ecclesiastical communities.[41] This included songs about a murdered street child, a black leader, a worker, Archbishop Romero, and others. Widely distributed and of great interest were songbooks with titles like *Let's Sing, Comrades!*, *Struggling and Singing*, or *Songs of the Peasant Struggle*. The contents were as revolutionary as the titles: "Wake up peasants/ Come on, let's wake up/See that the land is ours/And we're going to fight to get it/There is so much land in the world/With nobody to plant it/Men are thrown off the land/So that cattle can graze/Peasants go into shanty towns/And have to live on nothing," and "Some people rolling in money/Others dying of hunger/Some have pleasure without love/Others disgust and pain/But this is not what God wants/No, this is not what God wants," and "The poor are exhausted/Badly fed/No way forward/ Low salaries/All they get/is exploitation."[42]

Political ephemera literally inundated the streets of Brazil during the extremely free elections at the end of the period of the abertura. Tons of paper were thrown from trucks or handed out at traffic signals; there was also some use of direct mail. The simpler election flyers just had a picture of the candidate with name and electoral number; these were known as *santinhas* because of their similarity with the pictures of saints carried by Catholics. The initials of the political party and simple slogans also commonly appeared on political handouts. More solid information, such as party platforms or the candidates' promises, was available from their brightly painted offices. These tended to be run with more enthusiasm than organization, and it was often necessary to make a couple of visits, or to buy a T-shirt and buttons, in order to obtain a significant document. T-shirts, entirely adequate for the Brazilian, became the uniform of the abertura; many millions were sold to support direct elections for the presidency, or on behalf of the candidacies of Tancredo Neves or Lula. Political buttons, car stickers, and mass-produced banners were also common in the later years of the abertura. One Brazilian company got so skilled in this area that it began to print propaganda for New York election campaigns. Because of difficulties in handling and storage, together with their often limited informational content, nonprint and ephemeral materials will rarely attract the attention of librarians or archivists, which is a pity because much of this material is visually exciting.

Organizations by Type

It was quite difficult to find right-wing political literature at the time of the abertura; the extreme right organization Tradição, Família e Pátria was more or less dormant, and, in fact, the subject of a book debunking its activities.[43] The landowners' political party União Democrática Ruralista published almost nothing; its stands at agricultural shows, for instance, did not sell pamphlets. It was, however, one of Brazil's very successful pressure groups and was able to block land reform in the Constituent Assembly despite the fact that the innumerable publications on the subject during this period were almost uniformly in favor of land reform. The right then went on to win the presidential elections, despite left-wing publishing and pamphleteering in the period of the abertura. Printed documents were only one factor influencing voting patterns; it is also necessary to consider such factors as ingrained attitudes built up over decades, the impact of television, and the orientation of political bosses and opinion-leaders. The wide editorial freedom established in Brazil during the abertura in this period had one unexpected result in that it permitted the emergence of a neo-Nazi, anti-Semitic publisher at the end of the eighties. This launched a widely sold defense of Nazi Germany and reprinted the *Protocols of the Elders of Zion*.[44] This type of activity would not have been imaginable a few years earlier.

The rapid rise of the left during this period of Brazilian history was fully reflected in political ephemera, which ranged from socially committed to hard left. To some extent this can be seen as a natural reaction against the twenty-one years of military rule when all left-wing writing was rigidly suppressed. In preparing a survey of popular poetry pamphlets from this period, I was unable to find a single right-wing example.[45] Political organizations flourished during the period; from two parties, closely controlled by the state, Brazil reached a near anarchic state in which dozens of mini-parties competed for the electors' attention. Some were created simply so that they could claim free television time or be used by potential candidates who did not have a party. Most political parties left few publications, apart from handouts cleared from the streets after elections. Elected politicians, especially left-wing mayors from major cities, published newspapers and pamphlets to maintain contact with their electors, but these materials were normally unobtainable outside the city. Beyond the scope of this paper is the publishing done by federal deputies and senators, usually reprints of speeches for distribution in their home states. Elected representatives had a right to print their speeches in this way, and numerous volumes, often quite substantial, were published. The impact of this material on the political process was minimal; it is common to find copies in mint condition on secondhand bookstalls.

The political parties that had significant publishing programs were all on the left: The Partido dos Trabalhadores (PT), the Soviet-influenced Partido Comunista Brasileiro (PCB), and the small but noisy Albanian-line Partido Comunista do Brasil (PC do B). The PT was the most interesting of these parties because it grew out of the workers' movement and the strikes in the industrial suburbs of São Paulo in the late 1970s, had a well-known leader, Lula, a former toolmaker, and was from the beginning strongly supported by intellectuals and writers. Their publications were among the best produced of the period; the PT quarterly magazine *Teoria e Debate* printed 20.000 copies of each issue, a significant number in Brazil. There was also a monthly newspaper,[46] and its electoral propaganda was well written and intelligently argued.[47] The numerous books published by or about the PT tended to come from commercial publishers.[48] The PCB had its own publishing house, Novos Rumos, a widely available weekly newspaper, and a periodical; its books and pamphlets were frequently sold alongside imported Soviet publications.[49] The PC do B, like many splinter groups, made a noise disproportional to its size, publishing both a magazine and a newspaper.[50] Its publications were sold alongside translations of Enver Hoxha's works and were sometimes decorated with portraits of the original gang of four, Marx, Engels, Lenin, and Stalin.

The PT grew out of the labor movement, and unions were prolific publishers of pamphlets during this period. Perhaps the most important single source was the CUT (Central Única dos Trabalhadores, usually referred to only by its acronym). It published numerous individual pamphlets and series such as *Boletim Nacional*, *Caderno de Formação*, and *Debate Sindical*.[51] Publications of individual unions are normally brief pamphlets on workers' rights or specific strikes and are generally difficult to obtain.

The major best-seller in Brazil at this time was the in-depth examination of torture during the military government, *Brasil, nunca mais*.[52] It was translated into English, ran to twenty-three editions, and stayed on the best-seller list for more than two years. It was conceived, organized, and published entirely by the Diocese of São Paulo. Religious organizations in Brazil at this time were important in the publishing context and worked hard to improve the conditions of the poor and the oppressed. The nature of their ephemeral publications frequently overlapped that of political parties and labor unions. A key term here is "pastoral work" or activities carried out with the masses to improve the situation of the disadvantaged.[53] The meaning in English is close to "committed" or "activist"; publications produced to support these activities are known as pastoral documents.

Perhaps the most important single organization for the distribution and preservation of activist publications was the São Paulo-based Centro de Pastoral Vergueiro; its activities were roughly similar to those of a documentation center, combining library, archive, and document distribution, both wholesale and via COD.[54] In rural Brazil a key organization was the Comissão Pastoral da Terra (CPT, translated here as Commission for Rural Pastoral Activities). A national network linked to dioceses coordinated work in rural areas, forming an important source of publications on land reform, migration, migrant workers, and landless peasants. Human rights groups also frequently worked in conjunction with religious organizations, offering legal support to the oppressed. They sometimes published pamphlets for local distribution and had a national newspaper.[55]

Key organizations in the religious field were the Comunidades Eclesiais de Base, or CEBs (the acronym is almost always used); these basic ecclesiastical communities were the grass-roots religious organizations among the population.[56] They did not actually publish (they were de-bureaucratized and did not even keep minutes of their meetings), but numerous publications were produced at the diocesan or national level for use by CEBs.[57] In Recife, for instance, it was at one stage possible to purchase thirty or forty mimeographed publications with titles like *The Struggle of Working Class Youth*, *Asking and Replying*, *Organizing*, *Youth Prayers*, *New Paths*, and so on.[58] When the much-loved liberal Archbishop Dom Helder Câmara was replaced by a conservative successor in 1985 this type of publication abruptly ceased and the information center for pastoral work was closed. It was possible to find institutions which had religious names or support but which were responsible for publishing programs that went far beyond traditional church activities. Perhaps the prime example was the Rio de Janeiro-based Instituto de Estudos da Religião—ISER (Institute for Religious Studies), which published a catalog of black organizations,[59] a newspaper for prostitutes,[60] and a general political newspaper called *Vermelho e Branco*.[61] A recent issue of the last was devoted entirely to the Romanian revolution.

Documents on land reform, migration, migrant farm workers, and rural unions were a common feature of this period and were produced in all parts of Brazil. A catalog of documents on rural workers listed publications from cities such as Erexim, Própria, Teresina, São Luís, and Goiânia.[62] A newspaper called *O Migrante* appeared regularly from the remote agricultural frontier city of Ji-Paraná, Rondônia.[63] Some national-level organizations were also important in this context, notably the Centro de Estudos Migratórios and the Movimento dos Trabalhadores Rurais Sem Terra, both located in São Paulo.[64] The latter organization was responsible for well-produced and widely distributed pamphlets, with titles like *The Struggle Continues*, *How to Organize*, or *Our Strength Depends on Our Dedication*.[65]

Brazil had a significant population of African descent, but a cohesive black movement never got off the ground, and the relevant publishing was often historical in nature, focusing on the abolition of slavery or communities of escaped slaves.[66] Other pamphlets tried to raise the consciousness of the black population; one example had a crude drawing of a policeman arresting a black worker, while a white thief walked away with the loot from a mugging.[67] Relevant publications tended to come from cities where a significant proportion of the population was of African descent, such as Salvador, where a thin newspaper was published irregularly.[68]

Indians did not, of course, publish pamphlets, but numerous relevant items were issued by groups that defended their rights. Here the key organization was the Centro Indígeno Missionário (CIMI), based in Brasília but with branches in many cities, often sharing the same building as the CPT.[69] The most important national publication was the newspaper *Porantim*; most other publications dealt with individual tribes or the Indians of specific regions.[70] One very elaborate example dealt with Indians in Minas Gerais state; it began with a general history of the colonization of the state, listing its tribes, then focused on a single community, examining the murder of an

Indian by a landowner's thugs.[71] The book included text, tables, photographs, reproductions of press clippings and Indian drawings; the murder of the Indian was detailed in an eleven-page comic strip.

Feminists became relatively well organized in Brazil at this time. The government even sponsored a National Council for Women's Rights, which published pamphlets such as *Women and the Constituent Assembly*.[72] Numerous other publications encouraged women to fight for their rights; an especially interesting example was the comic strip *Women and Domestic Violence*, published in one of the poorer suburbs of Rio de Janeiro.[73] It described disputes in an extended working class family; as each situation of conflict or violence was depicted, the booklet cited relevant legislation in an understandable form. Many other documents issued by feminist organizations dealt in simple terms with contraception and female physiology. Women's studies even had their own information center, Centro Informação Mulher, in São Paulo; it did significant bibliographical work but was inactive by the end of our period.[74] The same fate overtook the nationally distributed feminist newspaper *Mulherio*.[75]

Homosexuals also had a widely circulated newspaper, *Lampião*,[76] at the beginning of this period, but, like *Mulherio*, it did not last long. It was extremely difficult to maintain a nationally published newspaper for a special interest group; a few left-wing political parties succeeded, but they sold basically to a cohesive membership. Apart from *Lampião*, some gay poetry and occasional items dealing with AIDS, I noted few homosexual publications. A further indication that little came out was the fact that homosexual publications did not gain separate treatment in either the Library of Congress microfilm project or the CPV catalogs; the only special group categories used were those for blacks, Indians, and women.[77] Other groups that published widely overseas, but had not yet had significant impact within Brazil, were the green or ecologically oriented parties. Their ideas only began to enter Brazil at the end of our period; another factor was that in the Northern Hemisphere the Greens often attracted people who were reacting against traditional political parties, whereas in Brazil during this period such persons gravitated toward the Partido dos Trabalhadores.

Principal Collections

Librarians generally consider ephemeral items difficult to preserve or not worth handling; programs to acquire and process the publications of developing countries also face special problems. It was therefore natural to find few institutions interested in ephemeral political publications from Brazil. It was difficult to obtain these materials on a systematic basis; a significant number could be obtained via the Centro de Pastoral Vergueiro, but the remainder had to be requested, purchased, or subscribed to individually from a wide variety of organizations and locations. Documentation centers attached to organizations working in this field could organize exchange programs with other activist groups; this practice is somewhat similar to the exchange arrangements of publishers of poetry magazines and small presses in the Northern Hemisphere, but can rarely be used by libraries outside the field. Processing of materials received is also made more complex by failure to print place and date of publication in pamphlets, incorrect numbering of periodical parts, lack of standardization of series titles, and so on. Newspapers and periodicals may arrive irregularly and it is difficult to claim missing issues. Many organizations print on poor paper, making early microfilming essential. Publications come in a variety of sizes and formats, including audiovisual materials. Collections that aimed to be truly complete would have to include buttons and T-shirts, considered realia by libraries and archives.

Within Brazil the principal general collection of ephemeral material of this period was located at the Centro de Pastoral Vergueiro in São Paulo.[78] This was a documentation and distribution center for the publications of activist groups of all types. A well-organized library preserved copies of all relevant materials and offered a photocopy service. The CPV also distributed publications, by COD within Brazil, and produced numerous catalogs, many of them computer produced. Many catalogs included both recent publications and items held only in the library, so that the user could either buy an original or order a photocopy. The CPV also published books, not necessarily in a very obvious manner; I came across one item where the only link to the CPV was the post office box number on the verso of the title page.[79]

A recent paper, one of the rare Brazilian discussions of preservation measures in this field, spoke of the "fragmentation" of documents among numerous institutions. This view coincided with the impression that I had of the field: numerous small, limited collections of relevant documents can be found in CPTs, political party offices, human rights centers, feminist and similar groups all over Brazil. At the same time there is little or no coordination of this work nor are resources available to form larger, systematically preserved and organized collections. The documentalists working in the area have taken preliminary steps, organizing regular meetings with the representatives of up to twenty documentation centers.[80]

The authors of that paper worked for the CEDI (Centro Ecumênico de Documentação e Informação) with offices in both Rio de

Janeiro and São Paulo.[81] Among other relevant institutions was IBASE, the computerized information service for pastoral agents located in Rio de Janeiro.[82] Also in Rio was the multifaceted Institute for Religious Studies.[83] The National Council for Woman's Rights recently established a documentation center, CEDIM (Centro de Estudos, Documentação e Informação sobre a Mulher).[84] They have begun to issue *Acervo Mulher*, printed from a database of documents of feminist interest, using the Micro Isis software which is being promoted in Brazil at the moment.[85] The Centro de Estudos e Ação Social in Salvador is an important source for the publications of Northeast Brazil.[86] An active documentation center in Minas Gerais state, named after the murdered president of a rural workers' syndicate, printed an appeal for further information.[87] The center intended to document CEBs, land disputes, and unions in the state and asked participants to tell their stories to the Center so that the memory of their struggles might be preserved.

I have listed names and addresses of organizations, but it is necessary to point out that publishing or selling copies of documents to foreign libraries is not their chief objective. Many will be happy to have contact with foreign institutions; IBASE produces publicity materials in English, and several of the better-organized magazines quote a subscription price in dollars. Other organizations may be more reticent, reserving sensitive documents for internal use or even being unwilling to sell large quantities of documents to institutions overseas. Such attitudes will seem alien to persons brought up on the concept of freedom of information within the North American and British library tradition. But such ideals are little known in Brazil, where many of the people working in this area have suffered severe repression in the past for their beliefs and activities.

The Library of Congress has maintained a dynamic field office in Rio de Janeiro for many years; they noted the growing importance of ephemeral materials in 1984 and set up a major collection and preservation program, extending back to 1966 imprints. Materials were collected by the Library of Congress office in Rio, cataloged and prepared for microfilming. The first collection of these materials covered 803 pamphlets, 200 serial titles, and 143 posters published 1966 to 1986, preserved on 28 rolls of microfilm. The collection was divided into categories; relation and theology was the largest, followed by agrarian reform.[88] A second collection of ephemeral materials was being organized to cover the years 1987-1989.

I know only one other foreign institution with a significant collection in this area: Princeton University. This university had previously microfilmed ephemeral material from Chile and extended the scope of its program to cover other Latin American countries.

Conclusions

Brazilian history is notable for rapid cyclic movements and little stability. At certain periods vigorous mass movements arose, only to be heavily repressed a short time later. There were periods in which the entire country discussed its future, printing and publishing at an almost frenetic rate, alternating with decades when the authorities decided what was to be said and done, while intellectual life retreated into silence and censorship.

Libraries must continue to acquire materials at all times and should clearly give priority to more formal books and periodicals. But at times of intellectual ferment, such as the abertura política in Brazil, there will be changes in publishing patterns and a significant quantity of ephemeral materials will be produced. Librarians must be aware of this process and be ready to set up collection and preservation programs for ephemeral materials. The acquisition and organization of such items requires an understanding of the currents of thought within society, contact with a wide variety of organizations, and the handling of materials that are more complex and varied than those normally collected by libraries. The task is daunting but the rewards are great, because libraries and archives will be preserving the working material used by society to think through and discuss its process of change and development.

BIBLIOGRAPHICAL NOTES

General Note: I have personally examined all pamphlet and book materials and at least one issue of every periodical cited in these notes. In certain cases I had to infer the date of the first issue of a periodical from its volume number. The subtitles of Brazilian periodicals tend to vary; political newspapers frequently cease publication temporarily to be relaunched later in a new series.

1. Thomas Skidmore, *Brasil: de Castelo a Tancredo, 1964–1985* (Rio de Janeiro: Paz e Terra, 1988), 608 pp., a translation of his *The Politics of Military Rule in Brazil, 1964–1985.*

2. The publications of Editora Abril are essential reference sources for this period; the most established Brazilian weekly, *Veja*, was a major source of information and above all was comprehensively indexed from 1972. Brazil's major almanac, *Almanaque Abril*, describes events of the previous year. In turn the events in the almanac were summarized in *Brasil dia-a-dia* (São Paulo, April, 1988), 258 pp.

3. *Pasquim* (Rio de Janeiro, 1968—).

4. *Hora do Povo* (Rio de Janeiro, 1979-1980).

5. *Voz da Unidade* (São Paulo, 1980—), Newspaper of the Partido Comunista Brasileiro.

6. Paolo Marconi, *A censura política na imprensa brasileira, 1968–1978*, 2d ed., rev., Passado e presente, 44 (São Paulo: Global, 1980), 312 pp.

7. *Lampião da Esquina: Jornal Gay* (Rio de Janeiro, 1978—).

8. *Beijo da Rua* (Rio de Janeiro, 1989—).

9. *Tempos Novos* (São Luís, 1982—).

10. *Opinião* (Rio de Janeiro, 1972-1979).

11. *Cadernos do CEAS* (Salvador: Centro de Estudos e Ação Social, 1977—).

12. *Lua Nova* (São Paulo: Centro de Estudos de Cultura Contemporânea, 1984—).

13. *Novos Rumos* (São Paulo: Editora Novos Rumos, 1985—). Editora Novos Rumos is the publishing house of the Partido Comunista Brasileiro.

14. *Reforma Agrária* (Brasília, 1972—).

15. *Teoria e Política*, Brasil Debates, no. 12 (São Paulo, 1989).

16. *Novos Estudos CEBRAP* (São Paulo: Centro Brasileiro de Análise e planejamento, 1981—).

17. *Ensaio* (São Paulo), no. 13 (1984).

18. *Mulher-Libertação* (São Paulo, 1985—).

19. *Teoria e Debate: revista trimestral do Partido dos Trabalhadores* (São Paulo, 1988—).

20. *Tempo e Presença* (Rio de Janeiro and São Paulo: CEDI [Centro Ecumênico de Documentação e Informação], 1978—).

21. *Presença da Mulher* (São Paulo: Editora Liberdade Mulher, 1986—).

22. Luiz M. Carvalho, "Imprensa sindical tem tiragem de 12 milhões por mês," *Jornal do Brasil* (20 November 1988), 19.

23. *Quinzena* (São Paulo: Centro de Pastoral Vergueiro, 1988—).

24. *Boletim do AGEN* (São Paulo: Agência Ecumênica de Notícias, 1986—). Some issues are titled simply *AGEN*.

25. *Aconteceu* (São Paulo: CEDI [Centro Ecumênico de Documentação e Informação], 1985—).

26. IBASE, Rua Vicente de Souza, 29, Botafogo, CEP 22.251, Rio de Janeiro, RJ.

27. *O lavrador: Produção e exploração* (São Luís: Caritas Brasileira, Escritório Regional de São Luís, 1986), 31 pp.

28. *Constituinte e Constituição: o que pensa o favelado* (São Bernardo do Campo: Movimento de Defesa dos Direitos dos Favelados, [1985?]), 22 pp.

29. *Greve no Paraíso*, História das lutas dos trabalhadores rurais de Minas Gerais, 2 (Contagem, MG: Comissão Pastoral da Terra de Minas Gerais, 1984), 34 pp.

30. Centro de Pastoral Vergueiro, Caixa Postal, 42.761, CEP 04229, São Paulo, SP.

31. *Igreja, o que?*, 9th ed., Coleção da base para a base, 7 (Petrópolis: Vozes, 1988), 46 pp. At head of title page: "Prelazia de São Félix do Araguaia." Preface signed by Pedro Casaldáliga.

32. Cavan McCarthy, "Recent Political Events in Brazil as Reflected in Popular Poetry Pamphlets (Literatura de cordel)" (Paper presented to the Thirty Fourth Seminar on Latin American Library Materials, Charlottesville, Virginia, May 27–June 1, 1989), 25 pp.

33. Crispiano Neto, *Cordel nas portas das fábricas* (São Paulo: Centro de Pastoral Vergueiro, 1984), 52 pp.

34. *Campanha de sindicalização*, Cadernos do trabalhador, edição extra (Santo André, SP: Sindicato dos Químicos do ABC, 1986), 8 pp.

35. *A situação do menor no meio popular*, Cadernos do CEAC, 10 (Nova Iguaçu, RJ: Centro de Estudos e Ação Comunitária, [1983?]), 13 pp.

36. See Millôr [Millôr Fernandes], *Diário da Nova República*, 3 vols. (Porto Alegre: L&PM, 1987–1989). Political cartoons and comment. See also Ique, *Brasileiras & brasileiros* (Rio de Janeiro: Lumiar, [1989]). Political cartoons about the Sarney government, 1986-1989.

37. "Dor no adeus do riso," *Isto É* 577 (13 June 1988), 50-54. The career and death of the cartoonist Henfil.

38. *Material didático para cursos de formação* (São Paulo: 13 de Maio—Núcleo de Educação Popular, [1989]), 6 pp.

39. *Mulher: catálogo de publicações* (São Paulo: Centro de Pastoral Vergueiro, 1988), 34 pp.

40. "*Folha* mostrará o vídeo militante," *Folha de São Paulo* (23 May 1984), 26.

41. *Caminhada dos mártires* (São Paulo: Verbo Filmes/Paulinas, 1986), (VE-07/86). Phonograph record; also available on cassette.

42. *Vamos cantar, companheiros!* (S. 1, s.d.), 40 pp. *Lutando e cantando* (Fortaleza: CNBB, Secretariado Regional Nordeste I, 1987), 114 pp. *Canções da luta camponesa* (Recife: Centru, s.d.), 24 pp.

43. Giulio Folena, *Escravos do profeta* (São Paulo: EMW, 1987), 193 pp. Discusses the right-wing organization Tradição, Família e Pátria.

44. S. E. Castan, *Holocausto judeu ou alemão? Nos bastidores da mentira do século*, 27th ed. (Porto Alegre: Revisão, 1988), 328 pp. Justavo Barosso, ed., *Os protocolos dos sábios de Sião*, texto completo e apostilado por Gustavo Barosso, 3d ed. (Porto Alegre: Revisão, 1989), 172 pp.

45. McCarthy, "Recent Political Events in Brazil."

46. *PT Boletim Nacional* (São Paulo: Partido dos Trabalhadores, 1985—).

47. *Brasil urgente, Lula presidente* (São Paulo: [Partido dos Trabalhadores], 1989). Set of five pamphlets: *Economia, Democracia, Questão agrária, Questão urbana, Sociedade.*

48. Adhemar Gianini et al., *PT: um projeto para o Brasil: economia*, Organização Francisco C. Weffort (São Paulo: Brasiliense, 1989), 251 pp. Apolônio de Carvalho et al., *PT: um projeto para o Brasil: política*, Organização Francisco C. Weffort (São Paulo: Brasiliense, 1989), 193 pp.

49. See nn. 5 and 13, above.

50. *Princípios: revista teórica, política e de informação* (São Paulo: Editora Anita Garibaldi, No. 15, May 1988). Published by the Partido Comunista do Brasil. *A Classe Operária* (São Paulo: Partido Comunista do Brasil, [1980–]).

51. *Debate sindical* (São Paulo: Central única dos Trabalhadores [CUT], 1987—).

52. *Brasil: nunca mais; um relato para a história*, Prefácio de Paulo Evaristo Arns, 23d ed. (Petrópolis: Vozes, 1989), 312 pp. First published 1985; copyright by the Archdiocese of São Paulo.

53. Clodovis Boff, *Agente de pastoral e povo*, Teologia orgânica, 1 (Petrópolis: Vozes, 1984), 29 pp.

54. See n. 30, above.

55. *Jornal dos Direitos Humanos* (São Paulo: Movimento Nacional da Defesa dos Direitos Humanos, 1988—).

56. Álvaro Barreiro, *Comunidades Eclesiais de Base e evangelização dos pobres*, 2d ed., Coleção teologia e evangelização, 1 (São Paulo: Loyola, 1981). Translated into English and Spanish. Faustino Luiz Couto Teixeira, *Comunidades Eclesiais de Base: bases teológicas* (Petrópolis: Vozes, 1988), 222 pp.

57. See n. 31, above.

58. *Lutas dos jovens do meio popular* (Recife, CNBB: Pastoral da Juventude, 1981), 23 pp.

59. Caetana Damasceno et al., *Catálogo de entidades de movimento negro no Brazil*, Comunicações do ISER, 29 (Rio de Janeiro: Instituto de Estudos da Religião, 1988), 89 pp.

60. See n. 8, above.

61. *Vermelho e Branco: transformações no socialismo* (Rio de Janeiro: Instituto de Estudos da Religião, 1990—).

62. *Trabalhador rural: informe bibliográfico* (São Paulo: Centro de Pastoral Vergueiro, 1988), 20 pp.

63. *O Migrante* (Ji-Paraná, RO: Centro de Estudos e Pastoral dos Migrantes, 1985—).

64. Centro de Estudos Migratórios, Caixa Postal 42.756, CEP 04299, São Paulo, SP. Movimento dos Trabalhadores Rurais Sem Terra, Rua Ministro de Godoi, i.484, CEP 15015, São Paulo, SP.

65. *A luta continua: como se organiza os assentados*, Cadernos de Formação, 10 (São Paulo: Secretaria Nacional do Movimento dos Trabalhadores Rurais sem Terra, 1986), 34 pp. *Como se organiza*, Cadernos de Formação, 5 (São Paulo: Secretaria Nacional do Movimento dos Trabalhadores Rurais Sem Terra, 1986). *Nossa força depende da nossa dedicação*, Cadernos de Formação, 13 (São Paulo: São Paulo: Secretaria Nacional do Movimento dos Trabalhadores Rurais Sem Terra, 1987), 12 pp.

66. *Palmares de liberdade e engenhos de escravidão*, Caminhos de Libertação, 1 (São Paulo: Paulinas, 1985), 44 pp.

67. *Negro tem valor*, 2d ed. (São Paulo: Paulinas, 1987), 30 pp. ". . . elaborado pelo Grupo Contra a Discriminação Racial, Comissão Justiça e Paz, Salvador. . . ."

68. *Nego: jornal nacional do Movimento Negro Unificado* (Salvador, 1988—).

69. Conselho Indigenista Missionário (CIMI), Caixa Postal 11-1159, CEP 70.084, Brasília, DF.

70. *Porantim: Em Defesa da Causa Indígena* (Brasília: Conselho Indigenista Missionário [CIMI], [1972—]).

71. *A luta dos índios pela terra: contribuição à história indígena de Minas Gerais* (Contagem, MG: Centro de Documentação Eloy Ferreira da Silva, 1987), 120 pp.

72. *Mulher e Constituinte* (Brasília: Conselho Nacional dos Direitos da Mulher, 1985), 16 pp.

73. *A mulher e a violência doméstica*, Cadernos do CEAC, 11 (Nova Iguaçu, RJ: Centro de Estudos e Ação Comunitária, s.d.).

74. *Catálogo*, 2 vols. (São Paulo: Centro Informação Mulher, 1985), 251 pp. Citations to books and articles on feminism. *Boletim* (São Paulo: Centro Informação Mulher), no. 6 (dez. 1985).

75. *Mulherio* (São Paulo, 1981-1988).

76. See n. 7, above.

77. *Brazil's Popular Groups 1966–1986: A Collection of Materials Issued by Socio-Political, Religious, Labor and Minority Grass-roots Organizations in Brazil between 1966 and 1986* (Washington, DC: Library of Congress, 1988). 28 reels of microfilm. (Microfilm 88/5259). *Listagem de preços de publicações* (São Paulo: Centro de Pastoral Vergueiro, 1988), 46 pp.

78. See n. 30, above.

79. Antonio Ozai da Silva, *História das tendências no Brasil: origens, cisões e propostas*, 2d ed. rev. and enl. (São Paulo, 1987), 293 pp.

80. Nelson de Oliveira and Marita Regina de Carvalho, "Memória: do silêncio ao banco de dados," *Tempo e Presença* 11, 247 (November 1989), 11-12.

81. Centro Ecumênico de Documentação e Informação (CEDI), Rua Cosme Velho, 98, fundos, CEP 22.241, Rio de Janeiro, RJ. Av. Higienópolis, 983, CEP 01.238, São Paulo, SP.

82. See n. 26, above.

83. Instituto de Estudos da Religião (ISER), Ladeira da Glória, 98, Glória, CEP 22.211, Rio de Janeiro, RJ.

84. Centro de Estudos, Documentação e Informação sobre a Mulher (CEDIM), Conselho Nacional dos Direitos da Mulher, Edifício-Sede do Ministério da Justiça, 4. andar, sala 409, 70.064 Brasília, DF, Brazil.

85. *Acervo Mulher* (Brasília: Centro de Estudos, Documentação e Informação sobre a Mulher [CEDIM], 1989—).

86. Centro de Estudos e Ação Social (CEAS), Rua Aristides Novis, 1-1, Federação, 40.210 Salvador, BA.

87. Centro de Documentação Eloy Ferreira da Silva (CEDEFES), Rua Tiradentes, 2564, Sala 04, primeiro andar, Bairro Industrial, 32.230 Contagem, MG. The appeal for documents was published in *A luta dos índios pela terra*. (See n. 71, above).

88. See n. 77, above.

7. Muestra bibliográfica de la acción en la investigación frente al proceso de transición del autoritarismo a la democracia en Chile

Marta Domínguez

En el año 1983, después de diez años de dictadura militar, surgen las protestas nacionales y con ello un fortalecimiento de la Oposición al régimen, Oposición que va no abandonará su lucha, hasta reconquistar la democracia perdida. Es así, como el 5 de octubre de 1988 la Oposición gana el Plebiscito convocado por Pinochet. La derrota del pinochetismo en este Plebiscito de octubre, creó condiciones más favorables para la existencia social y política del país. Ella facilitó la ruptura del aislamiento de la civilidad e inició la desocupación militar de Chile y la recuperación de los espacios sociales perdidos a raíz del Golpe Militar de 1973.

El país avanza en la reconquista de los derechos políticos, en la recuperación de libertades, en la legitimidad para organizarse y expresarse. La mayoría del país se inclina por un acuerdo de consenso entre la civilidad y los militares y el gobierno y la oposición, para ir paulatinamente avanzando en la transición a la democracia. Sin embargo persiste una confrontación en la sociedad chilena, entre los que desean la prolongación de la institucionalidad creada por Pinochet y los que desean reformas radicales de la Constitución de 1980.

La compleja situación que significaba este proceso de transición, demandó la creación de instancias académicas y populares de discusión, por fin, y análisis de lo obrado por el régimen en los distintos ámbitos del quehacer nacional. Es así como hemos visto surgir centros de estudios, que por su condición de independencia del gobierno, se les ha llamado las ONG, es decir Organizaciones No Gubernamentales, que en la mayoría de los casos, tienen el apoyo financiero de fundaciones y agencias extranjeras. De estos centros no oficiales surgirán, tanto los análisis críticos de las políticas implementadas por el gobierno militar, como las bases de la propuesta democrática en desarrollo.

Los estudios, investigaciones, mesas redondas, seminarios, encuentros, encuestas de opinión que realizaban en cada de sus sedes, iban generando innumerables publicaciones emitidas periódicamente en forma de documentos de trabajo, materiales de discusión, publicaciones restringidas, publicaciones clandestinas, cuadernos de difusión, libros, publicaciones periódicas, etc.

Dentro de este marco de estudios especializados o multidisciplinarios se fueron destacando uno a uno dichos centros, y por su perfil investigativo, comenzamos a conocer a FLACSO por sus estudios políticos; a CED para el sector económico y estudios sobre las Fuerzas Armadas; el CEM para el sector Mujer; SUR para el sector juvenil y comunidades indígenas; ICHEH en el sector justicia; CERC y CEP para las encuestas de opinión; la Comisión Chilena de Derechos Humanos, para los estudios sobre el tema, y muchos otros que habría que agregar a este ejemplo.

Actualmente, gran parte de las personalidades que constituían estos centros, han sido llamadas a integrar los equipos del nuevo gobierno democrático. Este hecho podría provocar la desintegración de ellos, como de hecho ha ocurrido en algunos casos, con el consiguiente deterioro de la investigación en varios sectores y la disminución de materiales escritos. Se espera sin embargo, que en un futuro próximo, la nueva Oposición al gobierno de Patricio Aylwin, comience a generar sus propias instancias, como ya se ha visto con la creación del Instituto de la Libertad y el Desarrollo, liderado por don Hernán Büchi, ex candidato presidencial, contendor de Patricio Aylwin, y ex ministro de gobierno militar.

La particular transición chilena va a ser muy difícil y compleja; estará continuamente amenazada por intentos desestabilizadores desde las reservas de poder del régimen anterior. Pero también estará amenazada por los estallidos sociales, producto de demandas largamente reprimidas y postergadas, sobre todo en lo que se refiere a los derechos humanos y la pobreza de 5 millones de chilenos, de los aproximadamente 12 millones que conforman la población.

Como complemento a esta breve exposición, y seguramente más ilustrativa de las implicancias que en el campo de la documentación e información ha tenido el proceso chileno de transición del autoritarismo a la democracia, anexamos una muestra bibliográfica, ordenada cronológicamente y por sectores de estudio, y un índice de las fuentes bibliográficas que han generado dichos materiales. El índice permite identificar a cada uno de los centros, conocidos principalmente por sus siglas, y apreciar en parte, su quehacer en materia de publicaciones.

BIBLIOGRAFÍA

Ciencias Sociales

1987 Rodríguez, Alfredo, et al. Marginalidad, movimientos sociales y democracia. Santiago: SUR. (En: *Proposiciones*, Santiago de Chile, no. 14, 1987) [1]

1988 Castells, Manuel, et al. *La ciudad de la democracia: urbanismo, poder local y tecnocracia.* Santiago: Ediciones Documentas/ VECTOR. 188 pp., notas, tablas. [2]

Gaete, M. Elena; Matthei, Evelyn. La privatización de la revisión social en Chile. Santiago: CEP. 8 pp. (En: *Puntos de Referencia*, Santiago, 32) [3]

1989 Zúñiga, Luis. *Fortalecimiento de la sociedad civil y superación de exclusiones: algunas dimensiones para las políticas de desarrollo social.* Santiago de Chile: CIDE. 18 pp., notas. (Documento de Discusión, 05/89) [4]

Comunicación de Masas

1986 Portales C., Diego. *La dificultad de innovar: un estudio sobre las empresas de televisión en América Latina.* Santiago de Chile: ILET. 126 pp. (Estudios ILET) [5]

1987 Altamirano, Juan Carlos, et al. *Televisión en Chile: un desafío nacional.* Santiago de Chile: CED/CENECA. 226 pp., notas. [6]

1989 Martínez, Guillermo. *El pluralismo informativo y político en la radio.* Santiago de Chile: Corporación de Estudios Liberales. 134 pp. (Documento de Trabajo, 3) [7]

Nómez, Naín. *Mito y realidad de la participación radial en Chile.* Santiago de Chile: CENECA. 56 pp. [8]

Portales, Diego, et al. *La política en pantalla.* Santiago de Chile: ILET/CESOC. 197 pp. [9]

1990 Fuenzalida, Valerio; Hermosilla, María E.; Navarrete, Jorge. *La televisión de los '90.* Santiago de Chile: CPU. 158 pp., cuadros, gráficos, tablas. [10]

Cultura

1989 Monckeberg B., Fernando. *Chile en la encrucijada: decisiones para una nueva era.* Santiago de Chile: Impresora CRECES. 136 pp., notas, gráficos, tablas. [11]

1989 Spoerer, Sergio. *Proyección cultural de Chile.* Santiago de Chile: ILET. 28 pp., notas. (La Política Internacional de Chile en la Década del '90, Serie) [12]

Derecho, Justicia

1987 Esponda, Jaime. *La dimensión educativa del hacer justicia en la transición a la democracia.* Santiago de Chile: CEAAL. [13]

1989 Squella, Agustín. *Positivismo jurídico y democracia.* Santiago de Chile: Instituto de Chile, Academia de Ciencias Sociales. 39 pp., bibliografía. [14]

1990 García Villegas, René (Juez). *Soy testigo: dictadura, tortura, injusticia.* Santiago de Chile: Ediciones Amerinda. 264 pp. [15]

Ysern, Juan Luis. *Verdad y justicia: el desafío del reencuentro.* Santiago de Chile: CESOC/Chile América Ediciones. 95 pp. [16]

Derechos Humanos

1988 Aldunate, José, s.j. *Derechos humanos: camino de reconciliación.* Santiago de Chile: Ediciones Paulinas. 60 pp. (Colección Reconciliación, 3) [17]

Andrade Millacura, Ricardo. *Testimonio de un proceso.* Santiago de Chile: Ediciones Ad Populi. 110 pp., fotografías. [18]

Olivares B., Eliana, comp. *Primer Seminario Los Derechos Económicos, Sociales y Culturales: desafío para la democracia.* Santiago de Chile: Comisión Chilena de Derechos Humanos, Programa de Derechos Económicos, Sociales y Culturales. 116 pp. [19]

Velasco, Eugenio. *Los derechos humanos y su protección después del restablecimiento de la democracia.* Santiago de Chile: CED. 24 pp., notas. (Material Discusión, 206) [20]

1989 Agrupación de Familiares de Detenidos Desaparecidos. *Actividades 1988.* Santiago de Chile. 209 pp., fotografías. [21]

Comisión Chilena de Derechos Humanos. *Situación de los derechos del niño y del adolescente 1973–1988.* Santiago de Chile. 32 pp., cuadros estadísticos. [22]

Croatto, Severino, et al. *Violencia, poder y opresión.* Santiago de Chile: Ediciones REHUE. 141 pp., referencias bibliográficas, notas. [23]

1989 Detzner, John A. *Después del Plebiscito: nuevas estrategias para la protección de los derechos humanos en Chile.* Santiago de Chile: Programa de Derechos Humanos, Academia de Humanismo Cristiano. 44 pp., tablas. (Cuaderno de Trabajo, 9) [24]

Domínguez Vial, Andrés. *La libertad de expresión en Chile.* Santiago de Chile: Comisión Chilena de Derechos Humanos. 64 pp., anexos. [25]

Laulie C., Max. *Abusos de publicidad en Chile: la información oficial. Una condena sin juicio.* Santiago de Chile: Comisión Chilena de Derechos Humanos. 93 pp., datos anexos. [26]

López Dawson, Carlos. *Derechos humanos y elecciones presidencial y parlamentarias.* Santiago de Chile: Comisión Chilena de Derechos Humanos. 287 pp., fuentes, cuadros estadísticos, gráficos, anexos. [27]

Mera F., Jorge. *Ley de seguridad interior del estado y derechos humanos.* Santiago de Chile: Programa de Derechos Humanos, Academia de Humanismo Cristiano. 51 pp., notas. (Documento de Trabajo, 8) [28]

Miranda, Pedro. *Terrorismo de estado: testimonio de horror en Chile y Argentina.* Santiago de Chile: Editorial Sextante. 476 pp., notas, fotografías, 3 anexos. (Colección Expediente Negro) [29]

Orellana, Patricio. *Violaciones a los derechos humanos e información: la experiencia chilena.* Santiago de Chile: FASIC. 191 pp., bibliografía, cuadros estadísticos, notas, gráficos. (Colección Documentos) [30]

Pesutic, Sergio, ed. *Persona, estado y poder: estudios sobre salud mental. Chile 1973–1989.* Santiago de Chile: CODEPU. 279 pp., referencias bibliográficas, tablas, notas. [31]

Verdugo, Patricia. *Caso Arellano: los zarpazos del puma.* Santiago de Chile: CESOC/Ediciones Chile América. 289 pp., notas. [32]

1990 Gómez Araneda, León. *Tras la huella de los detenidos-desaparecidos.* Santiago de Chile: Editorial Caleuche. 436 pp., bibliografía. [33]

Economía

1987 Aguilera, Máximo, et al. *Una nueva economía para Chile.* Santiago de Chile: Departamento de Investigaciones Económicas. 44 pp. [34]

1987 Arriagada S., Pedro, et al. *Desarrollo económico en democracia.* Santiago: Ediciones Universidad Católica de Chile. 418 pp., cuadros, bibliografía, notas, gráficos. [35]

Cortázar, René; Meller, Patricio. *Los dos Chiles y las estadísticas oficiales: una versión didáctica.* Santiago de Chile: CIEPLAN. 41 pp., referencias bibliográficas, notas, cuadros estadísticos, gráficos. (Colección Apuntes, 67) [36]

Foxley, Alejandro. *Algunas ideas sobre reencuentro nacional y cambios económicos.* Santiago de Chile: CIEPLAN. 19 pp. (Apuntes, 64) [37]

_______. *Los desafíos económicos de Chile.* Santiago de Chile: CIEPLAN. 18 pp. (Nota Técnica) [38]

Larraín, Felipe, et al. *Desarrollo económico en democracia.* Santiago: Ediciones Universidad Católica de Chile. 418 pp. [39]

Ortega, Emiliano. *Transformaciones agrarias y campesinado.* Santiago de Chile: CIEPLAN. 236 pp., notas, bibliografía, cuadros estadísticos, gráficos. [40]

Riveros, Luis; Labbe, Francisco J.; et al. *Orden económico y desarrollo en democracia: opciones distributivas.* Santiago de Chile: CED. 86 pp., bibliografía, cuadros estadísticos. (Documento de Trabajo, 33) [41]

Tironi, Ernesto. *Democracia y mejoramiento de remuneraciones.* Santiago de Chile: CED. (Material de Discusión, 178) [42]

________. *Otro rol para el Estado de Chile: de subsidiario a promotor.* Santiago de Chile: CED. (Material de Discusión, 163) [43]

1988 Bitar, Sergio; Edwards, Ernesto; Ominami, Carlos. *Cambiar la vida: una nueva economía para Chile.* Santiago de Chile: Ediciones Melquiades. 129 pp., notas, gráficos, anexos estadísticos. [44]

Dávila, Enrique, dir. *La economía chilena después del Plebiscito.* Santiago de Chile: Economic and Financial Survey. 100 pp., cuadros estadísticos, gráficos, tablas. (Informe Económico, 41) [45]

_______. *El futuro de la economía chilena.* Santiago de Chile: ECO Survey. 98 pp., cuadros estadísticos, gráficos, tablas. (Informe Económico, 43) [46]

1988 Labbe, Francisco J.; Yevenes, Marcelo. *Evolución del proceso de privatización chileno (1973–1987).* Santiago de Chile: CEP. 8 pp. (En: *Puntos de Referencia*, CEP, 3) [47]

Rozas, Patricio; Marín, Gustavo. *Estado autoritario, deuda externa y grupos económicos.* Santiago de Chile: CESOC. 229 pp., bibliografía general, notas, cuadros estadísticos, tablas. [48]

Sapag, Reinaldo, coord. *Empresa privada y democracia.* Santiago de Chile: Empresarios por la Democracia. 90 pp. [49]

Solimano, Andrés. *Política de remuneraciones en Chile, experiencia pasada: instrumentos y opciones a futuro.* Santiago de Chile: PREALC. 74 pp., bibliografía general, notas, cuadros estadísticos, gráficos, anexos. (Documento de Trabajo, 326) [50]

Universidad Academia de Humanismo Cristiano. Programa de Economía del Trabajo. *La conducción económica después del Plebiscito.* Santiago de Chile: PET. 6 pp., cuadros, gráficos, tablas. (*Indicadores Económicos y Sociales*, PET, Santiago de Chile, no. 63, octubre–noviembre 1988) [51]

1989 Cañas, Raúl. *Políticas y promoción del desarrollo científico y teológico chileno.* Santiago de Chile: CPU. 216 pp., notas, cuadros, gráficos, figuras. [52]

Caputo, Orlando; Navarro, Leonardo; Varela, Andrés. *Chile en la economía mundial.* Santiago de Chile: CISPO. 47 pp. [53]

Carey, Guillermo. *Chile sin U.F. Vivencias.* Santiago de Chile: Editora Zig-Zag. 156 pp., cuadros estadísticos. [54]

Corporación de Investigaciones Económicas para América Latina. *Balance económico social del régimen militar.* Santiago de Chile: CIEPLAN. 58 pp., cuadros estadísticos, gráficos, tablas, figuras. (Apuntes, 76) [55]

Dávila, Enrique. *El equipo económico sin Büchi.* Santiago de Chile: ECO Survey. 80 pp. (Informe Económico, 47) [56]

_______. *El programa de la concertación y proyecciones para 1990.* Santiago de Chile: ECO Survey. 80 pp. (Informe Económico, 50) [57]

Delano, Manuel. *La herencia de los Chicago Boys.* Santiago de Chile: Ediciones del Ornitorrinco. 209 pp., bibliografía, notas, cuadros estadísticos, gráficos, tablas, anexo estadístico. [58]

1989 Gómez, Sergio. *Desarrollo agrario y democratización*. Santiago de Chile: FLACSO. 35 pp., referencias bibliográficas, notas. (Documento de Trabajo, 430) [59]

GIA. *Desarrollo agrícola campesino: propuestas programáticas*. Santiago de Chile: GIA. 50 pp., notas, cuadros estadísticos, tablas. (Apuntes de Trabajo, 10) [60]

Huerta, María Antonieta. *Otro agro para Chile: la historia de la reforma agraria en el proceso social y político*. Santiago de Chile: CESOC/CISEC. 413 pp., notas, cuadros estadísticos, gráficos, tablas, mapas. [61]

Ibañez, María Angélica. *La industria textil chilena bajo el régimen militar.* Santiago de Chile: CES. 23 pp., bibliografía. [62]

Jansana, Loreto. *El pan nuestro: las organizaciones populares para el consumo*. Santiago de Chile: PET. 182 pp., notas, cuadros, tablas. (Colección Experiencias Populares) [63]

Jiménez Bermejo, Patricio. *Economía de la solidaridad (o el reencuentro con el hombre)*. Valparaíso: Ecogestión Editora. 171 pp., bibliografía, cuadros, tablas. [64]

Lavín Infante, Joaquín; Larrain Arroyo, Luis. *Chile, sociedad emergente*. Santiago de Chile: Empresa Editora Zig-Zag. 170 pp. [65]

Leiva V., Francisco Javier. *Economía social de mercado: perspectivas en el Chile del '90*. Santiago de Chile: ICHEH. 38 pp., notas. (Documentos, 38/89) [66]

Marcel, Mario. *La privatización de empresas públicas en Chile 1985–88*. Santiago de Chile: CIEPLAN. 107 pp., bibliografía, notas, cuadros estadísticos, tablas. (Notas Técnicas, 125) [67]

Marín, Gustavo. *Trayectoria de las privatizaciones en Chile durante el régimen dictatorial, 1973–1989*. Santiago de Chile: PRIES/CONO SUR. 47 pp., bibliografía general, referencias bibliográficas, notas. (Documento de Trabajo, 35) [68]

Martner, Gonzalo. *El hambre en Chile.* Santiago de Chile: GIA. 278 pp., bibliografía, cuadros estadísticos, tablas. [69]

Razeto, Luis; Calcagni, Rodrigo. *Para un proyecto de desarrollo de un sector de economía popular de solidaridad y trabajo: contribución a un proyecto de desarrollo y democratización.* Santiago de Chile: PET. 52 pp., cuadros, tablas. (Documento de Trabajo) [70]

1989 Universidad Academia de Humanismo Cristiano. Programa de Economía del Trabajo. *Las organizaciones de subsistencia en la transición a la democracia.* Santiago de Chile: PET. 85 pp. (Serie Trabajo y Democracia, 3) [71]

1990 Dávila, Enrique. *El equipo económico y los límites del realismo.* Santiago de Chile: ECO Survey. 65 pp., cuadros estadísticos, anexos. (Informe Económico, 57) [72]

Dávila, Enrique, dir. *Proyecciones económicas 1990–1993.* Santiago de Chile: ECO Survey. 57 pp., cuadros estadísticos, anexos. (Informe Económico, 56) [73]

Universidad Academia de Humanismo Cristiano. Programa de Economía del Trabajo. *El presupuesto 1990 y sus perspectivas.* Santiago de Chile: PET. 9 pp., cuadros. (Indicadores Económicos y Sociales, 76) [74]

Educación

1987 De La Maza, Gonzalo; Garcés, Mario. *La educación popular y los desafíos de la democratización.* Santiago de Chile: ECO. 70 pp., notas. (Documento de Circulación Interna, 15) [75]

Núñez Soto, Iván. *La gobernabilidad democrática del sector educacional: relación entre investigación y política.* Santiago de Chile: PIIE, Centro de Política Educativa. [76]

1988 Calvo, Carlos. *Des-escolarización de la escuela y democracia.* San Bernardo: Centro el Canelo de Nos. 14 pp., bibliografía. (Documento de Estudio, 4) [77]

Candia, Sergio; Castillo, Gabriel. *Aportes para una educación innovadora.* Santiago de Chile: Arzobispado de Santiago, Vicaría Episcopal para la Educación. 264 pp. [78]

Magendzo, Abraham, et al. *La educación particular y los esquemas privatizantes en educación bajo un estado subsidiario (1973–1987).* Santiago de Chile: PIIE. 205 pp., bibliografía, cuadros, gráficos, tablas. [79]

Oficina de Planificación Nacional. *Modernización del sistema educacional chileno.* Santiago de Chile: ODEPLAN. 21 pp., fuente de datos, gráficos. [80]

Ravela, Pedro. *Educación para la democracia y los derechos humanos.* Santiago de Chile: CEAAL. 12 pp., referencias bibliográficas. (Documento de Trabajo, 7) [81]

1989 Cox, Cristián. *Autoritarismo, mercados y conocimiento: evolución de las políticas de educación superior en Chile en los '80.* Santiago de Chile: CIDE. 47 pp., notas, figuras. [82]

García Huidobro S., Juan Eduardo, ed. *Escuela, calidad e igualdad: los desafíos para educar en democracia.* Santiago de Chile: CIDE. 275 pp., bibliografía, notas. [83]

_______. *La contribución de las organizaciones no gubernamentales de desarrollo a la educación de adultos.* Santiago de Chile: UNESCO, OREALC. 65 pp., bibliografía, notas. (Serie REDALF) [84]

Kirberg Baltiansky, Enrique. *Uruguay: transición democrática en la universidad.* Santiago de Chile: Ediciones LAR. 335 pp., bibliografía, notas, tablas. (Teoría y Sociedad) [85]

Letelier, María Luisa, et al. *Alfabetizar para la democracia: el CEAAL y el Año Internacional de la Alfabetización.* Santiago de Chile: CEAAL. 219 pp., referencias bibliográficas, cuadros. [86]

Programa Interdisciplinario de Investigación en Educación. *Educación y transición democrática: propuestas de políticas educativas.* Santiago de Chile: PIIE. 245 pp., referencias bibliográficas, notas, cuadros, tablas. [87]

_______. *Ruptura y construcción de consensos en la educación chilena.* Santiago de Chile: PIIE. 96 pp., notas, tablas, cuadros. [88]

Vio Grossi, Francisco, et al. *Educación popular y política en América Latina.* Foro-Panel. Santiago de Chile: CEAAL. 26 pp. (Serie Educación Popular y Democracia, 1) [89]

Fuerzas Armadas

1987 Navarrete, Jorge. *Inserción de los cuerpos armados en el sistema democrático.* Santiago de Chile: CED. (Material de Discusión, 179) [90]

Silva Bascuñán, Alejandro. *Bases constitucionales de una nueva institucionalidad castrense.* Santiago de Chile: CED. (Material de Discusión, 174) [91]

Varas, Augusto. *Las fuerzas armadas en la transición y consolidación democrática en Chile.* Santiago de Chile: CED. (Material de Discusión, 175) [92]

1988 Centro de Estudios Socioeconómicos para el Desarrollo. *Fuerzas armadas, estado y sociedad: el papel de las fuerzas armadas en la futura democracia chilena.* Santiago de Chile: CED. 156 pp., anexo. [93]

1989 Centro de Investigaciones Socioeconómicas. *Armas para otro Chile: fuerzas armadas y democracia.* Santiago de Chile: CISEC. 8 pp., notas. [94]

Molina Johnson, Carlos. *Chile: unidad y fuerzas armadas.* Santiago de Chile: Estado Mayor General del Ejército de Chile. 107 pp., bibliografía, notas, tablas. [95]

Varas, Augusto. *La legitimidad social de las fuerzas armadas en política.* Santiago de Chile: FLACSO. 36 pp., notas, tablas, cuadros. (Documento de Trabajo, 424) [96]

Iglesia

1987 Comunidad Teológica Evangélica. *Democracia y evangelio.* Santiago de Chile: Ediciones REHUE. 319 pp., notas, láminas. [97]

Hourton, Jorge. *Combate cristiano por la democracia.* Santiago de Chile: CESOC. 283 pp. [98]

1988 Camus, Carlos; González, Tomás; Hourton, Jorge. *Reconciliación y participación.* Santiago de Chile: Ediciones Paulinas. 93 pp. (Colección Reconciliación, 4) [99]

Dooner, Patricio, ed. *La Iglesia Católica y el futuro político de Chile.* Santiago de Chile: CISOC. 269 pp. [100]

Vives P., Cristián; Hevia, Renato; et al. *Iglesia, acción social y democracia: jornada nacional 1988.* Conferencia Episcopal de Chile, Area de Pastoral Social, Santiago de Chile. 123 pp., cuadros estadísticos. [101]

1989 Chaparro Navarrete, Patricio. *La Iglesia cree en la democracia: elementos para una educación política democrática. La perspectiva de los obispos chilenos (1970–1988).* Santiago de Chile: Editorial Patris. 45 pp., bibliografía, notas, anexo. (Serie Nueva Evangelización) [102]

Dooner, Patricio. *Iglesia, reconciliación y democracia: lo que los dirigentes políticos esperan de la Iglesia.* Santiago de Chile: Editorial Andante. 228 pp. (Libros para la democracia) [103]

Jóvenes

1988 Partido por la Democracia, PPD. *Juventud y democracia: una generación para cambiar a Chile.* Santiago de Chile: CESOC/ CENPROS/IDEAS/INCH. 25 pp. (Educación para la Democracia) [104]

Weinstein, José. *Entre la ausencia y el acoso: apuntes bibliográficos sobre jóvenes pobladores. Vida cotidiana y estado en Chile hoy.* Santiago de Chile: CIDE. 27 pp., notas. (Documento de Discusión, 22) [105]

1990 Corvalán, Oscar, et al. *Juventud y trabajo: una opción de capacitación para el Chile democrático.* Santiago de Chile: CIDE. 74 pp., bibliografía general, referencias, cuadros.[106]

Justicia

1988 Nogueira A., Humberto. *El poder judicial chileno: su crisis actual y vías alternativas de solución.* Santiago de Chile: ICHEH. 264 pp. (Documento de Trabajo, 27) [107]

1989 Cánovas Robles, Rodrigo. *Memorias de un magistrado.* Santiago de Chile: Editorial Emisión. 134 pp. [108]

Cerda Fernández, Carlos. *Exigencias primordiales de la jurisdicción del presente y del mañana.* Santiago de Chile: ICHEH. 19 pp. (Documento, 35/89) [109]

Mujer

1987 Salinas, Cecilia. *La mujer proletaria: una historia por contar.* Concepción: Ediciones LAR. 108 pp., notas, fotografías. [110]

1988 Campero Q., Guillermo. *Movimientos sociales y movimientos de mujeres.* Santiago de Chile: La Morada/Casa de la Mujer. 26 pp. (Serie Cuadernos La Morada) [111]

Gaviola, Edda; Lopresti, Lorella; Rojas, Claudia. *Nuestra historia de mujeres.* Santiago de Chile: Ediciones La Morada. 54 pp., dibujos. [112]

Muñoz Dalbora, Adriana. *Fuerza feminista y democracia: utopía a realizar.* Santiago de Chile: Ediciones Documentas/ Instituto de la Mujer/Vector. 129 pp. (Serie Mujer) [113]

Valdés, Teresa. *Venid, benditas de mi padre: las pobladoras, sus rutinas y sus sueños.* Santiago de Chile: FLACSO. 396 pp., referencias, bibliografía, cuadros, gráficos, tablas. [114]

1989 Del Gatto R., Delia. *Actitud de la mujer hacia la política: análisis de su comportamiento electoral.* Santiago de Chile: ICHEH. 84 pp., bibliografía, notas, cuadros, tablas, anexos. (Documento 34/89) [115]

González D., Sandra. *Los derechos de la mujer en las leyes chilenas.* Santiago de Chile: CESOC, Red de Información de Derechos de la Mujer, RIDEM. 268 pp., vocabulario, anexos. [116]

González Moya, Carlos A. *Ley No. 18.802: Nueva Ley de la Mujer. Incluye todos los artículos del Código Civil, las modificaciones de la Ley 18.802 y sus comentarios.* Santiago de Chile: Publiley. 45 pp. [117]

Ley de la Mujer. *Ley No. 18.802: nueva legislación.* Santiago de Chile: Publigráfica. 32 pp. [118]

Matus Madrid, Verónica. *Las mujeres en la legislación chilena: una lectura comentada.* Santiago de Chile: CEM. 39 pp., bibliografía. [119]

Pollack, Molly. *Mujer y desarrollo: un enfoque diferente.* Santiago de Chile: PREALC. 24 pp., bibliografía, cuadros, tablas. [120]

Rozas Vial, Fernando. *Análisis de las reformas que introdujo la Ley No. 18.802 en relación con la capacidad de la mujer casada en sociedad conyugal y la salida de menores.* Santiago de Chile: Editorial Jurídica de Chile. [121]

Tomasello Hart, Leslie. *Situación jurídica de la mujer casada: la reforma de la Ley No. 18.802 al Código Civil.* Valparaíso: Edeval. 190 pp. (Colección Legislación Comentada, 10). [122]

Valdés, Teresa, et al. *Centros de madres 1973–1989: ¿Sólo disciplinamiento?* Santiago de Chile: FLACSO. 176 pp., notas, tablas. [123]

Pobreza

1987 Hardy, Clarisa. *Organizarse para vivir: pobreza urbana y organización popular.* Santiago de Chile: PET. 340 pp., cuadros comparativos, mapas. [124]

1988 Conferencia Episcopal de Chile. *Desarrollo y solidaridad: dos claves para la paz. Los pobres no pueden esperar. XVI Semana Social de Chile.* Santiago de Chile: Pastoral Social, Comité de Semanas Sociales. 221 pp., anexos. [125]

1988 Fuenzalida, Luis Arturo. *Ocupación, desigualdades y pobreza: aspectos crónicos y política de largo plazo.* Santiago de Chile: CEP. [126]

Serrano, Claudia; Raczynski, Dagmar. *Crisis y recuperación: realidad cotidiana de algunos hogares urbanos pobres.* Santiago de Chile: CIEPLAN. 52 pp. (Apuntes, 71) [127]

1989 Hardy, Clarisa; Schkolnick, Mariana; Teitleboim, Berta. *Pobreza y trabajo.* Santiago de Chile: PET. 117 pp. (Serie Trabajo y Democracia, 4) [128]

Martner, Gonzalo D. *El hambre en Chile.* Santiago de Chile: GIA. 278 pp., bibliografía, cuadros estadísticos, tablas. [129]

Tironi, Ernesto. *Es posible reducir la pobreza en Chile.* Santiago de Chile: Editora Zig-Zag. 188 pp., cuadros estadísticos, tablas. [130]

Política

1985 Zaldívar, Andrés. *Chile, traspaso del poder: busquemos una solución por la razón y no por la fuerza. Plebiscito.* Santiago de Chile. 35 pp. [131]

1986 Oxhorn, Philip. *Democracia y participación popular.* Santiago de Chile: FLACSO. 116 pp., bibliografía, notas, cuadros comparativos. [132]

1987 Centro de Estudios Políticos Camilo Henríquez. *Democracia y constitución de 1980.* Santiago de Chile: Pehuén Editores. 89 pp. (Manuales de Educación Cívica, 1) [133]

Conferencia Episcopal de Chile. *Etica de la transición a la democracia.* Santiago de Chile: Comisión Nacional "Justicia y Paz", Area Pastoral Social. [134]

Flisfisch, Angel. *La política como compromiso democrático.* Santiago de Chile: FLACSO. 370 pp., datos bibliográficos, índice. [135]

_______. *Gobernabilidad y consolidación democrática: sugerencias para la discusión.* Santiago de Chile: CED. (Material de Discusión, 184) [136]

Garretón, Manuel Antonio. *1986–1987, entre la frustración y la esperanza.* Santiago de Chile: Instituto para el Nuevo Chile. 30 pp. [137]

_______. *Reconstruir la política: transición y consolidación democrática en Chile.* Santiago de Chile: Andante Editorial. 294 pp., notas. (Libros para la Democracia) [138]

1987 Geisse, Francisco; Gumucio, Rafael. *Elecciones libres y plebiscito: el desafío democrático*. Santiago de Chile: CESOC. 342 pp., notas. (Serie Educación y Democracia) [139]

Huneeus, Carlos. *Los chilenos y la política: cambio y continuidad en el autoritarismo*. Santiago de Chile: ICHEH. 241 pp., bibliografía. [140]

_______. *Para vivir en democracia: dilemas de su consolidación*. Santiago de Chile: CERC. 392 pp., notas, gráficos, tablas. [141]

Lavín Infante, Joaquín. *Chile: revolución silenciosa*. Santiago de Chile: Editora Zig-Zag. 155 pp. [142]

Larraín, Hernán. *Gobernabilidad en Chile luego del régimen militar*. Santiago de Chile: CED. (Material de Discusión, 186) [143]

Lechner, Norbert, comp. *Cultura política y democratización*. Santiago de Chile: FLACSO/CLACSO/IIC. 264 pp., notas, cuadros comparativos. [144]

Orrego Vicuña, Francisco. *El papel de las fuerzas armadas en la redemocratización de Chile*. Santiago de Chile: CED. (Material de Discusión, 172) [145]

Pérez Silva, Enrique. *El régimen autoritario y la transición a la democracia en Chile: una aproximación*. Santiago: Instituto de Ciencia Política, Universidad Católica de Chile. 70 pp., referencias bibliográficas, notas. [146]

1988 Albuquerque, Mario; Jiménez, Gustavo, eds. *Actores sociales más allá de la transición*. Santiago de Chile: Programa de Actores Sociales, Proyecto Alternativo. 209 pp., bibliografía general, notas, cuadros, gráficos. [147]

_______. *Los movimientos sociales en la coyuntura post plebiscitaria: un tiempo peligroso*. Santiago de Chile: ECO. 44 pp., fotografías. (Taller de Análisis de Movimientos Sociales, Informe 3) [148]

Alvayay, Rodrigo; Ruiz, Carlos, comp. *Democracia y participación*. Santiago de Chile: CERC. 365 pp., referencias bibliográficas, notas. [149]

Aylwin, Patricio. *Un desafío colectivo*. Santiago de Chile: Planeta Chilena. 157 pp., notas. [150]

1988 Aylwin Oyarzún, José. *La reforma municipal: un mecanismo para la proyección del régimen.* Santiago de Chile: Comisión Chilena de Derechos Humanos, Departamento Jurídico. 61 pp., notas, cuadros estadísticos. (Documento de Trabajo, 63) [151]

_______. *La recuperación de las juntas de vecinos: un primer paso para la democratización de la vida comunal.* Santiago de Chile: Comisión Chilena de Derechos Humanos. 16 pp., notas, tablas. [152]

Bitar, Sergio. *Chile para todos.* Santiago de Chile: Planeta Chilena. 170 pp. [153]

Calderón Azócar, Carlos. *Chile puede más: mil medios.* Santiago de Chile: CEPLA. 340 pp., notas, anexo. [154]

Campero, Guillermo. *Los empresarios en la alternativa democrática.* Santiago de Chile: ILET. 25 pp. (Cuadernillo de Contribución al Debate) [155]

Cárdenas, Juan Pablo, et al. *Chile, una esperanza.* Santiago de Chile: CEPLA. 83 pp. [156]

Comité Ejecutivo Nacional, Organización Nacional de Profesionales y Técnicos. *14 propuestas del Partido Radical.* Santiago de Chile. 134 pp., fuentes, notas, cuadros estadísticos, gráficos. [157]

Errázuriz E., Maximiano. *Nueva ley de municipalidades y consejos regionales de desarrollo.* Santiago de Chile: Editorial Jurídica de Chile. 182 pp. (Ediciones Populares) [158]

Foxley, Alejandro. *Chile puede más.* Santiago de Chile: Planeta Chilena. 299 pp., notas, láminas. [159]

Gallardo, Bernarda. *El modelo de transformación autoritaria de la política.* Santiago de Chile: FLACSO. 49 pp., bibliografía general, notas. [160]

_______. *De la municipalidad: el autoritarismo y la democracia.* Santiago de Chile: FLACSO. 61 pp., notas. (Documento de Trabajo, 423) [161]

García Barzelatto, Ana María. *Ley orgánica constitucional de partidos políticos: historia de su establecimiento y debate doctrinario.* Santiago: Editorial Jurídica de Chile. 281 pp., referencias bibliográficas, notas, cuadros sinópticos. [162]

Garretón, Manuel Antonio; Walker, Ignacio. *La transición a la democracia en Chile.* Santiago de Chile: Fundación Rafael Campalans, Barcelona. 171 pp., notas. [163]

1988 _______. *El plebiscito de 1988 y la transición a la democracia.* Santiago de Chile: FLACSO. 29 pp. (Cuadernos de Difusión) [164]

Gleisner, Hagen. *Centralismo en Latinoamérica y descentralización en Chile: un camino hacia el desarrollo y la plena democracia.* Santiago: Universidad Católica de Chile. 199 pp., bibliografía general, notas, tablas, índice temático. [165]

Gumucio R., Rafael Luis; Vásquez Lazo, Claudio. *El desafío de la soberanía popular: democracia y partidos políticos.* Santiago de Chile: CESOC. 129 pp., anexos, notas, cuadros, gráficos, figuras. [166]

_______. *Rol político de los cristianos en la construcción de una nueva sociedad.* Santiago de Chile: CESOC. 14 pp. (Documento de Apoyo) [167]

Instituto para el Nuevo Chile. *El no de los cristianos.* Santiago de Chile: Taller de Cristianos y Política. 101 pp. [168]

Jara, Eduardo. *Normas o principios internacionales que debiera contemplar una constitución democrática.* Santiago de Chile: ILET. 20 pp. [169]

Larraín, Hernán. *Ideología y democracia en Chile.* Santiago de Chile: Andante Editorial. 195 pp., referencias bibliográficas, notas. (Libros para la Democracia) [170]

Maira, Luis. *La constitución de 1980 y la ruptura democrática.* Santiago de Chile: Emisión Editorial. 337 pp., fuentes bibliográficas, cuadros, gráficos. [171]

Martínez, Fernando; Valladares, Julio. *La joven democracia: el movimiento estudiantil en Chile (1973–1985).* Santiago de Chile: Instituto para el Nuevo Chile. 100 pp. [172]

Ministerio Secretaría General de Gobierno. *Chile, realidad y futuro.* Santiago de Chile. 52 pp., ilustraciones a color. [173]

_______. *Chile nuestro compromiso: 1989–1997.* Santiago de Chile. 58 pp., ilustraciones a color. [174]

Oficina de Planificación Nacional. *15 años de realizaciones en Isla de Pascua.* Santiago de Chile. 24 pp. [175]

_______. *Chile 1997: un país con visión de futuro.* Santiago de Chile. 33 pp., fuentes, cuadros, gráficos, láminas a color, fotografías. [176]

1988 Pérez de Arce, Hermógenes. *Sí o no. Qué puede pasar . . . ¿Habrá democracia en Chile?* Santiago de Chile: Editora Zig-Zag. 205 pp., notas. [177]

Pozo, Hernán. *Administración interior del estado y sistema de participación: coredes y codecos.* Santiago de Chile: FLACSO. 90 pp., notas, anexos. (Cuadernos de Difusión) [178]

_______. *La reforma municipal: propuestas, problemas y perspectivas.* Santiago de Chile: FLACSO. 42 pp., referencias bibliográficas, notas. [179]

Ramos A., José D. *Nunca será tarde.* (Seguridad Democrática). Santiago de Chile. 191 pp. [180]

Rodríguez Quiroz, Ambrosio. *Una cuestión de principios: la defensa de la libertad y la democracia en la constitución de 1980.* Santiago de Chile: Ministerio del Interior. 562 pp. [181]

Santibáñez, Abraham. *El Plebiscito de Pinochet (cazado) en su propia trampa.* Santiago de Chile: Ediciones Atena. 166 pp. [182]

Servicio de Paz y Justicia. *Exigencias concretas para la reconciliación: llamado a los partidos políticos de la oposición chilena.* Santiago de Chile. 24 pp. [183]

Urzúa Valenzuela, Germán. *Los partidos políticos chilenos: las fuerzas políticas.* Santiago de Chile: Ediar Conosur. 471 pp., notas. [184]

Varas, Florencia; González, Mónica. *Chile entre el sí y el no.* Santiago de Chile: Ediciones Diario la Epoca. 223 pp. [185]

Verdugo, Mario, dir. *Leyes políticas.* Santiago de Chile: Ediar Conosur. 393 pp., notas, anexos. [186]

Vio Valdivieso, Rodolfo. *Manual de la constitución 1980.* Santiago de Chile: Ediciones Colchagua. 318 pp., notas. [187]

Vodánovic, Hernán. *Un socialismo renovado para Chile.* Santiago de Chile: Andante Editorial. 181 pp. (Libros para la Democracia) [188]

1989 Alaminos, Antonio. *Percepción de los partidos políticos al comenzar la transición.* Santiago de Chile: FLACSO. 102 pp., cuadros estadísticos, tablas. (Documento de Trabajo, 422) [189]

1989 Aravena, Pedro. *Reformas constitucionales: legitimación o cuestionamiento*. Santiago de Chile: CINTRAS. 15 pp. (Serie Estudios Revista Reflexión) [190]

Aylwin Azócar, Patricio. *Programa de gobierno: concertación de partidos por la democracia.* Santiago de Chile. 48 pp. [191]

_______. *"Llamo a mis compatriotas a construir el país que queremos".* Santiago de Chile: Concertación de Partidos por la Democracia. 8 pp. (Documentos) [192]

Bucca Arancibia, Pedro. *Chile: nueva oportunidad para la democracia.* Santiago de Chile: Merchan Editores. 118 pp. [193]

Büchi Buc, Hernán. *Lineamientos fundamentales del programa de gobierno de Hernán Büchi.* Santiago de Chile: Publiley Editora Jurídica. 31 pp. [194]

Buenaventura, Pablo, et al. *¿Transición a la democracia? Un modelo de análisis y una propuesta.* Santiago de Chile: Terranova Editorial. 70 pp. [195]

Cavarozzi, Marcelo; Garretón, Manuel Antonio. *Muerte y resurrección: los partidos políticos en el autoritarismo y las transiciones del Cono Sur.* Santiago de Chile: FLACSO. 522 pp. [196]

Centro de Estudios Públicos. *Estudio nacional de opinión pública, marzo 1989.* Santiago de Chile. 121 pp., cuadros, gráficos, tablas. (Documento de Trabajo, 119) [197]

_______/ADIMARK. *Estudio nacional de opinión pública, septiembre–octubre 1989.* Santiago de Chile. 178 pp., cuadros, gráficos, tablas. [198]

_______. *Informe encuesta CERC Gran Santiago julio 1989.* Santiago de Chile. 16 pp., cuadros, gráficos. [199]

Centro de Estudios Sociales. *Construir la democracia en la región y en la comuna.* Santiago de Chile: Partido por la Democracia. 47 pp., figuras. (Cuaderno de Capacitación) [200]

Comité de Defensa de los Derechos del Pueblo. *La constitución de 1980 y sus reformas.* Santiago de Chile. 45 pp. (Cuaderno para la Difusión, 2) [201]

Contador, Ana María, sel. *Continuismo y discontinuismo en Chile: discursos de asunción al mando, Jorge Alessandri, Eduardo Frei, Salvador Allende, Augusto Pinochet.* Santiago de Chile: Bravo y Allende Editores. 69 pp., notas. [202]

1989 Universidad Academia de Humanismo Cristiano. Centro de Estudios de la Realidad Contemporánea. *Informe de encuesta, abril 1989.* Santiago de Chile. 20 pp., cuadros estadísticos, tablas, gráficos. [203]

Corporación de Estudios Liberales. *Institucionalidad democrática y dinámica de la economía.* Santiago de Chile. 296 pp., cuadros, gráficos. [204]

Chile. Leyes, decretos, etc. *Constitución política de la república de Chile 1980: actualizada con las reformas aprobadas en el plebiscito del 30 de julio de 1989.* Santiago: Editorial Jurídica de Chile. 91 pp., notas. [205]

Dávila, Enrique, dir. *Informe político a marzo 1989.* Santiago de Chile: ECO Survey. 55 pp. (Informe, 1) [206]

_______. *Peligros y temores en la transición a la democracia.* Santiago de Chile: ECO Survey. 73 pp. (Informe Político, 2) [207]

_______. *La transición en marcha o la marcha de la transición.* Santiago de Chile: ECO Survey. 40 pp. (Informe Político, 3) [208]

Durán, Claudio; Reyes Matta, Fernando; Ruiz, Carlos. *La prensa: del autoritarismo a la libertad.* Santiago de Chile: CERC/ILET. 208 pp., tablas. [209]

Friedmann, Lenka, comp. *Floreció el desierto: vivencias del 5 de octubre.* Santiago de Chile: Ediciones Diario La Epoca. 194 pp. [210]

Fuentes Wendling, Manuel. *Chile al borde de una trampa.* Santiago de Chile: Glomar Editor. 197 pp. [211]

Gallardo, Bernarda. *De la municipalidad, el autoritarismo y la democracia.* Santiago de Chile: FLACSO. 64 pp. (Documento de Trabajo, 423) [212]

Garretón, Manuel Antonio. *La posibilidad democrática en Chile.* Santiago de Chile: FLACSO. 72 pp., notas. (Cuadernos de Difusión) [213]

_______. *Propuestas políticas y demandas sociales.* Santiago de Chile: FLACSO. 3 vols., bibliografía, notas, cuadros estadísticos. [214]

_______. *La transición a la democracia y el caso chileno.* Santiago de Chile: FLACSO. (Material de Discusión, 116) [215]

1989 Geisse, Francisco; Ramírez, José A. *La reforma constitucional.* Santiago de Chile: CESOC. 241 pp. [216]

Hevia, Renato. *Camino a la democracia.* Santiago de Chile: CESOC/MENSAJE. 382 pp. [217]

Jiménez, Marcelo, et al. *Desarrollo local, municipio y organismos no gubernamentales.* Santiago: Universidad Católica de Chile. 217 pp., notas, tablas, anexos. [218]

Molina Johnson, Carlos. *Chile: los militares y la política.* Santiago de Chile: Editorial Andrés Bello. 261 pp., referencias bibliográficas, notas. [219]

Montero, Cecilia. *Modernización vs democratización.* Santiago de Chile: FLACSO. 25 pp. (Documento de Trabajo, 425) [220]

Oficina de Planificación Nacional. *15 años de realizaciones en Isla de Pascua.* Santiago de Chile. 24 pp., gráficos. [221]

Ortega Riquelme, Eugenio. *Pensar de nuevo la política.* Santiago de Chile: Fundación Eduardo Frei. 164 pp. [222]

Partido por la Democracia. *Participación política y social de la mujer.* Santiago de Chile: CESOC. 28 pp., dibujos. (Cuadernos de Capacitación Política) [223]

Pinochet Ugarte, Augusto. *Mensaje presidencial, 11 de septiembre 1988–1989.* Presidencia de la República de Chile, Santiago. 555 pp., cuadros estadísticos, tablas, anexos. [224]

Portales, Carlos. *Los factores exteriores y el régimen autoritario: evolución e impacto de las relaciones internacionales de Chile en el proceso de transición a la democracia.* Santiago de Chile: FLACSO. 28 pp. (Documento de Trabajo, 419) [225]

Pozo, Hernán. *La reforma municipal: propuestas, problemas y perspectivas.* Santiago de Chile: FLACSO. 42 pp., referencias bibliográficas, notas. [226]

Programa de Seguimiento de las Políticas Exteriores Latinoamericanas. *Programas internacionales de las candidaturas de Büchi, Errázuriz y Aylwin.* 16 pp. (En: *Carta cronológica,* Santiago de Chile, octubre, 1989) [227]

Rosenfeld, Alex. *Descentralización y participación en el régimen militar chileno.* Santiago de Chile: SUR. (Documento de Trabajo, 104) [228]

Sabrovsky, Eduardo. *Hegemonía y racionalidad política: contribución a una teoría democrática del cambio.* Santiago de Chile: Ediciones del Ornitorrinco. 168 pp., notas. [229]

1989 Sepúlveda, Leandro, et al. *Los límites de la transición y los desafíos de la democratización desde la base.* Santiago de Chile: ECO. 49 pp., notas. (Taller de Análisis de los Movimientos Sociales y Coyuntura, 5) [230]

Silva Cimma, Enrique. *Una democracia eficiente para Chile.* Santiago de Chile: CIEDES. 192 pp. [231]

Sunkel, Guillermo. *Las encuestas de opinión pública: entre el deber y el poder.* Santiago de Chile: FLACSO. (Documento de Trabajo, 439) [232]

Tomic, Esteban. *1988 . . . Y el general bajó al llano.* Santiago de Chile: CESOC. 326 pp. [233]

Valdés, Teresa. *Organizaciones de pobladores y construcción democrática en Chile: notas para un debate.* Santiago de Chile: FLACSO. 36 pp. (Documento de Trabajo, 434) [234]

Varas, Augusto. *Crisis de legitimidad del autoritarismo y transición democrática en Chile.* Santiago de Chile: FLACSO. 49 pp. (Documento de Trabajo, 445) [235]

Vásquez Muruaga, Luciano. *Transición a la chilena.* Santiago de Chile. 187 pp., fotografías. [236]

Vial, Alejandro. *El consenso, la izquierda y los comunistas en el sistema de partidos.* Santiago de Chile: FLACSO. 45 pp. (Documento de Trabajo, 421) [237]

Viera-Gallo Q., José Antonio. *Chile: un nuevo camino.* Santiago de Chile: CESOC. 363 pp., notas. [238]

Vodánovic H., Antonio. *Constitución política reformada.* Santiago de Chile: Ediar Conosur. 147 pp., notas. [239]

1990 Conejeros, Senén. *Chile: de la dictadura a la democracia.* Santiago de Chile. 351 pp. [240]

Godoy Arcaya, Oscar. *Hacia una democracia moderna: la opción parlamentaria.* Santiago: Universidad Católica de Chile. 190 pp., referencias, cuadros. (Encuentros) [241]

González Parra, Raúl. *El presidente Patricio Aylwin Azócar y su pensamiento político social.* Santiago de Chile. 55 pp. [242]

Garretón, Manuel A. *Partidos, transición y democracia en Chile.* Santiago de Chile: FLACSO. 42 pp. (Documento de Trabajo, 443) [243]

Pozo, Hernán. *La nueva Ley de Junta de Vecinos: otro obstáculo para la democracia local.* Santiago de Chile: FLACSO. 39 pp. (Material de Discusión, 124) [244]

1990 SUR, Educación, Documentación, Estudios. *Chile: sociedad y transición.* Santiago de Chile. 301 pp. (En: *Proposiciones*, 18) [245]

Tironi, Eduardo. *La invisible victoria: campañas electorales y democracia en Chile.* Santiago de Chile: SUR. 110 pp., referencias bibliográficas. [246]

Política Exterior

1989 Instituto Latinoamericano de Estudios Transnacionales. *La política exterior de Chile en la década de los noventa: documento de síntesis.* Santiago de Chile. 62 pp. [247]

Muñoz, Heraldo, et al. *Chile: política exterior para la democracia.* Santiago de Chile: Ediciones Pehuén. 262 pp., notas, cuadros estadísticos. [248]

Varas, Augusto. *Hacia el siglo XXI: la proyección estratégica de Chile.* Santiago de Chile: FLACSO. 275 pp., bibliografía del tema, cuadros estadísticos, tablas. [249]

Sindicalismo

1986 Frias F., Patricio. *Prácticas y orientaciones del movimiento sindical en la lucha por la democracia.* Santiago de Chile: PET. 58 pp., cuadros estadísticos. [250]

1987 Moreno Beauchemin, Ernesto. *Sindicalismo y democracia.* Santiago de Chile: Andante Editorial. 150 pp., notas, bibliografía. [251]

1988 Lira, Pedro, ed. *La concertación para la paz y la democracia: los trabajadores chilenos.* Santiago de Chile: Comisión Sudamericana de Paz/Vicaría Pastoral Obrera. 159 pp. (Colección Posiciones y Debates) [252]

Maturana, Víctor. *Negociación colectiva: realidad y alternativas de cambio.* Santiago de Chile: CEDAL. 15 pp. (En: *Informativo Laboral*, 6) [253]

Universidad Academia de Humanismo Cristiano. Programa de Economía del Trabajo. *Concertación social y reformas institucionales.* Santiago de Chile. 6 pp., cuadros estadísticos. (Indicadores Económicos Sociales, 64) [254]

Ruiz Tagle, Jaime. *En el centenario del 1° de mayo: pasado, presente y futuro 1886–1988.* Santiago de Chile: PET. 24 pp. [255]

1989 Barrera, Manuel. *Cambios en la relación entre sistema económico y sindical: el caso de Chile.* Santiago de Chile: CES. 41 pp., bibliografía, referencias bibliográficas, cuadros estadísticos, tablas. (Material de Discusión, 12) [256]

Bengoa, José, ed. *Industria, obreros y movimiento sindical.* Santiago de Chile: SUR. 226 pp., bibliografía, cuadros estadísticos, láminas. (En: *Proposiciones,* no. 17) [257]

Centro de Estudios Sociales. *Propuestas de la CUT para la transición.* Santiago de Chile. 37 pp. (Herramienta de Trabajo, 14) [258]

_______. *Educación sindical en la transición.* Santiago de Chile. 40 pp. (Seminarios) [259]

Cortázar, René. *Sindicalismo y política: propuestas y programas para la transición.* Santiago de Chile: CES. 31 pp. [260]

Frias Fernández, Patricio. *El movimiento sindical chileno en la lucha por la democracia.* Santiago de Chile: PET. 193 pp., bibliografía, cuadros, tablas. [261]

Garretón, Oscar Guillermo. *Cambios estructurales y movimiento sindical en Chile.* Santiago de Chile: CES. 33 pp., notas. (Material de Discusión, 10). [262]

MacClure, Oscar. *La acción reivindicativa sindical en Chile.* Santiago de Chile: CEDAL. 30 pp., bibliografía, gráficos. [263]

Mihovilovich E., Milenko. *1000 datos: 15 años de retroceso para el trabajador y su organización.* Santiago de Chile: Editorial Ariete. 242 pp., notas, cuadros estadísticos, gráficos, tablas. [264]

Quevedo, Agustín. *El marco de las relaciones laborales en Chile durante el régimen militar.* Santiago de Chile: CES. 23 pp., notas, tablas, anexos. (Material de Discusión, 14) [265]

Trabajadores

1988 Humeres Magnan, Héctor; Humeres Noguer, Héctor. *Derecho del trabajo y de la seguridad social.* Santiago: Editorial Jurídica de Chile. 548 pp. [266]

1989 Centro de Estudios Sociales. *Los trabajadores y los cambios en la estructura económico social del país: primera y segunda parte.* Santiago de Chile. 130 pp., cuadros estadísticos, gráficos, tablas. [267]

INDICE DE FUENTES BIBLIOGRÁFICAS CITADAS*

*No se incluyeron las editoriales comerciales en el índice.

Toward Democratic Change: The Role of Interest Groups in Brazil, 1964–1990

8. O movimento ambientalista: a democracia e o acesso à informação

Rubens Harry Born

A organização da sociedade civil no Brasil para a discussão e defesa do meio ambiente é relativamente recente, quando comparada a outros movimentos sociais, organizados ou não, tais como os ligados à defesa de direitos humanos, da mulher e da criança, contra a discriminação e preconceito de qualquer tipo.

Embora existam registros de diversos personagens e movimentos dedicados ao estudo ou defesa dos recursos naturais em épocas anteriores, de fato foi nos últimos trinta anos, mormente na década de 80, que presenciou—se a formação ou o aparecimento de diversas campanhas e grupos voltados para os "assuntos ecológicos." De certa maneira, tal situação também ocorreu em outros países, e é fruto da recente e gradativa conscientização da opinião pública e dos governantes para os problemas ambientais e suas conseqüências. De fato, considera-se como marcos históricos dessa conscientização o lançamento do livro "Silent Spring," de Rachel Carson,[1] em 1962, e a primeira Conferência das Nações Unidas sobre o Ambiente Humano,[2] em 1972, na cidade de Estocolmo.

No Brasil, as primeiras denúncias de má qualidade ambiental partiram da sociedade civil, organizada ou não. Os grupos formados no final da década de 60 e início da de 70, elencam suas denúncias e cobravam soluções perante um governo (federal) que procurava sempre negar os problemas de poluição ambiental. Técnicos e cientistas, alguns deles atuando em órgãos públicos setoriais, contribuíram (e contribuem) para tal postura crítica das organizações não-governamentais (ONGs). Tal contribuição ocorreu significativamente em outros movimentos sociais importantes para a redemocratização do país. Organizações de profissionais, tais como Organização dos Advogados do Brasil (OAB), Instituto de Arquitetos do Brasil (IAB), Sociedade Brasileira para o Progresso da Ciência (SBPC), tiveram um papel de destaque nesse processo.

Entretanto, inicialmente havia um certo estigma contra as organizações e ativistas de defesa do meio ambiente. Esse estigma registrava-se, de um lado, junto aos detentores do poder político e econômico, com críticas pela críticas pela falta de embasamento técnico e econômico e com adjetivos classificando os ecologistas como "românticos, alienados, retrógrados, inimigos do progresso, etc.," ou ainda de que as ações dos ambientalistas acabavam beneficiando interesses estrangeiros que não desejariam o Brasil como uma grande potência econômica ou nuclear; de outro lado, subestimados por outros ativistas e organizações da sociedade civil mais voltadas à campanha pela redemocratização do país que não consideravam a defesa do meio ambiente como uma luta prioritária ou capaz de contribuir para tal redemocratização.

Um exemplo claro de tal situação é o caso da poluição ambiental em Cubatão, São Paulo, que ficou conhecida como "a cidade mais poluída do mundo": os ambientalistas vinham desde meados da década de 70 fazendo denúncias sobre a degradação residente junto às indústrias; na época os sindicatos de trabalhadores criticavam os ambientalistas, afirmando que as teses por esses defendidas poderiam afetar a oferta de empregos (reduzindo-a) e diminuir os rendimentos "salariais" pela eliminação eventual do adicional de indenizaçao por insalubridade. Em geral os sindicatos pautam suas ações por questões salariais sendo, que só recentemente, a questão do ambiente, mormente do ambiente de trabalho, está sendo alvo de suas ações; os partidos políticos ignoraram também a questão, sendo que somente em 1983 a Companhia de Tecnologia de Saneamento Ambiental (CETESB), órgão oficial de controle da poluição, admite a gravidade da situação de Cubatão (apesar de estudos da própria CETESB de 1978 e 1979). Para tanto, movimentos sociais específicos, entre eles o movimento ambientalista, que contribuiram para a formação da Associação das Vítimas e das Más Condições de Vida da População de Cubatão, tiveram um papel importante na pressão que levou governantes a estabelecerem providências visando o controle da poluição.

Os ecologistas no Brasil, como em outros países, elegiam alguns grandes temas, que tanto nos anos dos 70 e início dos 80, eram: a política nuclear, especialmente a construção da Usina Atômica Angra I e o Acordo Brasil–Alemanha; a Amazônia e determinados mega-empreendimentos, tais como o Projeto Jari (especial destaque teve o Movimento de Defesa da Amazônia—MDA), a Usina Hidrelétrica de Tucuruí, etc.; a poluição do ar nas cidades, como conseqüência do excessivo número de veículos motorizados e da ausência do controle da poluição industrial; a caça às baleias, como campanha—símbolo da predação dos recursos naturais.

Do ponto de vista político, pode-se dizer que inicialmente as campanhas dos ecologistas eram de oposição ao governo, sem serem campanhas de caráter ou vinculadas a partidos. Os movimentos contra a construção de usinas atômicas, contra a construção do Aeroporto Internacional de São Paulo em Reserva Florestal na região de Caucaia e o Movimento de Defesa da Amazônia são alguns exemplos dessa fase. A seguir, ambientalistas reinvindicam maior participação nas decisões e nos planos governamentais que potencialmente podem causar degradação ambiental. Em 1981, ao ser promulgada a Lei da Política Nacional de Meio Ambiente (lei n. 6938/81), os ambientalistas logram o "direito" de ocupar cinco vagas do Conselho Nacional de Meio Ambiente, órgão superior (até 1989) do Sistema Nacional de Meio Ambiente (SISNAMA) e definidor das diretrizes políticas para a questão ambiental. Em 1983, o Governo do Estado de São Paulo cria o Conselho Estadual de Meio Ambiente, também permitindo a participação de representantes da sociedade civil, situação que vai se repetindo em outros estados, e assim respondendo, formalmente, à reinvindicação por participação.

No discurso dos ambientalistas, mormente na década de 80, passam a aparecer reflexões e críticas quanto à organização e divisão (social e espacial) do trabalho; ao uso e desenvolvimento de tecnologias consideradas como brandas face àquelas de grande potencial poluidor; ao crescimento industrial como falácia do desenvolvimento e bem-estar social; ao acesso à informações visando permitir a participação da sociedade civil bem como maior transparência dos órgãos governamentais, etc.

Para alguns, o marco dessa crescente e gradual politização do discurso e das ações dos ambientalistas brasileiros ocorreu em 1986, quando o país discutia e preparava-se para eleger os parlamentares encarregados de elaborar a nova constituição do país. De fato, pela primeira vez, as ONGs dedicadas aos assuntos ecológicos, articulam-se e realizam o I° Encontro Nacional de Entidades Ambientalistas Autônomas, quando procuraram estabelecer propostas comuns aos Constituintes e discutem estratégias de ação e participação. Como resultado, organizam-se "listas verdes" de políticos sensíveis à questão ambiental; ativistas das ONGs lançam-se candidatos à Assembléia Nacional Constituinte; elencam-se propostas constitucionais, não só sobre assuntos de meio ambiente, mas notadamente sobre tópicos vinculados a um Estado mais democrático. Entre essas propostas, o direito e acesso à informações; a realização de audiências públicas prévias para decisão quanto à execução de empreendimentos com grande impacto ambiental e social; a ação popular isenta de custas judiciais, etc.

Com a instalação da Assembléia Nacional Constituinte, em fevereiro de 1987, a OIKOS—União dos Defensores da Terra encabeça uma articulação de ONGs ambientalistas que resultam na formação da Frente Nacional de Ação Ecológica na Constituinte, públicamente lançada em 5 de Junho do mesmo ano. A meta principal dessa Frente era conseguir introduzir no texto constitucional, as teses ambientalistas acima mencionadas, entre outras. Entretanto, à época, novamente os temas relativos ao meio ambiente eram menosprezados e não considerados de nível constitucional pelos partidos políticos, pela imprensa e até pela opinião pública.

Para enfrentar tal situação e lograr sucesso da inscrição na Constituição das teses ambientalistas, OIKOS organiza, em nome da Frente, uma campanha e audiências públicas (em diversas capitais) visando a conscientização da opinião pública e dos políticos sobre tais teses. Elaborou-se cartaz com as cores da bandeira brasileira e texto "Verde, amarelo, cor de anil, são as cores do Brasil. Por enquanto," sobre uma imagem cinza, simbolizando a destruição dos recursos naturais e do país. As propostas de ação e as teses ambientalistas foram divulgadas através de cartilha, que tendo a mesma figura estampada na capa, tinha, entretanto, a frase-resposta "O meio ambiente por inteiro." Ou seja, em linguagem coloquial, apresentava-se a idéia de que os problemas ambientais são resultantes de modos de desenvolvimento, e que portanto, a sociedade, no processo constituinte, teria a chance de fixar diretrizes quanto ao modelo de desenvolvimento do país e a ampliação da democracia e dos direitos políticos, jurídicos e sociais necessários para uma melhor qualidade ambiental e de vida.

Entretanto, o sucesso dessa campanha esbarrava em uma dificuldade: uma relativa falta de preocupação da mídia (TV, rádio e imprensa) para assuntos de meio ambiente. Não se obteria a necessária pressão da sociedade sobre os parlamentares, se a primeira não fosse suficientemente e convenientemente informada. Elaborou-se, então, um dossiê sobre os principais problemas ambientais brasileiros (poluição nas cidades, espécies em extinção, desmatamentos na Amazônia, etc.), do qual foram feitos duas mil cópias distribuídas à profissionais da mídia. Esse dossiê continha também lista indicativa de instituições e pessoas especialistas na questão ambiental ou que dispunham de informações mais detalhadas e completas aos assuntos abordados no documento.

Neste caso, e em diversos outros, tais como na luta contra a construção do Corredor Viário Sudoeste-Centro em São Paulo, um conjunto de obras com custo superior a quinhentos milhões de dólares e que ficou conhecido por um dos seus túneis—o Túnel sobre o Parque e que ficou conhecido por um dos seus túneis—o Túnel sobre o Parque Ibirapuera, apelidado de Túnel do Jânio Quadros, então prefeito da cidade)—OIKOS procurou reunir, sistematizar e distribuir informações junto a outros setores da sociedade, inclusive outras ONGs.

Parece-nos que esse é um dos aspectos característicos, e uma das dificuldades, das ONGs ambientalistas: a reunião, sistematização, a análise e posterior utilização das informações existentes (não tratamos das informações muitas vezes inexistentes e necessárias, para as quais seriam necessárias pesquisas científicas ou tratamento adequado do informações primárias, já que este não é um objetivo de atuação dessas ONGs). A dificuldade torna-se mais relevante, quanto mais abrangente a questão ecológicas "stricto sensu," mas também e fundamentalmente os aspectos econômicos, políticos e sociais envolvidos. À esta dificuldade agrega-se o fato de que a maioria das ONGs ambientalistas estarem insuficientemente estruturadas, não dispondo, na maioria delas, dos recursos financeiros ou humanos para uma maior eficácia de suas ações.

Contribuir para uma avaliação holística e ampla dos problemas ambientais e de desenvolvimento, inserindo-os inclusive no contexto das relações internacionais, parece-nos que seria um dos objetivos fundamentais das ONGs. Os problemas ambientais e de desenvolvimento são, em geral, vistos pela opinião pública de uma maneira simplista, pasteurizados por certos agentes da mídia, e sobre os quais só identificam-se certos interesses econômicos ou políticos locais ou específicos.

Na maior parte, as lutas das organizações ambientalistas não governamentais sofrem da falta de informações mais detalhadas ou precisas e da omissão de diversas variáveis que devem ser consideradas para uma correta compreensão dos problemas, tanto globalmente como internamente.

O provérbio ambientalistas, "pensar globalmente, agir localmente," é uma quase realidade. Embora os ambientalistas utilizem freqüentemente em seus discursos de argumentos globais para a defesa da vida no planeta, na prática pouco tem-se conseguido para uma mudança dos paradigmas mas que regem as relações internacionais no campo econômico, político e social.

Uma avaliação do contexto global dos problema regionais ou locais de maio ambiente e desenvolvimento pode permitir a identificação de diversos agentes e instrumentos que podem contribuir para um melhor equacionamento dessas questões, seja ecologicamente ou socialmente.

Há, entretanto, muitos ainda que considerem que as questões ambientais podem ser equacionadas ou discutidas sem uma profunda reflexão e alteração dos padrões de consumo, da reformulação das estruturas econômicas e políticas das sociedades humanas, da adoção de tecnologias apropriadas ao uso sustentado dos ecossistemas, etc. Discutir meio ambiente é discutir desenvolvimento, e portando encontraremos, nessas discussões, diferentes linhas de abordagem, face às diversas concepções sobre o que seja "desenvolvimento," a quem ele se destina e qual o grau de compromisso com os demais seres do planeta, inclusive os das futuras gerações.

Assim o movimento ambientalista, no Brasil com centenas de entidades criadas na maioria ao longo de última década, também abriga em seu interior ativistas e organizações que postulam e atuam segundo essas diversas concepções sobre a nossa sociedade e meio ambiente. Parece que o futuro no reserva uma diferenciação crescente dessas correntes. Não obstante é preciso, para conferir maior eficiência e maturidade ao movimento ambientalista, encontrar pontos mínimos ou comuns de avaliação, articulação e atuação a fim de acelerar o processo de transformação da sociedade para uma sociedade tecnologicamente, economicamente e ecologicamente mais sustentável e socialmente mais justa e democrática.

A próxima Conferência das Nações Unidas sobre Meio Ambiente, que ocorrerá em 1992 no Brasil, criará a oportunidade histórica ao movimento ambientalista brasileiro para apresentar, aos representantes de mais de uma centena de nações bem como aos ambientalistas de outros países, a visão que tem dos problemas ambientais, nacionais e planetários. Não pode deixar de apresenta, devidamente articulado com ambientalistas latino-americanos e de outros países do terceiro mundo, as nossas propostas para as florestas tropicais e seus povos, para as questões da dívida desses países com os do primeiro mundo, para uma nova ordem nas relações internacionais—notadamente as "norte/sul." Urge organizar, aprofundar e disseminar tais reflexões, para que em 1992 possamos contribuir decisivamente na (re)construção de um mundo melhor.

Assim, as contribuições que os movimento ambientalista, enquanto movimento a sociedade civil, pode dar ao aperfeiçoamento da democracia, no Brasil ou em outros países da América Latina, como por exemplo a disseminação de informações amplas e específicas, a "tradução" de seus aspectos econômicos e sociais para o restante da população, a obtenção de dispositivos legais que concretizem e ampliem os direitos do cidadão e do interesse difuso, etc., dependem, entre outros fatores, se as ONGs disporem de um quadro geral dos problemas de desenvolvimento, proteção do meio ambiente e dos direitos humanos, o qual fornecerá os dados necessários para o estabelecimento estratégias de ação, local, regional ou global.

Tais contribuições dependem, por sua vez, do acesso a documentos, relatórios, estudos, e informações produzidas pelos órgãos governamentais, ou a estes fornecidas ou submetidas para o licenciamento de empreendimentos privados e públicos. Bibliotecas de universidades, de institutos de pesquisa, além de outras bibliotecas mantidas por municipalidades e órgãos governamentais setoriais, poderiam incorporar ao seus respectivos acervos, as informações referentes aos planos e problemas de desenvolvimento regional, as questões de meio ambiente e de direitos humanos e sociais decorrentes desses planos.

Enfim, como sugestões aos participantes do XXXV SALALM, indicamos:

1. Incorporação, ao acervo das bibliotecas, de publicações relativas aos problemas e planos regionais de desenvolvimento relativos à região de onde se localiza a biblioteca; em especial os Estudos de Impacto Ambiental (EIA) e relativos Relatórios de Impacto Ambiental (RIMA); os planos de macrozoneamento ou zoneamento geoambiental; os Relatórios (anuais) de Qualidade Ambiental; os relatórios sobre impactos econômicos, sociais e ambientais de empreendimentos apoiados por agências multilaterais ou de financiamento, bem como de instituições vinculadas às organizações unidas, e por essas elaborados. Vale lembrar que no Brasil os Estudos de Impactos Ambiental e os respectivos RIMAs, por força de dispositivo constitucional e da Resolução CONAMA n. 001/86, são acessíveis ao público, inclusive durante o período de análise técnica, sendo que cabe ao proponente do empreendimento objeto do EIA/RIMA o custo do fornecimento de "pelo menos cinco cópias" aos órgãos públicos.

2. Empréstimo gratuito de publicações às organizações não governamentais sem fins lucrativos dedicadas à defesa dos interesses difusos, como os relativos à defesa do consumidor, do patrimônio histórico e cultural, do meio ambiente, e para outras organizações sociais específicas.

3. Nesse quadro, o papel dos profissionais e das instituições destinadas e dedicadas à organização de informações, parte aqui reunida nesta conferência, e fundamental. A democracia, na América Latina e no mundo, passa também pela mão desses profissionais e instituições. A coleção e adequada disposição ao público das informações que afetam a vida dos bilhões de seres que habitam nosso planeta é função social inadiável. Contamos com ela.

NOTAS

1. Rachel Carson, *Silent Spring* (Boston, MA: Houghton Mifflin, 1962).

2. United Nations Conference on the Human Environment, 1972, Stockholm, Sweden. *Report of the United Nations Conference on the Human Environment, Stockholm, 5-16 June 1972* (New York, NY: United Nations, 1973).

9. Uma reflexão ético-teológica sobre o símbolo da maternidade e suas implicações práticas

Margarida Luiza Ribeiro Brandão

Abordar o tema da maternidade não significa conformismo ou acomodação a valores e padrões de comportamento estabelecidos. Ao contrário, quer indicar mudança cultural e perspectiva transformadora, iluminada pela fé cristã, na ótica da inculturação.

O que se pretende neste estudo é captar o novo paradigma da maternidade, que brota da práxis comunitária das mulheres. É perceber como o novo jeito de vivenciar a maternidade é caminho de libertação, abertura para o mundo e compromisso com a vida. Um compromisso fundado na compreensão da história, como lugar por excelência da experiência de Deus.

Não faremos um estudo de caso, mas temático. A base de nossas reflexões está fundada na experiência adquirida como integrante do grupo Mulher e Teologia.[1] Trata-se de um grupo ecumênico, de maioria católica, formado por teólogas leigas, religiosas, pastoras evangélicas, que trabalham especialmente com mulheres pobres, em várias regiões brasileiras.

Temos a certeza de que a temática da mulher não ocupa um lugar periférico na extrema complexidade de conflitos e tensões do mundo em que vivemos. Muito menos se pode dizer que é uma questão que interessa apenas à metade feminina da população. Isto significa adotar uma postura na qual o discurso da mulher sobre si mesma não está desligada de situações históricas concretas. Nosso estudo situa-se dentro de um discurso ético-teológico. A articulação fundamental desse procedimento diz respeito à maneira como a práxis das mulheres e a teoria que elaboram (seja ela popular ou acadêmica) se interpenetram e se reabastecem mutuamente.

Um compromisso ético

O empenho ético de transformação da realidade está na base da reflexão teológica na perspectiva da mulher. Quando falamos realidade, queremos nos referir à sua dimensão cultural, social e histórica na perspectiva da inculturação da fé. O que é importante no processo de inculturação é a busca da identidade de cada sexo, de cada raça, de cada povo, de cada pessoa, respeitando a sua identidade própria. É ir ao encontro dessa identidade sem confiná-la na repetição de modelos preestabelecidos por padrões culturais que a anulam.[2] O que caracteriza a inculturação é o caminho de uma práxis destinada a reconciliar as contradições que brotam numa sociedade, cujo sistema tradicional foi profundamente sacudido por necessidades reveladas ou introduzidas pela presença do novo, ou seja pelas sementes do Evangelho na vida das pessoas e das comunidades.

A experiência da esmagadora maioria de mulheres brasileiras é de extrema pobreza. A luta diária pela sobrevivência de seus filhos e a própria é a experiência cotidiana de muitas mães. Espalhadas numa multiforme variedade de grupos e organizações de mulheres, nos mais distantes rincões do território brasileiro, encontram força para enfrentar todo tipo de violência, que recai sobre elas.

Se queremos ouvir o que as mulheres dizem de si mesmas, é importante captar o que há na cultura feminina no que diz respeito à maternidade. Na base das considerações ético-teológicas sobre a maternidade, está o respeito à dignidade da mulher como pessoa, como sujeito consciente de suas descobertas sobre si mesma e de suas decisões. Ao iniciar o caminho de superação da ideologia dominante que pretende manter as mulheres confinadas em papéis estereotipadas na esfera da reprodução, as mulheres constroem um novo paradigma da maternidade. Isso significa romper barreiras, abrir novas perspectivas, tomar consciência de que é possível não só superar a divisão entre os mundos da mulher e do homem, mas também as divisões entre culturas, nações, raças, classes e religiões diversas. A dignidade da mulher, a sua luta por igualdade e reciprocidade mulher–homem como valores éticos e sócio-culturais indispensáveis, não se restringe a meras relações inter-subjetivas, mas diz respeito à construção conjunta de uma nova humanidade. Uma nova humanidade numa nova terra, sempre associada a metáforas de cunho materno e comparadas com a corporeidade feminina: terra-mãe, terra onde corre leite e mel, "Pachamamma," etc.

O tema: delimitação e significado

O tema central de nosso estudo aparece sob os mais diversos enfoques na vida contemporânea, tais como mudanças na legislação brasileira, declaração dos Direitos da Mulher da Organização das Nações Unidas, considerações sobre o sentido social da maternidade. Examinado à luz da fé cristã e na perspectiva das mulheres, apresenta nuances próprias como veremos. Tendo em vista a presença de grande contingente de mulheres nos movimentos populares, este tema tem aparecido em textos recentes, com relativa freqüência.

A predominância dos estudos é de cunho biológico, psicológico ou sociológico, uma vez que a prioridade maior é dada ao caráter educativo contido no papel de mãe, na sociedade em que vivemos. O que está por detrás de tais estudos são mulheres concretas, mães com seus filhos, como se pode depreender do gênero literário "depoimentos" ou "histórias de vida," presente em muito deles. Não nos deteremos na problemática ligada ao parto, às violências sofridas, embora saibamos que a tomada de consciência progressiva de que elas existem e devem ser combatidas é caminho de libertação conquistado pelas mulheres.

Nossa ênfase é, pois, o enfoque teológico, mais precisamente ético teológico a partir de uma hermenêutica feminista. Em outras palavras, uma postura epistemológica que situa o discurso teológico da mulher numa perspectiva libertadora e criativa. Não pretendemos fazer uma compilação, nem uma sistematização, de todo um material de que dispomos, com alguns textos inéditos ou produzidos numa teologia vivida, espontânea, passada por via oral.

Nossa opção metodológica é captar o que há de experiência e reflexão, de crise e transformação, num símbolo cultural que serviu, durante milênios, para alimentar a ideologia da subordinação da mulher, tal qual é expresso nas palavras das mulheres sobre sua própria experiência. A pergunta chave é: um novo paradigma da maternidade significa um processo de inculturação em curso? O trabalho pastoral das teólogas junto aos clubes de mães e outros grupos de mulheres abre um espaço significativo de vida e expressão cultural do povo e acolhida à palavra de Deus?

Um aproximação histórica

Queremos dar uma ênfase maior à virada de nosso tempo, concretizada pelo redespertar das culturas que se afirmam na sua identidade, lutam por seus direitos e por suas expressões próprias. É a época da eclosão dos clubes de mães, da multiplicação das comunidades de base e de inúmeros grupos de mulheres.

Não é o caso de fazer uma tipologia dos grupos existentes, mas indicar o lugar ocupado pelos clubes de mães nos movimentos populares de reivindicação social e política. Na experiência vivida, nas pesquisas feitas, na elaboração teórica do papel dos clubes de mães, é possível captar o encontro e (até o desencontro) das mulheres pobres que fazem parte desses grupos e as mulheres que delas se aproximam para um trabalho pastoral e ou educativo.

Os clubes de mães são grupos de mulheres criados na periferia de muitas cidades no Brasil e na América Latina. A grande maioria desses clubes foram formados principalmente através do trabalho pastoral da Igreja Católica, como também de outras igrejas cristãs. As mulheres se reunem para fazer reflexões sobre a Bíblia e para tratar de assuntos de interesse das mulheres, das comunidades, do bairro e do país. Os clubes de mães estão intimamente ligados às comunidades eclesiais de base e foram como a "mãe de muitos movimentos de bairro," para usar a expressão de uma participante nesses clubes, na cidade de São Paulo. Podemos notar uma correlação acentuada dos clubes de mães com o movimento do Custo de Vida, a luta pela anistia política, a associação de grupos de produção, a participação na luta pela terra, bem como nos movimentos de direitos humanos e em diversos grupos ecológicos. Sabemos que esses clubes têm características bem precisas, quando situados nos meios urbanos e rurais, na periferia das grandes cidades, ou nas cidades satélites das metrópoles, como é o caso dos clubes de mães da Baixada Fluminense.[3]

Nos últimos anos, observa-se um aumento acentuado desses grupos, bem como cresce o número de mulheres que iniciam a temática da mulher, como sujeitos da própria reflexão. É também nesta década que renasce um trabalho pastoral, numa perspectiva da inculturação de fé cristã. A partir de 1985, o labor teológico feminista se torna visível no Brasil, na América Latina e outros continentes do mundo como uma atividade articulada e comprometida com o processo de libertação. A Campanha da Fraternidade de 1990 tem contribuido para que novos grupos sejam formados, abrindo novos espaços de participação para as mulheres. A teologia feminista passa a ser conhecida fora do seu círculo mais próximo de atuação, levantando controvérsias ou angariando novos adeptos.[4]

Essa nova maneira de fazer teologia implica alguns esclarecimentos preliminares. Começamos por situá-la historicamente a partir de duas vertentes que se interpenetram: (a) a que parte da Comissão de Teologia na Perspectiva da Mulher da Associação Ecumênica de Teólogos do 3° mundo. (EATWOT—Ecumenical Association for Third World Theologians). (b) a que parte dos encontros realizados no Brasil, desde 1985.

(a) Esta associação foi fundada em 1976, em Dar-es-Salaam, Tanzania.[5] Os teológicos do terceiro mundo constroem seu próprio modo de teologar refletindo sobre sua experiência de vida, sua herança cultural como povos da Asia, Africa e América Latina, cônscios do impacto das condições políticas, sociais, econômicas, raciais e religiosas na teologia.

A Comissão da Teologia na perspectiva da mulher dessa associação foi criada em Genebra, em 1983, no sexto encontro da EATWOT. A presença da teologia feminista foi uma "novidade" nesse encontro, e a comissão surgiu como resultado de um processo de reflexão que teve início em Nova Delhi, em 1981, por ocasião da primeira Assembléia da EATWOT. As teólogas presentes lutaram para criar uma comissão das mulheres e não sobre as mulheres, buscando um companheirismo criativo com os teólogos da Associação.

Os ecos dessa comissão deram lugar ao nascimento da teologia na perspectiva da mulher no Brasil, através do entendimento entre teólogas latino-americanas e brasileiras. Em 1985 inicia-se um trabalho mais consciente e articulado entre as teólogas latino-americanas e brasileiras.[6] Já havia predisposição para isso, especialmente entre algumas religiosas e algumas leigas que se destacaram.

Dois acontecimentos marcantes podem ser lembrados como inspiradores tanto dessa primeira vertente aqui indicada, bem como daquela que abordaremos, em seguida: o Concílio Vaticano II e o Ano Internacional da Mulher em 1975 e a Década da Mulher que lhe seguiu. (Estamos em plena Década da Mulher do Conselho Mundial de Igrejas.) O processo de libertação da mulher é um dos sinais dos tempos lembradas por João XXIII, ao convocar o Concílio Vaticano II, em 1962. A Igreja quer ser a Igreja de todos, mas sobretudo a Igreja dos pobres. As mulheres com seus filhos e dependentes são os rostos mais presentes entre os pobres.[7]

(b) A segunda vertente gira em torno do grupo Mulher e Teologia, que procura coordenar e/ou articular a reflexão teológica na perspectiva da mulher, que vem sendo produzida nos últimos cinco anos. No âmbito nacional, já foram realizados quatro encontros, além de alguns regionais no Rio de Janeiro, São Paulo, e Rio Grande do Sul. Esses encontros, com a sua temática, sua preparação e realização, podem ser sintetizados em quatro passos.

(1) Refletindo, em conjunto, sobre seu trabalho pastoral, sua experiência de vida e de fé as teólogas presentes no primeiro encontro, realizado em Petrópolis (1985), tematizaram que as mulheres começam a "desconhecer o seu lugar," um lugar que lhes foi anteriormente designado numa cultura patriarcal e androcêntrica.[8]

Saindo da esfera doméstica para o mundo do trabalho, para a experiência comunitária, as mulheres põem em crise a sua identidade pré-estabelecida e ganham o espaço público, no qual são chamadas a novos desafios e a uma visão mais ampla de sua responsabilidade social e eclesial. Este passo está ligado à descoberta da memória histórica das mulheres na Bíblia e na vida atual.

(2) No segundo passo, tematizado no encontro de 1986, as mulheres começam a romper o silêncio em que foram mantidas na sociedade e na Igreja. Rompendo o silêncio, tornam-se visíveis e se descobrem discípulas de Jesus, tais quais as mulheres que seguiam e serviam a Jesus, na comunidade primitiva (cf Mc 15,41; 8,18). Neste ponto, é importante a releitura da figura de Madelena, Marta e Maria, do encontro de Jesus com as mulheres, bem como dos textos bíblicos da criação, no Antigo Testamento (Gn 2 e 3). Nesses textos do Gênesis estão as raízes profundas da subordinação da mulher ao homem, quando lidos na perspectiva patriarcal e androcêntrica. Dentre as releituras latino-americanas das figuras das profetizas, de Agar, de Tamar, das discípulas e tantas outras, podemos situar o resgate de Maria, a mãe de Jesus, como figura fiel no meio do povo, como mulher e como discípula atuante numa comunidade de discípulos (Jo 2, 1-12: 18, 25-27). Nos diálogos de Jesus com sua mãe no Evangelho de João, Jesus a trata por "mulher," da mesma maneira como se dirige a todas as outras figuras femininas que aparecem no Evangelho.[9]

(3) No terceiro passo, as mulheres fazem teologia no feminino plural e o tema escolhido para o terceiro encontro, realizado em 1988 "Mulher, terra, teologia" fundamenta todas as analogias e comparações da mulher com a simbologia cultural, bíblica e religiosa da terra-mãe, onde corre leite e mel. Também o recurso à exegese é importante, para regastar o núcleo bíblico teológico da criação. A terra é comparada ao corpo da mulher e se poêm em destaque todas as lembranças da herança cultural latino-americana, que foram esquecidas e anuladas.[10]

(4) O quarto passo estamos vivenciando agora. É a descoberta comum de uma hermenêutica bíblica feminista. Parte da realidade vivida pelas mulheres, para reler toda a Bíblia numa nova ótica, com uma metodologia própria, na qual se mesclam a proximidade e a escuta da palavra de Deus bem como a suspeita pela maneira em que foi registrada e tradicionalmente interpretada. E o Espírito sopra e acontece algo de belo, que cumula de alegria e felicidade o coração das mulheres. Inspira e ilumina a vida de cada dia, dando ânimo para viver e enfrentar com dignidade e coragem os conflitos e tensões. Multiplicam-se os textos escritos por teólogas, que refletem um caráter eminentemente missionário e libertador, em busca de um inculturação adequado no universo cultural das mulheres. No quarto encontro, realizado em fevereiro de 1990, foi possível estabelecer um contato mais articulado com o grupo de Rede Mulher, coordenado por Moema Wiezzer, que vem fazendo um trabalho educativo com mulheres pobres, há alguns anos, no Brasil e na América Latina.[11]

A teologia feminista é teologia da libertação. Como ato primeiro é uma espiritualidade e uma práxis; como ato segundo é reflexão e discurso metódico. É uma teologia que tem as mesmas metas e preocupações da teologia da libertação, mas de uma maneira distinta, uma vez que a subordinação do gênero feminino ao gênero masculino existe em todas as raças e culturas. É uma teologia crítica da libertação e como tal luta pela emancipação e libertação da mulher, usando para isso de todos os recursos de uma nova perspectiva bíblica, um resgate de mitos e símbolos que não se confinam a uma luta pura e simples por direitos iguais. Em última análise, libertando a mulher, quer libertar também o homem, a teologia, exercendo uma missão profética face à Igreja e à sociedade. O que se quer afirmar é que a expressão da teologia na perspectiva da mulher deve ser ouvida e visibilizada ao lado da perspectiva do homem. Juntas e articuladas produzem uma teologia que se inspira nas vivências próprias das duas metades da humanidade.

Os quatro passos acima elencados, tematizados em momentos especiais de encontros, sempre precedidos de trocas mútuas e recíprocas entre as teólogas, agentes de pastoral e algumas mulheres da base, nos ajudam a refletir sobre o núcleo central deste estudo—a descoberta de um novo paradigma da maternidade. O processo de inculturação busca inserir progressivamente a mensagem cristã numa cultura determinada. No caso da cultura feminina, na práxis das mulheres que se encontram nos grupos a que estamos nos referindo, observa-se um aprendizado mútuo, uma troca de informações, uma busca constante de relações igualitárias e recíprocas. Evidentemente, não se está minimizando aqui os tropêços os entraves a nível pessoal que refletem estruturas de injustiça e opressão, de pobreza e violência.

O aprendizado mútuo

O aprendizado mútuo existente no processo de inculturação "pretende articular e integrar, de modo vital, pessoa—comunidade—cultura—sociedade e fé cristã."[12] Ora este aprendizado entre as mulheres é extremamente comunitário. Os passos que enumeramos acima não são momentos estanques de um passado recente, mas etapas sucessivas e entrosadas umas com as outras do processo de libertação empreendido pelas mulheres. Trata-se de um processo ativo, de mútua acolhida, de diálogo constante, em busca de transformação e crescimento. Um processo que leva à procura dialética de uma nova síntese. Isso significa estar presente na vida das mulheres, como um lugar privilegiado de evangelização, o que supõe um longo e corajoso processo de inculturação da fé.

A busca da identidade da cultura feminina implica o respeito à sua alteridade. Em outras palavras, supõe empenho em respeitar o seu espaço de criatividade e de expressão. Os momentos privilegiados desse empenho ético acontecem nos encontros e nas reuniões dos grupos diversos, nos quais se vivência uma experiência de comunidade, que permite o discernimento sobre a vida cotidiana. Quando se fala em comunidade no sentido teológico, estamos usando também mediações antropológicas, especialmente quando se fala do carácter comunitário do trabalho das mulheres. Elas vivenciam um tipo de cultura, como comunidade. No modelo de cultura como comunidade, as pessoas se confrontam umas com as outras integralmente e não de uma maneira segmentarizada em status e papéis. Comunidade aqui é tomada como um conceito que responde à convicção de que mulheres e homens foram colocados juntos por sua humanidade e articula o desejo utópico de ve-los interagirem de maneira igualitária.[13] É interessante observar o decálogo estabelecido pelas mães pobres de Canoas, Rio Grande do Sul, em que se privilegia a partilha, o se:viço e o carácter missionário da libertação dos pobres.[14]

A passagem da vida comum para a experiência da comunidade é importante. Nos períodos de experiência comunitária mais acentuada, muitos dos relacionamentos, valores, normas que prevalecem no domínio das estruturas diárias são suspensos, reinterpretados, ou substituidos por outros. Isto significa que os símbolos ou estruturas da experiência de comunidade são distintos daqueles observados na vida cotidiana.

Há duas correntes que foram sendo construídas pela reflexão antropológica e sociológica para conceituar a cultura em sua complexidade. Uma primeira corrente está relacionada com os símbolos e com os significados e quer responder à seguinte pergunta: O que querem dizer as instituições presentes numa sociedade? A segunda corrente pergunta sobre a cultura na sua vertente política. (Marx, Weber, Gramsci e Bourdieu) O que explica a cultura são as relações de poder.[15]

A articulação das duas correntes simbólica e política na conceituação teórico prática de cultura pode ser feita pela análise da práxis das mulheres, como na sua experiência de "comunitas" nos clubes de mães, comunidades de base, etc. no exercício possível da liderança repensam a maternidade, um simbólico que visto na perspectiva do sistema confina a mulher no limite biológico de reprodutora da espécie, mas que vivenciado na perspectiva feminina é caminho de compromisso com a vida e de abertura para o mundo, numa perspectiva ecológica ampla. Temos a certeza de não se pode falar de abertura para o mundo, sem levar em conta essa perspectiva ecológica sobre a qual não há espaço para nos deter nesse estudo.

Um novo paradigma da maternidade

Poderíamos citar um número bastante grande de depoimentos de mulheres, que vivenciaram os passos acima mencionados, em relação à maternidade. Ultrapassando atividades rotineiras ligadas as tarefas maternas no seu sentido tradicional de cuidado do lar e dos filhos, abriram suas perspectivas de vida e se descobriram como pessoas atuantes e aptas a influir na transformação da sociedade.

No trabalho dos clubes de mães, estamos em presença de duas vivências distintas em relação à maternidade. Aquelas que são mães propriamente ditas, que realmente geraram filhos de suas entranhas. As que são mães "espirituais," as que se dedicam ao trabalho nos meios populares, sobretudo numa nova visão de vida religiosa, mais aberta a realidades que não se limitam à estrutura interna das congregações de que fazem parte. O que está por trás dessas duas vivências é a emergência do corporeidade feminina, a tomada de consciência do próprio corpo, como algo de bom e querido por Deus.

Maternidade implica corpo, recipiente, abertura para o outro, serviço, solidaridade, participação. Serviço que como trabalho realizada pela mulher em favor do filho a quem oferece com amor, a primeira experiência de proximidade humana, significa um profundo comprometimento da mulher com o mistério da vida (cf J. Paulo II, M.D. 5, 17, 18). Serviço que desperta a mulher para o trabalho solidário na comunidade em que está naturalmente inserida, ou da qual se faz próxima, não como mãe, ou exercendo funções maternas, mas como pessoa humana aberta aos outros, a partir de seu amor a Deus, no seguimento de Jesus (cf Mc 10, 41-45). Este ultrapassar das fronteiras da maternidade biológica, com os condicionamentos que são inerentes ao cuidado dos filhos e da casa, um dos "efeitos libertadores" do aprendizado nos clubes de mães e grupos de mulheres é notada também em outros países da América Latina. O relacionamento com outras mulheres é uma oportunidade para sentirem-se úteis, tornando-as capazes de falar umas com as outras de seus problemas, dando-lhes novas idéias, abrindo-lhes novos horizontes.[16]

É também a partir desse trabalho com os pobres, que a "maternidade espiritual" vem sendo reinterpretada, vivida, desinstitucionalizada. Dois outros fatores contribuiram para este repensar: a tomada de consciência da estrutura patriarcal da sociedade e da Igreja e suas conseqüências na vida das mulheres, em especial das religiosas; a presença dos movimentos feministas com a sua articulada luta contra a ideologia da subordinação da mulher ao homem. Cresce a convicção de que não é possível fazer teologia na perspectiva da mulher, sem a mediação dos movimentos feministas.[17] Nos meios populares, as fronteiras da maternidade espiritual se alargaram. Não se destacam mais, prioritariamente, o que pode distinguir modos de vida das mulheres, à luz da fé. Quem são essas mulheres? Queremos fazer nossas as palavras de nossa companheira teóloga Ivone Gebara, religiosa, professora universitária, vivendo há quinze anos num bairro pobre da periferia de Recife.

> Essas mulheres são em primeiro lugar as líderes populares, mulheres sábias que por sua estreita ligação às coisas da vida são capazes de ouvir, sentir, aconselhar, ajudar aqueles e aquelas que delas se aproximam. São elas, que sem nenhum título, sem instituição oficialmente reconhecida, 'ampliam o espaço de suas tendas' para dar sua parcela de amor no processo de construção da vida. Elas sempre existiram em todos os momentos da história, mas como seres socialmente 'ausentes,' como gente sem importância, da qual não valia a pena assinalar a existência.
>
> Essas mulheres viúvas, casadas, mães solteiras, com poucos ou muitos filhos, vivem a 'maternidade espiritual' nos meios populares sem mesmo chamar essa doação cotidiana da vida, essa geração no Espírito, de 'maternidade espiritual.'
>
> Pobres, misturados ao cotidiano dos pobres, provadas nos mesmos sofrimentos, conhecedoras de seus sonhos e esperanças, são capazes de, de diferentes maneiras, aliviar a orfandade popular. Às vezes é um tempo dado a uma vizinha, um chá de ervas oferecido, outras vezes é na direção de uma associação de moradores de um bairro ou na liderança num grupo de mulheres que aquilo que chamamos 'maternidade espiritual' se exerce, mas agora no seu significado mais amplo, modificado pelas exigências da vida.[18]

Todo esse trabalho de evangelização na perspectiva inculturadora tem como referência máxima a pessoa de Jesus.[19] Quando se fala que o critério é o Homem e Jesus de Nazaré, mesmo inconscientemente a ênfase está no masculino. Cristo revela a Deus e ao ser humano não por ser varão, mas por ser humano. A dimensão da sexualidade, assumida de dentro pelo filho de Deus, o homem concreto Jesus de Nazaré, atenta para um carácter mais olvidado desta característica humana, o seu aspecto transcendente. Aí está a referência máxima da afetividade, da sensibilidade, que se encontra em cada pessoa humana, seja ela homem ou mulher, na sua unidade antropológica, cuja referência última é a vocação ao Transcendente.

Conclusão

Retomando as nossas perguntas iniciais cremos poder afirmar que a formulação de um novo paradigma da maternidade é um processo de inculturação em curso. Um processo lento, de contínuo recomeçar, de um caminho de libertação empreendido pelas próprias mulheres. A inculturação da fé aproxima uma cultura viva e uma fé viva. A vida supera esquemas ou reflexões que se possam fazer sobre ela.

A temática da maternidade dá uma nova perspectiva à questão da mulher, impedindo que sua identidade própria seja absorvida, quando se envolve por inteiro nos movimentos populares e nas comunidades de base. É na práxis comunitária, na sua relação como pessoas, que as mulheres encontram forças para serem elas mesmas e para mudar a sua posição face ao homem, da subordinação ao companheirismo partilhado, em todas as esferas da vida pessoal, social e eclesial.

Essa práxis comunitária é o lugar por excelência de novas relações éticas, fundadas na igualdade e na reciprocidade.

NOTAS

1. Sobre o resgate da alteridade feminina, ver Margarida L. R. Brandão, "Mulher e homem: igualdade e reciprocidade," ensaio de aprofundamento ético-teológica; H. Ribeiro, et al., *Mulher e dignidade: dos mitos à libertação* (São Paulo: Paulinas), pp. 96-108.

2. O Grupo "Mulher e Teologia" tem sede no ISER (Instituto de Estudos da Religião), Rio de Janeiro.

3. A título de exemplo, escolhemos dois textos sugestivos que abordam a temática do clube de mães: Moema Viezzer et al., "Que história é essa? Clubes de mães e grupos de mulheres de São Paulo" (São Paulo: Rede Mulher/Puc SP, 1987); Ana Alfonsin et al., *Mulher comunidade pastoral da mulher pobre* (Petrópolis: Vozes, 1988).

4. Na avaliação da Campanha da Fraternidade, notam-se os avanços e recuos da temática da mulher na Igreja Católica no Brasil. Um dos avanços é o aumento dos grupos de mulheres e a multiplicação de encontros e seminários sobre a mulher.

5. Sobre a sua origem ver E. Dussel, "Teologias da 'periferia' e do 'centro': encontro ou confronto?," *Concilium* 191 (1984) i, pp. 212-133.

6. Ver *Revista eclesiástica brasileira* (REB) 46 (1986), p. 181. *Teologia feminista na América Latina*, onde se encontram os principais textos e o "Documento final" do Encontro Latino Americano de Teologia na Ótica da Mulher em Buenos Aires, de 30/10 a 3/11 de 1985.

7. O documento dos bispos americanos sobre a mulher (1985) reflete sobre a "feminização da pobreza," um fenômeno mundial, regional e nacional, ver "Carta pastoral do episcopado americano sobre a participação das mulheres na missão da Igreja," Serviço de Documentação (SEDOC) (1988) 21, p. 394, nota 93. Para a elaboração deste documento foram entrevistadas 25,000 mulheres, e da equipe de redação participaram 7 mulheres, além dos bispos, sendo algumas delas teólogas e uma escritora.

8. Ver Ana Maria Tepedino, "A mulher: aquela que começa a desconhecer o seu lugar," comunicado do Encontro sobre a Questão da Mulher nas Igreja Cristã, *Perspectiva Teológica* 43 (1985), pp. 375-379.

9. Maria Clara Bingemer, ". . . e a mulher rompeu o silêncio," A propósito do Segundo Encontro sobre a Produção Teológica Feminina nas Igrejas Cristãs, *Perspectiva Teológica* 46 (1986), pp. 371-381.

10. Tereza Maria Cavalcanti, "Produzindo teologia no feminino plural," *Perspectiva Teológica* 52 (1988), pp. 359-370.

11. Ver Moema Viezzer, *O problema não está na mulher* (São Paulo: Cortez, 1989).

12. Marcello de Carvalho Azevedo, *Comunidades eclesiais de base e inculturação da fé* (São Paulo: Loyola, 1986), p. 302.

13. Ver G. A. Arbuckle, "Evangelisation and Cultures," *Australian Catholic Record* (1979), pp. 247-258.

14. Cf. *Mulher-comunidade*, pp. 18-19.

15. Jorge Paleari, "Inculturação (Teologia, história e libertação)," *Convergência* (1988) 215, pp. 402-420.

16. Trata-se de um estudo publicado pelo Instituto Bartolemeu de Las Casas, em Lima Rimac, citado por Arthur McGovern, *Liberation Theology and Its Critics: Toward an Assessment* (New York: Orbis Books, 1989), p. 94.

17. Sobre a participação feminina nos movimentos sociais no Brasil ver Fanny Tabak, "Movimentos sociais e participação feminina," em *Desarrollo, semillas de cambio: comunidade local atraves del ordem mundial* (1985) 2, DID, pp. 79-89.

18. Ivone Gebara, "A madre superiora e a maternidade espiritual: da intuição à institucionalização," *Concilium* 226 (1989) 6, p. 53.

19. Ver Marcello Azevedo, "A vertente feminina da Igreja," *Convergência* (1989) 221, p. 166-175.

10. Violência contra trabalhadores rurais e a omissão do poder judiciária

T. Miguel Pressburger

Raízes históricas da violência no campo

A história brasileira desde sempre foi marcada pela violência exercida sobre o povo: a dos colonizadores sobre as populações indígenas; a dos senhores, no Brasil-Reino e Império, sobre os escravos; e, do Império até a República a dos fazendeiros sobre os trabalhadores rurais; a dos latifundiários sobre os camponeses; a dos latifundiários sobre os operários; a dos poderosos sobre os que lutam pela liberdade e maior igualdade social.

Não se pode abstrair um fator psico-social, reflexo, por sua vez da estruturação jurídica implantada para regular as relações sociais: o escravismo. Após mais de três séculos, esta relação social e de trabalho institucional, teve seu fim decretado em 1888, ou seja, completando agora apenas 101 anos de extinção formal.

Coexistiram com o escravismo outras formas de relações, mas todas elas profundamente marcadas pelo caráter estamentário das classes dominantes, economicamente diferente do feudalismo europeu, mas portador dos mesmo privilégios e até mais agudizados, vez que neste caráter incluiu-se também, o fator étnico. Criou-se o mito (até hoje repetido na historiografia oficial) de que além de índios e negros era o povo composto de degredados e de suas sucessivas gerações, em contrapartida aos fidalgos, componentes das elites dominantes. Dito de outra forma, os trabalhadores desde o marco inicial da história brasileira foram estigmatizados por marcas de "inferioridade racial" ou de supostos crimes cometidos em terras européias, cujas penalidades eram cumpridas sob forma de trabalhos forçados em terras brasileiras.

O regime colonial e, posteriormente, o regime imperial nacional deixou, dentre outras marcas, o caráter cartorial e concessionário até hoje vigente nas elites dominantes: as concessões de imensas extensões territoriais, as concessões de monopólios comerciais inclusive de tráfico negreiro, as concessões para captura de povos indígenas (bem como eliminação física de seus chefes), as concessões de exploração de serviços públicos, etc. Os objetos das concessões, como é fácil entender, passaram a se constituir propriedade dos agraciados, como propriedades também passaram a ser os trabalhadores envolvidos nestas concessões, fossem eles escravos ou livres.

Em meados do século XIX, já no declínio do tráfico negreiro, escasseou a mão de obra disponível, em razão da baixa taxa de sobrevida dos escravos (em média, a expectativa de vida dos escravos não ultrapassava a sete anos de trabalho), pelo acréscimo da demanda de força de trabalho nas fazendas cafeeiras, cada vez mais prósperas, e pela inexistência de trabalhadores "livres." Neste período se inicia um processo dirigido de importação de mão de obra européia, conseguindo os fazendeiros, sobretudo os de café—a classe social que se tornava hegemônica—atribuir ao Estado o custo desta imigração. O programa de colonização (expresso em produções legislativas que simultaneamente criaram a propriedade privada capitalista da terra) na prática operou substituindo o trabalho escravo pelo dos imigrantes italianos, poloneses, alemães, japoneses, espanhóis, etc. que, internamente nas fazendas, continuaram a receber o mesmo tratamento dado aos escravos. Mesmo porque não fazia sentido para os proprietários reconhecê-los como trabalhadores, habituados que estavam a três séculos de escravismo.

Nem os métodos de coerção eram muito diferenciados. Se por um lado o trabalho escravo era impulsionado pelo castigo físico, este também não estava ausente na coerção exercida sobre o imigrante. Tanto escravos quanto trabalhadores "livres" eram impedidos de abandonarem as fazendas, para o que os proprietários mantinham milícias armadas. Talvez a coerção suplementar aplicada aos imigrantes tenha sido a ideológica: foi imposta a mistificação do trabalho através da convicção de que era necessário trabalhar bem e muito para conseguir poupar e se tornar proprietário.

Nas ligações com os novos trabalhadores brancos, subsistia a necessidade de dominação defensiva em relação a qualquer perigo de desestabilização. É elucidativa a observação, em 1842, do escravocrata Lacerda Wernek, em Vassouras (Estado do Rio de Janeiro), segundo a qual o trabalhador branco sería, na hora do perigo, um aliado na luta contra o negro insurgente.

O quadro atual do massacre de camponeses

Inicia-se naquele período histórico um acelerado processo de privatização da propriedade fundiária, tornando-se a terra uma mercadoria como outra qualquer, sujeita à compra e venda, portanto sem outras restrições que não fossem a do pagamento do preço imposto pelo proprietário. É fácil entender que o acesso à terra se vai fechando para os não capitalistas, e todas as outras formas, como a ocupação por meio do trabalho, vão sendo dificultadas. Este processo tem momentos de maior ou menor aceleração, dependendo do regime político vigente: a história política brasileira é marcada por um movimento pendular de períodos de relativa democracia e outros de regimes ditatoriais clara ou veladamente militares.

Com o advento da chamada Nova República, que secedeu o regime militar iniciado em 1964, não ocorreu simultaneamente a implantação de uma nova ordem democrática. Isto porque nossos governantes têm origem oligárquica e, ainda hoje, a democracia que se conseguiu está comprometida por "*alianças familiares e . . . acordos de tipo clientelístico . . . que escamoteiam o direito de participação do povo e até o anulam.*"[1] A oligarquia é ainda a forma de poder dominante, embora assuma, na aparência, a ideologia liberal. Dá-se o renascimento político dos mesmos antigos donos do poder, revestidos de roupagem mais moderna.

É exatamente a partir do último golpe militar, de 1964, que se conhece a maior aceleração na concentração fundiária simultaneamente com uma nunca vista escalada de assassinatos de camponeses, advogados, sacerdotes e outros profissionais que tentam prestar apoio aos movimentos populares no campo.

Numa rápida demostração estatística, dos 85.119.650 hectares do território brasileiro, 17.956.266 hectares (equivalente a 21% do território nacional) estão nas mãos de apenas 18 (dezoito) proprietários rurais (pessoas físicas e jurídicas). Desses, apenas um detêm 4.111.538 hectares.

Desde o genocídio das populações indígenas, que teve início com os primeiros dias da colonização portuguesa, nenhum outro processo foi marcado por tamanha violência e ao mesmo tempo pela impunidade de que gozam os assassinos e, principalmente, os seus mandantes. O pacto empresariado-militares que em 1964 realizou o golpe, implantou a Doutrina da Segurança Nacional, desencadeando a violência institucional em níveis jamais conhecido na história brasileira. Violência não apenas policial, mas violência econômica, violência social.

"*As oligarquias sempre foram, e continuam sendo, grupos armados com exércitos privados e, freqüentemente, com grande capacidade de mobilizar as polícias estaduais militarizadas, para, pela violência, impor sua vontade política e econômica.*"[2] Verdadeiros exércitos particulares, formados por jagunços, capangas e pistoleiros de aluguel, impunemente assassinam trabalhadores rurais, suas lideranças e assessores. Esta demonstração de poder, visa não só amedrontar exemplarmente, mas também eliminar quaisquer impecilhos à manutenção da ordem que defendem.

Para assegurar a fluidez e continuidade dos programas de modernização o Estado atribuiu imensos subsídios e favorecimentos ao grande empresariado nacional e multinacional, juntamente com garantias implícitas de impunidade aos crimes por ele e por seus mandatários cometidos. Está clara que o quadro de injustiça social e violência só vai ser alterado mediante conquistas da sociedade civil, dentro de um contexto de democracia, onde a oportunidade de acesso à terra seja um fato. Para isto deve ocorrer, necessariamente, uma conjugação de esforços do movimento social e dos governantes que, com determinação e vontade política, garantirá a implantação de reformas na estrutura sócio-econômica e jurídico-legal brasileira.

Pelo levantamento realizado pelo Movimento dos Trabalhadores Rurais Sem Terra e pela Comissão Pastoral da Terra, nestes 25 anos (de 1 de janeiro de 1964 a 31 de dezembro de 1989) foi registrado um total de 1.566 assassinatos de trabalhadores rurais, índios, advogados, religiosos e religiosas e de outros profissionais vinculados aos movimentos populares no campo e à luta pela terra.

> Os dados fornecidos não dão conta de todo o volume e da diversidade dos conflitos. Só foram registrados os casos em que se conseguiram denúncias e documentos com fontes comprovadas . . . Além disso, foram registrados apenas dados envolvendo a questão da terra, deixando de lado índios, garimpeiros e bóias-frias (até 1986). Dezenas de trabalhadores rurais (sobretudo aqueles ligados às Ligas Camponesas do Nordeste) mortos depois do golpe de 64, deixaram de figurar por falta de documentação confiável.[3]

Confrontando com este quadro, que alguns juristas já tendem a denominar de genocídio, os julgamentos promovidos pela justiça brasileira apresentam os seguintes resultados:

Relação dos Julgamentos—Tribunal do Juri de Assassinatos de Trabalhadores Rurais, Índios, Advogados e Agentes Pastorais
De 1 de janeiro de 1964 a 15 de março de 1990 *

Julgados:	17
Condenações:	8
Criminosos Identificados	
mandantes:	23
pistoleiros:	53
Condenações	
mandantes:	0
pistoleiros:	11

*As condenações ocurreram em julgamento de homicídios de: índios (dois casos); sacerdotes (três casos); advogados (três casos). Em nenhum caso de assassinato de trabalhador rural houve condenação dos criminosos.

É importante sublinhar que, sendo a república brasileira organizada sob forma de federação, com algumas poucas execuções, a competência judicial e policial é autônoma em cada Estado da federação, e tanto os crimes quanto a impunidade são idênticos em todos os Estados, independentemente do caráter mais ou menos democrático ou mais ou menos arbitrário dos diversos governadores. Isto aponta claramente para o imenso poder político dos latifundiários, que através dos tempos têm subordinado aos seus interesses, mesmo quando criminosos, o poder público local e mesmo nacional.

Iniciativas e respostas no terreno institucional

As organizações representativas dos trabalhadores e as entidades de apoio sempre tentaram usar todos os instrumentos políticos e legais ao seu alcance para interromper esta escalada de violência e fazer com que seus responsáveis respondessem por ela perante a justiça. Em que pese sempre a existência de legislação penal (e a brasileira atual nem é das mais arcáicas), os latifundiários permanecem impunes e, implícita ou explicitamente, suas vítimas mesmo quando fatais, são rotuladas como bandidos, malfeitores, merecedores da sorte que tiveram. E, note-se que não estamos nos referindo a indivíduos tanto de um lado como de outro; e sim a classes sociais. Como se a sociedade fosse dividida entre "bons" e "maus," aos primeiros tudo sendo permitido.

Entre aquelas iniciativas é possível apontar: petições de providências às autoridades competentes; a designação de advogados para acompanhar os processos como assistentes de acusação; levar previamente ao conhecimento das autoridades as ameaças sofridas por sindicalistas, sacerdotes, advogados; além de ampla campanha junto à opinião pública nacional.

Também instâncias internacionais foram acionadas, numa tentativa de que elas interviessem junto ao governo brasileiro. Assim, logrou-se registrar fundamentada denúncia perante a 36ª sessão de Conselho Econômico e Social das Nações Unidas, em agosto de 1983. Desta denúncia resultou uma interpelação formal, apresentada ao governo brasileiro em fevereiro de 1987, pela Comissão dos Direitos Humanos das Nações Unidas. Da mesma forma, em 1988 a Anistia Internacional publicou um alentado o comprovado relatório que também foi encaminhado às autoridades brasileiras com pedidos de providências. Diversas outras organizações governamentais e não governamentais (Parlamento Europeu, Pax Christi, Comissão Internacional de Juristas, Associação Americana de Juristas, etc.) tem pressionado o poder público brasileiro, mas todas essas iniciativas não conseguiram, das autoridades brasileiras, as respostas desejadas.

Em 1986, novo marco nessa luta: constituição, em caráter permanente, do Tribunal Nacional dos Crimes do Latifúndio. Diversas entidades da sociedade civil, vendo frustradas todas as tentativas de se dar paradeiro à violência impune, decidiram, com a criação dessa instância social de julgamento, lançar ao público e às autoridades, uma carta-denúncia, que ao mesmo tempo informa da decisão em constituir aquele Tribunal.

A organização e metodologia deste Tribunal incorporou várias experiências nacionais e internacionais, que foram avaliadas e adaptadas para a finalidade que se desejava. Experiência como o Tribunal Bertrand Russell e as posteriores sessões realizadas pelo Tribunal Permanente dos Povos, até tribunais temáticos de opinião levados a cabo por entidades de Direitos Humanos, contribuíram para o desenho final do Tribunal Nacional dos Crimes do Latifúndio. O que se julga não é o crime cometido, pois esta tarefa cabe ao poder judiciário e mesmo porque, uma condenação emanada do Tribunal Nacional dos Crimes do Latifúndio não poderia ser executada. Submete-se, isto sim, à investigação e apreciação de renomados juristas, em cada caso concreto, a atuação das autoridades brasileiras, notadamente da organização policial, do judiciário local e do Ministério Público. O material investigado é o próprio processo em curso na instância judiciária, e dele pode-se extrair as nulidades propositalmente plantadas, as delongas injustificadas, as apurações não feitas ou feitas defeituosamente, a parcialidade das autoridades incumbidas da investigação e julgamento, etc. O conjunto de eminentes juristas que compõem o Tribunal, no final de seus trabalhos produze um substanciado parecer que é um documento de inestimável valor jurídico não só para efeitos de denúncia mas, principalmente, para ampliar a eficácia de atuação dos advogados no acompanhamento dos processos como assistentes de acusação. A par disto, estes pareceres têm servido, com bastante eficácia, para interpelações às mais altas instâncias do poder público estadual e federal, que numa postura defensiva se vê obrigado a dar algum nível de resposta.

O Tribunal, em sua linguagem instituinte, num certo sentido, cria para o poder constituído, outros vínculos de responsabilidade ético-social. Independentemente do juízo sobre a eficácia maior ou menor desse desdobramento do Tribunal, um dado é nítido: possibilidade de inserção de novas exigências da sociedade e conseqüências para a omissão do Estado. Isto significa que não basta ao Poder atender apenas o que está exigido pela lei, mas sim à sociedade atenta.

Das sessões até agora realizadas, alguns ensinamentos podem ser apontados:

(a) O peso das conclusões apresentadas pelo Tribunal reside em seu caráter de pronunciamento jurídico, lastreado na legislação, doutrina e jurisprudências brasileiras, como categorias inerentes a um diagrama valorativo-cultural envolvendo conceitos de justiça. Não é um pronunciamento apenas político;

(b) Por ter característica de investigação, com depuração crítica de procedimentos judiciais, e não apenas de condenação política *a priori*, o Tribunal tem logrado sensibilizar e mobilizar setores sociais que se mantinham ausentes da problemática, especialmente no mundo jurídico e acadêmico, introduzindo a discussão mais ampla entre formadores de opinião e produtores de pensamento;

(c) Pedagogicamente, apresenta para alguns setores sociais, especialmente de trabalhadores, o confronto entre a justiça estatal e uma "outra justiça," deixando claro não apenas a incompetência, morosidade e omissão do poder judiciário, mas a sua conivência com os criminosos, o favorecimento e a tomada de posição classista;

(d) Ainda quanto ao efeito pedagógico, oferece a possibilidade de se ir formando as bases teóricas e metodológicas de um direito e de uma justiça a serem construídos em aliança entre as classes trabalhadoras e os intelectuais com elas comprometidos;

(e) É evidente a capacidade que o Tribunal tem demonstrado em mobilizar apoios internos e internacionais. Não somente durante as sessões públicas, mas em caráter permanente, entidades de direitos humanos, de juristas, sindicais e políticas, constante e ativamente expressam solidariedade e apoio;

(f) Finalmente, por tudo isto e mais pela cobertura que periódicos e outros meios de comunicação têm prestado ao Tribunal, ele vai se legitimando como interlocutor e interveniente perante os órgãos do Estado, obrigando-os a prestar informações sobre sua atuação ou omissão.

Do ponto de vista jurídico, o Tribunal Nacional dos Crimes do Latifúndio, por suas decisões, está caminhando na direção de reverter a tendência de inpunidade, até agora dominante. O que tem possibilitado a continuidade da violência, é o procedimento do poder público, e especialmente do Poder Judiciário, claramente comprometido com os interesses do latifúndio.

O Tribunal Nacional dos Crimes do Latifúndio, a par de sua especificidade, é mais um instrumento na luta pela constante reconceituação dos direitos humanos mediante a concretização prática dentro do próprio espaço judicial, e pelo acesso à justiça. Mas os caminhos que podem conduzir a estas metas passam também—e principalmente—por novas concepções do próprio direito que deve se vincular à realidade social e, pelo menos, não servir de obstáculo ao processo de sua transformação. Da mesma forma, passa também pela reconstrução do Poder Judiciário, que deve se abrir à toda a sociedade (e não apenas a uma minoria, cujos privilégios assegura) como também efetivamente assumir tarefa de proteção dos direitos dos oprimidos.

NOTAS

1. José de Souza Martins, "As lutas dos trabalhadores rurais na conjuntura adversa," *Direito Insurgente II: Anais da II Reunião [do] Instituto Apoio Jurídico Popular, 1988–1989* (Rio de Janeiro: Instituto Apoio Jurídico Popular, n.d.), 9.

2. Ibid.

3. *Jornal do Tribunal Nacional dos Crimes do Latifúndio* (Rio de Janeiro: Instituto Apoio Jurídico Popular, 1989). (Exact issue unknown. Ed.)

Economic Trends and Prospects in Brazil and the Southern Cone

11. La economía del Uruguay: Evolución y perspectivas

José Antonio Pini Martínez

Introducción

Un análisis de la situación y perspectivas de la economía del Uruguay, difícilmente pueda ser cabalmente comprendido e interpretado sin una referencia al proceso o las etapas que precedieron a la actual coyuntura.

Estancamiento estructural

La economía de Uruguay padeció durante el período 1950/80 un fuerte estancamiento. El Producto Interno Bruto (P.I.B.) creció durante los años 50 a un promedio anual del 2.1%; en los años 60 del 1.5% y en los 70 del 3.2%. Al inicio de los 50 las exportaciones anuales eran de U$S 200 millones; al inicio de los 60 habían caído a 150 millones anuales y en los 70 seguían estando en U$S 200 millones.

La cantidad de personas empleadas en el sector industrial quedó estancada entre 1959 (206.642) y 1974 (207.200). Luego aumentó hasta 1979 (275.700) para volver a bajar a menos de 200.000 en 1982.

Las causas más importantes de este estancamiento crónico fueron factores político-institucionales. Durante mucho tiempo no hubo obligación alguna para diversificar las exportaciones. La segunda guerra mundial y luego la guerra de Corea, hicieron que las exportaciones de los productos básicos del agro (carne, lanas y cueros) permitieran una financiación fácil de desarrollo interno y la continua ampliación de la red de servicios sociales. Ello facilitado por una población también estancada, con una tasa de crecimiento neto de la población de tan sólo el 0.5% en los últimos 25 años.

A su vez, los gobiernos de la época centraron su atención no en una apertura de la economía sino más bien en un modelo cerrado de sustitución de importaciones y fuerte protección a la industria local.

Intervencionismo estatal

Fue este además un período de gran intervencionismo estatal. Controlar de precios, cupos de importaciones y exportaciones durante todos los años 50—otorgados con demasiada frecuencia no por razones de interés general sino de intereses particulares—líneas de redescuentos bancarios subvencionadas; control del tipo de cambios e inconvertibilidad del peso; líneas de crédito bancario obligatorias para determinados fines promocionales, etc. Fue un período en que primó la concepción intervencionista y paternalista del Estado y en donde la política monetaria y de emisión respondieron más a las necesidades de la tesorería que a criterios de una sana administración económica.

Cuando las deficiencias de la base económica quedaron en evidencia y la política de desarrollo industrial basada en la sustitución de importaciones agotó sus posibilidades, los gobiernos y las empresas privadas probaron ser demasiado débiles para iniciar un proceso de adaptación y reestructuración.

El sector privado de la economía—salvo excepciones— mostró ser poco dinámico. No estaba acostumbrado a situaciones que significaran un reto, estando en cambio familiarizado con medidas estatales de protección, intervención y fomento.

El sistema político no tuvo la creatividad y la visión necesaria. La forma más efectiva de solucionar las carencias de oportunidades ocupacionales y reducir las tensiones sociales que las mismas generaron, fue la de utilizar al sector público como esponja ocupacional, creciendo en forma desmesurada la cantidad de funcionarios públicos.

La crisis institucional y económica y el replanteo de la política seguida

El estancamiento y la crisis económica que precipitó aquella crisis institucional de 1973 (golpe de estado, disolución del parlamento y gobierno cívico-militar), junto con los efectos y las consecuencias que imponía la crisis del petróleo (Uruguay importa el 100% de su consumo de petróleo), trajeron al escenario político nuevas concepciones sobre el rol del Estado (menos intervencionista) y sobre la necesidad de promover en forma agresiva una "apertura hacia afuera" a través del fomento de las exportaciones.

La apertura fue preparada en las primeras etapas del gobierno de facto (1973 hasta mediados de 1974). Hubieron luego tres fases (1974/75; 1976/78; 1979/82), seguidas de una profunda crisis en 1983/84. En su transcurso se aplicaron diferentes conceptos económicos neoliberales. Estos se sucedieron el uno al otro, porque parecía que la ejecución práctica de ideas monetaristas sólo podía hacerse gradualmente (el gradualismo forma parte de la cultura uruguaya, en la que ni el sistema político ni el sistema social perciben como deseables medidas profundas o de choque).

Fase I: Inicio de la apertura (1973-1975)

Prioridad: lucha contra el desequilibrio externo.

Políticas: fomento de las exportaciones; apertura comercial e inserción de la economía en el contexto mundial.

Los primeros intentos de una apertura cautelosa pueden identificarse en el "Plan Nacional de Desarrollo 1973–77" aprobado por el gobierno cívico-militar en agosto de 1973. En él se opta por un fortalecimiento de los elementos de economía de mercado, especialmente con respecto a la asignación de recursos a través de mercado y al aumento de las perspectivas de ganancia para la economía privada, con énfasis en las exportaciones.

La tarea del estado debía ser la concepción de la estrategia global de desarrollo; la determinación de los sectores económicos prioritarios; la elaboración de políticas sectoriales orientadas hacia la exportación y la canalización del fomento estatal hacia las ramas correspondientes. Por lo demás, el estado debía limitarse a aquellas actividades estratégicas o que la actividad privada no pudiera cubrir o atender (principio de subsidariedad del Estado).

En el marco de esta nueva política fueron adoptadas diversas medidas que se pueden agrupar en cuatro categorías:

Medidas para el fomento de la exportación.— El objetivo de reducir el desequilibrio del comercio exterior adquirió prioridad a raíz del aumento del precio del petróleo y del proteccionismo agrario de la comunidad europea. También se tuvo la esperanza de superar el estancamiento a través de la exportación de productos agropecuarios e industriales no tradicionales con mayor porcentaje de valor agregado.

Al contrario del ejemplo chileno, se fomentó primero la exportación para equilibrar la balanza comercial y con el fin de restaurar una capacidad de importación suficiente, para pasar después de haber obtenido los éxitos correspondientes, a la segunda fase de la apertura comercial, es decir a la reducción de la alta protección.

Los instrumentos utilizados fueron fundamentalmente:

Reintegros y bonificaciones, cuyo objetivo era estimular la apertura de nuevos mercados protegiendo a los exportadores de los costos más elevados internacionalmente comparados, proveniente de impuestos internos incluidos en los costos, de sus propias ineficiencias productivas y de la de los sectores abastecedores.

Prefinanciación de exportaciones, con intereses subvencionados, cubriendo la falta de capital propio, para financiar la producción por períodos a veces largos que van desde que se toma el pedido e inicia la producción hasta que se entrega y se cobra.

Una serie de convenios comerciales con países vecinos, en particular con Argentina, a través del CAUCE (Convenio de Cooperación Económica entre Uruguay y Argentina) firmado en 1974 y con Brasil, a través del PEC (Protocolo de Expansión Comercial Uruguay-Brasil) acordado en 1975.

Sus efectos fueron sin embargo relativos, aunque significaron el inicio de una corriente comercial que luego se incrementaría en forma sensible, especialmente con Brasil. La relatividad del éxito obedeció a trabas burocráticas y por las sobre y sub-valuaciones de las monedas de los referidos países en relación al peso uruguayo que provocaron una gran discontinuidad e inseguridad en las corrientes comerciales entre ambos países.

Reducción de las restricciones de las importaciones.— Se eliminaron los requisitos de prefinanciación externa de las importaciones; se redujeron las tarifas aduaneras para algunos productos y se inició un programa gradual de baja de los aranceles aduaneros.

Apertura financiera.— En septiembre de 1974 se estableció la libre convertibilidad del peso; se eliminó todo control sobre el movimiento de divisas y de capitales. El objetivo era apoyar la apertura comercial y hacer jugar las fuerzas del mercado en la cotización de las divisas extranjeras, las que podían ser compradas y vendidas por los particulares en bancos y casas de cambio sin restricción alguna; situación ésta que se mantiene hasta el presente.

Las empresas podían negociar sus divisas a través de todo el sistema bancario, con tasas de cambio pre-fijadas. Una política de mini-devaluaciones frecuentes e irregulares tenía por objetivo evitar distorsiones abruptas del tipo de cambio. Tenía además por finalidad evitar que las facturas de las exportaciones fueran falsificadas, indicándose montos menores, intentando así que los ingresos de divisas fluyeran hacia el mercado bancario nacional, en vez de desaparecer en el mercado paralelo.

Reducción de los salarios reales.— Para apoyar la orientación de la industrial hacia la exportación, se produjeron importantes reducciones del poder adquisito del salario. Sobre una base 100 de 1968 fueron bajando hasta el 62.4% en 1980 para de allí volver a subir.

Fase II: Creación de un mercado de capitales

Una vez reducidos los mecanismos de intervención estatal, pasó a considerarse prioritaria la creación de un mercado de capitales eficiente, cuyo financiamiento sin problemas fue considerado decisivo para la asignación eficiente de recursos en los restantes mercados.

Se procuró como parte de la apertura, que Uruguay se constituyera en plazo financiera, rememorando el período de los años 50 en que se le denominaba "La Suiza de América."

Una de las primeras medidas fue tomada en marzo de 1974 permitiéndose la libre circulación de divisas. En 1976 se incluye la realización de contratos en cualquier moneda. Los topes de intereses activos y pasivos fueron abolidos. Se suspendieron las líneas de redescuentos preferenciales a que se hizo referencia al analizar la primera fase. A partir de 1977 se autorizó la fundación de casas bancarias, especializadas en la importación y colocación de capitales extranjeros.

Las importaciones de capital financiero en su mayoría fueron de plazo corto y de carácter especulativo. A pesar de ello permitieron un aumento del total de las inversiones de un 12% del P.I.B. en 1974 al 18.3% en 1978, elevándose al mismo tiempo la inversión industrial del 2.7% al 6.6%.

Este crecimiento obedeció no sólo a la liberalización del mercado de capitales sino también a una demanda acumulada por inversiones de reposición, como resultado de anteriores trabas a la importación de bienes de capital.

Las elevadas importaciones de capital tuvieron como consecuencia que se anulara la contracción en la creación de dinero interno, obtenida a través de la reducción de los déficits presupuestarios. Así no se pudo contener la inflación, lo que se había tratado de lograr, al menos como objetivo secundario.

Fase III: Lucha contra la inflación (octubre 1978 a diciembre 1982)

Llegado a esta etapa, se consideró que la economía estaba madura para abordar el objetivo verdadero y final de la política implantada: la contención de la inflación. El instrumento elegido fue la fijación preanticipada del tipo de cambio del dólar por períodos que proyectaban la misma hasta en seis meses. Fue conocida como la política de "la tablita". Mirada retrospectivamente, esta política fue el mayor de los errores entonces cometidos que, junto con otros factores, llevaron a la economía a partir de 1982 a un estado de postración y endeudamiento.

Las devaluaciones previstas en "la tablita" fueron menores que la tasa interna de inflación. Esta medida reducía el riesgo de cambio del inversor extranjero, de lo cual se supuso que se produciría rápidamente una caída del nivel de intereses por el equivalente a la tasa de cobertura del riesgo, justificada por la inseguridad con respecto a la siguiente devaluación.

La creación interna de dinero debía disminuirse a través de la continuación de la reducción del déficit presupuestario, para así oponerse a futuras expectativas inflacionarias.

En forma consciente se aceptó la presión que se esperaba sobre la exportación. Se partió del supuesto que después del "fomento redundante" de los años previos (subvenciones que supuestamente permitían amplios márgenes de beneficios incluso con métodos de producción ineficientes), ahora los exportadores se podrían exponer a la competencia del mercado internacional de acuerdo al principio de una "reorientación eficientista".

Los hechos demostraron que:

1. Durante el primer ano, la lucha antiinflacionaria fracasó. La sobrevaluación del peso argentino generó capital de fuga, compras de stocks, boom de la construcción en Punta del Este, provocando un fuerte aumento de la demanda que se tradujo en alzas de precios en las ramas correspondientes (bienes inmuebles y de consumo fundamentalmente) que, agregadas a la subida del costo del petróleo, se reflejó en un aumento generalizado del nivel de precios. Mientras en 1977 la tasa de inflación fue del 57.3%, en 1978 fue del 46.0% y en 1979 del 83.1%.

2. Luego quedó en evidencia que el mercado crediticio no era un "mercado perfecto". El paulatino final del "boom" y la reducción de la inflación que sí se dio en 1980, no fue acompañado por una reducción correspondiente de los intereses (tabla 1).

Tabla 1

Año	Interés por préstamos[a] (%)	Incremento precios al consumo[b] (%)	Devaluación del dólar[b] (%)
1979	65.48	83.1	20.1
1980	66.60	42.8	18.4
1981	59.88	29.4	15.7

[a] Promedio de tasas más frecuente a fin de mes para operaciones en moneda nacional.
[b] Tasa anualizada.

Las tasas por endeudamiento en dólares resultaban menos caras ya que, al estar controlado por "la tablita" el tipo de cambio, el costo anual entre diferencia de cambio e intereses estuvo por debajo del costo financiero en moneda nacional.

La ley promulgada a fines de 1981, permitiendo la instalación de una cantidad limitada de nuevos bancos, fue un primer intento para tentar una reducción del costo del dinero a través de una mayor competitividad del sistema financiero.

Concomitante con ello, la apertura financiera de 1979 había traído al sistema financiero importantes flujos de capitales del exterior, particularmente argentinos, cuyo reciclaje rápido no resultaba fácil. En tales condiciones, prácticamente se lo ofrecían en condiciones de total fluidez y espontaneidad (por no decir irresponsabilidad) a las empresas, incentivando el endeudamiento en dólares y desestimulando, a través de la tasa de costo financiero, el endeudamiento en moneda nacional.

La industria, por su parte, cayó en la tentación de realizar, aún en 1980/81, amplias inversiones a raíz del crecimiento de las exportaciones y, posteriormente, de las ventas en el mercado interno como consecuencia del "boom".

En valores constantes, los créditos al sector industrial se duplicaron entre los inicios de 1980 y 1982. La mayor parte fue endeudamiento en dólares, estimado en el 50 a 60% del endeudamiento total.

La exportación agropecuaria fue fomentada. La liquidez de la plaza fomentó un "boom" también en el sector primario, lo que tuvo como consecuencia que también aquí se produjeran grandes endeudamientos de empresas de este ramo, por inversiones en infraestructura y en ganado en pie que subió fuertemente de precio en 1980/81 y cayó luego también fuertemente en 1982/83.

4. No siempre la industria exportadora pudo recoger para sí los beneficios económicos de los estímulos e incentivos que la política gubernamental les ofrecía. La dimensión de la industria exportadora de Uruguay no le permite fijar precios, sino tomarlos. Los compradores del exterior, conocedores del margen obtenido por el fabricante a través de las bonificaciones y los reintegros, se apropió de hecho de ese margen, ofreciendo precios que obligaban al productor promedio, con escasa capacidad de negociación frente a las grandes empresas internacionales, a trabajar con escasa y a veces nula rentabilidad.

5. Por último y no menos importante, la sobrevaluación del peso frente al dólar quitó competitividad a las exportaciones. Las empresas encontraban cada vez más dificultades para vender sus productos al exterior, con una tasa de conversión del dólar artificialmente deprimida

y costos internos que crecían más rápidamente que aquella. Ello llevó a que muchas empresas exportadoras tuvieran pérdidas importantes y descapitalización.

La crisis de 1982/83

Si bien es cierto que la tasa de inflación cedió considerablemente en el transcurso de 1982, llegando al 20%, los tipos reales de intereses subieron. La contracción del comercio internacional y la generalizada situación de endeudamiento con elevadas tasas de costo financiero, hicieron inviables a muchas empresas. Mientras que entre 1965 y 1980 se habían presentado en promedio 17 solicitudes anuales de concordato, en 1981 hubieron 102, en 1982 fueron 1.940 y en 1983 superaron las 1.200.

La conjunción de todos estos factores, la falta de credibilidad en el mantenimiento de la tablita y el continuo drenaje de divisas que significaba para el Banco Central una constante huida del peso hacia un dólar subsididado, obligaron al gobierno—al que la situación se le hacía insostenible—, a abandonar la "tablita" y liberalizar el tipo de cambio. Ello sucedió el 26 de noviembre de 1982.

En poco más de dos meses, el dólar casi triplicó su valor. Muchas empresas, tanto de exportación como de producción local, con abultados pasivos en dólares en relación a su capital propio, entraron en nuevas cesasiones de paso. De "boom" se pasó a la recesión profunda. El P.I.B. cayó abruptamente, al igual que las exportaciones (tabla 2).

Tabla 2

Año	P.I.B. (millones de U$S)	P.I.B. (millones N$ base 1978)	Exportaciones (millones de U$S)
1980	10.132	34:808	1.058
1981	11.328	35:469	1.215
1982	9.239	32:138	1.023
1983	5.355	30:257	1.045
1984	5.246	29:816	935
1985	5.126	29:905	853

El Banco Central acudió en ayuda del sistema bancario que, receptor de las quiebras de las empresas, entró también en crisis. Les compró cartera "pesada" contra préstamos al gobierno de dinero fresco que aumentaron en forma sensible la ya abultada deuda externa. Esta medida benefició sólo a la banca extranjera, que era la que estaba en condiciones de aportar nuevos flujos de capitales. Los bancos nacionales no pudieron usufructuar este beneficio y años después (1987) en una operación salvataje, fueron absorbidos por el Banco de la República, banco estatal.

Concomitante con la liberalización del tipo de cambio, se eliminaron la mayoría de los reintegros y la prefinanciación de las exportaciones, medidas éstas criticadas por el GATT que exigía su derogación. Dichos beneficios fueron substituidos por una devolución de los impuestos indirectos, que se mantuvo hasta fecha reciente.

Paralelamente un plan de refinanciación de las deudas internas fue puesto en práctica para paliar la situación. Una ley obligó a las instituciones bancarias a refinanciar las deudas de las empresas a través de créditos a largo plazo.

Retorno a la democracia

El año 1984 fue un año de transición política. El gobierno saliente no adoptó decisiones importantes en el campo económico, mientras la recesión se acentuaba. El retorno a la vida democrática a partir de marzo de 1985, cambió el clima desde el punto de vista psicológico, abriéndose una cuota de esperanza.

Situación económica

La economía uruguaya al momento de asumir el gobierno democrático en marzo de 1985 presentaba una situación crítica con profundos desequilibrios, internos y externos:

a. En el período 1982-84, la actividad económica había experimentado una caída del orden del 17%.

b. El déficit público total representaba el 10.3% del P.I.B. al fin del primer trimestre de 1985. En períodos de recesión, el déficit fiscal se agudiza fácilmente como consecuencia de que el sistema tributario está basado en un porcentaje muy elevado de la recaudación (60%) en dos impuestos al consumo: el IVA y el IMESI.

c. La tasa de inflación proyectada para 1985 se estimaba en un guarismo superior al 100%.

d. La balanza de pagos había sido negativa en 1984; se habían perdido reservas internacionales y fuga de capitales.

e. El endeudamiento externo a fines de 1984 era de 4.671 millones de dólares, con obligaciones de amortización e intereses imposibles de cumplir en los términos pactados.

f. Un abultado sobreendeudamiento de los sectores productivos (agrarios, industriales y comerciales) que adicionaba limitaciones para una reactivación económica.

g. En el sector monetario de la economía se verificaba una alta dolarización y negativas expectativas de los agentes económicos.

h. Un deterioro en el salario realista y alta desocupación, del orden del 14.3%, efectos que conjugados habían provocado una baja en la participación del salario en el ingreso nacional.

i. Las tasas de interés reales eran positivas en dólares y negativas para los créditos en moneda nacional lo que apuntalaba el proceso de dolarización de la economía.

La política económica aplicada

A mediados de 1985, el gobierno define un programa gradualista de estabilización con objetivos de reactivación económica para el período junio de 1985 a diciembre de 1986. Dicho programa comprendía medidas de ajuste fiscal y monetario así como para el control de la inflación.

Preveía una tasa de crecimiento del producto situada entre el 2 y el 4% para el período de programación, una reducción del déficit fiscal y parafiscal a menos del 5% del P.I.B. a fines del año 1966, un abatimiento significativo en el déficit en cuenta corriente de la balanza de pagos; un aumento de la tributación en porcentaje que implicaba un 2.5% del P.I.B., incremento de las tarifas públicas y baja del gasto público del 10% en términos reales.

Se inicia la renegociación de la deuda externa con los bancos internacionales para un reescalonamiento plurianual de vencimientos y financiación voluntaria a mediano plazo.

En cuanto a los componentes de esa política económica:

Política fiscal.— En esta área los objetivos perseguidos fueron una reducción del gasto público y una adecuación de los ingresos, sin que la presión tributaria se transformase en un freno a la reactivación económica. No obstante esa reducción del gasto público se promueve un incremento, en términos reales, del gasto en los sectores salud y educación.

En cuanto al servicio de la deuda, se busca un menor costo en ese servicio a través de la refinanciación con los bancos internacionales y por un cobro más efectivo de las carteras bancarias adquiridas por el

Banco Central del Uruguay en el período anterior. En este último punto los logros fueron mediocres.

Se aplica una política de realismo tarifario en el ámbito del sector público empresarial, con ajustes cuatrimestrales, con el fin de lograr un superávit de operación en ese sector.

En el sector de la seguridad social se privilegian las pasividades menores y se reduce el gasto corriente en la administración de los servicios.

Se realiza un ajuste tributario ampliando la base imponible del impuesto al patrimonio y persiguiéndose una racionalización de la estructura tributaria.

Política monetaria.— En este campo se reducen los requerimientos de crédito por parte del sector público y se logra desacelerar el crecimiento de los agregados monetarios, evitando generar restricción en la oferta de crédito a los sectores productivos, en particular los destinados a la exportación.

En materia de tasas de interés se aplica una política que consolida niveles de tasas moderadamente positivas.

Se promueve una política de tipo de cambio flotante, con intervención selectiva, aplicándose esa política en forma coordinada entre la autoridad monetaria (Banco Central) y el Banco de la República O. del Uruguay, con el objetivo de mantener un nivel adecuado de competitividad acorde con la estrategia de crecimiento liderado por las exportaciones.

Se mantiene la política de libertad cambiaria y de movimientos de capitales y retorno de dividendos.

Política salarial.— En el área de la política de ingresos el objetivo básico es la recuperación progresiva del salario realista así como el incremento de la productividad en forma compatibilizada con el aumento del salario.

La renegociación de la deuda externo.— Se culminan a mediados de 1986, las gestiones para la refinanciación de la deuda externa. Se logra una reprogramación de vencimientos por U$S 2.142 millones que representaban más del 80% del endeudamiento externo total, con un horizonte de 12 años de plazo y tasas de interés más convenientes que las pactadas anteriormente. A fines de 1987 se obtiene una segunda reprogramación de pagos externos por U$S 1.800 millones que comprende los vencimientos entre 1986 y 1991. Se logra una mejoría en las tasas de interés y un plazo de amortización de 17 años, ampliando en cinco años el término acordado el año anterior.

La promoción de las exportaciones.— A principios de 1987 el gobierno aprueba el programa de mediano plazo de 1987–89 con el objetivo de lograr un crecimiento sostenido de la producción basado en las actividades de exportación de bienes y servicios.

Al igual que en 1973, en la dinamización de la economía se asignaba un papel esencial al sector privado correspondiéndole al Estado un rol de orientación y promoción.

El programa establecía metas para las principales variables económicas; un marco de políticas e incentivos para expandir las exportaciones y un programa de inversiones públicas para el período 1987–89.

Los resultados obtenidos

La variación del P.I.B..— En la segunda mitad de 1985, se aprecia una progresiva recuperación de la economía que se afirma y consolida durante el bienio 1986–87. La reactivación económica fue significativa en el crecimiento del producto interno bruto con tasas de 7.5% y 5.9% para 1986 y 1987, respectivamente y una desaceleración para 1988 y 1989, años en que la tasa alcanzó al 0.5% y 1.5% respectivamente.

Las exportaciones.— Durante el bienio 1986–87 hay un alto dinamismo en las distintas variables, pero con cambios de significación. Si bien la demanda interna es el factor dinamizante, por una importante recuperación del poder adquisitivo, las exportaciones aumentan su contribución en 1986, se detienen en 1987 y se recuperan en 1988, creciendo nuevamente en 1989.

A su vez, las importaciones se incrementaron fuertemente en el bienio mencionado, lo que contribuyó a que la balanza comercial verificara un deterioro, recuperado en 1988 y 1989 (tabla 3).

Tabla 3

Año	Exportaciones (miles de dólares)	Importaciones (miles de dólares)	Saldo
1985	853.6	707.8	145.852
1986	1.087.8	870.0	217.850
1987	1.189.1	1.141.9	47.195
1988	1.404.5	1.176.9	227.578
1989	1.598.0	1.195.9	402.896

La inversión bruta.— La inversión bruta fija crece durante 1986 y 1987 (con tasas de 12.6% y 19.6% respectivamente) y también en 1988 pero ese año, a una tasa del 4% para decrecer en 1989 un 10% en relación a 1988.

La inflación y los salarios.— En cuanto a los precios internos, examinando la variación del índice de precios al consumidor a fin de cada año presenta la evolución siguiente: 83% en 1985; 70.7% en 1986; 57.3% en 1987; 69.0% en 1988; y 89.6% en 1989.

La evolución de las remuneraciones, que en el trienio 1982–84 registrara una caída del orden del 30% del salario real, en 1985 tiene una recuperación del 14.1%. Esa recuperación continúa hasta 1988 a tasas menores (5.8% en 1986; 4.7% en 1987; 1.5% en 1988 para decrecer un 0.5% en 1989).

Empleo y desempleo.— El aumento del nivel de actividad económica hizo que la tasa de desempleo, que como promedio anual fue del 13% en 1984, se sitúa en 12.8% en el segundo semestre de 1985, baja al 9% durante el año 1986, oscila entre el 10% y el 8% según los trimestres durante 1987 y alcanza al 8% durante el último trimestre de 1988, pasando al 9% en 1989.

Situación fiscal.— El déficit público total del sector público, financiero y no financiero, que incluye las pérdidas del Banco Central representaba el 9.5% del P.I.B. en 1984, se abate al 6.4% en 1985, al 4.9% en 1986, al 4.1% en 1987, se sitúa en 4.6% del P.I.B. en 1988 y sube al 5.5% en 1989. Aquí se aprecian también logros hasta 1987 y luego una reversión de la tendencia.

Los esfuerzos por reducir el gasto público no obtuvieron resultados significativos, quedando en evidencia una vez más la poca flexibilidad de esta variable y a su vez que no se actuó sobre ella con la debida energía.

Endeudamiento externo.— La deuda externa bruta que en 1985 era de 4.900 millones de dólares, en 1988 alcanza a 6.330 millones de dólares. En relación al producto interno bruto representaba el 93% en 1985 y pasa a representar en 1988 el 80%. El servicio de la deuda externa como porcentaje de las exportaciones de bienes y servicios que era del 47.1% en 1985 es a fines de 1988 del 35.7% de esas exportaciones. Es decir que el perfil del endeudamiento mejoró en cuanto a su peso relativo.

La situación actual

La situación a fines de 1989 presenta indicadores muy inquietantes. La misma constituía el cierre de un período de gobierno que, partiendo de una crisis muy importante, tal como fue señalado, había logrado administrarla con resultados muy positivos en 1986 y 1987 (reducción del déficit fiscal; recuperación de poder adquisitivo; aumento de las exportaciones; tendencia decreciente de la inflación y de la tasa de desocupación).

Sin embargo, en 1988 se comienza a notar un enlentecimiento del proceso. El P.I.B. detiene su crecimiento, al igual que el poder adquisitivo de los salarios. La inflación vuelve a tomar fuerza, alentada por un déficit fiscal en crecimiento. El control de la inflación es el punto más débil de toda la política del período, al no haber podido obtener resultados positivos perdurables, con tasas que, de no ser severamente controladas, pueden ser la antesala de la hiperinflación.

A pesar del éxito relativo de la política económica del período, particularmente si se le compara con los avatares de los países vecinos como Argentina y Brasil, la inflación uruguaya se encuentra entre las 10 más importantes a nivel mundial y es la cuarta en importancia a nivel latinoamericano, sólo superada por los extremos de Argentina, Brasil y Perú.

Ello ha significado a su vez, tasas de intereses durante estos años que han oscilado en el 80 y 90% efectivo, llevando una carga muy pesada a la estructura de costos de producción de las empresas que ya venían fuertemente endeudadas desde la crisis de 1982. Nuevamente muchas empresas y ramas enteras de actividad se hallan en crisis económico–financiera, reiterándose aunque a un menor nivel, la situación de 1983.

Dos grandes rubros contribuyen al déficit del sector público. Uno de ellos son los aportes al sistema de seguridad social, el que se encuentra sumamente desfinanciado, debiendo el gobierno central aportar anualmente U$S 300 millones para poder pagar sus haberes a los jubilados y pensionistas. Otro son los intereses de la deuda externa, ubicada en 6.500 millones de dólares.

En las elecciones de 1989 triunfa el partido Blanco o Nacional, opositor del gobernante partido Colorado. Asume el gobierno en marzo de 1990. La preocupación por el crecimiento del déficit fiscal y de la inflación se ve aumentada con la aprobación en un plebiscito realizado en forma conjunta con las elecciones nacionales, de un nuevo sistema de actualización de las jubilaciones y pensiones que sirve el Estado que agregarán a los egresos fiscales una suma adicional de U$S 180 millones, equivalentes al 2.2% del P.I.B. Con ello, el déficit total del sector público, alcanzará fácilmente al 8% del P.I.B. con el consiguiente impacto en el crecimiento de la tasa de inflación que se estimaba podría alcanzar al 180% no fueran adoptadas medidas muy duras para su contención.

Las perspectivas

Contención de la inflación

En el marco de este contexto, el nuevo gobierno ha fijado como prioridad número uno la contención de la inflación, con medidas que procuran obtener un abatimiento muy importante en el transcurso de 1990, con el objetivo de que en 1991 no exceda del 20%.

Estas medidas comprenden un importante ajuste fiscal basado en:

1. Un severo ajuste del sistema de fiscalización y de recaudación de los impuestos y de los aportes al sistema de seguridad social, a fin de reducir al mínimo posible la fuerte evasión existente.

2. Un aumento del 1% en los impuestos al consumo y del 3.5% en las tasas de aportación al sistema de seguridad social, tanto patronales como obreras, así como un impuesto a los sueldos que va desde el 3.5% al 7%, fondos estos destinados a financiar el déficit adicional generado por el plebiscito a que se hizo referencia. Ello significará una pérdida del poder adquisitivo de los trabajadores en el transcurso del presente año del orden del 6%.

3. Una reducción de los gastos de todos los organismos estatales, excepto la educación, así como de las empresas públicas del orden del 15%.

4. La eliminación—por ahora temporal—de los reintegros de impuestos indirectos que gravan los insumos de los productos destinados a la exportación.

5. Una lucha frontal contra el contrabando que por las relaciones de precios con los países limítrofes, particularmente Brasil, había adquirido un volumen muy significativo, repercutiendo negativamente en la producción y la venta de las industrias de productos para el consumo interno, con el agregado del crecimiento del sistema informal de comercialización que, al margen de las normas legales, retacea ingresos por concepto de impuestos a las arcas estatales.

Las referidas medidas ya fueron adoptadas y por ser de fecha muy reciente (mes de abril) es difícil todavía evaluar sus resultados y sus efectos. De ellas, la que más impacto inmediato ha provocado es la de la lucha contra el contrabando, favorecida por un cambio en las relaciones de intercambio que ya no hacen tan atractivos los precios de las mercaderías provenientes de Brasil y de Argentina. Ello ha tonificado a algunas industrias para el consumo interno, fundamentalmente en el área de la alimentación.

Principales medidas proyectadas

Reforma del Estado.— Otras medidas complementarias se anuncian. Algunas de ellas son destinadas a generar condiciones de mayor competitividad y eficiencia en las empresas y servicios públicos, así como reducir el tamaño del aparato estatal. Las mismas pasan por quitar el monopolio de algunos servicios a cargo del Estado (puerto de Montevideo; ciertos tipos de seguros); por admitir el ingreso de capitales privados en empresas como la estatal de aeronavegación, la de teléfonos y servicios conexos; por cerrar definitivamente una de las empresas estatales (ILPE—Industria Lobera y Pesquera del Estado) y por ofrecer a la actividad privada compartir la explotación y comercialización de la producción de alcoholes y de portland.

Adjustes al sistema de seguros sociales.— Otra de las vertientes de las medidas anunciadas es la relativa a la reestructuración del servicio de prestaciones sociales de seguros de enfermedad, de jubilaciones y pensiones, imposible de autofinanciarse con la relación de activos y pasivos que desde hace años tiene el sistema y que requiere en forma permanente de la ayuda del gobierno central con fuertes erogaciones a su cargo. La misma es de 1.2 activos por cada pasivo, cuando, en un sistema de solidaridad, la relación no debe ser inferior a un activo por cada 3 pasivos. Las medidas a adoptar van encaminadas a una reducción del monto de las prestaciones jubilatorias, a una ampliación de la edad para jubilarse y a promover un sistema basado en el ahorro personal que pudiere estar a cargo en forma indistinta de instituciones privadas y estatales.

Las relaciones obrero-patronales.— Un cuarto curso de acción anunciado es el relativo a la regulación de las relaciones obrero-patronales. El nivel de conflictividad ha sido muy alto, con efectos distorsionantes sobre la producción y las exportaciones, habiendo obligado al anterior gobierno a declarar "esenciales" varios servicios, poniéndo la paralización de los mismos al borde de la legalidad. Las medidas a proponer apuntan a establecer el voto secreto y obligatorio en las decisiones de los gremios de ir a la huelga y a establecer un debido proceso que asegure que aquella es adoptada como último recurso y luego de agotadas otras instancias. Ello permitiría asimismo establecer un sistema de negociaciones salariales entre las partes en las que el Estado quiere ser gradualmente prescindente.

La deuda externa.— Uruguay ha tenido en los últimos 15 años un prolijo cumplimiento de los compromisos asumidos en materia de deuda externa. Este hecho lo habilita a acogerse a los posibles beneficios del Plan Brady, a cuyos efectos el gobierno está realizando las gestiones del caso con perspectivas alentadoras.

Oportunidades en áreas no tradicionales

También existen oportunidades en el futuro mediato en áreas no tradicionales como la de los servicios, que pueden coadyuvar a un necesario proceso de reactivación económica.

El turismo internacional.— Uruguay ofrece atractivas condiciones naturales para el desarrollo del turismo internacional. Se carece sin embargo de la debida infraestructura que ofrezca las comodidades requeridas y que prolongue la temporada turística más allá de los tres meses de verano. A vía de ejemplo, no posee un solo hotel cinco estrellas. Como consecuencia, está al margen de las corrientes turísticas de mayor poder adquisitivo, europeas y americanas, que normalmente llegan a los países vecinos, alimentándose la industria solamente con la afluencia del turismo zonal (Argentina, Brasil y Paraguay). Si se otorgan las debidas facilidades, puede generarse una atractiva corriente de inversiones extranjeras conectadas con la red del turismo internacional.

La hidrovía.— La ubicación geográfica y las crecientes dificultades y costos para mantener operativo al puerto de Buenos Aires, hacen de Uruguay y sus puertos, particularmente a través de la hidrovía Paraguay-Paraná-Uruguay, una zona en la que puede desarrollarse una intensa actividad de servicios vinculados con el comercio internacional del Cono Sur. Una ley de zonas francas procura ofrecer condiciones ventajosas para la instalación de empresas que, tomando como base la ubicación geográfica, fraccionen, realicen procesos o industrialicen productos a serie re-exportados luego.

Barreras a superar

Inversiones insuficientes; tecnologías envejecidas.— Un bajo porcentaje de inflación es un requisito necesario para un desarrollo sano de la economía, pero no suficiente. Si no se realizan inversiones que repongan el desgaste del capital fijo del país, lo aumenten y lo tecnifiquen, la capacidad de producción no aumentará ni al ritmo ni a los costos necesarios.

La tasa de inversión interna bruta ha sido insuficiente, no cubriendo durante largos períodos ni siquiera la reposición de la obsolescencia de los activos fijos (10% anual), con lo cual se está produciendo un proceso de desinversión y de insuficiente actualización del parque productivo (tabla 4). Ello está indicando que la expansión de la producción y del P.I.B. así como de las exportaciones, se basó más en la existencia de capacidad ociosa instalada que en nuevas inversiones.

Tabla 4

Año	P.I.B. (millones de N$, base 1978)	Formación bruta de capital en relación al P.I.B. (%)	Exportaciones (millones de dólares)
1970/ 74	25.839	9.9	288:577
1975/ 79	30.025	14.8	602:406
1980/ 84	32.498	14.4	1.053:560
1985	29.905	8.4	853:614
1986	32.148	8.2	1.087:830
1987	34.048	9.6	1.189:086
1988	34.217	9.8	1.404:527
1989	34.730	8.6	1.598:775

De ahora en más se requerirán nuevas inversiones si se aspira a que aumente el P.I.B. y que las exportaciones continúen creciendo, ya que el mercado interno tiene un horizonte bastante acotado por su propio tamaño. Paralelamente, la competitividad de los mercados internacionales exige una renovación tecnológica que sólo puede lograrse con nuevas inversiones. Sin embargo, no se aprecian indicadores que permitan suponer que las mismas se realizarán en forma fluida y constituye una barrera cuya superación no surge clara.

En lo interno, el país no presenta una capacidad de ahorro que haga presumir la existencia de capitales de riesgo de cierta importancia. Los existentes encuentran en el sistema bancario una alternativa más segura y rentable. Si la inflación fuere efectivamente controlada, podría surgir un mayor interés por las inversiones de riesgo. Paralelamente las empresas presentan un alto nivel de endeudamiento que hace dificultoso aumentar el mismo para realizar nuevas inversiones, sin perder su equilibrio económico-financiero natural.

En lo externo, los esfuerzos por atraer inversores extranjeros de riesgo a través de la apertura del mercado de capitales, del libre tránsito de los mismos y de la garantía de giro de las utilidades, no han dado resultados. Los capitales ingresados han sido fundamentalmente de especulación financiera y buscando la seguridad y rentabilidad que ofrece el sistema bancario, la mayor parte proveniente de los países limítrofes. La continua conflictividad sindical; un régimen laboral que genera rigidez y poca flexibilidad en la adaptación de la mano de obra a los cambios tecnológicos y a las readaptaciones empresariales; un sistema judicial lento e inoperante en cuanto a la rápida ejecución de los créditos y derechos son señalados, entre otros, como factores que no estimulan al inversor extranjero.

Fraccionamiento del sistema político.— Uruguay se caracterizó durante más de 90 años por el bi-partidismo. Los dos partidos tradicionales, el Colorado y el Blanco, dominaron la vida política del país. En el año 1973 surgió una colación de izquierda, el denominado Frente Amplio, que ha venido acreciendo su participación electoral, al punto que en las recientes elecciones nacionales obtuvo el gobierno del departamento de Montevideo, donde está asentada casi la mitad de la población del país. Una cuarta fuerza minoritaria de orientación social-demócrata, el denominado "nuevo espacio," completa el menú de opciones políticas para el electorado.

Siendo el de Uruguay un sistema presidencialista, el Partido Blanco ahora gobernante ha buscado un acuerdo político con el principal partido opositor, el Partido Colorado, para llevar adelante un programa que posibilite introducir los cambios antes mencionados. El país, sin duda, necesita en forma urgente pero para los cuales el gobierno no cuenta con las mayorías parlamentarias necesarias para su aprobación.

Este acuerdo está resultando muy difícil de concretar. El Partido Colorado está actualmente dividido en su liderazgo en cuatro fracciones que representa cada una de ellas, aproximadamente un 25% del mismo con posiciones con frecuencia encontradas. El partido de gobierno encuentra a su vez dificultades internas, por la presencia de dos grupos con filosofía política sensiblemente diferenciada: la fracción mayoritaria partidaria de un enfoque neo-liberal y la fracción minoritaria pero importante, que propugna un modelo más tradicional, con fuerte intervención y participación del Estado.

Ello puede llevar a que no se logre el consenso político necesario para aprobar las medidas que el país necesita y que, una vez más, predomine el estancamiento en las decisiones políticas relativas a cambios de naturaleza estructural y que ni la economía, ni el estado, ni el régimen jurídico-comercial, ni el sistema de relacionamiento entre el trabajo y el capital se modernicen y actualicen para dar al país el dinamismo y la competitividad internacional que su desarrollo requiere.

Endeudamiento interno.— La crisis de 1982 dejó como resultado negativo—entre otros—empresas fuertemente endeudadas en dólares. Una parte sustancial de las mismas arrastra aún el problema. Desde entonces, los altos costos financieros y el atraso tecnológico en muchas ramas industriales han ido acumulando un endeudamiento creciente de las empresas que sobrevivieron a la crisis. Ello compromete la viabilidad de muchas de ellas, que una previsible situación recesiva como parte de la lucha contra la inflación recien iniciada puede agudizar.

Resumen conectivo

1. La economía de Uruguay padeció un estancamiento estructural durante más de 30 años. Una filosofía intervencionista y parternalista del Estado y una política de sustitución de las importaciones y fuerte protección a la industria local, generaron condiciones de poco desafío y competitividad. La fácil colocación de los productos naturales durante la segunda guerra mundial y la guerra de Corea, disimularon las falencias del sistema, que gradualmente se agudizaron.

2. Este deterioro y el aumento del precio del petróleo en la crisis de 1973, llevaron a un cambio de la política económica, promovido por el gobierno cívico-militar que en ese mismo año había tomado el poder. Se pasó entonces a una política neo-liberal, reduciendo la acción planificadora e intervencionista del Estado y dando mayor peso al mercado como asignador de recursos.

3. Bajo este marco general se adoptaron varias medidas tendientes a desregular la actividad económica y el funcionamiento de los mercados.

A través de diversos incentivos se fomentaron las exportaciones.

Se puso en vigencia una liberalización comercial eliminando los controles a las importaciones y reduciendo gradualmente las tasas y aranceles de protección efectiva para que la industria manufacturera sea competitiva a nivel internacional.

Se produjo la liberalización financiera y la desregulación de la actividad bancaria, con libre circulación de capitales para el mejor desplazamiento de los préstamos y la inversión extranjera, los retornos de intereses, amortizaciones, utilidades, pagos de tecnología, etc., así como la libre contratación activa y pasiva de las tasas de interés.

También fue liberado el mercado cambiario con libre oferta y demanda de todas las monedas.

4. Luego, en un intento por abatir la inflación, se adoptó la denominada política de "la tablita" con tasas de cambio prefijadas con meses de anticipación y con una tasa de devaluación sensiblemente por debajo del aumento de los precios internos. Esta política resultó

desastrosa para todo el sistema. El dólar artificialmente barato y un exceso de disponibilidad en los bancos junto con el "boom" de los años 79/80 llevaron a un fuerte endeudamiento de todo el sistema empresarial y a una continua demanda de dólares por parte del público.

5. Desbordado por la situación, el gobierno devaluó abruptamente el dólar en 1982, el que triplicó su valor frente al peso, generando una crisis de graves proporciones y una fuerte recesión durante los años 83 y 84 que, como aspecto positivo, facilitó en cierto modo el retorno a la vida democrática por lo insostenible que se le hacía al gobierno militar el mantener bajo control una situación por demás deteriorada.

6. El nuevo gobierno democrático que asumió en marzo de 1985 mantuvo las líneas generales de la política de apertura de la economía. Inicialmente, en 1985/86/87 pudo reactivar la economía, contener el déficit fiscal y el aumento de la inflación y lograr una recuperación del salario real que incrementó el consumo interno. Sin embargo, a partir de 1988 el proceso de crecimiento se enlentece, la inflación retoma un nuevo empuje, potencialmente agravado por la aprobación de un plebiscito que adiciona 180 millones de dólares a las obligaciones de pago del Estado al sistema de seguridad social. La única variable que no se deteriora son las exportaciones, las que, a pesar del "enfriamiento" de la economía siguieron creciendo favorecidas por buenos precios internacionales en los productos agropecuarios.

7. En marzo de 1990 asume el gobierno el hasta entonces opositor Partido Blanco. Como primera medida aplicó un fuerte ajuste fiscal a fin de aumentar la recaudación, contraer el gasto y contener la inflación creciente. El gobierno muestra una firme decisión a profundizar este camino y el lograr resultados positivos resulta imperativo para lograr una posterior reactivación de la economía sobre bases más sólidas que las logradas en el período 85/87. De no lograrse dichos resultados, una fuerte crisis sobrevendrá.

Sin embargo, los mismos son necesarios pero no suficientes. El ritmo de las inversiones internas no viene siendo suficiente ni para reponer el desgaste del capital ya invertido. No se aprecian condiciones que hagan vislumbrar un flujo de inversiones que asegure un crecimiento regular del P.I.B. Este problema, ya crónico, sigue sin tener una solución a la vista. El fuerte endeudamiento de las empresas hace más difícil aún que éstas inviertan y se actualicen tecnológicamente.

8. A diferencia del anterior gobierno, se propone ahora con bastante decisión el encarar medidas más profundas que el país requiere, en particular:

Acciones de reforma del Estado.
Prohibición de ingreso de nuevos funcionarios.
Reforma del sistema de seguridad social, que con un pasivo por cada activo resulta inviable y un factor inflacionario importante.
Regulación de las relaciones obrero-patronales y del ejercicio del derecho de huelga, como forma de encauzar y reducir la permanente conflictividad sindical.
Negociación de la deuda externa en el marco del Plan Brady.

No resulta claro al momento que el gobierno, que no tiene mayorías parlamentarias propias, pueda llevar adelante las soluciones que propone. Un acuerdo se gestó en los inicios del nuevo período con el opositor Partido Colorado, pero en la práctica su operativización está resultando sumamente difícil. El riesgo de que dichas medidas queden detenidas o demasiado desdibujadas aparece como importante.

9. El estímulo de áreas de servicios como el turismo internacional y los servicios de transporte, almacenaje, carga y descarga, zonas francas, etc. vinculados con la puesta en operación de la hidrovía Paraguay-Paraná-Uruguay promete en el mediano plazo nuevos e importantes rubros que se pueden agregar a los tradicionales de la industria y la agricultura.

ANEXO

Algunos Indicadores Macroeconómicos

Año	(1)	(2)	(3)	(4)	(5)	(6)	(7)	(8)
1980	10.132	34.808	1.059	42.8	18.4	6.461	2.161	130.22
1981	11.328	35.469	1.215	29.4	15.7	5.888	3.129	139.95
1982	9.239	32.138	1.023	20.0	188.9	4.815	4.201	139.50
1983	5.355	30.257	1.045	51.5	49.6	3.052	4.572	110.58
1984	5.246	29.816	.925	66.1	69.2	3.111	4.671	100.48
1985	5.126	29.905	.854	83.0	72.9	2.524	4.900	114.68
1986	6.454	32.148	1.088	70.6	42.9	2.630	5.239	122.42
1987	7.734	34.048	1.189	57.3	54.7	3.258	5.888	128.15
1988	7.944	34.217	1.405	69.0	61.2	3.338	6.330	130.07
1989	8.400	34.730	1.598	89.6	76.9	2.992	6.500	129.56

(1) Producto interno bruto (P.I.B.) en millones de dólares.

(2) Producto interno bruto (P.I.B.) en millones de nuevos pesos a valor constante a N$ de 1978.

(3) Exportaciones en millones de dólares.

(4) Porcentaje de crecimiento anual del índice de precios al consumo (IPC) = % inflación.

(5) Porcentaje de crecimiento anual del valor del dólar.

(6) Inversión bruta de capital en millones de nuevos pesos a valor constante a N$ 1978.

(7) Deuda externa en millones de dólares.

(8) Indice del valor de los salarios (base 100 = 78/84).

12. Trends in the Brazilian Economy of the 1990s and Scenarios for the Year 2000

Enrique Saravia

Introduction: The Scenario Method

Indicating prospects for a given economy has always been difficult. It has been said that economists are very good at explaining the past but very poor at planning the future. More cynical commentators maintain that modern economic forecasting is at the same scientific level as astrology.

Almost every failure in this field is attributable to the isolation of economics and economists from other scientists and disciplines. The huge mistakes made in the past thirty years have led economists to interdisciplinary research with other social scientists, and planning has benefited from this interaction, especially when it is applied to corporate planning.

Strategic planning means a radical change in relation to traditional organizational planning. In fact, the former introduces environmental concerns and requires permanent scanning of external variables. But, as in any plan, it is necessary to establish objectives to be achieved in the near or distant future. Since the permanence of objectives is independent of managers' or politicians' willingness, accurate and convincing instruments for identifying future prospects have to be created. Strategic management makes it possible to seek these moving targets.

An accurate planning instrument which has improved in recent years is the method of scenario construction. Older prospective techniques built their forecasting on the basis of quantitative data projections. Their premise was that the future is the product of the past or, in other words, that quantitative projections reflect immutable tendencies. This belief affected the prestige of planning in the 1970s. The two oil crises and the financial problems preceding them and resulting from them rendered useless many governmental and corporate plans. It appeared as if no one had foreseen the events that were to profoundly modify the commercial and financial markets.

Shell Corporation planners acknowledged that they had qualitative data that should have enabled them to anticipate the 1973 oil crisis, but they were not considered, since they did not conform to conventional planning models. As a result of that experience, planning instruments combining quantitative and qualitative elements came into use. That is the basis of the scenario method, allowing planners to deal with the uncertainty implicit in every forecast and to describe an imaginary future situation that will be taken into consideration in all planning activities.

Several governments and corporations are now using the scenario technique. Air transportation in France is planned on the basis of scenarios.[1] In Brazil the Banco Nacional de Desenvolvimento Econômico e Social (BNDES) (National Bank for Economic and Social Development) prepared scenarios for the Brazilian economy in the period 1985–2000 and for the freight transportation sector.[2]

Scenarios for the Brazilian Economy

This paper deals with the application of scenario techniques to the Brazilian economy. It is based on the scenario I constructed that is being used by certain multinational and local private enterprises as an element in their strategic planning. The conclusions arrived at using the scenario construction techniques were compared with those arrived at by the Banco Nacional de Desenvolvimento Econômico e Social, and projections made by the Instituto Brasileiro de Geografia e Estatística (IBGE) (Brazilian Institute of Geography and Statistics), the Fundação Getúlio Vargas (Getúlio Vargas Foundation), and both private and state-owned enterprises.

The scenario includes subsystems and variables that interact; they are, in other words, mutually dependent. The subsystems are: macro-economic, technological, social, political, and international.

Variables of the Macro-economic Subsystem

Two variables dynamize the macro-economic subsystem: (1) the export-oriented agriculture sector with high levels of technology incorporated will continue its growth; and (2) exports will maintain their increasing rhythm and the concomitant trade balance surplus will continue (tables 1, 2). It is important to note that the growth of both sectors developed as a result of the dynamic of the economic structure, and not as a consequence of governmental policies. In fact, the 1984 trade surplus was twice the amount expected by the government, which had not expected manufactured goods to be so high a share of total exports. Agricultural growth—higher than that reflected in official statistics—occurred in spite of government measures that might have indirectly discouraged it.[3]

Table 1. Brazilian Trade Balance
(US$ million FOB)

	January–December											
	1980	1981	1982	1983	1984	1985	1986	1987	1988	Average 1980-1988	Average 1985-1988	1989
Exports (A)	20.132	23.293	20.175	21.899	27.005	25.639	22.349	26.224	33.789	24.501	27.000	34.392
Imports (B)	22.955	22.092	19.395	15.429	13.916	13.153	14.044	15.052	14.605	16.738	14.214	18.281
Balance (A – B)	-2.823	1.201	780	6.470	13.089	12.486	8.305	11.172	19.184	7.763	12.786	16.111
Total Trade (A+B)	43.087	45.385	39.570	37.328	40.921	38.792	36.393	41.276	48.394	41.239	41.214	52.673

Source: Banco do Brasil S.A.
CACEX/DEPEC/ANEDI/SEANE

Table 2. Brazilian Exports
(US$ million FOB)

	January–December													
	1980		1981	1982	1983	1984	1985	1986	1987	1988	1980–1988		1989	
	Amount	Percent									Average	Percent	Amount	Percent
Primary (A)	8.488	42.16	8.920	8.238	8.535	8.706	8.538	7.280	8.022	9.411	8.460	34.53	9.599	27.91
Manufactured (B)	11.376	56.51	13.999	11.686	13.058	18.004	16.821	14.895	18.014	24.079	15.770	64.36	24.400	70.95
Semimanufactured	2.349	11.67	2.116	1.433	1.782	2.872	2.758	2.491	3.175	4.892	2.652	10.82	5.806	16.88
Manufactured	9.027	44.84	11.883	10.253	11.276	15.132	14.063	12.404	14.839	19.187	13.118	53.54	18.594	54.07
Special Operations (C)	.268	1.33	.374	.251	.306	.295	.280	.174	.188	.299	.271	1.11	.393	1.14
Total (A + B + C)	20.132	100.00	23.293	20.175	21.899	27.005	25.639	22.349	26.224	33.789	24.501	100.00	34.392	100.00

Another variable that potentially limits expansion is the possibility of a shortage of electricity caused by the slowdown of electric power production plans and diminished oil prospecting and production investments. Electric power rationing is expected to begin in 1992, and it is foreseen that in 1994 the available electricity supply will be 20 percent less than needed. Investments in 1988 were US $2.3 billion and in 1989 almost US $4 billion, whereas US $7.7 billion in investments per year were required to avert the coming power shortage (table 3).[4]

Table 3. Electricity Consumption/Gross Domestic Product

	1987	87/86 (%)	1988	88/87 (%)	1989	89/88 (%)
GWh	165,431	2.8	172,486	4.5	180,959	4.7
GDP (US$ millions)	268,663	3.6	279,492	0.0	303,452	3.6

Source: Banco Central do Brasil

Government-owned enterprises will improve their performance through the adoption of methods and technologies better suited to their corporate condition. This improvement is required by the economic system, and is necessitated by both the lack of government resources and the shortage of foreign credit.

The privatization process will continue, and enterprises no longer considered strategic as a result of changes in the role of the State and its priorities will close. The majority of state enterprises now operating, however, will continue to be run by the government.

The trend toward corporate concentration through mergers and takeovers, and cooperation through joint ventures will become stronger.

Technological Subsystem

There will be a strong incorporation of technology in the productive sectors as a consequence of the needs of the economic system and of its insertion in the international market. This trend will modify the manpower profile. The number of employees will not decrease (it will probably grow), but more specialization will be required. The question is whether the formal educational system will be able to provide the professionals needed by the market. If not, a parallel educational system will appear in order to meet the needs of enterprises and government alike.

Domestic technological development will accelerate, in research and development activities as well as in the establishment of efficient mechanisms for technology transfer and negotiation. As several countries have learned, there can be no solid productive structure without domestic technological development.[5]

Social Subsystem

The population projection for the year 2000 is 179 million inhabitants. Estimated population on July 1, 1989 was 150,051,784. But the basic needs of the Brazilian population (health, education, housing, social security) are ill-attended. The income of the majority is progressively decreasing. The economic growth of the last decades has accelerated the concentration of wealth in the groups located at the top of the socioeconomic pyramid: 10 percent of the wealthiest members of society receive about 51 percent of the national income.

Social indexes show stagnation and in some cases, even regression. For instance, the Brazilian child mortality rate, which ranked 58th in the world in 1960, ranked 65th (63 deaths per 1,000 children) in 1987. Whereas 82 percent of Korean teenagers attend school, in Brazil the proportion is 20 percent. From the economic point of view these social problems mean the loss of a huge potential market, since sound and dynamic economies—such as that of Japan—are based on solid domestic markets.

The tendency up to the year 2000 will be the reverse of this characteristic. The domestic market will grow as a consequence of salary increases reflecting an improvement in employment levels, which in turn will result from a slow increase in the economically active population and a more rapid growth of employment. The basis for this statement is data that show that the Brazilian urban population rate is close to that of industrialized countries (about 77 percent in developed countries, and 73 percent in Brazil in 1987). The female labor force is becoming similar to the rate for males, meaning that traditional sources of cheap manpower (rural workers and women) are drying up.

Driving forces will be trade unions which are growing stronger and maturing; the Congress—strengthened by the Federal Constitution of 1988—and a growing awareness among businessmen of the importance of the domestic market.

Political Subsystem

Difficulties in the redemocratization process were useful for learning how to live in a democracy, but weaknesses are still evident. For example, periodic legitimation of leadership through elections and a growing consciousness of the importance of the ballot are favorable signs, but the very slow modernization of the political system, especially in aspects related to civil participation, is a negative variable.

Brazil needs to solve the deep conflict between modern sectors (basically represented by business interests—urban and rural—from São Paulo and other Southeast, South, and Middle West regions), and traditional sectors (Northeast landowners and the urban professional groups attached to them). The Constitution of 1988 did not improve this situation. In terms of representation in Congress, for instance, 1 vote from the state of Acre is equivalent to 17 votes from São Paulo; and 1 vote from the new state of Roraima has the same power as 46 votes from São Paulo.[6]

The judicial system remains slow and complicated. Some innovative measures (e.g., establishment of small claims courts) and social pressure—wisely acknowledged by some of the more aware judges—allow one to foresee some improvements. The present judicial system, however, appears as a delaying variable in the overall scenario.

International Subsystem

Brazil is immediately affected by certain international factors. The first element is the stabilization of the world economy, with the consolidation of large regional blocs (European Economic Community, North America, Japan, and other Far East "tigers," and the apparent "integration" of the socialist economies into the global market and the internal transformations of them: 1992 European economic union; the U.S.–Canada Common Market with the possible incorporation of Mexico; Far East countries expansion; *glasnost, perestroikc*, and profound changes in the relationships of Eastern European countries.

Second, maintenance of moderate growth rates and, especially, the increase in international trade will dynamize the market. World trade expands rapidly: 4 percent growth was expected for 1988, but the actual rate was 9 percent. The growth rate for 1989 was 6.9 percent.

International transfer of capital increases rapidly, but this movement has not had an immediate effect upon Brazil. In fact, the capital flow takes place almost completely among industrialized countries.[7]

Conditions for a more favorable external debt negotiation will improve. At the same time, interest rates remain stable in absolute terms and diminish in relative terms. The Brazilian external debt is shrinking in relation to the GNP, exports, and trade balances (table 4).

Table 4. External Debt Indicators

	1984	1985	1986	1987	1988	1989
1. Total debt/GDP (%) (debt)(GDP)100	50	46	44	45	41	38
2. Total debt/exports (%) (debt)(exports)100	378	410	497	462	336	334
3. Total debt/trade bal. (debt)(trade bal.)100	nd	nd	1337	1084	591	713

Source: Banco Central do Brasil

Two aspects of the U.S. economy constitute a negative variable: the huge fiscal deficit and the external sector deficit. There is a slight tendency toward improvement, but the situation is dangerous: American GNP is slightly less than a quarter of world gross product.

Brazil in the Year 2000

All of the factors mentioned above interact to determine the possible future: a scenario is a set of mutually coherent determinants. According to the possible and negative variables considered above, what might be the Brazilian scenario for the beginning of the next century?

Let us see, through some key indicators, how the developed, market-economy countries can be expected to behave during the '90s (table 5).

Table 5. Forecast to the Year 2000 of Industrial Economies

GNP growth	2.5% annual
Inflation	4% annual
Price of oil per barrel	US$ 52
LIBOR rate	7% (real rate: 2.9% annual)
World trade growth	4% year

Possible Brazilian scenarios can be reduced to two, with a clear and increasing likelihood that the first will occur. The BNDES has named them the scenario of the competitive integration of Brazil into the world economy and the scenario of stagnation. Key figures of the first scenario are shown in table 6.

Table 6. Brazil: Scenario of Competitive Integration

Exports	1990-2000: annual growth of 7% (1970-1980: annual growth of 13%) 1989: US$ 34.392 billion
Trade balance surplus	US$ 12 billion until 1991, growing after. 1989: US$ 16.111 billion
Investments	Growth of 5.8% annual (around 21% of GNP)
Industry	Increase of 7% annual
Consumption	7% annual (average)
GDP	1989: US$ 303.452 million (Japan: US$ 2.700 trillion 2000: about US$ 700 billion (1986 prices)
Per capita income	1989: US$ 2058.64 2000: US$ 4000 (1986 prices) (Near that of Spain in 1990)

The second scenario—stagnation—would be determined by the preponderance of the following two variables:

1. Growth of both the U.S. fiscal deficit and the external debt could lead to protectionist measures and, consequently, to the shrinkage of world trade. This situation would impact the U.S. dollar exchange rate: it would decline and the interest rate would increase.[8]

2. Brazil could fail to take advantage of economic opportunities that arose. If this issue depended entirely on the government bureaucracy, there would be good reason for concern. In reality, however, the economic system is able to overcome many obstacles. The growth of the informal economy is, paradoxically, a symptom of good health.[9]

NOTES

1. Michel Godet, "Scenarios of Air Transport Development to 1990 by SMIC 74: A New Cross-Impact Method," *Technological Forecasting and Social Change* 9 (1976), 279-288.

2. National Bank for Economic and Social Development, scenarios are for the Brazilian economy, 1985–1990; the Brazilian economy, 1987–2000; and the Brazilian freight transportation sector.

3. For example, the freezing of foreign exchange rate in early 1989 at the time of the sale of the soybean harvest.

4. Eletrobrás, the state-owned power company, reports that investments in electric power, which were about 2 percent of the GNP during the '70s, shrank during the '80s to 0.3 percent. Consumption of electricity is growing faster than GNP expansion rates (table 3): Eletrobrás says that the consumption rate increased annually by an average of 6 percent during the last eight years, while economic growth averaged 3 percent annually.

The private sector is trying to decrease the deficit. The Votorantim group built seven medium-sized hydroelectric plants and is planning the eighth; Belgo-Mineira, Paraibuna Metais, Italminas, Alcoa, and Alcan have become partners in the construction of fourteen plants. The Serra Quebrada project will be funded by Alcan, Alcoa, Billington, Dow Chemical, and Camargo Correa.

5. South Korea invests 2.2 percent of its GDP in R & D; Brazil invests only 0.6 percent.

6. Article 45 of the 1988 Federal Constitution establishes that each State will have no fewer than 8 representatives and no more than 70. Senate representation is equal for all states: 3 senators per state.

7. Between 1982 and 1988 the international capital flow grew from $50 billion to $150 billion (three-quarters of the movement occurred among countries of the industrialized world, whereas in Latin America foreign investment fell by 50 percent. For example in 1986–1988 Spain received $34 billion in foreign investments, while from 1900 to 1988 American investments in Brazil were about $9.9 billion, according to a statement by Ambassador Rubens Ricupero in the *Jornal do Brasil*, June 4, 1989, p. 30.

8. The U.S. deficit was $152.1 billion for the fiscal year ending September 30, 1989. There was a reduction of 2 percent in comparison with fiscal year 1988.

9. More conservative estimates consider that the informal economy is about 28 percent of the Brazilian GNP, but some calculations make it as high as 40 percent. The Italian informal economy is calculated to be more than 30 percent, and India's is 80 percent.

Trends in Contemporary Literature of Brazil and the Southern Cone

13. O conto brasileiro contemporâneo

Berta Waldman

Já dizia Mário de Andrade que conto é o que a gente chama de conto. Essa afirmação traz à tona a rebeldia do autor com relação a conceitos que funcionaram durante bom tempo como verdadeiros espartilhos, enquadrando o conto como o texto ficcional curto, em oposição à novela e ao romance mais extensos.

De gênese desconhecida, o conto remonta aos primórdios da própria arte literária. Alguns exemplos de contos podem ser localizados centenas ou milhares de anos antes do nascimento de Cristo. Na *Bíblia*, os episódios de Salomé, do Filho Pródigo, podem ser considerados contos, assim como, na Pérsia e na Arábia, as "Mil e Uma Noites," "Simbad," "Marujo," "Ali Babá e os Quarenta Ladrões."

No nosso século, o conto desenvolve sutilezas que, acentuando-lhe a fisionomia estética, o aproximam de uma cena do cotidiano poeticamente surpreendida. Vários mestres na matéria surgiram nas primeiras décadas do século, como Katherine Mansfield, Virginia Woolf, James Joyce, Franz Kafka, Máximo Gorki, e outros. Até os nossos dias, o conto vem sendo praticado por uma legião cada vez maior de ficcionistas, que nele encontram a forma adequada para exprimir a rapidez com que tudo se altera no mundo moderno.

Gênero ágil, Julio Cortazar[1] comparava-o analogicamente à fotografia, enquanto o romance equivaleria ao cinema, na medida em que um filme é, em princípio, uma "ordem aberta," enquanto uma fotografia bem realizada pressupõe uma justa limitação prévia, no recorte que faz de um fragmento da realidade, fixando-lhe determinados limites de um modo tal que o recorte atue como uma explosão que abra para uma realidade mais ampla.

Enquanto no cinema, como no romance, a captação dessa realidade mais ampla é alcançada através do desenvolvimento de elementos parciais, acumulativos, numa fotografia ou num conto se procede inversamente, isto é, o fotógrafo ou o contista sentem necessidade de escolher e limitar uma imagem ou um acontecimento que sejam significativos, que valham não só por si mesmos, mas sejam capazes de atuar no espectador ou no leitor como uma espécie de abertura, de fermento, que projete a inteligência e a sensibilidade em direção a algo que vai muito além do argumento visual ou literário contido na foto ou no conto. O contista sabe que não tem o tempo por aliado e seu único recurso é trabalhar verticalmente, em profundidade.

Daí que o conto seja uma unidade tensa e intensa de onde se eliminam todas as situações e idéias intermediárias, todo e qualquer recheio ou frase de transição que o romance permite e mesmo exige.

Proteiforme, ele não só consegue abraçar a temática toda do romance, como põe em jogo os princípios de composição que regem a escrita moderna em busca do texto sintético e do convívio de tons, gêneros e significados.

Em face da História, o contista é um pescador de momentos singulares, que explora no discurso ficcional uma hora intensa e aguda de percepção. Esta, por sua vez, não cessa de perscrutar situações narráveis na massa aparentemente amorfa do real.

E, entre nós, o que tem representado essa percepção?

Como se sabe, o Modernismo paulista de 1922 caminhou em direção a mitologias globais, chamadas Pau-Brasil, Antropofagia, etc., e através delas articularam sua relação estética com o espaço nacional. Era o momento áureo do primitivismo como eixo artístico da cultura brasileira.

Depois de 1930, começam a desenhar-se as novas fisionomias regionais, enfocando a crise material e a depressão que se estende da cidade ao campo, ambos cada vez mais invadidos pela frente capitalista do primeiro pós-guerra.

Com João Guimarães Rosa, cessa a urgência do diálogo dos regionalismos com a cultura dominante e o mito tende a fechar-se às contradições com a sociedade englobante.

Do ponto de vista das conquistas formais do conto brasileiro de hoje, vê-se que não se deu em vão a intensa experiência estética que foi o Modernismo.

Aqui, é bom distinguir entre os primeiros frutos das vanguardas de 1920/30, ora futuristas, ora expressionistas (penso na prosa experimental de Oswald de Andrade, Mário de Andrade e Antônio de Alcântara Machado), e a condição de um realismo novo e depurado que se formou depois de 1930: a prosa nua de Graciliano Ramos, José Lins do Rego, Marques Rebelo, Aníbal Machado, Dionélio Machado. É no tronco desta escrita que se inserem os modos de dizer e de narrar mais correntes do conto contemporâneo.[2]

Por outro lado, deve-se apontar a presença de narradores estrangeiros que entraram na atmosfera literária brasileira a partir da Segunda Guerra, aproximadamente.

O nosso conto intimista é devedor tanto de certos modos alusivos de Katherine Mansfield e de Virginia Woolf, quanto do gosto da análise moral de Gide e Mauriac.

A prosa fantástica e metafísica segue as trilhas de Poe, Kafka, Borges, a que se pode acrescentar a sugestão, na época avassaladora, que o teatro de Pirandello produziu em um escritor como Murilo Rubião, sensível ao tema da mudança da pessoa por trás da rigidez das máscaras sociais.

Há alguma ressonância norte-americana, de Hemingway, Steinbeck e de Faulkner, na pungência cruel de Dalton Trevisan. E há muito brutalismo yankee na concepção da linguagem de Rubem Fonseca e de seus seguidores.

O segundo modernismo e a literatura de fora mais divulgada a partir de 1940 foram, portando, o principal quadro de referências estilísticas do conto brasileiro dos últimos vinte e cinco anos.

É difícil esquematizar os caminhos que o conto contemporâneo brasileiro vem percorrendo, sem que algumas tendências fiquem omitidas. O certo é que ele compre hoje, no Brasil, a seu modo, o destino da ficção contemporânea. Variável e variado, ele se põe entre as exigências da narração realista, os apelos da fantasia e as seduções do jogo verbal. Quer dizer, o contista explora no discurso ficcional uma hora intensa e aguda da percepção e submete sua matéria a um registro que pode ser realista documental, realista crítico, intimista na esfera do *eu* (memorialista), intimista na esfera do *id* (onírico, visionário, fantástico) e experimental no nível do trabalho da linguagem.

A percepção do contista reconhece vários graus de lesão que a sociedade de classes não pára de produzir. Lesões que vão da subvida do pequeno marginal das histórias de João Antônio, que se passam nos bairros pobres de São Paulo, à subvida dos altos marginais cariocas, empresários à cata de travestis, executivos em férias, agentes da prostituição grã-fina que formam o mundo de Rubem Fonseca.

A violência pode inscrever-se no nível das relações familiares transformadas em pelejas amorosas, onde um destrói o outro e se auto-aniquila, como ocorre nos contos de Dalton Trevisan.

O estilo urbano tem, como a cidade grande, zonas e camadas distintas. Entre delinqüentes e bandidos sobrevive a classe média bem representada em suas idiossincrasias no conto de Zulmira Ribeiro Tavares.

A mesma tensão com o presente pode levar também a uma relação dramática com o passado. Recuperar a imagem do que já foi, mas que ficou para sempre, é o esforça que se nota na prosa de Lygia Fagundes Telles, Autran Dourado e no sinuoso jogo de Osman Lins.

Mas o conto brasileiro tem procurado atingir também a dimensão metafísica e, número certo sentido, atemporal, das realidades vitais: Guimarães Rosa foi mestre na passagem da narrativa plana à constelação de imagens e símbolos.

Já, em Clarice Lispector, temos uma visão "existencial do mundo," onde o espírito paira inquieto sobre coisas e pessoas e, não sabendo que sentido lhes atribuir, faz do texto uma constante perplexidade. Como o discurso psicológico não dá conta desse universo, Lispector vai descobrindo, reinventado, o caminho que vai do *eu* narrativo aos objeto. Este caminho está sempre presente quer a autora fale de amor, crianças, desencontros ou animais, o que imprime um caráter especulativo à sua linguagem. Partilham com Clarice esse caráter especulativo da linguagem escritores como Samuel Rawet e Nélida Piñon.

Mesmo que as situações, em Clarice Lispector, se confinem num estranho mistério, este não é tematizado nem explorado para produzir efeitos insólitos como é o caso de Murilo Rubião. Neste contista, o insólito irrompe em meio ao cotidiano, mascara suas feições, para em seguida, revelá-lo de modo inexorável. Já Clarice Lispector dispensa os instrumentos de magia e do fantástico porque suas palavras avançam para uma estranheza mais radical, alicerçada, por exemplo, no fato banal e ao mesmo tempo misterioso de que existem fora e além do eu, as coisas e outros consciências.

Ao contrário de Clarice Lispector, Murilo Rubião compraz-se em tratar diretamente o estranho em si mesmo. Mas, para dizer as suas mágicas, não se vale, como se poderia esperar, das ousadias formais do surrealismo. O seu estilo não está longe do padrão alcançado por outros escritores mineiros como Ciro dos Anjos, Autran Dourado, Otto Lara Resende, no que todos têm em comum: as andanças da memória, as paradas freqüentes para a análise subjetiva dos acontecimentos e o talhe vernáculo da frase.

À diferença de J. J. Veiga e de Murilo Rubião, Modesto Carone inscreve o insólito no espaço estritamente cotidiano e, à semelhança de Kafka, trata da degradação do homem num mundo altamente administrado e fantasmagórico.

Outro categoria de conto a se destacar é aquela que, para além de veleidades etnocêntricas, procura estabelecer a identidade nacional através da valorização do emigrante, dando continuidade ao caminho iniciada por Antônio de Alcântara Machado em "Brás, Bexiga e Barra Funda." É o caso de Samuel Rawet, Moacyr Scliar e Lya Luft.

Quanto ao experimentalismo verbal, pensando-o de modo radical, é apenas discreto nesse *corpus*. Encontra-se em Guimarães Rosa, e, confrontada com essa literatura, a narrativa breve brasileira poderá parecer lingüisticamente conservadora. Embora voltada a uma comunicação clara e inovando pouco o código lingüístico, há trechos antológicos de força representativa nessa linguagem de conto que tem seus modelos em Graciliano Ramos, Marques Rebelo, Eça de Queirós e Machado de Assis, junto com os estrangeiros já citados. Para evidenciar esse uso de alta expressividade da linguagem detenho-me no conto de Dalton Trevisan, que considero o maior contista brasileiro vivo.

Dalton Trevisan é um contista que reúne, hoje, vasta obra: dezoito livros de contos, três antologias de contos e um romance. Rastreando essa obra "por dentro," percebe-se um caminho indiciado pelas repetições—marca registrada do autor. Repetem-se, em seus contos, situações, personagens (João e Maria), temas, sendo que a repetição esconde uma operação dupla: progressivo-regressiva, algo como um movimento estático, já que retomar supõe que se está a caminho e que se insiste em progredir. Mas caminho que aponta para o retorno. Que melhor que a metáfora do vampiro para traduzir esse universo seriado e repetitivo? Lembre-se aqui que o mesmo, o sempre igual é o universo do vampiro, já que não são necessários dois para que surja um terceiro: a vítima de um vampiro torna-se semelhante a seu algoz. A multiplicação, portanto, dá origem a um *outro* que, paradoxalmente, é o *mesmo*.

Conforme se vê, o vampiro comporta tanto o movimento como a fixidez. É por isso que ele, enquanto metáfora, tem a força de traduzir a obra de Dalton Trevisan. Nela, o vampiro perde a capa, a sofisticação e a nobreza, constituindo-se numa multidão de funcionários públicos, lojistas, prostitutas, donas de case, domésticas, profissionais liberais, trabalhadores da terra.

A família é o lugar privilegiado pelo autor para enfocar a vida como vampirização. É principalmente em seu âmbito que se explicita a impossibilidade de convívio com a diferença, através da prática de verdadeira guerra conjugal, onde a existência acaba por se confinar a um cerco de onde o *outro* é expulso e só é admitido o *eu*.

No limiar da angústia, da crueldade, da agressividade, da lubricidade, as personagens reduzem-se a peças silenciosas de um espetáculo sempre igual, indiferenciado e terrível: o do cotidiano. Visto como o domínio da tautologia, da repetição, universal plano gerador de formas embalsamadas, de um modelo que se reproduz perpetuamente, o domínio do cotidiano e o do vampiro se identificam.

A linguagem que conta esse universo achatado pela multiplicação do mesmo é feita de grandes elipses, pausas, cortes abruptos, frases reduzidas. Pode-se observar nessas marcas um caminho que aponta para a redução da linguagem que passa a incorporar o não dito, o implícito, uma área de silêncio que caminha na contramão da linguagem, emperrando o seu curso.

Um dos principais responsáveis pelo entranhamento do vazio no corpo da narrativa de Dalton Trevisan é o clichê, entendido aqui, como molde, linguagem pronta, o *ready made*. Dessas linguagens, a predileção do autor recai sobre a fotonovela para expressar o universo feminino, e sobre o relatório policial, quando pretende expressar a violência.

O *ready made* vai precipitando a criação de um espaço oco no interior da linguagem e é esse vazio um dos fortes responsáveis pela fragmentação do conto de Dalton Trevisan.

Se é certo que seus contos são sobre a província, sobre o vampiro, sobre Curitiba, é também certo que o vampiro e Curitiba são antes de tudo formas de contar a sociedade liberal de arremedo que o chamado capitalismo tardamente avançado produziu no Brasil.

Se é certo, ainda, que seu trabalho de linguagem não estabelece a ruptura com relação à tradição, ele se enriquece e muito, na hora das grandes sínteses, alcançando alta voltagem de força representativa.

É muito provável que o conto oscile ainda por bom tempo entre o retrato fosco da brutalidade corrente e a sondagem mítica do mundo, da consciência ou da pura palavra. Essas faces de mesmo rosto talvez componham a máscara estético possível para os nossos dias. Desse modo, como superá-la?

NOTAS

1. Cf. Julio Cortázar, "Alguns aspectos do conto," em *Valise de cronópio* (trad. Davi Arrigucci, Jr. e João Alexandre Barbosa), (São Paulo: Ed. Perspectiva, 1974).

2. Para esse apanhado geral do conto contemporâneo brasileiro, vali-me muito da apresentação de Alfredo Bosi ao livro por ele mesmo organizado, *O conto brasileiro contemporâneo* (São Paulo: Ed. Cultrix/Ed. da Universidade de São Paulo, 1975).

14. The Seventies Generation of Argentine Prose Writers: Identity and Decline

May Lorenzo Alcalá

When the literary generations issue is discussed in Argentina, apparent contradictions arise between specialized terminology on the one hand and that of ordinary discourse on the other.

Since the decline of the long-lasting influence exerted on the liberal sectors of the Argentine intelligentsia by the Spaniard Ortega y Gasset, who advanced the theory of generations with its fifteen-year cycles and other deterministic constants fashionable in those circles, it is almost *de rigueur* for it to be categorically rejected in all its manifestations and nuances in the various branches of thought and artistic creation, and not merely in the literary sphere. The Dilthey-Petersen formulation, that is, Julius Petersen's development of Dilthey's basic premises, establishes eight variables that should be verified in order that a literary generation be considered as such: close personal contact, experience as a generation, a mentor or charismatic leader, a heritage, educational factors, date of birth, language, and the stagnation of the older generation. There is no need even to try to test this theoretical model for us to be able to predict that, owing to its rigidity, it would exclude any contemporary human group we might care to analyze.

A more flexible formulation associates the concept of generation exclusively with the fact of its members being contemporaries, in the sense that a generation would consist of those writers, whatever their ages, whose stages of literary initiation and creative maturity coincided. This can also be refuted by textual analysis because of the tremendously dynamic influence of social and historical factors in Argentina during the stage when the individual's personality is formed which, according to this formulation, does not necessarily occur at the same time in all members of the generation.

More detailed formulations turn out to be all exclusive because their requirements are excessive, and the more flexible models are unsatisfactory by default. It is common, however, to hear the expression "literary generation" in everyday language, where it is applied with the vagueness typical of intuitive or nonrational codes which, for precisely this reason, are understood by those who send and receive them but which they find difficult to define.

It is within this framework, the rational rejection of the theoretical model and the acceptance of everyday usage, that one speaks of the "forties generation of poets" or the "fifties generation of writers" to refer, in the latter case, to the heterogeneous group as far as age and literary stance were concerned, that began to publish at the time of the fall of the constitutional government in 1955. It is also within this framework that we talk about the "seventies generation of prose writers," an expression which was coined around 1973 and which came to be used especially since 1980 in a number of interviews and newspaper articles published in various media, particularly the "Cultura y Nación" supplement of the Buenos Aires daily *Clarín*.[1]

The writers we are referring to were born between approximately 1935 and 1950 and began to publish between 1965 and 1973; they make up the prominent, visible part of the new Argentine writing. They are not a movement, since they show marked aesthetic differences, and it is possible to deduce from their work that they observe reality from diverse ideological positions. The marking of a chronological band in Argentine literature may not be arbitrary, however, if it is directed at showing how a section of it, the novel, responded to the challenge of survival during our most recent history. These writers, the so-called "seventies generation," lived the decisive period of their formative years and early maturity in the sixties and seventies which, except for short intervals, were unfortunately typified by the increasingly rapid decay of Argentine society. The symptoms of this increasing decline were: institutional instability, violence, intolerance, repression, social and economic degradation, halting of attempts to get the country out of its underdeveloped state, and weakening of cultural identity. These experiences, common to the seventies writers and different from those of their predecessors—not because they did not experience the same conditions but because they did so at a different stage in their individual development—link them inexorably, whether they are from the provinces or Buenos Aires, regardless of their class origins, and whether or not they have a university education. In any case, these factors constitute conditions to be borne in mind to explain the differences that distinguish them, without this preventing the collective social and historical factor from exerting a subtle influence, like fine sand once the coarse grain of literary forms and ideologies has been sieved out.

It is, therefore, no coincidence, nor is the connection idle, that those first works I referred to appeared at the same time as *Lugar común*,[2] an anthology selected and with a prologue by Santiago Kovadloff, who collected works of some of the best poets of the seventies. In the introduction, Kovadloff admits that "there seems to be no doubt that the adoption of chronology as a criterion lacks methodological reliability, but the need to adopt it arises from the evidence that the poets who begin to publish in the seventies emerge on to a very different stage: events involving greater conflict, their development more tragic and the outcome bloodier . . . Controversies become intolerance; party political fervor, merciless violence; factional fighting becomes generalized and the everyday atmosphere takes on features that make it anxiety-laden, uncertain, stifling." And he concludes that "inevitably, these circumstances exert their influence on the course of poetic creation. Argentine society, and consequently its culture, have been struggling between extinction and survival: in this context it is understandable that sampling of and theorizing on the generationally most dynamic sectors of our literature have been attempted from different theoretical and ideological angles."

In my particular case, those initial works—supplemented by surveys, interviews and comparative analysis of texts—have culminated in an anthology published by the Celtia Publishing Company of Buenos Aires, entitled *Cuentos de la crisis*.[3] For the anthology I selected a dozen short stories by the most representative writers of the so-called generation of the seventies, who met the requirement that they demonstrate the many aesthetic trends it follows and an understanding of its thematic concerns. And I have restricted the anthology to this genre, which has a great tradition in Argentine literature, because its unity helps the separate reading and comprehension of the texts, without this suggesting that there should be a division in the literature, which is analyzed as a whole.

Many of the aspects that are examined in this paper were developed in my prologue to this book, which is in fact the first *systematic* work to be published in Argentina on the writing of the seventies generation.

A Little Bit of History

In 1965 Beatriz Guido wrote a newspaper article in which she mentioned the most precocious members of the seventies generation, who at that time had published in newspapers and magazines and only a few of them in book form, referring to them as "young writers." It may seem odd that even today, twenty years later, they are given the same title, in some cases in a somewhat pejorative sense, but otherwise as a mere reflection of reality: although in almost any country in the world a group of writers of between thirty and forty-five years of age would be considered an intermediate generation, in Argentina the term has not undergone its natural decanting, since there is no significant flow of younger writers in print who mark a logical sequence.

This vacuum—which is only apparent, since the attendance of young people at literary workshops and the unpublished works offered to publishers are sufficient to refute it—is caused principally by the economic crisis and the lack of protection provided for local industry, which makes it difficult for publishers to take risks with names that do not guarantee sales. But in 1965 we were still experiencing the aftermath of the publishing and creative euphoria that had started years before, with the application of a policy designed to establish an integrated economy, in the context of which and with the exercise of freedom, genuine cultural manifestations were encouraged.

"The start of the presidency of Arturo Frondizi, in 1958," Josefina Delgado and Luis Gregorich were to say in *Capítulo de la literatura argentina*, published in installments in 1968, would mark "too the start of a period of social and economic reforms. . . . The winning candidate's background foreshadowed this transformation and it was also based on the broad coalition of forces from different social classes which had given Frondizi his electoral victory."

The structural changes set in motion during this period were sufficiently profound for their repercussions still to be felt in all aspects of sociocultural life even a considerable time after the democratic process was cut short in 1962. It is from this point that there was a return to the sequence of events initiated with the 1930 revolution when the crisis of the agro-import model became evident, a sequence that was to be repeated in 1955—when the handout system, without an adequate wealth-generating structure, ran out of steam—and with all abrupt changes of government after 1962, whether constitutional or not: a deepening of the crisis, leading to social dissatisfaction and demands on the government, repression, a propitious environment for the development of violence, lack of freedom, and institutional instability. The publication quoted stated further on that, after the break in the institutional order occasioned by the overthrow of Arturo Illia, "there was an increased tendency towards authoritarianism" and "cultural life was stunted and circumscribed . . . despite the obstacles referred to and the difficult circumstances the country had to go through. . . . There is no doubt that after 1962 Argentine literature continued to reach remarkable heights, generally well beyond those of the past." Three years after the first reference, under the generic title of "The Latest Batches" in that same publication in installments, Miguel Briante,

Aníbal Ford, Liliana Heker, Ricardo Piglia, and Fernando Sánchez Sorondo were mentioned in a rather chaotic list that included writers of different ages and volume of production.

But it was only around 1970, and hence the name, perhaps arbitrary from the literary, but not from the sociohistorical point of view, when they began to publish regularly and to make the break with writers slightly older than themselves, such as Manuel Puig, Eduardo Gudiño Kieffer, and Sara Gallardo who, despite their individual contributions, are distinguished from the writers of the seventies because of their attitude to both writing and the writer's craft.

It is true that the sociohistorical conditions that encouraged cultural activities and facilitated publication changed in the seventies owing to the sharp new decline deriving from the recessive policy of the so-called Argentine Revolution. The failure of its electoral platform, however, which was once again to provoke widespread social pressure demanding thoroughgoing changes and an immediate election toward the end of Alejandro Lanusse's presidency, forced the opening of some safety valves that made it possible, albeit only in part, to satisfy the needs of the reading public, who were avid for works tackling Argentine themes and treating them in depth. Hence the occurrence of phenomena such as the mass publication of the historical or political essay, their sale outside the traditional bookshop environment, and renewed interest in writing by Argentine authors. Not unconnected with this situation is the so-called boom in Latin American literature, which was simply the sometimes legitimate, on occasion contrived, manifestation in publishing and the press of authors' efforts to delve into each nation's own peculiar characteristics, the turning in of their vision toward the depths of their collective nature and reality. Since these varied in the different countries involved, the resulting tone, themes, and styles were also diverse.

Around 1970 the following published or had already published works: Juan Carlos Martini, Germán Leopoldo García, Liliana Heker, J.C. Martini Real, Ricardo Piglia, Luis Gusmán, Héctor Libertella, Blas Matamoro, Héctor Lastra, Fernando Sánchez Sorondo, Marcelo Pichón Riviere, Antonio Dal Massetto, Fernando De Giovanni, Osvaldo Lanborghini, Miguel Briante, Aníbal Ford, among others.

Stressing the popularity of three works—*La manifestación* (1971) [4] and *Don Abdel Salim* (1972) [5] by Jorge Asís, and *Las tumbas* (1973) [6] by Enrique Medina (the latter the best-selling novel of the decade in Argentina—Germán García was to mark 1973 as the "symptomatic chronological centre" of the seventies generation. It is curious that that year also marks the final dividing line, since it saw the first public appearances—they won prizes and published in newspapers, magazines, and in book form—of Eduardo Belgrano Rawson, Rodolfo Rabanal, Fernando Sorrentino, Osvaldo Soriano, Reina Roffé, Antonio Brailovsky, Pacho O'Donnell, Diego Angelino, Jorge Manzur, Mario Schisman, Leonardo Moledo, Javier Torre, Hugo Corra, Ramón Plaza, Alicia Steinberg, Osvaldo Seiguerman, Silvia Plager, and myself, among others. And so was finally constituted, this time without the conflicts that are usual in Argentine literature, this group of writers that from then on would exhibit one of their essential characteristics, diversity—a characteristic analyzed below.

And Some Geography

Owing to structural reasons—the lack of integration of the country's territory and the excessive influence of Buenos Aires on cultural objectives—the members of this group of writers, finally organized in 1973, were either born in Buenos Aires and environs or were born in the provinces but were living in the capital when their works were published. The fact is that neither the regional distribution of some Argentine provincial newspapers nor the ever less frequent attempts at publishing in the provinces can manage to alleviate the lack of communication among our different geographical regions and the anachronistic difference in economic capacity and infrastructure between the provinces and Buenos Aires, which is the result of the old agro-import scheme. This means that Buenos Aires not only decides what she will consume but also what the rest of the country will consume.

Local production, which we would call "provincial literature," either remains practically unknown, limited to public debate only in its area of origin, or becomes known in Buenos Aires, which means that the authors are almost inexorably obliged to move to the capital. Exceptions to this rule are: Diego Angelino, who is from Entre Ríos but lives in El Bolsón in the Province of Río Negro and who had to win a prize in Buenos Aires in order to be published, and Juan Carlos Martini, who went from his birthplace in Rosario into exile in Barcelona and has recently returned to Argentina. The latter had, in fact, joined the long list of intellectuals who were forced to emigrate for either economic or political reasons, as was only logical in a society in a permanent state of crisis. Hence, because they belonged to the more active elements, many of the writers of this generation lived—and some, like Blas Matamoro, still live—outside Argentina during the last military regime. This gave rise to a so-called literature in exile, a phenomenon that has been exaggerated for ideological reasons, and regarding whose existence and nature heated arguments took place between, for example, Julio Cortázar and Liliana Heker, and Manuel Puig and Pacho O'Donnell.

It should be pointed out that the longest period in exile of the writers of this generation in no case exceeds eight years which, at least in Argentine literature, has proved insufficient for distinguishing characteristics to appear in the works written outside this country. This statement does not intend to ignore the brief flowering of the "themes of exile" which now, some years after the constitutional government came into power, seems to be in decline, and which has undoubted antecedents in works written in the nineteenth century. This double polarity of provincial versus Buenos Aires literature and literature written inside and outside of Argentina loses substance if it is analyzed on the basis of the texts instead of the context; that is, regardless of the actual fact—painful though it may be in the case of an exile—of living in a specific place. This does not appear to prevent the careful reader from finding clear connections among the works, whether written in the provinces, in Buenos Aires, or outside Argentina. The connections are vertical, owing to a shared rich and deeply rooted heritage and a common literary genealogy, and horizontal in that these writers have shared experiences that are unprecedented in the country's history at a decisive stage in their literary development.

Argentine literature, like many other cultural manifestations, gives rise to individual peculiarities and regional characteristics, and even forms that originate in specific circumstances, because it is not a polished, static product, but rather something dynamic, which reflects both endogenous and exogenous influences. To the extent that the different influences can be assimilated and synthesized, this continuous flux enriches, and therefore fortifies, the nation's identity. When this metabolic process is hindered in periods of decline, owing to the fact that the social body as a whole, or a group or class, lacks its normal defenses, we see mechanical imitations of models from the countries of the center.

The Links

Synthesis, Genealogy, and Shared History

Before analyzing the specific characteristics that are more or less exclusive to these writers, and therefore distinguish them from other generations of Argentine authors, it is worth considering briefly the processes that have determined and still do the existence of an Argentine literature, regardless of the age of its members. Prior to this generation, there have been long and not always peaceful processes of cultural integration, acculturation, and the complex assimilation of successive influences, which have produced an identity of a dynamic nature.

These processes include the incorporation of the original indigenous–Spanish elements, the subsequent influences of the numerous and varied waves of immigrants at the end of the nineteenth and first half of this century, and the influences we receive continuously without any human intermediary due to advances in technology and communications. This reality, which is a complex and ever incomplete synthesis, cannot be avoided when ideas are communicated in writing, even if we were thinking of uncultured writers, which is not the case, because cultural identity has to do with character and not with knowledge. This character, which is incorporated almost unconsciously, traces a global unifying link embracing even those aspects of literature that could be regarded as bastard: even comic strip stories will have different features if the author is American or Argentine.

To this factor, cultural synthesis, should be added another which acts at two levels of consciousness: their predecessors' work. It is part of the overall feedback of cultural identity and thus one of the ingredients of the synthesis. However, since the writers we are talking about, aside from their varying degrees of technical preparation, have a declared and manifest unsatiable passion for reading, and particularly for reading their predecessors' work, the influence of a common literary genealogy appears systematically in their writing. An example would be a paragraph of the document on the Argentine situation signed by almost all the writers of the group we are dealing with. The untitled paper, informally known as "Documentos de los escritores de la generación del 70," was published in two Buenos Aires newspapers in January 1981: in *Tiempo Argentino* in its totality and in *Clarín* in a partial version (exact pages unknown). In it they recognize a "genuine genealogy running from José Hernández to Sarmiento, from Macedonio Fernández to Roberto Arlt, from Borges to David Viñas, from Leopoldo Marechal to Ernesto Sábato, from Cortázar to Haroldo Conti."

As mentioned, both the dynamic cultural synthesis and the influence of a literary genealogy are common but not exclusive characteristics of this generation. The exclusive constant features that appear in the works of the seventies writers are the result of the sociohistorical element referred to earlier, which has had a particularly active influence on this group of writers, given the stage of their development at which it was operative.

In an interview published in the daily *Clarín* on March 19, 1981, Héctor Lastra said:

> Most of those of us [writers] who have appeared over the 1965–1975 period have many points in common: more or less the same age, no debts to literary patronage and above all a highly complex, hostile historical heritage, and that despite the fact that our work may have different lines of argument, different influences and even different tones and approaches. . . . [That historical constant] is the principal and decisive effect on us. . . . In most of our books the themes of Peronism, repression, alienation and decadence are practically a constant feature. . . . Besides, the characters we tackle are typically searchers for identity, which in my opinion is one of the key points in the literature of my generation.

One could only disagree with Lastra if this list is interpreted as categorical and exclusive, and that it refers only to thematic elements and not thematic influences.

It is true that in literature of a realistic nature thematic elements occur clearly as such; but that is not the only angle from which reality can be recounted. The artist absorbs data which he reworks, sieves, and expresses in the most diverse forms. This provides a broad framework for a literature with many different meanings, where the reader's role is not limited to consuming, but rather is forced to rework what he reads, thus becoming coauthor and accomplice.

Despite the difficulty, albeit not insurmountable, of detecting the thematic influences listed by Lastra as well as some others we could add, such as the lack of freedom and fear, in the nonrealistic texts, it can be stated that they underlie all the work of this generation. But the strongest link among the seventies writers is the desperate and at times incoherent search for and reaffirmation of cultural identity. This seems a logical reaction if it is borne in mind that these writers belong to the chronological group of Argentines most sensitive to a consciousness of its possible loss. On May 17, 1984, once again in the previously quoted "Cultura y Nación" supplement to *Clarín*, I published an article that the newspaper entitled "La imaginación anda por aqui," whose second part consisted of a report of a round table discussion with Liliana Heker, Juan Carlos Martini, Héctor Lastra, and Jorge Asís. When asked about the more or less explicit presence of the problems of identity in their work, the authors all agreed that, although those problems are on occasion unconsciously incorporated by the author into his work, they can nevertheless be perceived by the reader. This statement acquires greater relevance if we bear in mind that they are writers with very different ideological backgrounds.

It could be argued that other Argentine authors, who do not belong to this generation, have also attempted to plumb the depths of our identity. They have indeed, but only in isolated cases, not as the constant feature of a whole generation, and without the passion that moves the seventies writers who, rather than approaching it as a theme, strive to recover it.

Until relatively few years ago, Argentines maintained that somewhat mythical belief in the indestructibility of a country favored by the hand of God that would inevitably survive all passing squalls. Due to this form of fatalism in reverse, in the immediate past only a few isolated intellectuals raised the possibility of the loss of their traditions and their future, because certain values were considered invulnerable. On the other hand, the sociohistorical reality it was their lot to experience created the conscious or unconscious need in the seventies writers to recover the features that define the cultural identity they have inherited through genealogy and synthesis. And it is here that textual analysis leaves no room for doubt: Piglia's senator's monologue and his dialogues on Argentine literature in *Respiración artificial*[7] and those of Martini Real's escapist characters in *Copyright*[8] attempt this search from the structuralist side; the novels of historical reconstruction and fiction of Belgrano Rawson, *No se turbe vuestro corazón*,[9] set in the arid west toward the end of the last century and of Antonio Brailovsky, not entitled *Identidad*[10] by chance, that unfolds in the far-off years of the Inquisition, clearly have this intention; likewise *El tigrecito de Mompracen* by Pacho O'Donnell[11] and *Risas y aplausos* by Fernando Sánchez Sorondo,[12] which deal with themes of adolescence. Exactly the same need moves the characters of *La vida entera* by Juan Carlos Martini,[13] written in Barcelona, and those of *Sobre la tierra* by Diego Angelino,[14] written in the midst of a valley in the Andean cordillera in the south of Argentina.

Plurality and Diversity

In my interview with him called "Las ratas contraatacan" for the magazine *Extra* in April 1981, Rodolfo Rabanal said that "two trends can be shown in contemporary Argentine literature: Robert Arlt's and Borges'." "There are writers of my generation," he went on, "who can be classified in the former, some might admit less definite links with the latter, but most of us lie in that grey area that enables us to develop our own peculiar characteristics." On the same occasion, Jorge Asís was more categorical: "Almost as many trends as authors could be found among us."

Both statements represent one-sided views in the analysis of Argentine literature; in the first case, because it repeats the doubtful division between the Florida Street and Boedo Street literary groups raised, seriously or otherwise, from the thirties between the contributors to two magazines. Those from the former, whose ranks included Borges, were apparently the experts in literary forms, and those from the latter in dealing with social problems. Asís's position is also one-sided, since he stresses only the factor of individual originality. What is certain is that, from a reading of the texts, and despite the constant features we have pointed out, one can appreciate the undeniable diversity of the literary results, which Asís and Rabanal somehow indicate. This is not, however, incompatible with the recognition of a shared literary genealogy and of cultural synthesis, but rather ratifies the fact that they have operated in a national society constantly struggling for freedom.

It is unusual to find in a national literature at one specific time such a broad range of tone and nuance, and it makes it an uphill task to fit these writers into schools or trends, so any attempt to do so will be merely that. Even more so since, due to the ages of the members of the seventies generation, it can be assumed that individuals will still both develop aesthetically and mature, which may separate present trends from the final ones.

Aside from the essential feature of individuality or personal characteristics that, the more original it is, encourages the germ of diversity, it should also be considered that the latter is the result of a double plurality, in both observing reality and recounting it. Given that the seventies writers do not constitute a movement, they also hold a multiplicity of ideological positions and aesthetic affiliations. The mere numerical combination of the variables contained in those who are recipients of aesthetic ideas and ideology gives an idea of the spread of possibilities covered by these authors.

Trend toward Dispersal and Group Consciousness

Plurality that results in *diversity* are two characteristics of this generation that were pointed out by J. C. Martini Real in his controversial article "La promoción de las ratas," published in *La Opinión Cultural*[16] on September 7, 1980. A third characteristic should be added to these two; one that he calls dispersal, which he describes as a consequence of pluralism and of the need for individual survival. This trend, which being such contains its own contradiction, appears at two levels in the social relationships of the members of the generation. On one level it appears in their links with political reality: during more or less the same periods they have shown an inclination for party political commitment—rather erratic, as can be seen from a simple comparison of the groups of intellectuals who participated in the 1973 and 1983 election campaigns—alternating with a tendency to act from independent positions, to issue judgments from more or less undefined ideological sectors, to act in opposition on humanitarian principles or under banners representing general demands, or else to take refuge in nonparticipation. This generation, which seeks only to define a trend, does not presume to ignore the fact that some members of this generation maintain a consistent political stance and show understanding of the fact that a commitment to truth requires the exercise of freedom, which can only be achieved when the community one belongs to is on the rise.

On the second level, the trend of dispersal appears in the relationships among the members of the generational group themselves and with their colleagues in general. Perhaps due to painful experiences in the past, or to the individualistic nature of a solitary task like writing, or to the example of some of their illustrious predecessors, the members of the seventies generally reject more or less institutional ties, even when they may be of a purely professional nature. In this sense it should be observed that these writers are almost totally absent from organized groups of intellectuals. Nevertheless, their gregarious instinct, their common concerns—either sectorial or general—and their shared history have prevailed on occasions, so that they have been able to undertake collective tasks or actions. Suffice it to recall in this respect that during 1981 almost all the writers of the seventies generation who were resident at that time in Argentina met every week to discuss and undertake activities in support of freedom of expression, of the reappearance alive of missing writers, of the abolition of censorship. These activities culminated in a controversial document, to which we have already alluded, which the press at large refused to publish, that saw the light of day in only two newspapers and was considered "dangerous" by the military authorities. It is with particular affection that I keep the original of that manifesto of human dignity, with the personal signatures of about thirty writers who, despite representing a wide range of very different aesthetic and ideological positions, could stand united against a fearsome enemy.

This shows that, despite the plurality, and perhaps thanks to it, despite their individual reticence, and despite their shyness in publicizing their ties of affection, they have a latent group consciousness and recognition—though it may imply rejection—of the other members of the generational group. Asked what the future of this group of writers was, one of them answered unhesitatingly: "The future or the collapse of Argentina's great literature." One should fully agree with this statement, which lacks all conceit or desire to be in the limelight.

At all events, one lone writer may manage to introduce new avant-garde fashions, or turn readers' preferences toward writing of a particular tendency. No matter how talented or popular he is, though, he will not be able to play a decisive role on his own at this stage in Argentina's cultural development. That task, if it is what is proposed, is for a generation of individuals aware of their duty as intellectuals and as Argentine citizens.

NOTES

1. *Clarín* (Buenos Aires).

2. *Lugar común*, ed. Santiago Kovadloff (Argentina: Ediciones El Escarabajo de Oro, 1981).

3. *Cuentos de la crisis*, ed. May Lorenzo Alcalá (Buenos Aires: Editorial Celtia, 1986).

4. Jorge Asís, *La manifestación* (Buenos Aires: Centro Editor de América Latina, 1971).

5. *Idem*, *Don Abdel Zalim: el burlador de dominico* (Buenos Aires: Corregidor, 1972).

6. Enrique Medina, *Las tumbas* (Buenos Aires: Ediciones de la Flor, 1973).

7. Ricardo Piglia, *Respiración artificial* (Buenos Aires: Editorial Pomaire, 1980).

8. Juan Carlos Martini Real, *Copyright* (Buenos Aires: Editorial Sudamericana, 1979).

9. Eduardo Belgrano Rawson, *No see turbe vuestro corazón* (Buenos Aires: Ediciones de la Flor, 1974).

10. Antonio Elio Brailovsky, *Identidad* (Buenos Aires: Editorial Sudamericana, 1980).

11. Pacho O'Donnell, *El tigrecito de Mompracen* (Buenos Aires: Editorial Galerna, 1980).

12. Fernando Sánchez Sorondo, *Risas y aplausos* (Buenos Aires: Editorial Sudamericana, 1980).

13. Juan Carlos Martini, *La vida entera* (Barcelona: Brugera, 1981).

14. Diego Angelino, *Sobre la tierra* (Barcelona: Editorial Pomaire, 1979).

15. May Lorenzo Alcalá, "Las ratas contraatacan," *Extra* 16, 190 (April 1981), 56-58.

16. *La Opinión Cultural* (Buenos Aires), September 7, 1980.

15. A Coleção Arquivos

Jorge Schwartz

Se o maior escritor em língua espanhola do século XX foi na sua juventude funcionário de uma biblioteca dos subúrbios de Buenos Aires e, posteriormente, homenageado com a direção da Biblioteca Nacional de Buenos Aires, não vejo porque eu, pobre professor de literatura latino-americana (e como diria o próprio Borges, quem não consegue escrever poesia, a ensina), não poderia participar de um encontro de bibliotecários latino-americanistas, aqui no Rio de Janeiro, embora não seja esta uma das minhas especialidades. Sem dúvida compartilhamos uma paixão comum: o livro. No Brasil a precariedade de grande parte de bibliotecas impede por enquanto a sofisticação das especialidades, como ser bibliotecário latino-americanista, modalidade que distingue este encontro. Nas universidades brasileiras, e para suprir a carência desta área profissional, o professor deve, em muitos momentos, assessorar os bibliotecários. Se por um lado isto provoca atividades paralelas imprevistas, por outro cria uma convivência salutar de educação mútua.

Como coordenador do volume dedicado a Oswald de Andrade da Coleção Arquivos da UNESCO, achei por bem fazer uma apresentação de caráter geral sobre o projeto (Archives, originalmente) cujos primeiros doze títulos começaram a ser publicados a partir de 1988. No Brasil, a coleção conta com o apoio do Conselho Nacional de Pesquisas (CNPq) e do Instituto de Estudos Brasileiros da Universidade de São Paulo (USP).

O maior projeto literário latino-americanista, a menos que eu me engane, foi até agora o da série, Biblioteca Ayacucho, da editora venezuelana do mesmo nome, sob inspiração de Angel Rama e ainda hoje em fase de produção de títulos. Entre os seus méritos, o fato de ser um dos primeiros projetos bibliográficos de ordem continental, ou seja, inclui o Brasil no seu vasto repertório. Para a parte brasileira, contou justamente com a assessoria de Antonio Cândido. Os textos da Biblioteca Ayacucho aparecem todos apresentados em língua espanhola, mesmo os brasileiros, com uma introdução à obra, mais um quadro cronológico final. Vejo dois problemas nesta coleção: o seu preço e a divulgação, já que os volumes são de difícil aquisição, limitando-se em geral a bibliotecas especializadas. Dificilmente encontramos exemplares da Ayacucho em livrarias comerciais.

O projeto Arquivos é muito diferenciado. Concebido com grande originalidade e inesgotável iniciativa, merece destaque o nome do Coordenador Geral da coleção, Amos Segala. Embora a agência central da Coleção Arquivos esteja sediada em Paris, por ser respaldada pela UNESCO, são responsáveis por ela as bibliotecas nacionais de oito países signatários: Espanha, França, Itália, Portugal, Argentina, Brasil, Colômbia e México. América Latina e o Caribe aparecem na coleção representados em quatro línguas: espanhol, português, inglês e francês. O resgate dos textos em suas línguas originais é fundamental para um contato mais fiel com o mesmo. A coleção tem a particularidade de ser uma edição crítica, ou seja, tem por finalidade elaborar o estabelecimento final dos textos através da recuperação dos manuscritos (autógrafos ou apógrafos), ou edições consideradas definitivas pelos próprios autores em vida. Assim, empreende um trabalho de crítica genética que permite recuperar a memória do texto, da maneira mais fidedigna possível. Este tipo de edição permite, nas palavras de Giuseppe Tavani:[1]

> A possibilidade de encarar o conceito de texto de uma maneira menos rígida: isto é, considerar o texto não como um dado mas como um processo; não como uma entidade estável mas como uma variável; não como um elemento estático mas como um elemento dinâmico, cujas facetas sincrônicas—as que conhecemos como variantes ou redações sucessivas—vêm a ser definidas por acidentes extra-textuais, e não por exigências do texto.

Como suporte teórico desta coleção, já foram realizados três colóquios internacionais sobre teoria e prática da edição crítica: 1983 e 1984 (Paris) e 1986 (Porto), publicados agora em forma de volume (op. cit.).

Hoje o conceito de manuscrito está chegando ao fim. A possibilidade de redigir e corrigir diretamente no computador faz da crítica genética uma profissão ou uma área de interesse circunscrita no tempo e, talvez no espaço, pois focalizará textos de escritores pertencentes a países de menor desenvolvimento tecnológico, forçados ainda ao uso da página manuscrita. Num futuro mais próximo do que imaginamos, só teremos acesso a uma versão única e final: aquela que aparece no disquete. Assim, os estudiosos ver-se-ão privados da arqueologia do texto. As próprias editoras solicitam hoje os originais dessa forma, permitindo-se inclusive fazer alterações próprias à preparação do texto diretamente no disquete. Isto vai uniformizar e pasteurizar de tal maneira os manuscritos, que será difícil termos uma dimensão diacrônica do processo construtivo de um original. O que seria dos estudos flaubertianos ou proustianos sem a riqueza das correções dos vários manuscritos? O preço da evolução tecnológica implicará na perda da 'aura' do manuscrito (do latim *manu scriptu*, escrito a mão). Sabemos, por exemplo, que hoje Gabriel García Márquez escreve os seus romances diretamente no computador.

Ocorrem-me ainda dois exemplos. No livro de ingresso das noviças, conhecido como o "Libro de Profesiones . . . del Convento de San Gerónimo" no México, pertencente à Biblioteca Latino-Americana "Nettie Lee Benson" da Universidade do Texas em Austin,[2] contamos com o registro do ingresso de Sor Juana Inés de la Cruz, cujo texto, de 8 de fevereiro de 1694, consta como tendo sido assinado pela freira mexicana "con mi sangre." Do fato, cotejando a cor da assinatura com as firmas das outros noviças, percebemos uma coloração mais tênue e avermelhada. Acredito que hoje um convento moderno e bem aparelhado registre as freiras através de um sistema de fichas no computador (IBM ou Macintosh), obliterando para a história a dramaticidade de semelhante voto.

Outro exemplo é o original do conto "El Aleph" de Jorge Luis Borges, adquirido recentemente de Estela Canto pela Biblioteca Nacional de Madrid. A possibilidade de estarmos próximos do manuscrito de esta obra prima equivale, como talvez diria o próprio Borges, a ver fugazmente o rosto de Deus: o papel quadriculado (originalmente dos típicos "cuadernos San Martín"), a letra minúscula de Borges, às vezes inclinada para baixo, e mais importante ainda, a possibilidade de ver as palavras grifadas com as várias alternativas que Borges percorre até chegar ao *mot juste*. Mesmo numa das passagens mais memoráveis do conto, a descrição do objeto mágico, o aleph, Borges vira a página de cabeça para baixo, para escrever, de forma invertida e numerada, a seqüência da famosa descrição. Além da extraordinária importância para a arqueologia e reconstrução do texto, ele possui grande beleza visual. Acredito que em pouco tempo teremos uma publicação sobre as variantes do "El Aleph," permitindo percorrer o trajeto pré-textual do conto, até chegar à sua versão final. Supondo que hoje a IBM, num golpe publicitário desse a Borges um computador com um teclado com letras em relevo, capaz de imprimir em Braile, o que lhe permitiria a correção das provas impressas, dispensado a ajuda de leitores, isto eliminaria de vez e para sempre a possibilidade de semelhante manuscrito. Permiti-me esta digressão, para falar do caráter quase obsoleto hoje do manuscrito e de uma profissão que, provavelmente, no século XXI será semelhante ao do paleógrafo ou do arqueólogo.

Neste sentido, a iniciativa da Coleção Arquivos, de reunir os originais mais importantes das nossas letras, de modo a estabelecer textos finais, com todas as suas variantes e histórias evolutivas dos textos, tem um mérito sem precedentes na reconstituição da identidade cultural latino-americana. Como mencionou Ernesto Sábato, estamos frente a uma espécie de *La Plêiade* do nosso continente. O plano original, de aproximadamente 120 títulos de autores do século XX, consagrados e já mortos, está projetado para os próximos dez anos. Cada volume está sob a responsabilidade de um coordenador geral e um número de colaboradores que pode variar entre cinco ou mais especialistas (o volume de Miguel Angel Asturias, por exemplo, conta com onze). Entre as várias normas previstas, foi estipulado que a equipe de especialistas deve ser internacional, de modo a ampliar os horizontes interpretativos. A coleção obedece a um esquema-tipo, dividido em dez partes. A introdução, conta com a "Liminar" de um reconhecido estudioso do autor; depois um introdução do coordenador com uma nota filológica preliminar e um estudo crítico-genético, assim como a explicação dos critérios gerais para a edição do texto. A seguir, a parte mais importante do volume, o texto em si, representado pela obra em questão, com todas as variantes e notas críticas. No volume dedicado a *Paradiso*,[3] de José Lezama Lima, por exemplo, há notas de autores diferentes no corpo de uma mesma página, contrastando assim pontos de vista, tornando a interpretação um verdadeiro diálogo de vozes diferenciadas. Dependendo do volume, há espaço para um glossário (como no caso de *Don Segundo Sombra* ou para a poesia de Vallejo)[5] e documentos fotográficos e iconográficos. A quinta parte é a histórica do texto, com estudos sobre a gênese e circunstância da obra, assim como os seus destinos. A sexta parte remete a leituras originais do texto: seja ela temática, seja intra-textual. Também há espaço para um quadro cronológico; não de ordem geral, como na Biblioteca Ayacucho, mas pensando sempre nos fatos históricos que de alguma maneira se vinculam à própria obra. A coleção prevê também um dossiê, com documentos, manuscritos e até correspondência. No final uma bibliografia seleta comentada e um índice. Embora este seja o esquema-tipo, os doze volumes até agora apresentados são idiossincráticos e, talvez, nas diferenças resida o interesse. Sem dúvida que a parte mais importante é aquela dedicada ao estabelecimento final do textos. As vezes não contamos com originais, nem provas corrigidas pelo autor, nem sabemos se algumas variantes são "erros" propositais ou deslizes tipográficos. O caso de César Vallejo é exemplar, pois sua obra póstuma contou com dois editores: Georgette de Vallejo e Juan Larrea; hoje sabemos que houve manipulação dos originais. Valha o testemunho de Américo Ferrari, coordenador do volume dedicado ao poeta peruano:[6]

Se ha dicho—con maldad—que Vallejo dejó dos viudas: Georgette y Larrea. Los dos editores han asumido la responsabilidad—o la irresponsabilidad—de hacer cortes no justificados objetivamente en el continuum de la escritura vallejiana y de fabricar libros que el poeta no compiló. Estas fabricaciones, desde luego, no son inocentes, y tienen claramente por objetivo imponer al lector una lectura orientada por intereses afectivos o ideológicos de los editores.

Em relação ao Brasil, dos doze volumes projetados, foram publicados até hoje dois títulos: *A paixão segundo G. H.*,[7] de Clarice Lispector, e *Macunaíma*,[8] de Mário de Andrade. O primeiro deles teve que limitar-se às edições em vida da autora, já que não foi possível localizar os originais manuscritos:

A falta de originais de *A paixão segundo G. H.* (1964), de que não têm notícia nem os herdeiros de Clarice Lispector, nem os editores deste romance, priva a presente edição da medula do seu aparato crítico. Mas a falta desses originais é apenas caso particular de uma carência generalizada, extensiva à obra da romancista. Para os vinte e cinco livros de Clarice Lispector só encontramos um original completo,

afirma Benedito Nunes, coordenador da edição (p. xxxiv).

Mário de Andrade representa, do ponto de vista da pesquisa, a antítese de Clarice Lispector. O autor de *Macunaíma* foi um intelectual de gabinete por excelência, consciente da dimensão histórica de sua obra, preservando ao máximo todo e qualquer tipo de documentação: "O bloco de bolso é bom companheiro para quem vive a febre da criação. Mário lê. Lê de tudo. Conversa com pessoas que lhe passam informações. Multiplica fichas, sublinha e destaca trechos, faz indicações nas margens das obras . . .," comenta Telê Porto Ancona Lopez, coordenadora do volume (p. xxvi). O acervo Marioandradino, no Instituto de Estudos Brasileiros da USP, representa até os dias de hoje um manancial inesgotável de dissertações, teses, edições fac-similares e edições críticas. Aliás, a riqueza das possibilidades fica comprovada pelo fato de ser esta não a primeira, mas a segunda edição crítica de *Macunaíma* realizada pela mesma coordenadora do volume (a primeira é de 1978[9]).

Gostaria ainda de me deter no meu próprio projeto. Ele coincide com o centenário do nascimento do Oswald de Andrade, mas infelizmente o volume, dedicado à poesia e aos manifestos, não será publicado este ano (espero que não tenha que esperar até o bicentenário . . .). Conto com vários colaboradores: Haroldo de Campos, Silviano Santiago, Vinícius Dantas, K. David Jackson, Diléa Zanotto Manfio, Luis Henrique dos Santos e Orna. Apesar de minhas insistentes e inúmeras circulares, até o momento só foi realizado o estabelecimento final do texto, parte central do projeto e sem o qual não podem ser empreendidos os estudos paralelos. Na medida em que foi impossível achar rastros dos originais manuscritos da poesia, *Pau Brasil* (Paris: 1925)[10] o estabelecimento final de texto, é um trabalho que se reveste de grande originalidade. Foram marcadas todas as variantes em vida do autor. Mas o lado mais fascinante empreendido por Diléa Zanotto Manfio foi a recuperação histórica da poesia. Oswald, especialmente nos poemas pertencentes à "História do Brasil," vai a fontes primárias, às crônicas de época, e faz um verdadeiro recorte do texto original, transfigurando-o em material poético. Assim, por exemplo, em o poema "A descoberta" que abre o livro, temos a transcrição de fragmentos da Carta de Pero Vaz de Caminha a El-rei D. Manuel,[11] onde aparecem grifadas as frases ou palavras selecionadas para compor o poema. O mesmo com processo seletivo e de posterior recomposição poética acontece com a *História da Província Săcta Cruz*, de Pero de Magalhães Gandavo,[12] ou a *História dos padres capuchinos*,[13] do capuchino Claude d'Abbeville. Oswald de Andrade: uma espécie de Pierre Menard tropical, que reescreve a história do Brasil quatro séculos mais tarde, para transfigurá-la em material poético, compondo uma obra cuja modernidade foi responsável por uma das maiores transformações estéticas da literatura brasileira.

Ainda uma informação final, sobre o projeto gráfico da Coleção Arquivos. Para a confecção das capas foram solicitados trabalhos de artistas plásticos de grande renome, de modo a formar uma espécie de pinacoteca original, com exposições previstas.

NOTAS

1. "Los textos del siglo XX," em *Littérature Latino-Américaine et des Caraibes du XXe siècle* 58 (Roma: Bulzoni, 1988).

2. Convento de San Gerónimo, "Libro de professiones y elecciones de prioras y vicarias del Convento de San Gerónimo, [1586–1713]," MS. (Benson Latin American Collection, The University of Texas as Austin).

3. José Lezama Lima, *Paradiso*, Cintio Vitier, ed., Colección Archivos 3 (Nanterre, France: ALLCA XX, 1988).

4. Ricardo Güiraldes, *Don Segunda Sombra*, Paul Verdevoye, ed., Colección Archivos 2 (Buenos Aires: Ministerio Relaciones Exteriores; Brasília: CNPq; Bogotá: Presidencia de la República; México: SEP; Madrid: CSIC, 1988).

5. César Vallejo, *Obra poética*, Américo Ferrari, ed., Colección Archivos 4 (Buenos Aires: Ministerio Relaciones Exteriores; Brasília: CNPq; Bogotá: Presidencia de la República; México: SEP; Madrid: CSIC, 1988).

6. Américo Ferrari, "Problemas de cronología y manuscritos en los *Poemas póstumos* de César Vallejo, em *Littérature Latino-Américaine et des Caraibes du XXe siècle* 58 (Roma: Bulzoni, 1988), p. 258.

7. Clarice Lispector, *A paixão segunda G. H.*, Benedito Nunes, ed., Coleção Arquivos, 13, (Trindade, Brasil: Editora da UFSC, 1988).

8. Mário de Andrade, *Macunaíma: o herói sem nenhum caráter*, Telê Porto Ancona Lopez, ed., Coleção Arquivos 6 (Trindade, Florianópolis, SC: Editora da UFSC, 1988).

9. *Idem, Macunaíma: o herói sem nenhum caráter*, Telê Porto Ancona Lopez, ed., Biblioteca Universitária de Literatura Brasileira, Série C: Ficção, Romance e Conto 1 (Rio de Janeiro: Livros Técnicos e Científicos, 1978).

10. Com exceção de um único poema, "Atelier."

11. Fac-simile e transcrição em Jaime Cortesão, *A Carta de Pero Vaz de Caminha* (São Paulo: Livraria Editora Livros de Portugal, 1943), pp. 133-189; "Fac-simile, transcrição paleográfica e versão em linguagem atual," em José Augusto Vaz Valente, *A carta de Pero Vaz de Caminha: estudo crítico, paleográfico–diplomático*, Série de História 3 (São Paulo: Fundo do Pesquisas do Museu Paulista, Universidade de São Paulo, 1975, pp. 113-196.

12. Pero de Magalhães Gandavo, *História da Província Sãcta Cruz* (Lisboa: 1576).

13. Claude d'Abbeville, père, *Histoire de la mission des pères capucins en l'Isle de Maragnan et terres circonvoisines* (Paris: 1614).

Actualizaciones en bibliotecología en el Cono Sur

16. Desarrollo de colecciones latinoamericanas: monografías editadas y tesis de graduación, problemas de su acceso

Teresa Fittipaldi de Gimeno

El camino que recorre el libro desde su concepción en la mente del autor hasta las manos del usuario es largo, complicado y esquivo. El proceso que va desde que el libro es conocido por el usuario, a través de una fuente de información secundaria, hasta que llega a sus manos depende de tantos factores externos a la voluntad de adquirir el libro que es necesario que tratemos de hacer este proceso lo más eficaz posible para poder agilizar la incorporación de documentos a los acervos bibliográficos.

Es responsabilidad del bibliotecólogo la identificación y clarificación del mismo para poder tener acceso a la mayoría de los documentos. La actividad que involucra editores, distribuidores, representantes, libreros y bibliotecólogos es complicada, pero indiscutiblemente básica. Sin acervo documental adecuado ninguna biblioteca puede prestar servicios efectivos por mejor procesada técnicamente que se encuentre. El conocimiento de la industria editorial es básico para la estrategia de la formación y desarrollo equilibrado de las colecciones. Por que si nos limitamos a los fácilmente accesible sin profundizar en la búsqueda y selección, podemos establecer una limitación que no responde a los principios básicos de la selección y lleva al estancamiento.

Para poder poner la producción científica y tecnológica al alcance de los interesados y promover de este modo el desarrollo económico y social de los países, es necesario ahondar aún más en los elementos que esta industria maneja, puesto que el riesgo que se corre al no poder acceder a esos conocimientos se acrecenta con el tiempo. El aumento constante del valor de los materiales bibliográficos ha sido un factor preponderante para jerarquizar la tarea de selección de libros y colocarlo al mismo nivel que la planificación de servicios.

Las medidas deben ser tomadas de inmediato porque si nos sentimos complicados en este momento, debemos pensar que el advenimiento del libro electrónico multiplica los problemas actuales. Estos inconvenientes no subsanados, han llevado en muchos casos a la utilización de la discutida reprografía cuando el acceso a las obras es muy difícil y el desequilibrio estructural de la industria editorial lo propicia. Si bien estas reproducciones no se hacen con fines de lucro podrían ser evitadas. A la producción editorial comercial se suma la producción editorial académica que crea un tipo particular de problemas producto de la escasa distribución.

Los libros de habla hispana que más absorbía el mercado uruguayo hasta hace muy poco provenían fundamentalmente de España. Hoy la situación ha cambiado mucho. Existen países latinoamericanos como México, Argentina y, en forma incipiente, Colombia, que van paulatinamente aumentando su producción editorial con éxito.

El desarrollo de la industria editorial latinoamericana en las últimas décadas produjo un aumento (crecimiento) tan importante en la producción de material bibliográfico que ha sobrepasado las previsiones de los bibliotecólogos. Se hace imprescindible en este momento contar con conocimientos de la industria editorial latinoamericana y de los canales de distribución de su producción.

Las recomendaciones efectuadas en general en los eventos internacionales apuntan a una coordinación entre editores, agentes, libreros, bibliotecas, y centros de documentación que difícilmente se logra en América Latina.

Hay además otros inconvenientes que se suman con las dificultades de adquisición de material y que son difícilmente subsanables: la extensión geográfica, los lentos y caros sistemas de transporte y correo, y las tarifas y aranceles.

Las distribuidoras nacionales no quieren correr riesgos y sólo trabajan con aquellas editoriales que les ofrecen un margen de ganancia tal que cubre todos los riesgos y es muchas veces en la producción de editoriales pequeñas no consideradas rentables en donde se encuentra el material bibliográfico de avanzada, sobre todo en profesiones como la nuestra que no tienen un prestigio demasiado difundido. Para obtener un nivel alto de satisfacción en los pedidos hay que recurrir generalmente a distribuidores de gran envergadura que se encuentran en nuestro caso fuera del país o a los distribuidores locales que señalan precios tan altos que no se pueden costear con los recursos escasos de que disponen en lo general las bibliotecas.

En nuestro medio se maneja con agentes especializados y generales que se dedican a obtener material por encargo, con libreros que poseen libros para venta directa y que también venden por encargo, libreros simples que cotizan sólo lo que tienen con representantes de editoriales extranjeras.

Los editores en general ven a la biblioteca en América Latina como una institución "anémica" derivada de su escasez de recursos, desconociendo por un lado los esfuerzos de racionalización, objetividad y pertinencia que se realizan en la misma referentes al desarrollo de sus colecciones y difícilmente reconocen que son muchas veces circunstancias externas derivadas del mercado editorial y de la forma de distribución las que imposibilitan el desarrollo específico que es más importante que el desarrollo exhaustivo.

Hemos intentado medir algunas de las dificultades externas a la biblioteca mediante el análisis de las respuestas a pedidos de cotización para compra de libros realizadas por la EUBCA[1] durante el bienio 1988–89:

Tabla 1. Dificultades de acceso a material bibliográfico, 1988–1989 (%)

Dificultades	Años		Bienio
	1988	1989	
Cotizan	70	43	54
No Cotizan	30	57	46
N =	(90)	(120)	(210)

En 1988 no se logró la cotización de un 30% del pedido efectuado a pesar de que los libros solicitados eran de fácil localización (tabla 1). Se trataba con este pedido de llenar carencias, atrasos que se habían producido en varios años en los que por falta de rubros y otros motivos la universidad no pudo destinar recursos para libros. Los libros solicitados eran en su mayoría básicos y de fácil localización.

En 1989 se trató de ir armonizando crecimiento de la colección y darle un sesgo realmente especializado a las adquisiciones. La selección se hizo más específica y actualizada, ya no se trataba de cubrir las necesidades básicas de información, sino ampliarla y hacerla lo más especializada posible. La tabla 1 señala para 1989 un aumento en la proporción de no cotización de libros: más de la mitad de los libros no fueron cotizados, esto lleva a un porcentaje en el bienio de 46% de no cotizados lo que indica una fuerte dificultad en el acceso al material.

Los libreros explican esta realidad como consecuencia fundamentalmente de problemas de orden cambiario. Como la universidad paga con retraso, los libreros cotizan con margen amplio de ganancias haciendo que los libros aumenten de costo. Además los libreros sólo cotizan libros cuyo origen implique cierta garantía de estabilidad en sus precios, ya sea por la moneda en la que están cotizados como por la editorial que los respalda.

También los libreros demoran su cotización, lo que produce un encarecimiento aún mayor en el costo de los libros y una disminución en la capacidad de compra de las bibliotecas.

Otra de las justificaciones de los libreros es que los plazos destinados a la cotización de libros son muy breves y les falta tiempo para poder localizar el material y establecer los precios.[2] Sin embargo esto no es explicativo de todo el fenómeno, ya que hay libros que no se cotizan en más de un período. En nuestro análisis éstos son considerados de máxima dificultad de acceso. Del pedido total de material bibliográfico para 1988 no se cotizan un 30%; estos fueron solicitados nuevamente en 1989, parte (12%) pasó a integrar la categoría de máxima dificultad de acceso. La tabla 2 da cuenta de este fenómeno.

Suelen justificarse las dificultades de la distribución de libros por las tasas aduaneras y las trabas legales. Legalmente podemos considerar que en nuestro país las puertas están realmente abiertas. La importación de libros está libre de impuestos desde la "Ley Rodó" N° 3.681 del 23 de julio de 1910 que exime de todo impuesto aduanero "a la importación de libros destinados a la lectura y al estudio".

Además, en la ley 15.913 del 27 de noviembre de 1987 en el artículo 8 inc.C) dispone las siguientes franquicias fiscales en beneficio de la difusión de libros: ". . . c) la importación de libros, folletos y revistas de carácter literario, científico, artístico, docente y material educativo, estará exonerado de proventos, precios portuarios y de todo tributo, incluidos recargos, impuesto aduanero único, tasa de movilización de bultos, tasas consulares y cualquier otro aplicable en ocasión de la importación. . . ."

Esta misma crea una comisión nacional del libro entre cuyas atribuciones están:

"LL) Propender a la eliminación de trabas directas o indirectas de carácter arancelario tales como cupo, facturas pro-forma, plazos para girar divisas, permisos previos o análogos."

"M) Propender al otorgamiento de prioridades en la asignación de divisas al tipo de cambio más conveniente para el cumplimiento de las obligaciones derivadas del comercio y producción de libros."

"N) Expedirse a requerimiento de los particulares o de las oficinas estatales intervinientes en las operaciones de importación de libros, sobre si éstos, así como los folletos y revistas a introducirse en el país, reúnen o no el carácter literario, artístico, científico y docente que exigen las disposiciones tributarias que establecen exenciones en su beneficio."

El problema de América Latina no se limita a la escasa producción editorial debido a los altos costos de edición, sino a las irregularidades en la comercialización y distribución de los mismos. Muchas veces un autor que tiene aceptación dentro de su especialidad, no recibe para sus obras la demanda que corresponde porque las vías de acceso a la adquisición del material editado no dejan llegar la demanda a su meta.

La tabla 2 presenta una distribución de las cotizaciones correspondientes al período 1988–1989 realizada en la Escuela Universitaria de Bibliotecología y Ciencias Afines en plaza según el lugar de edición de los distintos materiales. Las diferentes divisiones responden a un criterio eminentemente práctico, se diferencian los países a los que se les solicita mayor cantidad de material. Como se ha señalado, se utiliza como indicador de dificultad la no cotización de un libro por una sola vez y para indicar dificultad máxima cuando el libro no es cotizado tampoco al año siguiente.

Tabla 2. Procedencia del material bibliográfico solicitado en 1988–1989
%

Procedencia	Total	Dificultad	Dificultad Máxima
Brasil	20	40	36
México	4	7	9
Otros América Latina	8	15	9
Total América Latina	(32)	(62)	(81)
España	32	19	--
EE.UU.	36	13	9
N =	(90)	(27)	(11)

De los libros que ofrecen dificultades para su cotización observamos que sólo un 19% corresponde a España y EE.UU., porcentaje que está debajo del tercio que correspondería estadísticamente si la "dificultad" dependiera del simple azar. En cambio América Latina presenta el doble de dificultad de acceso a los libros editados en la región. Para los libros que presentan máxima dificultad también se destacan los porcentajes asignados a América Latina. Estas observaciones apuntan a subrayar las diferencias de los sistemas de información/distribución dentro de la región del material editado en América Latina, frente a los sistemas de información/distribución del material editado en EE.UU. o España.

El acceso a la literatura gris

La llamada literatura gris no ha sido objeto de suficiente atención desde el punto de vista de su acceso. Tomando conceptos de la definición de Helmut M. Arthurs podemos decir que la literatura gris es aquella que no ha sido editada pero que no tiene carácter de privada, confidencial, secreta o de distribución restringida, y que tiene un interés académico o práctico. La característica editorial de este tipo de literatura es que no fue hecha con la intención de ser editada y sólo en contadas ocasiones se edita.

Arthurs señala que la literatura gris ofrece: "rápida comunicación de los resultados de trabajos por parte de los investigadores". Señala además que su acceso es fácil debido a: "baratura y alta calidad de los sistemas reprográficos modernos". Esta última conclusión no se ajusta necesariamente a los países latinoamericanos en general y en particular a Uruguay. La literatura gris es muy abundante en nuestros países por la dificultad en que se encuentran los autores para publicar sus trabajos. Como ejemplo citaremos el caso de los licenciados que producen trabajos que no despiertan interés público que justifique intentar su edición, sin embargo estos trabajos son inscritos en el registro de autor o en la institución donde ejercen para asegurarse el reconocimiento de su autoría. Estos trabajos figuran en los currícula personales y eventualmente son usados en actividad docente. Este tipo de literatura no fue hecha con intenciones de ser publicada puesto que en nuestro ámbito la publicación es vista como quimérica. Sin embargo la intención latente es su máxima divulgación.

Existe por otro lado otro tipo de literatura que a mi juicio no debería considerarse como gris porque si bien sólo poseen el carácter de literatura gris en forma transitoria tienen el mismo inconveniente que la literatura gris propiamente dicha. Son los resultados de congresos que aunque no tienen la intención de ser restringidos su forma de distribución es fundamentalmente para los concurrentes al evento y su adquisición por la biblioteca es muy difícil y tardía. Si tenemos en cuenta que H. Arthurs menciona para EE.UU. que sólo un 24% de publicaciones de esta índole (resultados de congresos) se publicaron en revistas el año siguiente a su producción, poca es la esperanza que queda en países de menores recursos económicos para estas publicaciones.

Alfredo Sara Guitard resume en su comentario sobre Helmut M. Arthurs que:

1) la literatura gris tiene hoy día una gran importancia científica; 2) su importancia desde el punto de vista documental corre pareja a la científica, dado, sobre todo, que buena parte de ella no es recogida ulteriormente en revistas, libros y monografías; 3) la literatura gris es un objeto tan legítimo de atención documental como la oficialmente publicada; 4) se impone la tarea de concientizar debidamente sobre todos estos aspectos de la literatura gris a bibliotecarios y documentalistas, e incluso a científicos sociales.

Tesis de graduación

En la literatura gris que ha sido y definida, se puede distinguir una tipo particular que corresponde a la tesis de graduación académica. Este tipo de literatura tiene varias particularidades que la hacen muy buscada en el ambiente académico. En primer lugar son los resultados de una investigación documental o empírica que se realiza bajo la supervisión de un docente y que debe cumplir con determinadas exigencias puesto que se trata de la culminación de la actividad académica.

Por otro lado se encuentran entre ellas muchos casos de adaptación de tecnologías o innovaciones particularmente importantes para la región. En el intento de adoptar tecnologías que han sido elaboradas y perfeccionadas en otros lugares de la región, realizamos duplicaciones para acomodarlas a nuestra realidad y no siempre mejoramos porque en la mayoría de los casos ignoramos la existencia de estos esfuerzos realizados en el mismo sentido. Uno de los ejemplos más claros es la adaptación de las computadoras para los procesos técnicos en las bibliotecas y centros de documentación. Cada unidad de información elabora un plan, un programa, un formato distinto al otro y tiene que pasar por los mismos errores y pérdidas de tiempo y dinero que podrían evitarse si se conocieran más a fondo las experiencias y estudios hechos para experiencias similares.

También este material es de uso importantísimo para la docencia que lo utiliza, ya como ejemplo, apoyo o complemento de la literatura editada que muchas veces no es suficiente. Por estos motivos creo imprescindible encontrar una vía organizada para "captar", conocer su existencia, y adquirir ese tipo de literatura. En primer lugar hay muy pocos repertorios que las difunden ya sean publicadas o no.

Las tesis publicadas lo mismo que las publicaciones académicas son muy difíciles de obtener. Esto se debe a que si son publicadas en general lo hace la misma institución académica y lo distribuye como canje. Al no contar con suficientes publicaciones muchas bibliotecas no pueden obtener esas publicaciones porque no tienen con que canjear. Para ambas, quien edita y quien recibe, el sistema de fotocopiado es muy caro, tanto por la reproducción de ejemplares como por el alto costo que resulta su envío por correo; y muy pocas instituciones académicas cuentan con telefax al servicio de la biblioteca, que también es un servicio muy caro. No se posee, como es obvio, datos sobre las frustraciones que ocasiona no poder hallar esa literatura. En primer lugar cuando se realizan pedidos de esta índole ni siquiera se tienen en cuenta (no se registran), tal es el concepto de imposibilidad que ellos conllevan. Por otro lado, como ya se mencionó en la mayoría de los casos hay un desconocimiento absoluto sobre las posibilidades que este tipo de literatura ofrece, por falta, como ya se señaló, de repertorios que las identifiquen aunque existen esfuerzos para crearlos.

Si tenemos en cuenta los inconvenientes que tiene el material bibliográfico editado para ser obtenido por compra en Latinoamérica, estos deberían ser multiplicados por 50 para ejemplarizar los inconvenientes de acceso a la literatura gris y por 100 los que se derivan de la literatura académica en particular.

El caso específico de las tesis de graduación es preocupante puesto que muchas veces estas obras tienen valor de investigación y son citadas por otras impresas pero no pueden ser obtenidas fuera del ámbito local. Esto deja al estudioso con insatisfacciones que muchas veces interrumpen trabajo intelectual.

Se agrega a este trabajo un listado de las monografías seleccionadas que han sido presentadas para graduación en la Escuela Universitaria de Bibliotecología. Se excluyen las recopilaciones tales como bibliografías, índices, guías, catálogos e inventarios. Sólo se recopilaron aquellos repertorios bibliográficos que constituyen fuente de información secundaria para localizar tesis de graduación.

NOTAS

1. Escuela Universitaria de Bibliotecología y Ciencias Afines.

2. Los esfuerzos hechos en varias instituciones y fundamentalmente en el CICH de México para reunir trabajos publicados por latinoamericanos en revistas de la región y extranjeras son muy importantes. Pero no son suficientes para localizar la real producción editorial de Latinoamérica y menos solucionar sus problemas de acceso.

BIBLIOGRAFÍA

Augsburger, Alberto E. *El mercado del libro en América Latina: situación actual y perspectivas*. París: Unesco, 1981.

Garzón, Alvaro. *La promoción del libro y de la lectura*. Costa Rica: Unesco, 1979.

Impuesto al libro. Montevideo: Cámara Uruguaya del Libro, 1981.

Irazabel Nerpell, Amelia de, y Manuela Vázquez Valero. "Congreso Internacional sobre la Disponibilidad Universal de Publicaciones". *Revista Española de Documentación Científica* 5, no. 4 (1982), 375-388.

"Ley 15.913, del libro, del 27 de noviembre de 1987." *Diario oficial*, 1987.

El libro en América Latina y el Caribe. Bogotá: Centro Regional para el Fomento del Libro en la América Latina y el Caribe (CERLALC), 1987–.

Sandoval, Armando M. "Sobre la investigación y la producción bibliográfica en América Latina". *Revista Española de Documentación Científica* 5, no. 4 (1982), 347-367.

17. Desafíos bibliográficos sobre la educación paraguaya

Sofia Mareski

Introducción

El 35° Congreso del SALALM con buen acierto ha enfocado el tema de la investigación y las colecciones bibliográficas en el proceso de cambio en el Cono Sur, apuntando hacia el año 2000. Es oportuno destacar que este enfoque se inicie al comienzo en la década del 90, abarcando un área potencialmente rico y de recursos ilimitados. Se afirma que los recursos naturales del Cono Sur pueden dar alimentos para todo el mundo. Por lo tanto, el tema de la investigación y las colecciones bibliográficas ocupan en el desarrollo un lugar fundamental en la región, al igual, el acceso a las colecciones bibliográficas en esta vasta zona geográfica.

Para esta ocasión se eligió el tema de los recursos bibliográficos sobre la educación paraguaya durante la década del 80. Se trata de un programa de investigación educativa que forma parte de una red latinoamericana de información en educación. El diseño del sistema elaborado por Gonzalo Gutiérrez en 1978 abarca las siguientes características:

1. Global, que toma la educación como un todo y se refiere a todos los aspectos, niveles y tipos de educación.
2. Cooperativo, por cuanto se basa en la cooperación de los diversos centros asociados al sistema, bajo la coordinación de uno de ellos.
3. Orientado a un objetivo. No se refiere a una disciplina en forma exclusiva, sino que es interdisciplinario.
4. Regional, porque reune información sobre la educación en los países latinoamericanos y nacionales en materia educativa.
5. Los usuarios enfocados por el sistema son los investigadores en el campo de la educación, los profesores universitarios, sus alumnos y los ejecutivos que deben tomar decisiones en materia educacional y administrar sistemas educativos.[1]

Antes de entrar en el tema paraguayo que me toca desarrollar voy a referirme brevemente a los antecedentes de la institución central que coordina las actividades entre los 27 centros de los 18 países que componen la Red Latinoamericana de Información y Documentación en Educación, con sede en Santiago de Chile a cargo del Centro de Investigación y Desarrollo de la Educación (CIDE). La Red-REDUC constituye el acervo documental de la región latinoamericana del Caribe, contando para su operación con centros de documentación en cada país, los que actúan en su carácter de centros nacionales.

En el caso del Paraguay, el Centro Paraguayo de Documentación Social está comprendido dentro de la red para coordinar las actividades dentro del país y los demás centros participantes de la red, y operar en las siguientes modalidades:

1. Procesar documentos del país para una rápida recuperación de la información.
2. Redactar resúmenes de estos documentos y mantener un archivo completo del fondo documental en uno o más centros del país, los que pueden poseer a su vez sus servicios de información que forman la red nacional.
3. Mantener un sistema de capacitación de usuarios en el empleo de la información en el campo educacional y especialmente en la información microproducida.
4. Proporcionar asistencia técnica a los centros en la organización de sus servicios de documentación y afines.
5. Organizar subredes especializadas que cubren determinados campos o disciplinas de educación.
6. Elaborar el análisis de la información de los documentos a través de la publicación nacional *Resúmenes analíticos en educación* (RAE).[2]

Los criterios de selección de los documentos para la Red deben ser relevantes que se refieran a investigaciones o innovaciones en educación en su concepción más amplia. Dichos documentos son procesados de acuerdo a las normas internacionales del *Tesauro de la Educación* de *UNESCO-OIE* para la unificación de los criterios dentro de la Red y los centros integrantes de la misma.

Los campos temáticos se refieren a:

1. Determinantes de rendimiento
2. Niveles escolares
3. Problemas de aprendizaje
4. Niveles de repetición
5. Alfabetización
6. Educación de la mujer
7. Bilingüismo
8. Educación y trabajo
9. Factores de promoción.

La información en educación está orientada al siguiente grupo de usuarios, considerados como usuarios potenciales y en menor escala efectivos:

1. Investigadores en educación
2. Profesores universitarios del área de educación y afines
3. Estudiantes de pedagogía de todos los niveles
4. Estudiantes graduados en educación
5. Administradores y planificadores educacionales
6. Personas que desarrollan proyectos educativos
7. Analistas de información
8. Bibliotecarios y documentalistas
9. Personal docente a nivel básico, medio y superior.

Organización de la investigación educativa en el Paraguay[3]

Las características de las unidades que producen la investigación educativa son las siguientes:

1. Nacionalidad de la unidad que produce el documento, que puede ser: nacional; nacional con asistencia internacional; nacional con ayuda externo; de otro país de la región; de otro país fuera de la región; u organismo internacional.
2. Tipo de organización de unidades: nacionales que pueden ser gubernamentales, universitarias, o centros privados.
3. Tipo de documentos: estudio empírico, estudio formal, material de enseñanza, informe de experiencias, informe de avance, informe de reunión, recopilación de trabajos o documento oficial.
4. Niveles del sistema: sistema escolar, pre-escolar, básico, superior, o especial.
5. Tipo de educación: educación técnica, educación rural, educación de adultos, etc.
6. Materias tratadas: proceso de enseñanza, aprendizaje, alumnos, profesores, institucionalidad de la educación, educación y sociedad.

Partes componentes de los *Resúmenes analíticos en educación* (RAE)

1. Número del resumen.
2. País: al que se refiere el documento resumido. Cuando no corresponde a un país, se emplea región o sub-región o se escribe la palabra "general".
3. Autor: personal o corporativo.
4. Publicación: datos bibliográficos.

5. Unidad: patrocinadora del documento.
6. Palabras claves: tomadas de *UNESCO terminología: tesauro de la Educación UNESCO-OIE* (Paris: UNESCO, 1977, 304 p.).
7. Título del resumen.
8. Traducción: de este título al castellano.
9. Descripción: del documento y de su tema.
10. Fuentes: empleadas en la elaboración del documento.
11. Contenidos: principales del documento.
12. Metodología: empleada en el estudio que dio origen al documento.
13. Conclusiones: principales a las que llegó en ese estudio. A veces se suprimen algunos de estos párrafos.
14. Redactor: iniciales del analista que hizo el resumen.

Anexo 1 "Modelo de ficha"

Productos de los RAE-PAR

Entre los años 1981 y 1988, el Paraguay aportó a la red 433 documentos los que son insertados en la Red REDUC como producto y diseminados a través del sistema.

Productos de REDUC

1. *Resúmenes analíticos en educación* (RAE)
   Presentación resumida del contenido de informes de investigación y de experiencias innovativas en el campo de la educación. Los resúmenes son preparados sobre la base de una pauta que tiene por objeto maximizar el uso del espacio en la inclusión de todos los contenidos del documento que se resume. Tiene una extensión aproximada de 300 a 400 palabras cada uno. Se los prepara en dos tipos de ediciones: regional, que incluye documentos de interés para todos los países; nacional, con un carácter más limitado a los contextos locales.
2. Microfichas
   Reproducción, en microfichas de 60 cuadros, del texto completo de los documentos.
3. Indices de *Resúmenes analíticos en educación* en América Latina y el Caribe
   Medio de reproducción manual de la información contenida en el fondo REDUC, mediante listados por autores y numeración de RAE.

4. Diskettes
   La información contenida en los índices está disponible en diskettes.
5. Análisis de información
   Síntesis, a partir del fondo documental de REDUC, acerca de un tema específico. Algunos de estos análisis de información tienen la forma de un "estado de arte" sobre temas de particular importancia para la toma de decisiones en material educacional en la región.
6. Otros productos
   Además de los mencionados, algunos centros REDUC han preparado otros productos:
   Bibliografías nacionales.
   Bibliografías de artículos de prensa.
   Informes de seminarios y otros eventos.

Bibliografías especializadas

La serie de bibliografías especializadas está orientada a prioridades en determinados momentos del país, la que claramente se puede deducir de las investigaciones y la bibliografía de la prensa, las que abarcan la década del 80 y acompañan el proceso de la investigación.

La estructura de dichas bibliografías se ajusta a las normas de REDUC.

Las seis bibliografías que se describen a continuación son: *Bibliografía sobre bilingüismo en América Latina* [4] (1982) con 532 citas, de las cuales 160 corresponden al Paraguay; *Bibliografía sobre educación, producción y trabajo* [5] (1986) con 340 citas; *Bibliografía sobre educación técnica y vocacional en el Paraguay* [6] (1987) con 114 referencias; *Bibliografía sobre alfabetización y educación de adultos en el Paraguay* [7] (1988) con 154 documentos; *Bibliografía sobre juventud y educación en el Paraguay* [8] (1989) con 162 artículos; y *Bibliografía sobre educación superior en el Paraguay* [9] (1989) con 104 datos, totalizando 1034 documentos sobre temas específicos de la educación.

Bibliografías sobre bilingüismo

La *Bibliografía sobre bilingüismo en América Latina* constituye un aporte inicial para el estudio del bilingüismo paraguayo. Esta fuente de consulta sirve básicamente a investigadores en el área de la sociolingüística—aunque no exhaustiva—de los que se ha hecho en el país sobre esta temática.

Debido a que muchas de las referencias provienen de fuentes secundarias y terciarias, hecho que da lugar a que algunas de ellas no posean las referencias bibliográficas completas. La alternativa fue, obviamente, eliminarlas o dejarlas con dichas limitaciones. Se decidió por esto último, dando una oportunidad al interés del lector para continuar la búsqueda de los datos faltantes.

Dicha bibliografía reune 532 citas bibliográficas de las que 160 corresponden al Paraguay y que se encuentran en la Colección del Centro Paraguayo de Documentación Social, sede de REDUC.

Esta bibliografía sobre bilingüismo está dividida en 37 temas que conforman la Red Latinoamericana de Información (REDUC). No obstante, fue necesario agregar 8 temas no comprendidos en las divisiones mencionadas, resultando así 45 secciones. Además contiene un índice de autores personales, corporativos y temático.

En relación a la presente bibliografía se desea destacar que el Paraguay es el país que más investigó sobre este tema. Hecho que puede ser apreciado en el documento *Estado de arte del bilingüismo en América Latina.*[10] También una bibliografía más actualizada se encuentra al final de ese libro.

Bibliografía sobre educación, producción y trabajo

La bibliografía que se presenta es el resultado de una exhaustiva revisión de las investigaciones y trabajos realizados sobre educación, producción y trabajo. Esta bibliografía confirma la importancia de esta temática en nuestro país. El objetivo principal de la misma es constituirse en una herramienta importante de trabajo para los investigadores, docentes, estudiantes, planificadores y responsables de la toma de decisiones en el campo educativo.

Para la elaboración de este trabajo se realizó una investigación bibliográfica en varios centros de documentación y educacionales dedicados a la enseñanza técnica y vocacional del país. No obstante, siempre existe la posibilidad de omitir datos no detectados, cuya tarea debe continuar.

Se identificaron unos 340 trabajos sobre la educación técnica vocacional. Estos datos fueron ordenados conforme a la norma de la Red REDUC. Además, se cuenta con índices de autores personales, corporativos, temáticos y un índice por niveles de educación.

Bibliografía sobre educación técnica y vocacional en el Paraguay

Para compilar la presente bibliografía se consultó bibliotecas relacionadas con la educación técnica y vocacional en el país. Pero, dicha temática es muy nueva en nuestro país y debido a ello se pudo reunir solamente 144 documentos. No obstante, este aporte se constituye un elemento valioso de consulta para la investigación en esta área que es de tanta importancia en la enseñanza actual.

Siendo un tema relativamente nuevo, se han incluido todo tipo de publicaciones, sin tomar en cuenta la selectividad. De esa manera, se constituye en punto de partida para el estudioso del tema. Esta bibliografía sigue las normas de la red y cuenta con sus respectivos índices de autores y temáticos.

Bibliografía sobre alfabetización y educación de adultos en el Paraguay

La presente bibliografía cubre un tema específico que es la alfabetización y educación de adultos en el Paraguay, campo donde la actividad educativa, tal como puede apreciarse por el conjunto de material ofrecido, ha sido creciente durante los últimos 10 años.

Con relación al tipo de material incluido, se incorporó a esta bibliografía, libros y artículos de publicaciones periódicas. El conjunto conforma un total de 104 citas en las bibliotecas y especialmente en el Departamento de Alfabetización y Educación de Adultos, y el Departamento de Curriculum del Ministerio de Educación y Culto, y en la colección de REDUC-PAR.

Como se puede apreciar que la producción bibliográfica es bastante escasa y dispersa. Es un tema que evidentemente merece más atención.

En lo que respecta a su presentación, la bibliografía está dispuesta en orden alfabético por autores. Además, cuenta con un índice por autores, temas y cronológico. Este último permite apreciar la marcada diferencia del tiempo.

Bibliografía sobre juventud y educación en el Paraguay

Con la presente bibliografía sobre juventud y educación en el Paraguay REDUC incorpora a su producción un tema de gran interés y resonancia, tanto en el plano académico como en el social y político de nuestro medio.

El Paraguay, en especial en los últimos años, se ha caracterizado por su baja producción en el campo de la investigación y divulgación del tema educativo. A pesar de esto, es notorio comprobar que la materia que nos ocupa adquiere relevancia sobre todo a partir de la década del 80.

Un hecho igualmente interesante de destacar es que existe incremento de trabajo sobre juventud y educación, se da primordialmente por vía de libros, artículos breves de revistas y periódicos. Tal circunstancia podría explicarse por diversos motivos; en primer lugar, porque esta problemática es preocupación central de los organismos de acción y promoción social que acompañan sus acciones dedicando una parte de sus esfuerzos a producir una literatura especializada tendiente por lo general a sistematizar y divulgar los trabajos que realizan. En otro orden, las limitaciones que sigue experimentando la actividad investigativa en general ayuda la producción en esta área sea aún limitada.

A pesar de estas restricciones cabe considerar este nuevo aporte de REDUC como un instrumento indispensable y valioso para acceder a este crucial aspecto de la realidad paraguaya.

Bibliografía sobre educación superior en el Paraguay

La presente bibliografía pretende dar cuenta de manera bastante completa de lo que se ha escrito en el país sobre "Educación Superior". El objeto central de este estudio es el de divulgar el conjunto de investigaciones, y reflexiones educativas relacionadas al tema, comprendido entre los años 1960 y 1989.

Se incluyen aquí 162 documentos, elegidos después de un análisis minucioso de las fuentes de consulta existentes en el país, entre las que podemos destacar el Centro de Documentación de la Institución y las Bibliotecas del Ministerio de Educación y Culto.

La metodología seguida para la elaboración y presentación de esta bibliografía consistió en realizar inicialmente una selección de libros y artículos de revistas. Luego se clasificaron los títulos por autores de acuerdo a un orden alfabético. El documento cuenta con un índice de autores, temático y cronológico.

La actual coyuntura que vive el país donde los temas de la educación en general y la superior en especial, están en plena discusión, hace que la bibliografía que hoy damos a conocer se constituya en un valioso aporte para todos aquellos que están trabajando, analizando y diagnosticando sobre la educación superior en el Paraguay.

Bibliografía de artículos de periódicos sobre educación paraguaya[11]

"La presente bibliografía comprende los artículos sobre educación aparecidos en los diarios de mayor circulación del país: *ABC Color* y *Hoy* en el año 1981".[9] La clasificación de la información se llevó a cabo en base a la lista de 17 temas comunes a los países que conforman la Red Latinoamericana de Información y Documentación en Educación (REDUC). Se agregó tres temas que se relacionan con la educación, tales como educación y política, área idiomática y actividades educativas.

Es importante destacar que a diferencia de otros trabajos similares, que se tomaron como referencia, éste incluye todas las informaciones referidas a educación que aparecieron en los diarios analizados, por lo tanto, no se excluyeron las noticias repetidas. Se utilizó esta metodología para dar lugar a un análisis cuantitativo de la información, de manera a conocer su frecuencia y por lo tanto, establecer el énfasis dado a determinadas noticias.

En definitiva, se considera que se puede establecer prioridades de la prensa escrita en materia de noticias educativas.

Otro punto interesante de resaltar es que tanto el diario *Hoy* tiene un suplemento escolar que aparece todos los martes, durante el período escolar (desde la tercera semana de febrero hasta la última semana de noviembre). El suplemento tiene un total de ocho páginas con informaciones e ilustraciones para los alumnos y maestros del sistema primario. La información sigue el esquema del programa educativa de todo el año escolar. Esta información no aparece detallada dentro de las bibliografías.

En cada uno de los temas se han ordenado los artículos por orden cronológico. De acuerdo a este orden han quedado numeradas las referencias incluidas en este trabajo. Finalmente se hizo la clasificación por niveles de sistema educativa y por autores.

Todas las series siguen las mismas normas establecidas por la REDUC, las que abarcan un período de 4 años con un total de 8.715 artículos, como sigue: *Bibliografía de artículos de periódicos sobre educación paraguaya*—año 1981 con 3.161; 1982 con 2.989; 1983 con 1.568 y la edición 1984 con 1.605 artículos, y un total de 8.715 artículos.[12]

El uso de la información en educación

Se destaca el uso de la información a partir de cualquier de los productos de REDUC. En este caso se evidencia un análisis de los editoriales sobre el "impacto de la educación en la prensa" realizado por los investigadores Mirtha M. Rivarola y Ernesto Schiefelbein.[13]

Bibliografías generales sobre educación

La segunda serie de bibliografías se refiere a bibliografías generales sobre educación. Se remonta a la creación del Centro Paraguayo de Documentación Social, desde el comienzo de la década del 70 hasta principios de los años 80, como programa para la investigación en ciencias sociales: *Estudios sociolingüísticos en el Paraguay*,[14]

1976 (Grazziella Corvalán); *Datos y estudios sobre educación en el Paraguay,* [15] 1976, y *Estudios y datos sobre educación técnica y agropecuaria en el Paraguay,* [16] 1978 (Oscar Ferraro); *Bibliografía sobre la educación en el Paraguay, período 1970–1981* [17] (Sofía Mareski), con 355 datos; *Bibliografía sobre educación en el Paraguay, período 1980–1985* [18] (Mabel Centurión), con 160 documentos, los que ya forman parte del programa REDUC.

Dichas bibliografías reseñan los documentos, libros y artículos de publicaciones periódicas. Además, se trata de una bibliografía anotada en resúmenes informativos e índices de autores, temáticos y cronológicos.

Usuarios de la información

Los usuarios de la información educativa REDUC son dos grupos: regulares y esporádicos. Los regulares son estudiantes universitarios en la rama de pedagogía, educación parvularia y psicología, para la elaboración de la tesis.

El otro grupo incluye estudiantes graduados que vienen desde Estados Unidos, Canadá, Brasil y Argentina, profesores universitarios y secundarios, y el sector gubernamental.

Conclusión

El verdadero papel que desempeña el conocimiento científico, producto de la investigación, consiste en descubrir caminos nuevos para las decisiones, en cuestionar las decisiones tomadas o bien en formular diagnósticos y propuestas. El objeto de reunir la información bibliográfica de las investigaciones en educación es detectar los documentos, procesarlos y ponerlos a disposición de responsables de la política educacional del país.

Recomendaciones

Considerando que la información será un componente cada vez más importante de las decisiones educativas, desde los gobernantes hasta los padres de familia en la orientación de la educación de sus hijos, se recomienda lo siguiente:

1. Que dicha información llegue hasta los hogares como llegan los periódicos y la televisión.
2. Que se establezca una estrecha relación entre la información y los usuarios para transformar y mejorar el sistema educativo.

3. Que la información sobre educación llegue a los educadores populares que trabajan fuera del ámbito universitario (maestros primarios y secundarios), a los directores de escuelas y supervisores, y a los alumnos, quienes necesitan de información diversa sobre orientación vocacional o solución de problemas de aprendizaje y rendimiento.

NOTAS

1. Luis Brahm y Gonzalo Gutiérrez, *La Red Latinoamericana de Educación y Documentación (REDUC): análisis de una experiencia* (Santiago de Chile, 1989), p. 4.

2. *Resúmenes analíticos en educación*, Resúmenes 1-50—, 1981— (Asunción: Centro Paraguayo de Estudios Sociológicos; Centro Paraguayo de Documentación Social; Red Latinoamericana de Información y Documentación en Educación, REDUC-PAR).

3. Sofía Mareski, *Funcionamiento de la Red Latinoamericana de Información y Documentación en Educación—REDUC-PAR* (Asunción: Centro de Documentación Social, 1982).

4. Grazziella Corvalán, Mabel Centurión, y María Julia Duarte, *Bibliografía sobre bilingüismo en América Latina* (Asunción: CPES-CPDS-REDUC-PAR, 1982).

5. Mabel Centurión y María Julia Duarte, *Bibliografía sobre educación, producción y trabajo* (Asunción: CPES-CPDS-REDUC-PAR, 1986).

6. María Julia Duarte y Mabel Centurión, *Bibliografía sobre educación técnica y vocacional en el Paraguay* (Asunción: CPES-CPDS-REDUC-PAR, 1987).

7. Idem, *Bibliografía sobre alfabetización y educación de adultos en el Paraguay* (Asunción: CPES-CPDS-REDUC-PAR, 1988).

8. Idem, *Bibliografía sobre juventud y educación en el Paraguay* (Asunción: CPES-CPDS-REDUC-PAR, 1989).

9. Idem, *Bibliografía sobre educación superior en el Paraguay* (Asunción: CPES-CPDS-REDUC-PAR, 1989).

10. Grazziella Corvalán, *Estado de arte del bilingüismo en América Latina*, Serie REDUC-PAR 5 (Asunción: CPES-CPDS-REDUC-PAR, 1985).

11. Mirtha M. Rivarola, *Bibliografía de artículos de periódicos sobre educación paraguaya* 1981:7.

12. Idem, *Bibliografía de artículos de periódicos sobre educación paraguaya, año 1981* (Asunción: Centro Paraguayo de Estudios Sociológicos, 1983–). Vols. 2–, compilados por Mabel Centurión y María Julia Duarte.

13. Mirtha M. Rivarola y Ernesto Schiefelbein, *Impacto de la educación en la prensa: un análisis de los editoriales*, Serie REDUC-PAR (Asunción: CPES-CPDS-REDUC-PAR, 1989).

14. Grazziella Corvalán, *Estudios sociolingüísticos en el Paraguay*, 2d ed. (Asunción: Centro Paraguayo de Estudios Sociológicos, Centro Paraguayo de Documentación Social, 1976).

15. Oscar Ferraro, *Datos y estudios sobre educación en el Paraguay* (Asunción: Centro Paraguayo de Estudios Sociológicos, 1976).

16. Idem, *Estudios y datos sobre educación técnica y agropecuaria en el Paraguay* (Asunción: Centro Paraguayo de Estudios Sociológicos, 1978).

17. Sofía Mareski, *Bibliografía sobre la educación en el Paraguay, período 1970–1981* (Asunción: CPES-CPDS-REDUC-PAR, 1982).

18. Mabel Centurión, *Bibliografía sobre educación en el Paraguay, período 1980–1985* (Asunción: CPES-CPDS-REDUC-PAR, 1985).

18. Un especialista en bibliotecología e información para los nuevos desafíos profesionales

Priscila Leni Olivares

Antecedentes del problema

Ya no es posible definir con claridad los límites de la acción propiamente profesional, ni cuál es el campo ocupacional específico, ni qué tipo de especialista se requerirá en el futuro, ni cómo formarlo. De lo que no cabe duda alguna es que las antiguas fronteras disciplinarias y profesionales han sido superadas.

Si a esto se le unen las deficiencias que ha tenido la formación tradicional del bibliotecario, en Chile ha adolecido de deficiencias, que han sido percibidas con el correr del tiempo y los nuevos desafíos profesionales. Lamentablemente, existe muy poca información documental al respecto; sin embargo, la alta demanda da perfeccionamiento solicitada al Colegio de Bibliotecarios de Chile es un indicador de cuáles son las áreas más deficitarias: gestión administrativa; desarrollo de la tecnología computacional de la información disponible y de sus usos potenciales; aplicación de criterios de costo-beneficio.

Los desafíos que enfrenta el bibliotecario

Estas áreas son una pequeña expresión de los diversos desafíos que el bibliotecario ha ido asumiendo en los últimos tiempos, más con buena voluntad, que con la preparación profesional adecuada. Estos cambios en el campo profesional van acompañados de una disminución de las ofertas de trabajo tradicionales para el bibliotecario y, paradojalmente, de una creciente oferta de trabajo no tradicional, propia de un "campo ocupacional emergente" (Páez 1989) en torno a la generación, uso y diseminación de la información.

Como este constituye un campo no tradicional para el bibliotecario, la mayoría de ellos no se encuentran preparados para ejercer idóneamente, lo que dificulta que accedan a esas fuentes laborales. Las

---

Nota del autor: La ponencia sintetiza el proyecto, elaborado por la autora, para la *Formación de un especialista de la información*, elaborado para la Universidad de Playa Ancha de Ciencias de la Educación (UPLACED), Valparaíso, Chile, en 1989.

nuevas exigencias profesionales le demandan una sólida formación en áreas como: gestión de servicios, adaptación y desarrollo de la tecnología, procesamiento analítico de la información, producción de bienes y servicios.

Sin embargo, el rápido crecimiento del conocimiento científico y el deslumbrante y acelerado desarrollo tecnológico dificultan precisar los conocimientos, destrezas y habilidades que debe dominar para su desempeño futuro, por cuanto la mayoría de los conocimientos que son válidos hoy, habrán cambiado mañana, al igual que las tecnologías que llegarán a usarse mañana ni siquiera son posibles de imaginar hoy.

La formación del bibliotecario

Los desafíos que debe resolver el nuevo profesional son tantos y tan variados que es indispensable que adquiera una sólida formación universitaria, que lo capacite para responder creativamente a las nuevas exigencias tecnológicas, educacionales, científicas y empresariales. La experiencia demuestra que una formación no universitaria adolece de muchos defectos, entre otros, la falta de una formación integral que permita relacionar distintas áreas del quehacer científico y tecnológico, así como de interactuar con profesionales de alta especialización.

La formación universitaria de pre-grado puede realizarse en cuatro años, período que parece adecuado para adquirir las destrezas, conocimientos y competencias mínimas de la profesión. Dicha formación inicial debe complementarse con la especialización que podrá ser la especialización futura, cualquiera sea el campo que le corresponda.

El post-título se caracteriza por un marcado carácter de especificidad técnica, gracias al cual el bibliotecario, u otro profesional, puede conocer o profundizar algún tema de especialización técnica, como por ejemplo, administración de bibliotecas escolares, gestión de bases de datos, o redes y sistemas de información documental.

El post-grado, por su parte, no sólo profundiza en la especialización técnica, sino que avanza hacia la re-invención de la disciplina, especialmente a partir de las nuevas relaciones que se generan debido al rápido desarrollo científico y tecnológico en el campo de la información. En este sentido, el post-grado es selectivo; es útil para aquellos que tendrán que darle una nueva dimensión a su trabajo profesional, posiblemente aún inexistente.

Al bibliotecario hay que enseñarle los contenidos básicos de la bibliotecología, al mismo tiempo que inculcarle la capacidad de cambio a partir de la inquietud por preguntar y responder educativamente. Ya pasó la época en que bastaba que el bibliotecario diera una respuesta simple y directa al usuario. Hoy, más que antes, para el bibliotecario es posible asumir plenamente su rol de educador del usuario, puesto que los cambios actuales en el universo de la información facilitan su tarea.

El bibliotecario como educador

Ahora bien, el bibliotecario al ocuparse de la educación de los usuarios asume su rol de educador. En ese caso, no debe limitarse a entregar información relacionada con el horario y normas de funcionamiento de la biblioteca, que ha sido lo habitual en los talleres de formación de usuarios, sino que debe preocuparse por entregar conocimientos que permitan al usuario acceder a la información deseada en forma rápida, acertada y en el menor tiempo y costo posible.

Como objetivo de un taller de usuario, el bibliotecario debe preocuparse de:

Motivar al usuario en la búsqueda personal de la información;

Entregar los conocimientos indispensables para que el usuario no se extravíe ni confunda en el complejo universo de la información;

Entregar antecedentes teóricos y empíricos que permitan definir criterios prácticos y funcionales de utilización de los recursos disponibles en la especialidad del usuario.

Por su parte, al finalizar un programa de educación de usuarios, el filósofo, el profesor, el teólogo, el técnico, el cientista social, el ingeniero o el abogado, será capaz de:

Conocer las posibilidades con que actualmente cuenta para acceder a las fuentes de información requeridas;

Discriminar entre las fuentes de información propias de su campo de especialización;

Ponderar y decidir sobre las distintas posibilidades de acceso, uso, tiempo y costo de cada una de las alternativas.

Sin embargo, la realización de los talleres de formación de usuarios no es simple, pues requiere que el bibliotecario seleccione y utilice metodologías que le permitan entregar los contenidos en una forma adecuada y efectiva, para lo cual requiere de conocimientos de pedagogía.[1]

Finalmente, el bibliotecario debe aprender a evaluar la calidad de su gestión por la independencia idónea que vaya logrando de parte de los usuarios que frecuentan su unidad de información. Esto es, en la medida que el usuario sepa acceder a las fuentes de la información, menos dependerá de la ayuda del bibliotecario para instrucciones menores y sólo lo acudirá a él para búsquedas complejas, que exijan un fuerte trabajo interdisciplinario, con lo que el estatus profesional se consolida, antes que debilita. Esto podríamos compararlo al rol del médico, que es mejor en la medida que sus clientes no enferman.

El usuario desde su disciplina

Si nos referimos a los usuarios en particular, nos sorprende la diversidad y complejidad que encierra. Un filósofo no es el mismo tipo de usuario que un ingeniero o un artista. Por lo que, es indispensable que el bibliotecario conozca a cada usuario en su disciplina. Por ejemplo, si observamos al filósofo, como usuario de la información, vemos que la tarea del usuario filósofo es la reflexión, para la cual recúrre al texto con parsimonia, nunca con rapidez ni ligereza; se entusiasma con los misterios que encierra el texto, mientras trabaja en su develamiento. El filósofo, a diferencia del científico, del ingeniero y del técnico que se encuentran presionados por la urgencia de estar al día en el último descubrimiento o creación tecnológica, tiene una urgencia distinta, razón por la cual la explosión de la información no lo afecta de la misma manera que a los otros.

Nuevos medios para la transferencia de la información y el conocimiento

Los nuevos medios de comunicación permiten al filósofo un acceso más amplio y universal a la reflexión filosófica contemporánea. Hoy, por ejemplo, es posible solicitar una bibliografía especializada por medio de una consulta en línea vía satélite, a diferentes bases de datos disponibles en distintas partes del mundo, con un costo relativamente bajo. Igualmente, es posible establecer una teleconferencia vía satélite con el filósofo o científico que se desee, para dialogar acerca del tema de estudio. No hace mucho tiempo, había que esperar resignadamente a que se publicara la obra; más aún, en algunos casos, incluso, había que esperar la traducción de ella.

Evidentemente que jamás será suficiente conversar con el autor, pues siempre será necesario leer y estudiar pausada y reflexivamente el pensamiento impreso, pero tampoco puede menospreciarse la importancia que tiene conversar directamente.

Ciertamente que esto sorprende y hace pensar que se trata de una utopía. No lo es. Asistimos a la creación de nuevos medios sobre los cuales construiremos las comunicaciones y todavía no hemos sido educados para usarlas y gozarlas.

Las unidades de información y sus servicios

En Chile, las bibliotecas y los centros de documentación paulatinamente van incorporando las nuevas tecnologías en la creación de nuevos servicios para los usuarios, dependiendo de los recursos económicos y profesionales disponibles.

Los actuales servicios de referencia, paulatinamente han ido transformando la tradicional biblioteca parroquial en una biblioteca universal. No obstante, el usuario actual en poco difiere de aquel de comienzo de siglo, en gran medida, porque los cambios en las bibliotecas no han ido acompañados de la adecuada educación del usuario, que ha quedado a la zaga en este proceso innovador. Hay que educar al usuario sin más demora, de tal modo que los nuevos usuarios sean capaces de utilizar las nuevas tecnologías que se van creando y para lograrlo debemos formarnos los bibliotecarios, los especialistas en información obviamente.

El campo de la información

En estos últimos años asistimos a una verdadera revolución en el campo de la información y comunicación, generando cambios que afectan profundamente la actitud del intelectual contemporáneo. Si bien los libros continúan yaciendo en los estantes de una biblioteca, no sucede igual con mucha información puntual, incluso efímera, que fluye constantemente de y hacia los centros de investigación y desarrollo tecnológico.

Por estos desafíos ha sido necesario re-estudiar los curricula vigentes y readecuarlos a las nuevas exigencias, incorporando la identificación de los usuarios y de los generadores de información, los nuevos soportes de información, las nuevas tecnologías computacionales, los nuevos espacios que ofrecen las instituciones como empresas, industrias, bancos y otros que consideran imprescindible para ellos, la información como un insumo y un producto de mayor importancia en estos tiempos y que se mantendrá hasta el próximo siglo.

Volvamos a nuestra reflexión en el punto en que nos referíamos a la importancia de formarnos para responder como educador frente al usuario. Para que una respuesta sea educativa debe, por una parte, satisfacer alguna inquietud y, por otra, ser capaz de generar nuevas preguntas, para lo cual, el bibliotecario no puede limitarse a dar sólo una respuesta específica, sino que debe tener la formación que le permita sugerir al usuario nuevas relaciones científicas, técnicas, empresariales, o del tipo que sea, de tal modo que recodifique la información desde los códigos de su propia disciplina.

Los docentes

La idoneidad de los bibliotecarios dependerá, en gran medida, de la formación académica y experiencia bibliotecaria de los docentes que, se espera, realicen investigaciones interdisciplinarias que nutran su docencia, dinamizándola con los aportes de las otras disciplinas científicas y tecnológicas. De este modo, los docentes podrán estar en condiciones de innovar en el desarrollo de nuevas especialidades que se requiere de acuerdo a las circunstancias y exigencias científicas, técnicas, empresariales y profesionales.

Por ejemplo, el bibliotecario puede constituirse en un auxilio del filósofo, en su compromiso de pensar la historia; puede ayudarle a satisfacer la necesidad de conocer qué está sucediendo en el mundo de la investigación filosófica, básica y aplicada, así como en el arte y realidad social. Lo que hoy se descubre e inventa es tan apasionante como sorprendente y, a la vez, un real desafío al pensamiento y la reflexión filosófica. Por ejemplo, la clonación es una posibilidad técnica, la fertilización in vitro una realidad, al igual que la capacidad de aniquilamiento de la humanidad.

Del mismo modo que los otros intelectuales, el filósofo ha comenzado a escribir artículos para congresos y conferencias, monografías para simposios, a la vez que publica en revistas especializadas. Por otra parte, ya no alcanza a estar al día sin la lectura de estas publicaciones, consideradas menores hasta hace poco tiempo atrás y fundamentales para cualquier investigación filosófica.

Se hace urgente para el filósofo, como para otros usuarios, desarrollar la capacidad de acceder a las fuentes de información en una forma expedita, para lo cual requiere actuar interdisciplinariamente con el especialista en información, de modo de aprovechar adecuadamente los recursos técnicos disponibles. Los problemas del mundo contemporáneo demandan del filósofo una urgencia no antes conocida. Tampoco el acceso al conocimiento puede continuar igual.

Otra consecuencia adicional, pero no por ello menos importante, será la aceptación del bibliotecario—no la del profesor en un Escuela de Bibliotecología—como un académico en el mundo universitario chileno y no sólo como un invitado ocasional a algunas reuniones académicas. Hoy en muchas universidades, el bibliotecario es considerado como un para-académico, sin mayor ingerencia en el que-hacer universitario.

Experiencias chilenas

A partir de la experiencia del programa de formación de bibliotecólogos de la Carrera de Bibliotecología de la Universidad de

Playa Ancha de Ciencias de la Educación (UPLACED), de Valparaíso y, el de la Licenciatura en Transferencia de la Información Documental, que se imparte en la Universidad de la Frontera (UFRO), Temuco, analizaré el modo como han sido formalizados en los respectivos curricula, uno en pre-grado y el otro en post-grado,[2] los diferentes desafíos que tiene el nuevo profesional de la información.

Ambos programas coinciden en torno a los nuevos desafíos que enfrentan los profesionales de la información y en el tratamiento curricular que hacen de ellos, al enfatizar el rol como recurso e insumo importante que la información desempeña hoy día en el desarrollo de la ciencia, la tecnología y la sociedad.

Carrera de Bibliotecología
Universidad de Playa Ancha de Ciencias de la Educación

Históricamente, el Programa de la Carrera de Bibliotecología de la UPLACED, el único de pre-grado que se imparte a nivel universitario, se centraba por completo en las competencias, habilidades y conocimientos para dirigir bibliotecas tradicionales sin asumir la formación relacionada con los sistemas de información, lo que llevó a plantear su reformulación.

Al transformar el currículum se ha pretendido innovar creando un nuevo perfil del profesional de la información, capaz de responder a los requerimientos y exigencias actuales, tanto de los usuarios como de los generadores de información en sus distintos niveles y áreas de desarrollo, a partir del siguiente diagnóstico:

a. En términos operativos, se define bibliotecología como el área relacionada con el flujo de información y diseminación. Esta definición pone intencionalmente el acento en la información, antes que en las bibliotecas, como ha sido lo habitual.

b. En general, los currícula de formación se han centrado en la operación de las bibliotecas, produciendo una identificación entre el bibliotecario y la institución "biblioteca", que no es más que una reducción de su rol profesional.

c. La constante creación de instituciones donde la información constituya un recurso o insumo importante. En ellas, no sólo el concepto de biblioteca está ausente, sino también el mismo bibliotecario—entendido como el profesional que opera en el dominio de la información—, pues sus funciones son realizadas por otros profesionales.

d. En consecuencia, el currículum debe propender a que los profesionales del área de la información posean la capacidad de desempeñarse en esos dominios, con propiedad y eficacia.

e. En el diseño del currículum se ha considerado deseable que el estudiante entienda, utilice y comprenda el desarrollo de la tecnología vinculada con el desarrollo de la información, particularmente en las áreas de la computación y telecomunicaciones.

No obstante lo anterior, es importante explicar que la tecnología no se ha incorporado al currículum como un fin en sí misma. Se la considera un medio—hoy día indispensable—para obtener los objetivos que se persiguen y, en consecuencia, no acoge la tecnología como un tema aislado, sino que se visualiza integrado a los contenidos de los temas básicos de la "bibliotecología", de modo de asegurar que tanto el estudio, comprensión y eventual utilización de la tecnología esté siempre en contexto.

Perfil de bibliotecario

Este profesional podrá desarrollar sus funciones en diferentes organizaciones para las cuales la información constituye un insumo importante. Además este profesional:

1. Podrá administrar unidades de información, sean bibliotecas, centros de información o centros de documentación;
2. Estará en condiciones de seleccionar y aplicar la tecnología de comunicaciones y computacional disponible. Esto implica, en particular, la capacidad de discriminar si se requiere determinada aplicación y escoger de acuerdo a criterios de costo-beneficio;
3. Poseerá un vasto conocimiento de las fuentes de información en sus distintos formatos (impresos, magnéticos u ópticos);
4. Conocerá, a nivel operativo, los servicios de información nacionales e internacionales disponible parar acceder en línea a sus bases de datos (RENIB, DIALOG, BRS, ORBIT, etc.);
5. Organizará el material bibliográfico de acuerdo a normas nacionales e internacionales vigentes;
6. Administrará bases de datos institucionales;
7. Interactuará eficazmente con distintos profesionales para identificar y satisfacer sus necesidades de información;
8. Poseerá al conocimiento necesario para interactuar con ingenieros y analistas en la planificación y desarrollo de proyectos de automatización de diversas funciones de las unidades de información. También estará capacitado para

participar, junto a arquitectos y planificadores, en proyectos de construcción o readecuación del espacio físico de las unidades de información.

En suma, este profesional:

1. Poseerá la preparación necesaria para mantenerse actualizado en el desarrollo tecnológico en el área de la información;
2. Podrá aplicar la tecnología, disponible en Chile, adecuada a las necesidades de información de sus usuarios de acuerdo a criterios de costo-beneficio;
3. Poseerá una adecuada comprensión del rol de la información en el desarrollo socio-económico del país.

Campo ocupacional

Dado que en el perfil previsto, además de la formación tradicional del bibliotecario, se pone énfasis en el adecuado manejo de la información en la sociedad contemporánea, al campo también tradicional de las bibliotecas se agregan otras organizaciones para las cuales la información representa un insumo importante para el éxito de su gestión. Esto último es particularmente relevante para empresas privadas que se mueven en un ambiente competitivo y que, por lo tanto, el adecuado manejo de todas las variables claves, entre ellas, la información, determinará la posición de esa organización en el mercado en el cual compite. Esta necesidad, sin embargo, no es algo comúnmente identificado como un área de actividad especializada en las empresas. Por otra parte, el bibliotecario "tradicional" no está, en general, en condiciones de abrir este campo y desarrollarlo con efectividad.

Objetivos de las líneas curriculares

1. *Naturaleza de la información*
   Comprender el desarrollo y fundamentos teóricos del fenómeno de la información y su valor como recurso, de modo de estar capacitado para participar en la elaboración de las normas y políticas que regulen su inserción en la sociedad.
2. *Gestión administrativa*
   Generar competencia en la utilización de las técnicas modernas de administración para el manejo eficiente de las unidades de información. Esto implica estar en condiciones de establecer un diseño organizacional que integre los distintos componentes de una unidad de información y determinar los mecanismos óptimos de gestión y control.

3. *Organización de la información*
   Proveer conocimientos sobre la teoría y aplicación de los sistemas y normas utilizados en el procesamiento de la información.
4. *Servicios de información*
   Proveer las herramientas para el diseño, implementación y evaluación de servicios de una unidad de información.
5. *Tecnología de la información*
   Conocer e identificar la dinámica de desarrollo de la tecnología de información, para su aplicación en diferentes tipos de unidades de información. Proveer los conocimientos operacionales fundamentales para la integración armónica de dicha tecnología a estas unidades, con el propósito de optimizar su funcionamiento.
6. *Area complementaria*

Licenciatura en Transferencia de la Información Documental
Universidad de la Frontera

Este programa, iniciado en enero de 1990, privilegia el perfeccionamiento y actualización de los conocimientos de bibliotecólogos y documentalistas en ejercicio, sin ser excluyente de otros profesionales que se desempeñan en el campo de la información. El programa está diseñado de acuerdo a una modalidad educacional que combina la docencia presencial con el trabajo tutorial a distancia, dando lugar a una actividad académica directa e indirecta.[3]

El plan está constituido por cuatro áreas temáticas:

1. Lenguaje y comunicación de información;
2. Información y sociedad;
3. Tecnología de la información;
4. Gestión de la información.

Una innovación importante de este programa se refiere a la importancia otorgada a la transculturalidad propia de la zona. La ubicación de la Universidad de la Frontera en el centro de la cultura mapuche,[4] Región de la Araucanía, y lugar de fuerte inmigración europea, le confiere un carácter peculiar.

Objetivos de la licenciatura (Feliú 1989a)

1. Desarrollar en profesionales de información la capacidad para fundar teóricamente su campo de estudio permitiéndole adquirir competencia académica;
2. Capacitar al bibliotecólogo para interactuar con grupos interdisciplinarios, contribuyendo al desarrollo del sector de la información, a través de la formación de profesionales académicos e investigadores en el campo;
3. Contribuir al perfeccionamiento y actualización de conocimientos del bibliotecólogo y del profesional de la información, permitiéndole concebir la biblioteca, el centro de documentación y, en general, toda unidad de información como un sistema que interactúa con otras unidades y sistemas de información nacionales, regionales e internacionales;
4. Desarrollar en el profesional de información las habilidades necesarias para promover el concepto de información como un recurso nacional que se genera en los países y poner a disposición de quienes contribuyen a su desarrollo económico, social y cultural;
5. Desarrollar en el profesional de información el juicio crítico que le permita seleccionar y estimular el uso de la información necesaria en los distintos entornos laborales, facilitando la transferencia de información directamente, o a través de la organización de las unidades de información, el diseño de sistemas o la participación en redes de información.

En atención a los objetivos del programa y a la relación que guarden estos objetivos con los nuevos desafíos que enfrentan el profesional de la información, pensamos que debe ser capaz de:

1. Conocer, seleccionar y manejar las nuevas tecnologías;
2. Gestionar, planificar, organizar y administrar la transferencia de la información sobre la base de la aplicación eficiente de la tecnología disponible;
3. Transformar el ámbito de trabajo en virtud de la incorporación de nuevos desarrollos teóricos, enfoques y tecnologías;
4. Planificar y diseñar sistemas que operan con distintos formatos que se alejan de los convencionales como son los soportes magnéticos y ópticos;
5. Transformar las fuentes en recursos de información de tal modo que sustenten el proceso de transferencia de conocimientos y de información;

6. Utilizar los recursos para resolver los problemas de información del usuario;
7. Discriminar entre los usuarios, los distribuidores primarios (editores de todo tipo) y los distribuidores secundarios (unidades, redes y sistemas de información);
8. Generar metodologías que perfeccionen la educación de usuarios de acuerdo a sus necesidades de información.

Perfil del egresado

Considerando que el programa de licenciatura se entrega a profesionales, cuyo principal desempeño se desarrolla en el campo de la información, y que la esencia de su formación los ha conducido al dominio de técnicas y metodologías concretas, el egresado al finalizar el programa (Feliú 1989a) deberá poseer un:

1. Actitud crítica, asertiva y constructiva en relación con la gestión de los componentes del ciclo de transferencia de información documental;
2. Conocimiento de la naturaleza, estructura, funciones y dinámica que las unidades, redes o sistemas de información deben cumplir para facilitar el proceso de transferencia;
3. Conocimiento de la problemática de la interculturalidad y capacidad para crear las condiciones en las que la transferencia de información documental contribuya a la resolución de situaciones de desarrollo e integración de grupos sociales específicos;
4. Conocimiento de las tecnologías de información para su selección, aplicación y consiguiente optimización de los servicios de información;
5. Conocimiento y capacidad para supervisar la coordinación y organización de recursos de información requeridos por las comunidades de usuarios a las que sirve;
6. Conocimiento de los entornos políticos, sociales y económicos de los servicios de información—marcos nacionales, regionales e internacionales de interacción—para planificar nuevos servicios y desarrollar proyectos cooperativos;
7. Conocimiento de las metodologías de investigación y capacidad de investigar los mejores cursos de acción que optimicen los recursos existentes, a la vez que esté en condiciones de vincularse a otros proyectos de investigación y de desarrollo multidisciplinarios.

Estructura del programa

El programa se desarrolla a partir de cuatro áreas temáticas relacionadas con los componentes del ciclo de transferencia de conocimientos e información documental.

1. *Lenguaje y comunicación de la información*
   Esta área entrega conocimientos y comprensión acerca del rol de la lingüística y semiótica como base del proceso de producción y comunicación de conocimientos e información. La bibliotecología y la transferencia de la información documental basan en el lenguaje y en su manifestación escrita u oral, gran parte de sus herramientas de análisis, almacenamiento y recuperación de información.

2. *Información y sociedad*
   En esta área se entregan conocimientos y comprensión acerca del impacto de la información, su organización y difusión en la sociedad, especialmente como base de la educación, de la investigación científica y de la integración de los grupos étnicos específicos al desarrollo económico y social del país. Lo que también puede ser válido, con todas las salvedades y modificaciones del caso, para los distintos grupos sociales en el seno de la sociedad chilena.

   En esta área deben desarrollarse estudios y programas de investigación sobre las necesidades que originan los procesos de transculturación en las características y comportamiento de los distintos tipos de usuarios, especializados generales.

3. *Tecnología de la información*
   En esta área se entrega conocimientos y comprensión acerca de las aplicaciones de los programas y equipos computacionales y de telecomunicaciones, medios audiovisuales, tecnología micrográfica, y otros, al tratamiento de los procesos y componentes que intervienen la transferencia de información.

4. *Gestión de la información*
   En este caso, el área entrega conocimiento y comprensión acerca de la administración de los recursos y componentes del ciclo de transferencia del conocimiento y de la información.

NOTAS

1. Lo dicho se materializa en los talleres de formación de usuario que he diseñado y conducido en el Sistema de Bibliotecas de la Pontificia Universidad Católica de Chile/ Temuco, en el Sistema de Bibliotecas de la UPLACED, y en la Universidad de la Frontera (UFRO), como actividad del Proyecto OEA-UFRO, dirigido a académicos de las universidades locales.

2. La profesión de bibliotecólogo en Chile demora 4 años de cursos, más la práctica profesional y el seminario de tesis, ambos de un semestre consecutivo de duración, lo que da 5 años de estudio. La licenciatura se obtiene después de 2 años de estudio y la elaboración de una tesis, posteriores a haber cursado y aprobado al menos 4 años de estudios universitarios y haber obtenido el título profesional.

3. Esta modalidad que intercala períodos presenciales y a distancia, a través de tutorías personalizadas, permite la participación de profesionales que no cuentan con permiso para ausentarse de su trabajo por el tiempo que dure la licenciatura. Sin duda, que la modalidad implica un alto compromiso de los participantes para estudiar y elaborar los trabajos durante la fase "a distancia", que se complementa con encuentros entre los profesores y los alumnos en otras sedes del país, cercanas a las ciudades de residencia de los participantes.

4. Cabe hacer notar que en los últimos años se acordaron los criterios que permitieron uniformar el alfabeto del *mapudungum*, lengua del mapuche, por lo que actualmente se asiste a un creciente proceso de escritura en dicha lengua.

BIBLIOGRAFIA CONSULTADA

Calvo, Carlos

1989a "De la utopía a la eutopía." *El Canelo de Nos*, 4, no. 15, 29-33.

1989b ". . . esa es una canción que no enseñe." *Revista Temas de Educación*, no. 1 y 2, 3-18.

Feliú, Ximena

1989a *Programa de Licenciatura en Transferencia de la Información Documental.* Temuco: UFRO.

1989b "Formación y perfeccionamiento del bibliotecario para el pleno aprovechamiento de las nuevas tecnologías." Jornadas Bibliotecarios. *Las nuevas bibliotecarios: su impacto en las bibliotecas y los bibliotecarios.* Santiago: Colegio de Bibliotecarios de Chile, A.G.

Ferreiro, Soledad

1989 "Reflexiones de los bibliotecarios ante las nuevas tecnologías." Jornadas Bibliotecarias. *Las nuevas tecnologías: su impacto en las bibliotecas y los bibliotecarios.* Santiago: Colegio de Bibliotecarios de Chile, A.G.

Fleming, Lucy

1989 *Informe carrera de bibliotecología.* Santiago.

Jornadas Bibliotecarias

1989 *Las nuevas tecnologías: su impacto en las bibliotecas y los bibliotecarios.* Santiago: Colegio de Bibliotecarios de Chile, A.G.

Leni, Priscila

1989 "Acceso y utilización de las fuentes de información especializadas en filosofía." Tesis para optar al grado de Profesor de Estado con mención en Filosofía. Valparaíso: UPLACED.

Páez, Iraset

1989 *Mercado informacional emergente y perfiles de profesionalización para América Latina.* Caracas.

19. La información bibliográfica argentina

Iris Rossi

El análisis del estado actual de la información bibliográfica en la República Argentina, muestra una realidad que no se concilia con el nivel de las actividades desarrolladas en otras áreas como son las de la ciencia, la tecnología y la bibliotecología en particular.

Tres científicos argentinos fueron galardonados con el premio Nobel, lo cual hace resaltar el desarrollo de la investigación científica en el país. Este nivel alcanzado demanda una buena política nacional de información en lo científico-tecnológico y, en general, en todo lo que hace a la cultura de un país.

En cuanto a la situación de la bibliotecología Argentina, es bien conocido el rol preponderante que les cupo a nuestros bibliotecarios en América Latina, especialmente a algunos de la denominada "década del 40" y a otros de generaciones posteriores. Bibliotecarios argentinos contribuyeron al desarrollo profesional en varios países del continente sudamericano, y esos países se encuentran hoy a la vanguardia en el campo de la información bibliográfica porque supieron capitalizar los conocimientos y ponerlos al servicio de la comunidad. Pero esto no habría sido posible si esas iniciativas y esos proyectos no hubiesen contado con un seguro apoyo político que garantizara su desarrollo en cada uno de esos países.

Es comprensible que la política informática científica y tecnológica haya sido impulsada en algunas naciones de América Latina ya que contaron con la asistencia técnico-financiera de organismos internacionales. Fueron varios los estados miembros que supieron beneficiarse con esta asistencia, pero hubo otros que no tuvieron esa visión de futuro y no supieron justipreciar lo que representa la información para el progreso, quedando, como la Argentina, en un estado de postergación del que procuran salir a fuerza de voluntad y empeño. La crítica situación económica obliga a establecer prioridades para cubrir requerimientos de orden social. Se levantan entonces barreras y se establecen limitaciones que impiden organizar servicios de información eficientes, aún cuando es sabido que a través de la información se accede al conocimiento que lleva a mejorar la calidad de vida del hombre y por ende de la sociedad. A pesar de estas contrariedades, en el transcurso del tiempo y en determinadas circunstancias, vieron la luz varios trabajos bibliográficos que contribuyeron a posibilitar, en su momento, un buen servicio de información. Los mismos, que se iniciaron con fervientes anhelos de continuidad y permanencia, tuvieron, en muchos casos, una vida efímera. Si bien es cierto que el factor político o el factor económico gravitaban en la obra emprendida, también es cierto que, a veces, los proyectos carecían de buenos fundamentos, lo cual no favoreció su prosecución. Muchos esfuerzos argentinos quedaron así en intentos, sin llegar a concretarse.

Si se recorre en forma panorámica la actividad bibliográfica, remontándose al siglo pasado, se advierte la falta de continuidad: obras truncas o ediciones sin actualizar. Esto ocurrió tanto en el área oficial como en el área privada. En los niveles de decisión, la trascendencia de la bibliografía nunca fue comprendida. Y no es posible atribuir tal actitud a la ignorancia, porque es público y notorio que todos, sin excepción, debemos requerir su auxilio y, por lo tanto, no es difícil ni extraño apreciar sus bondades y saber de su utilidad. Sin embargo, pese a lo que se supone evidente, no siempre se tiene en cuenta lo que interesa a la cultura de la nación. Un ejemplo para ilustrar este hecho: quienes estamos en la actividad bibliográfica conocemos muy bien la riqueza y el valor de la colección de la biblioteca que perteneciera al investigador, bibliófilo y bibliográfico Pedro de Angelis. Cuando ésta se puesto a la venta, el gobierno de la República Argentina no supo apreciarla y retenerla y así fue cómo la adquirió un país vecino. Hoy esa importante colección se encuentra en la Biblioteca Nacional de Río de Janeiro.

En esta oportunidad no se hará referencia detallada de las bibliografías que se han producido en la Argentina, en distintas épocas y sobre temas diversos. De las del siglo pasado que son un orgullo para el país por la laboriosidad de aquellos eruditos, pioneros en este quehacer; tampoco de los trabajos posteriores, pues se considera que todo ello pertenece ya a la historia de la bibliografía Argentina y la misma fue considerada ya en otros estudios precedentes, como los de Josefa Emilia Sabor, Hebe Pauliello de Chocholous, Hans Gravenhorst, Roberto Couture de Troismonts y la autora de este trabajo.

Existen también en el país compilaciones bibliográficas individuales que responden, por lo general, a temas humanísticos (literatura, arte, etc.). Son ediciones de entidades privadas.

Pero sí corresponde hacer ahora especial referencia del repertorio que marcó una etapa en la bibliografía argentina, la *Bibliografía argentina de artes y letras* (*BADAL*), editada por el Fondo Nacional de las Artes. Bibliografía nacional, especializada, selectiva, corriente, con rigor técnico y exactitud en la información y, además, de periodicidad regular. En 1971, Irene Zimmerman dice: "... es al presente la mejor fuente de información a considerar en bibliografía corriente en la Argentina". Fue fundada y dirigida por un bibliotecario e investigador argentino de prestigio internacional, el doctor Augusto Raúl Cortazar, siendo Director del Fondo Nacional de las Artes. El primer número se editó en 1959 y el último corresponde al N°. 52, en 1974. La publicación quedó trunca a la muerte de quien fuera su fundador. Este valioso repertorio no sólo fue muy apreciado en el país, sino que alcanzó también a destacarse por su jerarquía en el exterior y fue ampliamente reconocido, en la Argentina y en el extranjero, por quienes fueron sus usuarios. La falta de continuidad de la *BADAL* hace suponer que esta empresa requería, además de mucha iniciativa, una especial creatividad y un gran esfuerzo para ser mantenida en el nivel donde la ubicó su fundador.

La Argentina cuenta, además, con dos bibliografías de bibliografías: *Bibliografía de bibliografías argentinas*, de Narciso Binayán (1919) y *Bibliografía de bibliografías argentinas: 1870–1970*, de Abel Rodolfo Geoghegan, edición preliminar, 1970. La Biblioteca Central de la Universidad Nacional de Mar del Plata se ha comprometido a actualizar esta obra.

También es bueno destacar en esta ocasión las actividades de investigación bibliográfica que lleva a cabo la Sociedad Argentina de Bibliografía (SAB), creada en 1987. Tiene su sede en la Biblioteca Central de la Universidad Nacional de Mar del Plata y organiza reuniones anuales a nivel nacional.

Los servicios de información en el país

La incorporación y el aprovechamiento de la electrónica para almacenar y obtener productos de información han iniciado una etapa próspera, que sería deseable no fuera interrumpida en el futuro. Pero es prudente tener en cuenta lo imprescindible de una estructura orgánica apoyada en sólida base, con una planificación cuyos objetivos estén bien definidos, que sea coherente en su accionar y que responda a intereses comunes y no sectoriales. Los servicios de información, es sabido, deben ser el resultado de trabajos en cooperación.

Hoy existe una gran demanda de información, especialmente en los campos de la ciencia y de la tecnología y hacia ella se encaminan la mayoría de los proyectos que nacen. Desde hace unos años, ya están funcionando redes, no sólo integradas a nivel nacional, sino también a nivel regional y/o internacional. La suma total de las mismas constituirán el Sistema Nacional de Información, de ahí la notoria conveniencia de que no existan limitaciones, para evitar lagunas imposibles de cubrir después. La apertura debe ser lo más amplia posible.

La necesidad de contar con fuentes que faciliten el acceso a la información ha llevado a una generación de bibliotecarios a buscar soluciones que les ayuden a resolver los problemas que cotidianamente les ocasiona la falta de servicios eficientes para satisfacer las demandas. Han sabido enfrentar la situación, aunando esfuerzos y voluntades con el fin de alcanzar objetivos comunes en el campo de la información. Cada uno actúa en su área temática, trabaja su propio producto y los aporta para beneficio de todos. Así es cómo, con verdadera dedicación y entusiasmo, se está logrando la efectividad del Programa de Información y Comunicación Científico-Tecnológica (PNNICCYT).

El PNNICCYT fue creado por Resolución N° 80/89 de la Secretaría de Ciencia y Tecnología que depende de la Presidencia de la Nación. Radica en el ámbito de la Subsecretaría de Informática y Desarrollo. La propuesta de un "Perfil del Sistema Nacional de Información" fue elaborada por los especialistas en Ciencias de la Información (bibliotecarios, archiveros, museólogos e informáticos) reunidos en dos Seminarios organizados por la Universidad de Buenos Aires (UBA) y el Consejo Nacional de Ciencia y Tecnología (CONICET) durante diciembre de 1987 y octubre de 1988. Estos Seminarios fueron auspiciados por la UNESCO. La propuesta que resultó de los mismos y que se refiere a la creación del Sistema Nacional de Información, fue entregada en su oportunidad a las autoridades del CONICET, con especial mandato de llevarla a cabo, compromiso que fue aceptado. Con el cambio de autoridades gubernamentales, en julio de 1989, se produjo también un cambio de estructura. La Secretaría de Ciencia y Tecnología se hizo cargo del mencionado mandato y, mediante una continuidad jurídica, colocó la propuesta en el marco del PNNICCYT, donde actualmente se está trabajando. La acción operativa de este Programa está plenamente en actividad y se espera que en un corto plazo brinde sus resultados. El Sistema está integrado por varias redes, especialmente en el área científico-tecnológica y no descuida otras áreas como son las de la Biblioteca Nacional, las bibliotecas públicas u otras.

En el Anexo se detallan algunos de los servicios de información existentes en la Argentina.

La Bibliografía Nacional Argentina

El problema de la Bibliografía Nacional ya fue analizado en trabajos anteriores. En esta oportunidad se hará referencia únicamente a los motivos por los cuales los planes para su elaboración nunca pudieron concretarse, a pesar de tener objetivos muy precisos.

La Biblioteca Nacional es la encargada de producir la Bibliografía Argentina. En el año 1971, por decreto–ley N° 727, se establece que debe editar dicho Repertorio. En esa ocasión, durante la gestión de Jorge Luis Borges, se elaboró el primer Plan. En 1974, siendo Vicente D. Sierra Director de la Biblioteca, se retomó la iniciativa. En 1976, con José Edmundo Clemente a cargo de la Institución, se actualizó nuevamente el Plan.

En las tres oportunidades mencionadas se gestionó, ante las autoridades de la Secretaría de Cultura de la Nación, la adjudicación de una partida presupuestaria para financiar solamente la publicación del primer número de la Bibliografía, pues en el Plan se había previsto la autofinanciación de la misma, a los efectos de garantizar su continuidad y evitar su dependencia de los fondos estatales. La partida presupuestaria nunca fue otorgada.

Entre los proyectos de las actuales autoridades de la Biblioteca Nacional, y aún entre los prioritarios, figura este insustituible Repertorio Bibliográfico. Es alentador y promisorio el hecho de que se tenga conciencia de su inapreciable valor. El país no puede continuar sin su Bibliografía Nacional, más aún cuando en un futuro próximo se establecerá el Sistema Nacional de Información. Ella será la que aporte el mayor caudal de datos al mismo.

Desde 1971, al elaborarse el primer Plan, la Biblioteca Nacional comenzó a preparar y a organizar el registro de datos destinados a la Bibliografía Retrospectiva. Pero cuando se inicie la publicación, lo hará con la Bibliografía Nacional en curso o corriente. A principios de 1980, la Biblioteca Nacional adoptó las últimas directivas internacionales para el registro de datos.

La legislación argentina sobre el depósito legal

Teniendo en cuenta que el depósito legal es la principal fuente de alimentación para una bibliografía nacional, la legislación respectiva en la República Argentina es deficiente, desde sus comienzos.

La ley N° 9.510 del 10 de octubre de 1914 modificó parcialmente la anterior ley, N° 7.092, sobre propiedad literaria y artística. La citada ley reformó el artículo 7°, reglamentándose el depósito que debían cumplir los impresores o editores y estableció las correspondientes sanciones por incumplimiento de esa obligación legal. Luego, por tres decretos que aparecieron en año 1931, se encomendó a la Biblioteca Nacional el registro y la administración del depósito legal de obras inéditas y éditas.

En 1933, se sanciona y promulga la ley Nº 11.723 que trata sobre el "Régimen legal de la propiedad intelectual". En ella se contempla más ampliamente lo que hace al depósito legal, tanto de trabajos monográficos como de publicaciones periódicas y otras formas de impresos.

Con fecha 3 de mayo de 1934, mediante el decreto Nº 41.233, se reglamenta la ley Nº 11.723. En su artículo 1º, dice: ". . . el Registro Nacional de la Propiedad Intelectual, que funcionará provisoriamente en la Biblioteca Nacional, se hará cargo de los libros de registro, correspondencia, ficheros y demás efectos de la Oficina del Depósito Legal". En el artículo 2º, dice: "Hasta tanto no se establezca el personal correspondiente, el Director de la Biblioteca Nacional desempeñará las funciones de Director del Registro de Propiedad Intelectual". En un plazo casi inmediato, el mencionado Registro Nacional sale del área de la Biblioteca Nacional y pasa a funcionar directamente en el entonces Ministerio de Justicia e Instrucción Pública de la Nación. El 22 de febrero de 1972, por decreto Nº 984, se denomina Dirección Nacional del Derecho de Autor y es un organismo centralizado de la Subsecretaría de Justicia de la Nación. Tiene a su cargo la aplicación de la ley Nº 11.723, aspectos registrales y administrativos. En 1986, dicha Dirección Nacional estableció convenios con entidades civiles a fin de delegar determinadas funciones que le son inherentes. Así es cómo la Sociedad Argentina de Escritores (SADE) se ocupa del registro de las obras inéditas y su depósito; la Cámara Argentina del Libro (CAL), de las obras éditas; la Asociación de Editores de Revistas, de las publicaciones periódicas y seriadas, y la Cámara Argentina de Productores e Industriales de Fonogramas (CAPIF), de todo lo relacionado con fonogramas y música. Si se analiza esta situación, respecto a los ingresos que estas entidades perciben en concepto de inscripción, no se puede dejar de pensar en lo que ellos significarían para financiar y producir la Bibliografía Nacional. Y respecto a la delegación de funciones en entidades privadas, en que afectan el buen funcionamiento del Sistema del Control Bibliográfico Nacional. A ello cabría agregar de qué manera fueron dispersadas las actividades que debería cumplir un sólo organismo.

Referente a la ley Nº 11.723 y su decreto reglamentario Nº 41.233/34, se les efectuaron varias modificaciones tanto en lo que hace al amparo autoral como a la cantidad de ejemplares a depositar y a sus destinos, pero, a pesar de esas modificaciones, el panorama no mejoró. Requeriría, por lo tanto, una revisión y una nueva redacción acordes con las exigencias actuales y que la responsabilidad y el control del depósito legal de impresos dependen de entidades ajenas a la Biblioteca Nacional. No existe un verdadero control de policía respecto al mismo y se estima una evasión aproximada del 45% del total de la producción impresa dentro del territorio argentino. Ese porcentaje de evasión incluye tanto ediciones privadas como gubernamentales a nivel nacional, provincial y municipal.

El tema del depósito legal en la República Argentina requiere pues un estudio serio y exhaustivo. Algunos países cuentan ya con una legislación exclusiva para el depósito legal.

El Sistema del International Standard Book Number (ISBN)

La ley Nº 22.399, sancionada y promulgada el 11 de febrero de 1981, establece en la República Argentina la obligatoriedad de que todo librero editado en el territorio nacional se identifique con el número correspondiente al Sistema Internacional Normalizado de Número para Libro (ISBN).

El Sistema comenzó a aplicarse a partir del mes de enero del año 1982 y el número que identifica al país es el 950.

Para el funcionamiento de la Agencia Nacional del ISBN estaba previsto el ámbito de la Biblioteca Nacional. Pero la Resolución Nº 407 del 16 de junio de 1981, del entonces Ministerio de Cultura y Educación de la Nación, determina que la Subsecretaría de Cultura de la Nación actúe como "Agencia Nacional del ISBN u Oficina Nacional de Grupo en todo el país. . . ." Pero, en sus considerandos, la mencionada resolución dice: ". . . que atendiendo a principios de subsidiariedad, la ley Nº 22.450 (en el Título II, art. 4, inciso b, puntos 3, 4 y 5) viabiliza y aún recomienda la transferencia de servicios técnicos de las actividades propias del ámbito privada". Y por ello, la Subsecretaría de Cultura de la Nación delegó las funciones vinculadas con la inscripción y registro de trabajos monográficos comprendidos en la ley Nº 22.399 en la Cámara Argentina del Libro (CAL), firmándose el correspondiente contrato.

El ISBN es uno de los Sistemas que hacen al Control Bibliográfico Universal (CBU/UBC) y las bibliografías nacionales son los principales aportes al Sistema del Control Bibliográfico Universal. Por esta razón es que, originariamente, la Agencia Nacional del ISBN debía tener su sede en la Biblioteca Nacional, responsable de editar al decir de la bibliógrafa Francesa Louise Noëlle Malclès, "... el inventario de la producción intelectual y tipográfica de una nación".

La Cámara Argentina del Libro (CAL) en cumplimiento de las exigencias de la Agencia Internacional del ISBN edita anualmente, desde 1984, *ISBN: libros argentinos*. El anuario correspondiente a 1989, está próximo a aparecer. A partir de julio de 1984, dicha entidad publicó también *LEA: libros de edición argentina*, cuyo último número (35) apareció en junio de 1989. La segunda sección de esta revista se titulaba "Información bibliográfica" y en ella se registraban todos los trabajos monográficos inscriptos en el ISBN. Desde el Nº 1 su periodicidad fue mensual y pasó a ser bimestral a partir del Nº 18 (1º marzo-30 abril 1986). Razones de índole económica dejaron trunca su continuidad.

En cuenta al International Standard Serial Number (ISSN), la Agencia Nacional funciona en el Centro Argentino de Información Científica y Tecnológica (CAICYT) que depende del CONICET.

Conclusiones

La importancia del intercambio de información radica en el hecho de que ella incide efectiva y decididamente en el proceso, no sólo económico sino también socio-cultural-científico y tecnológico, de cualquier país.

La falta de estrategias y de una política adecuada hacen imposible el crecimiento armónico y sistematizado de la información. Es menester que la planificación y el establecimiento de programas no se limiten sólo a las áreas de la ciencia y de la tecnología sino que abarquen otros campos a fin de ofrecer un panorama más amplio y general. El Sistema Nacional de Información debe abarcar la totalidad de los conocimientos.

La creación de una política global que se proyecte más allá de las fronteras territoriales, con la cooperación recíproca entre las naciones, como ya existe en algunos casos, podría lograr la formación de una unidad regional de la Información en el Cono Sur para el progreso de los países participantes y también para beneficio de toda la humanidad. Teniendo en cuenta la situación económica por la cual atraviesa esas naciones, sus proyectos deberían recibir asistencia de los organismos internacionales.

Además, y a fin de unificar criterios, sería conveniente que los países que pertenecen al Cono Sur revean su legislación sobre el depósito legal. Se propone para ello la organización de un encuentro interdisciplinario de profesionales especialistas en derechos de autor, legisladores y bibliotecarios de las Bibliotecas Nacionales, para analizar las legislaciones vigentes y elaborar un proyecto de ley para cada uno de los países participantes. Proyecto de ley exclusivamente dedicado al

Depósito Legal, que responda con eficiencia a las necesidades y aún a las exigencias que demanda un verdadero Control Bibliográfico Nacional.

ANEXO

En este Anexo se citan algunas de las redes que funcionan en la República Argentina y algunos trabajos bibliográficos útiles para la información.

1. *Catálogo colectivo de bibliotecas biomédicas*. Buenos Aires: Asociación de Bibliotecas Biomédicas Argentinas, 1983.
2. *Catálogo colectivo de bibliotecas empresarias*. Buenos Aires: CACOBE, 1980.
3. CID (Centro de Investigación Documentaria del Instituto Nacional de Tecnología Industrial–INTI).
4. *GREBYD/Noticias*. Boletín del Grupo de Estudios de Bibliotecología y Documentación. Ultimo número abril de 1990. Directora: Prof. Elsa Barber. Esta publicación ha sido muy bien recibida en el ambiente bibliotecario. Es una revista de resúmenes de trabajos sobre bibliotecología, documentación, etc.
5. *Indice de contenidos*. Serie 1, N°—, marzo 1990—. Buenos Aires: Centro Argentino de Información Científica y Tecnológica (CAICYT). Semestral.
6. *Publicaciones periódicas argentinas registradas para el Sistema Internacional de Datos sobre Publicaciones Seriadas (ISDS)*. Buenos Aires: CAICYT, Centro Argentino de Información Científica y Tecnológica del CONICET, 1981. 1er Suplemento, 1983; 2° Suplemento, 1989.
7. RED NAPLAN ARGENTINA. Producto: *Planindex argentina*, catálogos, bibliografías, etc.
8. REDICSA (Red de Información sobre Ciencias Sociales Argentinas). Establecida en 1986. Producto: *Bibliografía argentina de ciencias sociales*. Anual. N° 1, 1979. El correspondiente a 1989, aparecerá en mayo de 1990.
9. RENBU (Red Nacional de Bibliotecas Universitarias). Produce el *Catálogo colectivo de publicaciones seriadas para América Latina* (CCNAR), 1988; *Catálogo colectivo nacional universitario de libros* (CCNUL).
10. REFIPLAN (Sistema Federal de Información para la Planificación y el Desarrollo). Consejo Federal de Inversiones (CFI).

11. RENICS (Red Nacional de Información en Ciencias de la Salud). 1986. Forma parte de la Red Latinoamericana ya establecida por BIREME en otros países de América Latina. Está integrada por 17 unidades de información en salud. Produce: *Bibliografía nacional en salud*. Alimenta la base de datos ULACS, desarrollada por BIREME.
12. SIDI (Sistema de Información Documental del Instituto Nacional de Ciencia y Técnica Hídricas). El SIDI está organizado en forma de red. Produce: bibliografías, catálogos, etc. Integración: regional y/o internacional.
13. SIDINTA (Sistema de Información y Documentación del Instituto Nacional de Tecnología Agropecuaria–INTA). Produce: bibliografías y tiene proyectos de interés.
14. SIIAP (Sistema Integrado de Información Agropecuaria). Base nacional de datos bibliográficos del sector agropecuario, forestal y pesquero. Produce: bibliografía nacional del sector, tablas de contenido, etc.

BIBLIOGRAFIA CONSULTADA

Argentina. Leyes. N°s 9.510; 7.092; 11.723; 22.399; 22.450.

Argentina. Decretos. N°s 41.233/34; 727/71; 984/72.

Argentina. Ministerio de Cultura y Educación. Resolución N° 407/81.

Argentina. Secretaría de Ciencia y Tecnología. Resolución N° 80/89.

Atherton, Pauline. *Manual para sistemas y servicios de información*. París: UNESCO, 1978.

Becú, Teodoro. *La bibliografía en la República Argentina*. Buenos Aires: Comité Argentino de Bibliotecarios de Instituciones Científicas y Técnicas, 1945.

Bibliografía general de la literatura latinoamericana. París: Unesco, 1972.

Congreso Internacional sobre Bibliografías Nacionales. París, 1977. *Informe final*. París: Unesco, 1978.

Couture de Troismonts, Roberto. *Estado actual de la bibliografía corriente nacional argentina*. Buenos Aires: Fundación Interamericana de Bibliotecología Franklin, 1965.

Fussler, H. H., y K. Kocher. "Contemporary Issues in Bibliographic Control". *The Library Quarterly*, 47, n° 3 (1977): 237-252.

Geoghegan, Abel Rodolfo. *Bibliografía de bibliografías argentinas: 1870–1970*. Edición preliminar. Buenos Aires: Pardo, 1970.

Gietz, Ricardo Alberto. *Situación general de la información científica y técnica en la Argentina*. Buenos Aires: CAICYT, 1976.

Gravenhorst, Hans. *El panorama bibliográfico documental en la Argentina*. Washington, D.C.: Unión Panamericana, 1969.

Greer, Roger. "National Bibliography." *Library Trends*, 15 (1947): 350-277.

International Federation of Library Associations. International Office for UBC. *Guidelines for the National Bibliographic Agency and the National Bibliography*. París: Unesco, 1979.

__________. *Manual on Bibliographic Control*. París: Unesco, 1983.

Larsen, Knud. "Los servicios bibliográficos nacionales". *Boletín de la Unesco para las Bibliotecas* 15, n° 6 (1961): 313-322.

Malclès, Louise Noëlle. *Cours de bibliographie*. Genève: E. Droz; Lille: Giard, 1954.

Oliver Murra, Katherine. "Observaciones sobre la evolución del concepto de bibliografía nacional contemporánea completa." *Servicios bibliográficos*. Washington, D.C.: Library of Congress, 1971.

Pauliello de Chocholous, Hebe. *Hacia un sistema nacional de información*. San Juan: ABGRA, 1986.

Rossi, Iris. "La Argentina y su bibliografía nacional." *Documentación Bibliotecológica* N° 6 (1954): 15-24.

Sabor, Josefa Emilia. "Apuntes sobre el concepto de bibliografía." *Documentación Bibliotecológica* N° 6 (1976): 1-13.

———. "La bibliografía general argentina en curso de publicación." *Handbook of Latin American Studies*, vol. 25 (1963): 373-381.

———. *El inquietante futuro de la bibliografía argentina*. Mar del Plata: Universidad Nacional de Mar del Plata, Biblioteca Central, 1986.

———. "Bibliografía nacional de la República Argentina." En *Manual de fuentes de información*, pp. 194-210. 3ª ed. corr. y aum. Buenos Aires: Marymar, 1978.

———. *La referencia y los servicios bibliográficos en la biblioteca moderna*. Buenos Aires: ABGRA, 1978.

Servicios bibliográficos: estado actual y posible mejoramiento. Washington, D.C.: Library of Congress, 1950.

Zimmerman, Irene. *Current National Bibliographies of Latin America: A State of the Art Study*. Gainesville: University of Florida, Center for Latin American Studies, 1971.

Coleções especiais brasileiras

20. Arquivo Edgard Leuenroth: Centro de Pesquisa e Documentação

Rachel Meneguello

O Arquivo Edgard Leuenroth—Centro de Pesquisa e Documentação Social (AEL)—vinculado ao Instituto de Filosofia e Ciências Humanas (IFCH) da Universidade (UNICAMP) constituiu-se em 1974 através da incorporação do acervo do militante sindical e escritor Edgard Leuenroth composto de uma rica biblioteca e coleções de jornais, revistas, folhetos e manuscritos, que compreendem o período histórico desde a última década do século 19 até a década de 1960.

Desde meados dos anos 70 o AEL vem ampliando seus acervos através da incorporação de novos fundos e coleções, reunindo extensa documentação sobre a história social e política do Brasil Repubiicano. Os temas que dizem respeito ao mundo do trabalho, ao movimento operário e às ações sindicais, ao pensamento político e aos movimentos de esquerda, o processo de urbanização dos grandes centros e os movimentos sociais, o âmbito da cultura, do comportamento político e social e das manifestações artísticas, entre outros, têm constituído importantes fontes para a realização de inúmeras dissertações, teses e investigações nas áreas de pesquisa desenvolvidas nos programas de Pós-Graduação do IFCH, sobretudo pelos departamentos de História e Ciências Sociais.

A riqueza de acervos pessoais incorporados ao Arquivo Edgard Leuenroth ao longo destes anos é inestimável. Dentre os mais importantes estão os acervos de Hermínio Sacchetta, jornalista e membro do Bureau Político do Partido Comunista Brasileiro; Astrojildo Pereira, fundador e secretário-geral do PCB; Otávio Brandão, dirigente do PCB; Mauricio de Lacerda; Miguel Costa, líder da Revolução Tenentista de 1924 e comandante da Coluna Prestes; Lourenço Moreira Lima, comandante e secretário da Coluna Prestes/Miguel Costa, que constituem um complexo material sobre a história do trabalho e de sua organização política e do desenvolvimento da esquerda brasileira na primeira metade do século XX, composto de documentos, jornais, periódicos e manuscritos, além de significativas bibliotecas de apoio.

O intercâmbio com instituições de pesquisa e pesquisadores da América Latina tem possibilitado ao AEL, não apenas o aprofundamento de suas metas científicas, mas também o exercício de seu papel político-acadêmico de luta pela preservação da memória da resistência democrática. Neste contexto destaca-se a incorporação dos acervos de Liborio Justo, importante historiador argentino, e de Francisco Gaona, pesquisador do Banco Paraguayo de Dados, os quais permitem constituirmo-nos em importante centro para o estudo da história social e do movimento operário na América Latina nas últimas décadas, especificamente sobre o Chile, Bolívia, Argentina e Paraguai.

A área do estudo do trabalho e de sua organização política destaca-se como central no escopo temático dos acervos do AEL desde sua fundação. Além de exaustiva coleção de jornais e periódicos específicos, o AEL compreende dentro do estudo da organização do trabalho, a incorporação dos acervos de Roberto Mange, fundador do Serviço Nacional de Aprendizagem Industrial (SENAI) e do Instituto de Organização Racional do Trabalho (IDORT), viabilizando pesquisas no sentido da compreensão da implementação dos métodos de racionalidade técnica no Brasil no período iniciado a partir dos anos 30. Na história mais recente, a incorporação de acervos de sindicatos e o contato permanente com organizações sindicais compõem importante fonte documental sobre o movimento operário atual, onde destaca-se a recente incorporação do acervo do Sindicato de Volta Redonda.

A preservação da memória brasileira de resistência democrática é a tônica que permeia as metas de pesquisa e do aquisição de acervos do AEL. Neste conjunto cabe ser destacado o acervo Brasil Nunca Mais, composto de mais de 800 processos movidos pela Justiça Militar e de anexos com mais de 10.000 documentos compilados pela Arquidiocese de São Paulo sobre a tortura militar e a resistência política durante o regime militar de 1964 a 1979. O acervo BNM constitui a única fonte organizada de dados que viabiliza o estudo do aspecto institucional da violência política nas ditaduras militar da América Latina.

Ainda na área da história política brasileira, a AEL contém a coleção de Documentos Diplomáticos Sobre o Brasil, formada sobretudo por correspondências diplomáticas, relatórios e informes recolhidos nos National Archives de Washington, sobre a questão militar, econômica, política e de relações exteriores do Brasil entre 1910 e 1954, e o acervo sobre a história política do Movimento Estudantil, que traça uma completa reconstituição da memória política da resistência estudantil a partir dos anos 60 no Brasil.

No amplo campo da cultura, são várias as áreas de pesquisa que podem ser embasadas pelos acervos localizados no AEL. A área de opinião pública baseia-se nos fundos doados pelo Instituto Brasileiro de Opinião Pública e Estatística (IBOPE), compostos de três significativos acervos—o acervo político-eleitoral, formado de pesquisas políticas e de tendências eleitorais desde de 1945, e os acervos das pesquisas de mercado e de audiência de rádio, televisão e imprensa escrita, desde 1943. Esta área compreende ainda importante acervo de dados para o estudo da violência na cidade do Rio de Janeiro.

No campo dos movimentos sociais, os acervos dos movimentos feminista e de homossexuais têm se constituído em importante área de pesquisa, sendo este último composto de inúmeros acervos documentais pessoais e de grupo, fundados ainda em importante biblioteca de apoio e de obras raras sobre o assunto, viabilizando sobretudo a compreensão do processo de transformação comportamental ao longo dos últimos 30 anos no país.

O AEL possui importante setor iconográfico para a organização de acervos cinematográficos e teatrais. Destacam-se aqui os acervos do Teatro Oficina, movimento artístico de vanguarda dos anos 60, a coleção Vieira Pontes, composta de manuscritos e folhetos de peças teatrais do início do século, os acervos dos cineastas Leon Hirshman e Silvio Back, várias publicações específicas no campo do cinema, teatro, rádio e esporte. Este setor compreende ainda, mais de 30.000 materiais fotográficos desdobrado em acervos, coleção e álbuns, e de cerca de 500 discos abrangendo a música brasileira, latino-americana e européia.

Finalmente, vale destacar a numerosa coleção de jornais, revistas e periódicos nacionais e estrangeiros, que abrangem vários temas nas áreas de história e ciências sociais editados em diversos períodos desde o início deste século.

Apesar de sua vocação estar voltada prioritariamente para o apoio pesquisa, o AEL acolhe constantemente solicitações de sindicatos, jornalistas e demais interessados na temática social, além de receber pesquisadores de universidades brasileiras, e dos continentes americano e europeu, viabilizando pesquisas avançadas nos mais variados temas.

21. O acervo do CPDOC: características, especificidades e potencialidades

Adelina Maria Alves Novaes e Cruz

Breve histórico

Os centros de documentação surgem no Brasil, na década de 70, motivados, entre outros fatores, pelo despertar da sociedade brasileira para as questões de identidade nacional, a criação dos cursos de pós-graduação em história e o papel desempenhado pelos brazilianistas. Sobre esse tema está para sair um texto do CPDOC escrito por Regina da Luz Moreira, entitulado "Brazilianistas, historiografia e centros de documentação,"[1] onde a autora resgata o processo de criação dos centros e a importância dos brazilianistas para "revelação" dos arquivos enquanto fonte de consulta para a história. Esse termo "brazilianista" foi utilizado pela primeira vez por Francisco de Assis Barbosa, em 1969, na apresentação do livro de Thomas E. Skidmore, *Brasil: de Getúlio Vargas a Castelo Branco*[2] passando então a ser adotado por brasileiros e norte-americanos. Esses centros constituem-se, particularmente, dentro das universidades voltadas para a pesquisa histórica e passam a desempenhar as tarefas de coletar fontes privada dispersas pelo país. Nesse contexto surge o Centro de Pesquisa e Documentação de História Contemporânea do Brasil (CPDOC) da Fundação Getúlio Vargas, criado em 15 de junho de 1973 com a dupla finalidade de reunir, organizar, preservar e disseminar as informações relativas aos documentos privados de homens públicos com atuação no cenário político nacional do pós-30, além de desenvolver pesquisas sobre temas da historiografia brasileira do período. Dessa maneira, contou inicialmente com dois setores: Documentação e Pesquisa.

Desde o primeiro momento, a equipe de Documentação foi constituida por profissionais das áreas de biblioteconomia, de ciências sociais e de história.

A troca de informações entre a equipe multidisciplinar constituida e o incentivo da instituição levaram esses profissionais a complementarem sua formação com estudos na área acadêmica para aqueles formados em biblioteconomia e na área técnica, para os que tinham a formação exclusivamente acadêmica.

Posteriormente, outros setores foram criados além dos setores de Pesquisa e de Documentação—História Oral e Editoração. Foi desenvolvido também um projeto especial durante dez anos que veio a se constituir no *Dicionário Histórico-Biográfico Brasileiro*,[3] com 3.800 verbetes biográficos e 700 temáticos.

Estrutura organizacional

O acervo conta com uma Direção geral ligado diretamente à presidência da Fundação. A essa Direção estão subordinadas, como setores de apoio, uma Assessoria, uma Secretária Administrativa e uma Editoria que é responsável pela normalização e edição dos textos produzidos pelos demais setores.

O setor de Pesquisa desenvolve trabalhos de investigação vinculados a temas ou períodos da história contemporânea brasileira, como história das idéias, história regional, história da educação, história política.

O setor de História Oral se ocupa da constituição de um acervo de depoimentos gravados de homens públicos com atuação política no pós-30. Esses depoimentos na sua grande maioria são do tipo história de vida, existindo alguns temáticos como Centrais Elétricas Brasileiras, S.A. (ELETROBRÁS), Banco Nacional de Desenvolvimento Econômico (BNDES), Banco Central (102 entrevistas disponíveis para consulta).

O setor de Documentação encontra-se dividido em três subsetores e três núcleos. Os subsetores são Arquivo, Audiovisual e Impressos, e os núcleos de Microfilmagem, Linha de Acervo e Informatização. Os subsetores são encarregados do tratamento, organização e preservação dos arquivos doados ao CPDOC. E os núcleos, constituidos por profissionais que integram os subsetores, desenvolvem projetos específicos de trabalho. O de Microfilmagem define prioridades executa as tarefas próprias desse processamento técnico. O de Linha de Acervo define os trabalhos a serem desenvolvidos com o objetivo de complementar e disseminar informações relativas ao próprio acervo—manter um cadastro de arquivos prioritários para o CPDOC—localizando-os, identificando seus titulares e possibilidades de doação, no caso de se encontrarem com familiares; elaborar instrumentos de consulta, como o recente publicado, guia de acervo presidenciais, entre outras atividades. O Núcleo de Informatização é responsável pela proposta de reunir e recuperar as informações geradas pelo setor de Documentação de forma sistemática. Voltaremos a falar desse núcleo mais tarde.

O acervo documental

O acervo do CPDOC vem sendo constituido a partir da doação de arquivos privados. No momento, conta com noventa e seis arquivos e quarenta e quadro coleções fotográficas ou bibliográficas. Os documentos que integram esses arquivos são de diversos gêneros: textual, iconográfico e audiovisual.

O textual divide-se nos manuscritos, datilografados e impressos. Assim temos cartas, ofícios, telegramas, panfletos, folhetos, discursos, periódicos, livros, recortes de jornais, mapas, plantas, etc. Cada espécie de registro documental necessita de tratamento e acondicionamento específicos e isso é tarefa dos subsetores. Mantendo a indivisibilidade do fundo através de uma notação alfabética atribuida a cada arquivo, o tratamento desses documentos gera uma série de instrumentos de consulta como guias, inventários analíticos e sumários, catálogos e índices. O CPDOC desenvolveu uma metodologia específica voltada para a organização de arquivos privados pessoais. Essa metodologia é hoje reconhecida pelas instituições nacionais da área e adotada como modelo por muitas delas.

Com relação às características do seu acervo, além da variada tipologia documental, o arquivo privado pessoal, especialmente dos homens públicos, revela, quase sempre, a vontade do titular—daquele que gerou e acumulou aquele conjunto. Os documentos são guardados com o objetivo de revelar os fatos, de esclarecer acontecimentos, de enaltecer suas personalidades. Desde o rascunho de uma carta, passando por uma foto, um livro ou um recorte de jornal, enfim, qualquer tipo de registro tem uma razão de permanecer, resguardado do descarte ou destruição. Por exemplo, no arquivo de Pedro Ernesto encontramos documentos que comprovam sua atuação como prefeito do Rio de Janeiro, então Distrito Federal (1935–1936), bem como aqueles que revelam sua condição de réu em conseqüência da sua participação no levante comunista de 1935. No arquivo de Lindolfo Collor, avô do presidente Fernando Collor, temos os documentos que identificam sua proximidade com Getúlio Vargas, a Aliança Liberal, a Revolução de 30 e a criação do Ministério do Trabalho, bem como aqueles que revelam, em outro momento, sua mágoa com o mesmo Getúlio, o exílio, o afastamento do poder.

Um material que é bastante rico são os folhetos. Estando no limite entre o manuscrito e o impressos são considerados como fonte primária de consulta. Em sua grande maioria são publicações de sindicatos, partidos, associações com tiragem e circulação restritas, geralmente não existentes nas bibliotecas públicas e onde podemos encontrar estatutos, discursos, conferencias, editais.

Assim como os folhetos, as fotografias e os filmes são uma fonte histórica praticamente inexplorada. Até pouco tempo, a foto só era usada como ilustração de um texto. Hoje em dia a imagem, estática ou em movimento, já se revela como documento em si. Há que se desenvolver métodos e teorias de leitura desses registros—não só na história, como na antropologia, nas ciências sociais.

O acervo de CPDOC—seja textual ou audiovisual—cobre todos os temas da historiografia política contemporânea brasileira, sendo que alguns deles ganham destaque em função das origens da constituição desse acervo. Ele teve início com os arquivos de Getúlio Vargas, presidente do Brasil nos períodos de 1930 a 1945 e de 1950 a 1954 e de Osvaldo Aranha, seu ministro em quase todo esse período. A eles se juntaram os arquivos de outros colaboradores e correligionários—assumindo um formato próximo das bibliotecas presidenciais norte-americanas, sem contudo recolher os documentos públicos, a não ser aqueles que foram "esquecidos" nas gavetas e cofres de seus titulares. Mais recentemente, já praticamente esgotados o que poderíamos chamar "era Vargas" novos arquivos vêm sendo incorporados como o de Antonio Carlos Muricy, Nelson Mello, Hermes Lima, Anísio Teixeira, Clemente Mariani—personagens mais recentes da história do Brasil.

A automação das informações

Com cerca de dois milhões de documentos, a análise e a recuperação das informações são diferenciadas. Os documentos manuscritos e/ou datilografados são descritos nos inventários; os impressos recuperados pelas normas de catalogação e classificação e os visuais e sonoros por um método que adota tanto procedimentos biblioteconômicos quanto arquivísticos. Não existe entretanto uma interligação entre esses diversos tipos de instrumentos de consulta. Em função disso, está sendo desenvolvido um sistema de recuperação automatizada das informações aplicado aos arquivos permanentes. Como uma primeira etapa, coordenada pelo *Núcleo de Informatização*, foi desenvolvido um vocabulário controlado em história do Brasil e ciências afins que conta com 1.862 termos, incluindo assuntos, instituições, nomes geográficos e nomes próprios. A grande maioria dos termos diz respeito à história política contemporânea brasileira.

A segunda etapa, em andamento, é estudo dos diversos tipos de instrumentos de consulta para a definição dos campos—existem itens comuns a todos os instrumentos como código, outros específicos de alguns instrumentos como o local. Essa análise é imprescindível para a definição do software, bem como a previsão dos diversos tipos de cruzamento necessários a uma precisa e objetiva recuperação das informações. Esse trabalho será desenvolvido junto com a equipe do Centro de Processamento de Dados da Fundação Getúlio Vargas.

No momento, o Centro conta com uma base de dados do usuário onde os pesquisadores que consultam o CPDOC são cadastrados e o objetivo, além de se ter esses dados recuperados e sempre facilmente atualizados, é delimitar o perfil do usuário do Centro. Ficamos sabendo, por exemplo, que temas estão sendo mais consultados, qual a formação acadêmica desses pesquisadores, quais as finalidades de consulta ao acervo, enfim uma série de estatísticas e relatórios, são possíveis de serem extraídos.

Outro base que está sendo implantada é a dos guias de acervos—ela arrolará e cruzará as informações geradas pelos guias de arquivos do CPDOC, bem como todos os guias elaborados pelo Núcleo de Linha de Acervo—guia dos acervos presidenciais, guia dos ministros das Relações Exteriores etc. A recuperação dos assuntos/pessoas/locais dessas diversas bases é feita pelo vocabulário controlado acima referido.

Conclusão

Para concluir, gostaria de informar que o CPDOC funciona na Praia de Botafogo, nº 190, 12ºandar das 9:00 h. às 16.30 h. para consulta externa e tem como prática a liberação do seu acervo tão logo seja tratado. Cada arquivo é entregue ao CPDOC mediante um contrato de doação que nos garante o direito de liberar à consulta os documentos que o integram. Muitos poucos contratos fazem restrições ou limitações à consulta, acredito que por duas razões: por um lado a seriedade com que o CPDOC trabalha e por outro, pelo papel que as teses, os livros e os artigos elaborados a partir da consulta a fontes primárias representa para o resgate da história do nosso país.

NOTAS

1. Estudos históricos (Rio de Janeiro) 3, no. 5 (1990): 66-73.

2. Thomas E. Skidmore, *Brasil, de Getúlio Vargas a Castelo Branco: 1930–1964* (Rio de Janeiro: Paz e Terra, 1969).

3. *Dicionário histórico–biográfico brasileiro, 1930–1983*. 1ª ed. 4 vols. (Rio de Janeiro: Forense-Universitária, 1984).

Brazilian Non-Book Materials

22. A produção de vídeo independente no Brasil: dados para a sua história

Patrícia Monte-Mór

É com imensa satisfação que como produtores de cinema e vídeo independentes participamos deste seminário e, em especial, ficamos muito esperançosos pelo interesse que parece crescer pela produção dos chamados "non-book materials."

A produção de vídeo independente no Brasil, um histórico das instituições produtoras, o chamado vídeo popular e um inventário do que se tem feito nos últimos dez anos e sua relação com a produção da América Latina são alguns dos pontos mais gerais que pretendo traçar nesta comunicação. No entanto, acredito ser essencial contextualizar esta produção na trajetória da implantação da televisão comercial no país e sua penetração nos tempos atuais.

Num país de 154 milhões de habitantes, 8.5 milhões de Km2, encontramos hoje aproximadamente 36 milhões de aparelhos de televisão representando um universo potencial de 100 milhões de telespectadores e o 4. maior império televisivo do planeta: a Rede Globo de Televisão.

A televisão no Brasil possui hoje uma penetração de 60% do total de domicílios, percentual inferior ao dos Estados Unidos ou Japão, mas expressivo se levada em conta sua extensão territorial. Acrescente-se a isso o alto índice de analfabetismo e a situação sócio-econômica e cultural em que se encontra a maior parte do povo brasileiro. Impõe-se então a TV como o grande meio de comunicação no país e a Rede Globo, em especial, atingindo praticamente todo o território nacional hoje.

No dia 18 de setembro de 1950, começava a funcionar a televisão no Brasil, e com ela, a era da informação eletrônica no país. Fruto de empenho pessoal do empresário Assis Chateaubriand, a TV TUPI predominou no cenário até o golpe militar de 1964.[1]

Numa primeira fase, que durou até 1956, a televisão nada mais era do que o rádio visual, com o predomínio dos programas de auditório gravados ao vivo. Com o surgimento do vídeo tape, inaugura-se a revolução do tempo audiovisual. Com pesados equipamentos e de difícil mobilidade, o vídeo tape foi, no entanto, imediatamente incorporado por estações de televisão em todo o mundo, redimensionando os modos de produção da imagem eletrônica. A trajetória deste veículo, no Brasil, pode ser classificada em quatro momentos distintos: o primeiro, que é marcado pelo improviso e criatividade artística e administrativa, liderado pela TV TUPI, dura aproximadamente quinze anos. O segundo, a partir de 1965, por injunções políticas e tecnológicas, será marcado pela criação do império e do poder de Rede Globo de Televisão, assegurando a sua penetração horizontal por todo o território nacional e consolidando uma imbatível hegemonia até o final da década de 80. O terceiro momento é marcado pelo advento de dois novos grupos de comunicação: a Rede Manchete e o Sistema Brasileiro de Televisão (SBT). Uma inexpressiva concorrência se esboça, dessas redes junto com outros já existentes frente a Rede Globo, que mantem, no entanto, sua confortável liderança.

A década de 90 se abre com uma novidade: a TV GLOBO, com sua potência já internacionalmente reconhecida, com um gigantismo absoluto e responsável pela produção de informações para a divulgação ao povo brasileiro, vê a sua liderança abalada. Dona de uma linguagem própria, rápida, computadorizada, marcou toda uma geração de técnicos e realizadores, e começa a sentir a concorrência de outros redes, que passam a investir numa outra linguagem, a aproximar-se do cinema e de temas de interesse nacional.

Este é um pano de fundo do movimento que vai surgindo ainda no final da década de 70, que no Brasil se concretiza nos anos 80. O da produção independente de vídeo. O vídeo, de formato cada vez mais portátil popularizado neste período, favorece o surgimento de um movimento audiovisual que aqui denominou-se produção independente. Esta produção nasce definitivamente marcada pela confluência de várias vertentes: (1) os curta metragistas, documentaristas, com suas marcas do cinema novo da década de 60 com propostas estéticas e temáticas nacionais; (2) os movimentos populares e as organizações não governamentais (aqui denominadas ONGs), com uma necessidade crescente de comunicação na sua militância política, educativa, sindical, religiosa; (3) a vídeo-arte e os grupos alternativos e experimentais e (4) em termos de linguagem, marcada pela experiência ditada pela Rede Globo de Televisão.

As produções nascem já com um duplo caminho: o de buscar romper o monopólio estatal da informação, através da implantação de TVs em praça pública, de experiência com grupos indígenas, sindicatos, movimentos populares, onde o processo é o que essencialmente importa, e um universo de produção mais preocupado com o produto, que elege os festivais e mostras, inicialmente concentradas no eixo Rio-São Paulo para divulgar e exibir seus trabalhos.

No ano de 1982 surge a 1ª. Mostra Nacional de Vídeo, em São Paulo, seguindo em 1983 com o I Vídeo Rio, na cidade do Rio de Janeiro. O Festival Fotóptica de Vídeo que se realizará neste ano de 1990, em São Paulo, em sua 8ª. edição, é hoje a mostra mais importante no gênero no país e terá, pela primeira vez, a especificidade de ser um festival do Hemisfério Sul, congregando não só a América do Sul, como a Africa e a Oceânia. Outros festivais e mostras foram surgindo nesta década no Brasil.

Núcleos de produção extremamente ativos e criativos se organizaram na década de 80, em Minas Gerais, Rio Grande do Sul, e Pernambuco destacando-se aí a experiência pioneira no trabalho de vídeo popular de um projeto denominado TV VIVA, em Olinda, Pernambuco. Trabalho vinculado ao movimento popular que rapidamente incorporou o vídeo na produção e exibição de programas para comunidades locais, a partir de temas de sua vivência cotidiana, propiciando mostras e discussões em Praça Pública, levando ao desenvolvimento de novas produções. O projeto tem continuidade ainda hoje, em seus diverso desdobramentos, com a entrada de equipamento broadcast e um maior aprimoramento técnico da produção.

O surgimento do vídeo doméstico, na década de 80, o home-video, promove uma revolução nos hábitos e costumes televisivos dos espectadores. Os primeiros equipamentos encontrados no Brasil são contrabandeados, e as fitas, clandestinas. Em 1982, o primeiro aparelho é produzido em território nacional, a propósito da Copa do Mundo! Em 1984, os primeiros vídeo clubs são então reconhecidos.

A questão da circulação e distribuição da produção em vídeo passa a ser colocada com maior ênfase no país.

Os produtores independentes definiram a sua estratégia a partir do próprio conceito: produzir à margem do sistema convencional de TV sem, no entanto, prescindir deste no que se refere à difusão. Aí está o nó da questão!

No Brasil, as concessões de canais de televisão permanecem nas mãos do poder Executivo, que as utiliza como instrumento de manipulação política. Essa é uma das razões para não haver uma produção regional de TV no Brasil. Para o dono uma concessão regional sempre é mais interessante repetir uma rede sediada no Rio ou São Paulo, do que incentivar a produção local.

Se, nos EUA, as emissoras comerciais estão proibidas de produzir além de 20% de toda a programação por elas veiculada, no Brasil, a televisão se fechou contra a entrada do cinema nacional e seus técnicos, à produção independente, tornando-se autora da produção, e controladora absoluta da distribuição, optando pela importação de filmes estrangeiros de baixa qualidade, em detrimento da produção nacional. Esta empresa, assim organizada, foi se tornando inviável e para sobreviver hoje exige uma audiência acima de 70%.

Ao longo da década de 80 as experiências dos produtores independentes, sobretudo de linguagem, se desenvolveram ao ponto de interferir na própria estética da televisão comercial que, apesar de seu fechamento, acabou absorvendo em alguns de seus programas sinais desta gramática visual. Por outro lado, alguns dos grupos formados, como o Olhar Eletrônico, por exemplo, que já ficou como parte da história, passou a produzir para a TV, de fora da TV, numa experiência de emissora regional paulista. Rompeu com o que se chama "padrão de qualidade," adotando o VHS para maior agilidade jornalística, buscando mostrar como viabilizar uma concessão com um mínimo de recursos. Somos um país pobre, onde equipamentos são caros e ainda de difícil acesso.

E, no entanto, a respeito do que entre os independentes chamou-se vídeo popular que gostaríamos de nos deter nesta comunicação, onde uma gama multicor de programações e experiências encontra-se a disposição para veiculação e monta um panorama do Brasil de ontem, hoje e amanhã.

No futuro, os anos oitenta ficarão marcados pelo processo de redemocratização do país, com suas esperanças e desesperanças, assim como pelo desenvolvimento rápido das novas tecnologias de comunicação e informação.

Grupos e movimentos populares, a partir de 1982, contando inicialmente com o apoio de alguns setores da Igreja, de centros de educação popular, de sindicatos de trabalhadores, tem acesso aos equipamentos de vídeo. São mais leves e portáteis, mais baratos e ágeis como instrumento de registro, de análise, de divulgação de imagens e de reforço da prática política. Estes realizadores certamente ficarão para a história da década assim como os documentaristas do Cinema Novo para o movimento popular dos anos 60.[2]

A TV VIVA, já citada anteriormente, é um exemplo que já podemos chamar clássico, deste tipo de trabalho. Outros grupos, chamados organizações não governamentais (ONGs), como a Federação de Orgãos para a Assistência Social e Educacional (FASE), o Instituto de Estudos da Religião (ISER), o Instituto Brasileiro de Análises Sociais e Econômicas (IBASE), o Centro de Imagem de Criação Popular (CECIP), passam a trabalhar com o vídeo, como uma de suas estratégias de ação, adquirindo equipamentos, montando produtoras de porte profissional. A estes grupos não podemos deixar de incluir a Produtora dos Salesianos em Minas Gerais e a Verbo Filmes em São Paulo, com trabalhos semelhantes, só que diretamente vinculadas a Igreja Católica. A produção destes diversos grupos é para e com os movimentos sociais. Experiências com comunidades indígenas também são realizadas neste período, tendo o Centro de Trabalho Indigenista (CTI), em São Paulo, desenvolvido projeto sistemático com quatro grupos indígenas no Brasil central com equipamentos de vídeo, realizando várias produções conjuntas.

Em junho de 1986, começou a funcionar a Tevê dos Trabalhadores (TVT), vinculada ao Sindicato dos Metalúrgicos de São Bernardo e Diadema, São Paulo, a partir de uma câmara VHS doada ao sindicato. A idéia central era a de se criar um espaço onde os trabalhadores pudessem apropriar-se de sua própria imagem. O vídeo acabou sendo o instrumento mais eficaz de esclarecimento para a categoria nas suas questões centrais. A comunicação, a TVT e os direitos dos trabalhadores nesta área foram discutidos amplamente na maioria das fábricas da região. Atualmente existem duas TVTs: uma unidade em São Bernardo, totalmente controlada pelos trabalhadores, a outra, na cidade de São Paulo, integrada à Rede de Comunicação dos Trabalhadores (RCT), criada em maio de 1989. Entidade civil, autofinanciada, fundada por 68 líderes sindicais, populares, intelectuais, artistas, jornalistas e trabalhadores da cultura. A TVT de São Paulo é uma produtora profissional, equipamentos broadcast, mas produzindo essencialmente voltada para o interesse dos trabalhadores. No ano de 1989, a TVT realizou o programa político eleitoral do Lula (Luís Inácio da Silva) para Presidência da República. Na TV São Bernardo busca-se a autoformação: os próprios trabalhadores sujeitos da comunicação e protagonistas de ação. São responsáveis pela criação, produção, pós-produção e distribuição dos vídeos da categoria. Opta-se pelo processo, pelo militância. Na TVT de São Paulo, opta-se pelo produto, incorpora-se a experiência e o apoio de cineastas, jornalistas e artistas.

A área sindical, no entanto, tem sido muito mais receptora do que produtora de vídeo. A avaliação dos próprios grupos é de que "falta vídeo para ajudar os sindicatos do campo e da cidade."[3]

Podemos citar experiências variadas neste sentido. Dentre elas, o ISER–Vídeo, criado em 1986, no Rio de Janeiro, é hoje uma produtora em nível profissional, com os mais modernos equipamentos, órgão do Instituto de Estudos da Religião. Produzindo sobre temas da cultura, religião e dos movimentos populares sua programação tanto é destinada aos circuitos de distribuição alternativa quanto ao broadcast. Dedica-se prioritariamente a produção voltada para as diversas pesquisas e projetos do ISER junto aos movimentos populares, Igreja Católica, negros, prostituição, AIDS, favelas, etc.[4]

No ano de 1984 o vídeo popular ganha um novo impulso, quando cerca de quarenta grupos se reúnem no I Encontro Nacional de Vídeo do Movimento Popular, em São Bernardo do Campo, Estado de São Paulo. Do conjunto de reflexões e do interesse de trocas permanentes nasceu a Associação Brasileira de Vídeo Popular (ABVP).[5] Hoje com cerca de 180 grupos associados, é o Brasil o único país na América Latina que possui esta estrutura organizada permanente, em âmbito nacional.

Traçando um breve panorama da América Latina, podemos dizer que no Equador e no Uruguai não existe uma circulação organizada da produção. No Chile não há ação coordenada. No Peru, a Videored organiza uma rede de trocas já bastante ativa. Na Bolívia, a circulação de programas educativos ganha força como o movimento do Nuevo Cine e Video Boliviano. O vídeo popular e alternativo ganha cada vez mais espaço nos festivais de cinema, no Brasil no Festival Internacional de Cinema TV e Vídeo, do Rio de Janeiro e em Havana, Cuba, quando a categoria vídeo passa a ser incluída.

Em junho de 1989, realizou-se em Cochabamba, Bolívia, um encontro de vídeo Latino-Americano, com representantes de doze países da América Latina e do Caribe, e de dois da América do Norte.[6] Nesta ocasião foi discutida a possibilidade de uma articulação a nível continental. Entre as questões tratadas e as prioridades destes grupos estão: as diversas concepções de vídeo popular; capacitação dos realizadores; utilização do vídeo e aprofundar as diferenças e relações entre o vídeo-produto e o vídeo-processo. Em 1990, o novo encontro será em Montevideo, no Uruguai.[7]

Em 1987, a Associação Brasileira de Vídeo Popular inicia uma parceria com o Cinema Distribuição Independente (CDI) e começa a implantação do cinevídeo—um sistema de distribuição no formato VHS, com apoio da Ford Foundation. A CDI congrega produções realizadas por cineastas independentes de curta, média e longa metragem. Vai-se buscando consolidar assim um sistema de vídeo popular que torne acessível ao conjunto da sociedade e, em particular, aos movimentos sociais toda uma produção à margem dos veículos tradicionais. Entre outros passos, a compilação de um catálogo temático, que já se encaminha para a segunda edição, parece ser o avanço fundamental.[8]

No bojo deste processo, o vídeo passa a ser incorporado pelos mais diversos segmentos da sociedade, em projetos culturais e educacionais, numa gama de produtos e produções como: Vídeo Universidade, Pró-Memória Vídeo, Vídeo-escola, para citar algumas redes de produção e/ou distribuição de programas de vídeo para grupos específicos—escolas, universidades, centros culturais, de preservação de memória. Videotecas públicas também começam a ser implantadas, assim como setores específicos em algumas bibliotecas, arquivos, centros culturais nas principais capitais do país, ainda que de modo assistemático.

É neste universo que a chamada produção independente gravita, retratando este país plural, que vive de mudanças como processo cotidiano. O Brasil com seus desafios e diversidade, estimula a criatividade. É neste contexto que o vídeo popular em especial, significa um meio na construção da identidade social e cultural de cada um de nossos países da América Latina, juntos na mesma tela.

NOTAS

1. Ver Cândido José Mendes de Almeida, *O que é vídeo*, Coleção Primeiros Passos (Rio de Janeiro: Brasiliense, 1984). Ver também do mesmo autor, "TV e vídeo no Brasil: uma abordagem sintética," *VII Festival Fotóptica Vídeo Brasil, Outubro, 1989* (catálogo), 28-29.

2. Para este tema, ver artigo de autoria da Diretoria da ABVP, "A expansão do vídeo popular e a atuação da ABVP," *Proposta* 43 (Nov. 1989): 37-39.

3. Sobre a experiência da TVT ver, Regina Festa, Eliseu Marques, e Luís Fernando Santoro, "TVT uma rede sindical em expansão," *Proposta* 43 (Nov. 1989): 6-10.

4. Em Novembro de 1985, o n.16 do periódico *Comunicações do ISER*, sob a coordenação de Patrícia Monte-Mór, com o tema: "Cinema, TV e vídeo: as imagens da religião," já apontava para o início do ISER na área de vídeo.

5. Patrícia Monte-Mór, "Vídeo e Organizações Populares: algumas notas e referências," *Comunicações do ISER* 16 (Nov. 1985); e Diretoria da ABVP, "A expansão do vídeo popular e a atuação da ABVP," *Proposta* 43 (Nov. 1989): 37-39.

6. Ibid.

7. Os encontros Latino-Americanos já realizados: 1984—Havana, no Festival do Novo Cine Latino Americano; Seminário Vídeo, Cultura Nacional e Subdesenvolvimento, (com participação brasileira); 1987—Havana, no mesmo Festival, vários realizadores de vídeo se reunem e produzem o documento, "A vinte anos de Viña del Mar"; 1988—Montevidéu, O Vídeo na Educação Popular; Santiago, Primeiro Encontro Latino Americano de Vídeo; Costa Rica, Seminário Internacional sobre Vídeo, Comunicação Popular e Intercâmbio Tecnológico; Quito, Experiências de Vídeo na América Latina; 1989—Cochabamba, Encontro Latino Americano de Vídeo. Ver Mabel de Faria Melo, "D'América Imagem Latina," *Proposta* 43 (Nov. 1989): 40-44.

8. Catálogos reunindo a produção independente no Brasil são escassos: em 1986—uma primeira iniciativa de compilação foi publicada em *Comunicações do ISER*, n. 16, no artigo citado, de minha autoria, "Vídeo e organizações populares: algumas notas e referências." Alguns vídeos e sua localização (pp. 91-96). A distribuidora CINEVIDEO publicou, em São Paulo em 1989, o *Catálogo*, temático, da produção alternativa, popular, independente, brasileira, reunindo 320 vídeos disponíveis em VHS, na ABVP, São Paulo. Iniciativa de fôlego que estará ampliada em 1990.

23. Catálogos de microformas de periódicos brasileiros

Felícia Musikman e Maria José da Silva Fernandes

Estando há algum tempo atuando na área de microfilmagem de documentação cultural, mais especificamente na microfilmagem de periódicos, através das atividades desenvolvidas pelo Plano Nacional de Microfilmagem de Periódicos Brasileiros, criado oficialmente em 1978 e gerenciado hoje pela Biblioteca Nacional (BN), sentimos a necessidade de discutir a importância da existência de publicações (impressas ou em microformas), que venham contribuir para a divulgação e recuperação do já vasto número de coleções e/o acervos microfilmados, e que no entanto não são consultados em toda a sua potencialidade por um simples motivo: a escassez de instrumentos bibliográficos que permitam a todos os pesquisadores interessados o acesso direto a essa informação.

Nas modernas bibliotecas e centros de documentação, que historicamente têm sido os grandes responsáveis pela coleta e armazenamento da produção intelectual da humanidade, a disseminação da informação tem se apresentado como a grande preocupação dos profissionais da área.

Nesse sentido, a microfilmagem, desde os seus primórdios, foi vista como uma técnica capaz de permitir o rápido acesso a novas informações, a partir da transferência do conteúdo informativo de acervos convencionais—em papel—para um suporte que atenda as necessidades atuais do pesquisador, tendo em vista a facilidade do manuseio e transporte, a grande compactação de dados, a drástica redução de espaço ocupado, além de possibilitar o intercâmbio a nível nacional e internacional, e atuar, paralelamente, de maneira decisiva, como elemento de preservação e complementação desses mesmos acervos.

Nesse contexto, de extremo dinamismo, o catálogo, como instrumento de divulgação, quer assuma a forma de listagem, automatizada ou não, "folder," folheto, livro ou microfilme, torna-se fundamental como forma de registro e divulgação, constantemente atualizável, do universo documental disponível.

O nosso objetivo maior, nesse trabalho, é enfatizar que o acervo histórico cultural hoje disponível no Brasil em microformas já atingiu um estágio à nível qualitativo e quantitativo, de grande relevância, que ressente-se da insipiência e escassez de instrumentos que respondam, satisfatoriamente, às duas indagações básicas do pesquisador:

a. O que está microfilmado? e

b. Onde está disponível?

Do nosso ponto de vista, a maior circulação de informações sobre as coleções em microformas, evitaria não só a duplicidade de esforços, como resultaria também na economia da recursos e em um uso mais constante e racional dessas coleções.

O catálogo deve possuir características que permitam sua fácil e constante atualização e simples o suficiente para propiciar uma rápida consulta em qualquer local onde estiver o pesquisador. Caso se apresentem muito complicados ou específicos, e demandem custos muitos onerosos para sua publicação, não haverá interesse das instituições em elaborá-los, nem dos usuários em acessá-los. Dilui-se assim o objetivo primordial dos mesmos, ou seja, a divulgação dos acervos em microformas.

Essa preocupação não é recente à nível internacional, conforme podemos observar através do grande número de catálogos, de diversos países, que o Plano vem recebendo periodicamente, e que informam, de maneira clara e objetiva, cumulativamente ou não, quais as coleções microfilmadas—se periódicos, manuscritos, obras raras, teses, censos, relatórios, entre outros—disponíveis para consulta ou aquisição.

Que essa preocupação esteja presente em bibliotecas e centros de documentação é perfeitamente compatível com suas funções precípuas—coleta, guarda e disseminação da informação—participando assim, de forma plena, do ciclo evolutivo do conhecimento humano. No entanto, essa preocupação se apresenta de maneira muito nítida, e mais ainda, nos repartições de serviço, que sabem que se não divulgam, não vendem sua produção em microfilme.

Compreende-se assim, o apuro na apresentação dos catálogos, tanto intrinsecamente, no valor informativo dos ítens relacionados, quanto na parte estética, de apresentação visual e qualidade de gráfica, que tem o poder de transformar o próprio catálogo em instrumento de pesquisa atraente.

Catálogos Brasileiros

A divulgação dos jornais brasileiros em microformas e seus catálogos iniciou-se em 1976 através do trabalho pioneiro da Biblioteca Nacional, apoiada pela experiência técnica da Bibliotecária Maria de

Lourdes Claro de Oliveira, Chefe da então Seção de Reprografia, e sob a ótica modernizante de então Diretora-Geral da Biblioteca Nacional, a Professora Jannice Monte-Mór.

Em 1975, foi criado o Grupo de Documentação em Ciências Sociais, que congregava as maiores instituições culturais e de pesquisa do país, entre elas Arquivo Nacional, Fundação Casa de Rui Barbosa, Biblioteca Nacional, Instituto Histórico e Geográfico Brasileiro, Fundação Getúlio Vargas, Academia Brasileira de Letras, Conselho Federal de Cultura, Universidade Federal Fluminense, Universidade Federal do Rio de Janeiro para dinamizar quatro linhas de atuação com relação à documentação brasileira, de grande interesse para pesquisadores nacionais e estrangeiros:

- técnicas de história oral
- guias de fontes para a história
- restauração de documentos
- microfilmagem de jornais.

O estimulador do Grupo de Documentação e Ciências Sociais através de financiamento a diversos projetos foi a Fundação Ford.

O Projeto de Microfilmagem de Jornais Brasileiros, então embrionário, desenvolveu-se, transformando-se em 1978 no Plano Nacional de Microfilmagem de Periódicos Brasileiros.

A preocupação da Biblioteca Nacional ao iniciar o seu projeto de microfilmagem de jornais foi a de verificar quais as instituições no Brasil e no exterior que já haviam realizado microfilmagem de jornais brasileiros, a fim de que se evitasse superposição de recursos financeiros e humanos, duplicando inutilmente esforços já dispendidos por outros instituições, filosofia essa que norteou o início dos trabalhos, segundo palavras de Jannice Monte-Mór, na apresentação do catálogo preliminar, editado em 1976. [1]

Nascia assim, a primeira tentativa de catálogo coletivo de jornais existentes, sob a forma de microcópias, em instituições do Brasil e do exterior, contendo informações extraídas de repertórios estrangeiros e de outras fontes brasileiras e inspirado em serviço semelhante realizado pela Library of Congress, dos Estados Unidos. Tratava-se de uma modesta publicação, com apenas 31 páginas.

Este levantamento preliminar permitiu saber-se um determinado jornal brasileiro já foi microfilmado em algum país e se poderia ser obtido em microfilme positivo ou negativo, ou em microficha, se fosse o caso. Incluía o registro de 102 jornais correntes ou extintos, existentes no Brasil, nos Estados Unidos, na Alemanha e na Grã-Bretanha, e utilizava, para as indicações da forma e localização da microcópia, símbolo e abreviaturas adaptados dos empregados pela Library of Congress.

Dos 102 títulos de periódicos relacionados, apenas a metade estava acessível em microfilme no Brasil (desses cinqüenta e seis títulos, trinta e um haviam sido microfilmados fora das especificações técnicas, necessitando de nova microfilmagem), o que vem sendo realizado paulatinamente pelo Plano.

Algumas coleções de títulos de jornais brasileiros disponíveis em microforma apenas no exterior, foram duplicados e enviados ao Brasil, através de intercâmbios estabelecidos com a Library of Congress, Yale University, etc., o que permitiu, em pouco tempo (e isso veremos no catálogo editado em 1979) a disponibilidade quase que total dos títulos arrolados neste primeiro catálogo.

Enquanto que nos Estados Unidos vinte e sete instituições possuíam periódicos brasileiros em microformas, apenas dez possuíam no Brasil, sendo que três eram as próprias empresas editoras dos títulos.

Com a criação, em 11 de dezembro de 1978, do Plano Nacional de Microfilmagem de Periódicos Brasileiros, com o objetivo de identificar, localizar, organizar, recuperar e preservar—pela microfilmagem sistemática—o acervo hemerográfico brasileiro existentes nas diversas Unidades da Federação, visando sua reconstituição não só para a Biblioteca Nacional, órgão depositário da memória imprensa brasileira, mas também para os acervos das diversas cidades e Estados, facilitando o acesso à informação, foi possível, já em 1979, publicar a primeira edição do *Periódicos brasileiros em microformas: catálogo coletivo* [2] que passou a incluir, além dos jornais, revistas e outros tipos de periódicos.

Em apenas um ano, foram microfilmados oitenta e quatro títulos novos, que somando-se aos 102 anteriormente divulgados—dos quais vinte e dois atualizados—totalizavam 186 títulos de periódicos brasileiros em microforma.

Cresceu também de dez para dezessete, o número de instituições possuidoras no Brasil, de microformas para pesquisa.

O início efetivo dos trabalhos do Plano em 1979, estabelecendo as bases e diretrizes à nível nacional, foi a alavanca propulsora para o desenvolvimento sistemático da microfilmagem de jornais brasileiros.

Já na terceira edição do *Catálogo*,[3] através de Núcleos Regionais e/ou Estaduais de Microfilmagem, que se multiplicaram rapidamente por todo o território nacional, houve um salto de quase mil títulos, ou seja, em dois anos o *Catálogo coletivo* cresceu de cinqüenta para 296 páginas, tornando-se preciosa fonte de informação para os pesquisadores e historiadores brasileiros, que tiveram enormemente facilitadas suas pesquisas. Trinta e uma instituições brasileiras contavam já com cópias microfílmicas das coleções de periódicos.

O catálogo de 1981, editado graças ao apoio do Senado Federal, trazia algumas ilustrações de primeiros números de jornais brasileiros, e inclui toda a coleção microfílmica realizada pelo Arquivo Público Mineiro, sobre cujo catálogo falaremos oportunamente.

São já trinta e uma instituições, em treze estados brasileiros, que possuem coleções, em microfilme, para acesso e pesquisa. O índice alfabético dos títulos dos periódicos brasileiros existentes em microfilme no Brasil mostra a riqueza e a variedade dos títulos microfilmados, que incluía jornais literários, informativos, femininos, operários, estudantis, etc. desde o início da imprensa brasileira até jornais correntes.

Em 1985, finalmente a 4ª edição (e atual) do catálogo coletivo, *Periódicos brasileiros em microformas*,[4] foi publicada, consignando 2.700 títulos disponíveis em quarenta e dois instituições brasileiras, representando mais de dez milhões de páginas microfilmadas em cerca de 13.000 rolos matrizes.

A totalidade dos Estados da Federação, está pela primeira vez, representada no *Catálogo coletivo*, que foi enriquecido também com uma bibliografia sobre a imprensa brasileira e a cada um dos Estados, com 1.137 referências bibliográficas.

Dificuldades de toda ordem sempre coexistiram com o trabalho do Plano, e em especial o crescente aumento do custo de matéria-prima, a falta de mão-de-obra especializada no país, e mais recentemente dificuldades de ordem administrativo-financeira, o que inviabilizou a transferência de recursos para os órgãos estaduais e municipais, que vinham participando do Plano cada vez em maior número.

Entre os anos 1978 e 1984, foi possível implantar alguns núcleos de microfilmagem com repasse de recursos destinados à aquisição de equipamentos e aparelhos de leitura. O incentivo financeiro do Plano aumentou também a capacidade operacional de alguns núcleos, atingindo-se uma média de produção nesses anos de 1.450 rolos matrizes, o que permitiu divulgar na edição de 1985 do *Catálogo coletivo*, os 2.700 títulos já mencionados.

Neste catálogo aparecem em destaque as primeiras coleções especiais em microfilme que são os relatórios dos Presidentes das Províncias/Estados Brasileiros e os Relatórios Ministeriais (do Império à Primeira República), que foram levantados e microfilmados graças ao apoio do Center for Research Libraries/Latin American Microform Project (LAMP). A coleção compõe-se de 569 rolos matrizes, correspondentes a 3.808 documentos resgatados pela microfilmagem sistemática, em todo o território nacional.

Aparece também como coleção especial o conjunto de oitenta e um títulos de jornais operários, microfilmados em cinco rolos, em ordem cronológica, com títulos editados à partir de 1858 até 1959, sendo a maioria deles impressos no final do século XIX e início do século XX.

Adotando o mesma sistemática de apresentação de informações desde o primeiro catálogo, baseado no catálogo de microformas da Library of Congress, sempre que possível inclui-se na referência da microforma a quantidade de rolos correspondente a cada título.

Uma das maiores dificuldades com que nos deparamos para complementação dos dados no *Catálogo* foi a falta de informações sobre a data de início e fim dos periódicos, apesar da consulta à extensa bibliografia levantada.

Catálogo de Jornais dos Estados

O primeiro catálogo de jornais em microforma editado em um Estado da Federação brasileira, foi aquele publicado pelo Arquivo Público Mineiro, em sua tradicional *Revista*, em 1980,[5] existindo também em separata.[6] O catálogo seguiu a sistemática adotada pelo catálogo coletivo, *Jornais brasileiros em microformas*—Edição preliminar de 1976, o que permitiu fossem as referências ali indicadas inseridas integralmente no *Catálogo coletivo* editado pela Biblioteca Nacional em 1981.

Eram então 552 títulos editados em 140 cidades mineiras. A produção microfílmica do Arquivo Público Mineiro cresceu rapidamente, atingindo já em 1985, mais de 1.300 títulos que circularam ou circulam em 229 cidades do Estado de Minas Gerais.

Significativa quantidade de periódicos mineiros existentes em microforma permitiu a tiragem de separata de *Periódicos brasileiros em microformas* da Biblioteca Nacional de 1985.[7]

O Plano/BN ainda não dispõe na sua sala de leitura de microfilme cópia positiva de todos os títulos microfilmados, o que vem sendo feito paulatinamente, face as dificuldades de aquisição de matéria-prima para duplicação.

Sem dúvida a quantidade de títulos de jornais editados no Estado do Rio de Janeiro vem crescendo à cada nova edição do catálogo, não só por ter sido o Rio de Janeiro a capital do Brasil independente, até 1961, data de transferência da capital para Brasília, mas também pela demanda dos pesquisadores. No momento, inclusive, estamos empenhados em concluir a microfilmagem de todos os títulos do Rio de Janeiro existentes na Biblioteca Nacional e em outros instituições, editados até 1889—data marco do início da República Brasileira.

Mereceu também separata de *Periódicos brasileiros em microformas: catálogo coletivo 1984*, onde o Estado era representado por 544 títulos em microfilme.[8]

De lá para cá a coleção cresceu em 45,5%, o que significa que dispomos, no momento, em microfilme, de 791 títulos de periódicos publicados no Rio de Janeiro.

Por outro lado, concentra-se no Rio de Janeiro hoje, o maior número de jornais correntes microfilmados, entre os quais podemos citar o *Jornal do Brasil*, *Jornal do Comercio*, *Jornal dos Sports*, *O Dia*, *Tribuna da Imprensa*, *O Monitor Campista* e *O Fluminense*.

Em 1986, um ano após a edição do *Periódicos brasileiros em microformas: catálogo coletivo* foi publicado pelo núcleo estadual do Plano no Espírito Santo, sediado no Arquivo Público daquele Estado, o catálogo *Jornais e relatórios de Presidentes de Província ES em microformas*[9] relacionando os 69 títulos microfilmados até então, e acrescentando de forma sumária, interessante histórico de cada título.

O catálogo foi organizado dentro do critério cronológico, e apresenta índice de títulos e de municípios. Inclui também os relatórios de Presidentes da Província do Espírito Santo, à época do Império, contendo ainda algumas ilustrações.

Seguindo o exemplo do Espírito Santo, o núcleo de microfilmagem da Secretaria de Cultura do Estado do Ceará, dirigido com entusiasmo pela Historiadora Walda Maria Motta Weyne, publicou em 1988 um primoroso catálogo geral, *Jornais cearenses em microformas*[10] indicando 159 títulos de jornais, relatórios de Presidentes da Província do Ceará, do Império até a 1ª República, e alguns outros documentos avulsos.

Ilustrado com os primeiros exemplares dos mais significativos jornais da imprensa cearense, apresenta resumido histórico dos títulos microfilmados, além de discriminar rolo à rolo, o conteúdo das coleções.

O trabalho de microfilmagem dos jornais do interior dos estados tem caminhado muito lentamente. O Brasil possui quase 5.000 municípios, alguns muito antigos, e outros que acabam de ser criados. A extensão territorial brasileira e as dificuldades econômico-financeiras com que nos deparamos, torna sempre longínqua a meta de levantamento e microfilmagem sistemática dos jornais editados em cada município brasileiro. Mas as dificuldades não impediram que algumas excessões possam ser indicadas, além das centenas de municípios mineiros, que tiveram seus títulos microfilmados, talvez não de forma sistemática, mas numa tentativa de preservar os exemplares disponíveis à época do trabalho:

São elas,

- Blumenau e Joinville, em Santa Catarina
- Caxias do Sul, no Rio Grande do Sul
- Sobral, no Ceará.

Contudo, apenas Sobral editou pequeno folheto[11] com os títulos dos jornais microfilmados, graças ao apoio da Universidade Estadual Vale do Acaraú aos trabalhos de preservação da memória da imprensa cearense, e com o apoio financeiro do Banco do Nordeste do Brasil.

Apesar de não ser propriamente um catálogo, merecem destaque as informações sobre o levantamento de títulos de jornais publicados em Caxias do Sul, cidade típica de imigração italiana, com indicação dos já microfilmados pelo Plano através do Projeto de Recuperação e Microfilmagem dos Periódicos editados em Caxias do Sul, muitos dos quais em língua italiana.[12]

Os jornais microfilmados reunem diversas coleções particulares e de instituições públicas de Caxias do Sul, Porto Alegre, a da Biblioteca Nacional.

Muito se poderia divulgar no Brasil se as instituições detentoras de acervos microfílmicos percebessem a importância de divulgar os seus documentos através de catálogos com ampla distribuição, procurando atingir o usuário potencial. É o caso por exemplo, apenas para citar alguns, das publicações do Instituto Brasileiro de Geografia e Estatística (IBGE) (anuários, censos, etc.) disponíveis em microfilmes e microfichas, mas não relacionados em nenhum catálogo.

A informação da existência desses documentos em microforma é passada apenas aos usuários que se dirigem à Biblioteca do IBGE, através de pequeno folheto que fala sobre a rede de bibliotecas daquele órgão.

Queremos com isso incentivar a todos os que possuem publicações periódicas em microformas a pensar seriamente no possibilidade de divulgarem de maneira ampla junto aos usuários especializados os seus acervos microfílmicos, já que uma das vantagens principais do microfilme é transferir o conteúdo da fonte de pesquisa até os olhos, sempre ávidos, do pesquisador.

Conjuntos em microfilmes de jornais especializados, tais como operários, anarquistas, alternativos, maçônicos, católicos, israelitas, femininos, esportivos, econômicos, literários, de cinema, etc., certamente reunirão coleções esparsas, números avulsos e únicos, preservados quase que pelo acaso, sendo o microfilme quase o instrumento mágico capaz de reunir em alguns metros de filme informações coletadas aqui e ali, quase sempre com dificuldades.

É sempre com satisfação que recebemos a correspondência da Meckler Publishing Company e da Chadwyck-Healey, solicitando-nos atualização do nosso catálogo de microformas e dados para constarem das grandes publicações internacionais *Guide to Microforms in Print* [13] e *Micropublisher's Trade List Annual*, [14] que divulgam amplamente, em todo o mundo, as informações dos títulos de periódicos brasileiros já microfilmados. Certamente muitos de vocês conhecem as duas publicações mencionadas, e sempre que nos chegam pedidos de países longínquos, sabemos que as informações foram colhidas em uma dessas publicações.

As informações contidas no catálogo por nós enviado são inseridas em um banco de dados que congrega todos os títulos de todos os países do mundo.

Gostaríamos de concluir esta breve comunicação falando do incentivo e do apoio com que a Library of Congress sempre distinguiu o Plano Nacional de Microfilmagem de Periódicos Brasileiros da Biblioteca Nacional, apoio este temos procurado corresponder com esforço até além da nossa capacidade, e que pode ser avaliado no catálogo de jornais correntes recebidos na Library of Congress, onde em relação ao Brasil consta a informação do recebimento de vinte títulos, dos quais a maioria são enviados à partir do trabalho do Plano em todo o Brasil. Observamos na capa da última edição de 1988 do catálogo da Library of Congress de jornais estrangeiros recebidos correntemente,[15] o aparecimento de um jornal brasileiro (*Jornal do Brasil*), o que muito nos gratificou.

Peço licença à todos vocês e à Coordenadora do Painel, para em meu nome e em nome da minha colega Felícia Musikman, testemunhar de público a dedicação incansável e o entusiasmo contagiante com que Drª Esther Caldas Bertoletti, desde 1976, na Biblioteca Nacional e em tantas outras instituições por este grande Brasil afora vem impulsionando, apesar de todas as adversidades, o já conhecido e respeitado Plano Nacional de Microfilmagem de Periódicos Brasileiros, o grande responsável pelo resgate da preservação de milhões de páginas, testemunhas da trajetória sócio-política, econômica e cultural do povo brasileiro.

NOTAS

1. Biblioteca Nacional (Brasil), *Jornais brasileiros em microformas: catálogo coletivo*, Ed. preliminar (Rio de Janeiro: A Biblioteca, 1976).

2. Ibid., *Periódicos brasileiros em microformas: catálogo coletivo* (Rio de Janeiro: A Biblioteca, 1979).

3. Ibid., *Periódicos brasileiros em microformas: catálogo coletivo* (Rio de Janeiro: A Biblioteca, 1981).

4. Ibid., *Periódicos brasileiros em microformas: catálogo coletivo 1984* (Rio de Janeiro: A Biblioteca, 1985).

5. "I Catálogo dos jornais mineiros do A.P.M. em microfilme," *Revista do Arquivo Público Mineiro* 31 (1980): 5-72.

6. *I Catálogo dos jornais mineiros do A.P.M. em microfilme: separata da "Revista do Arquivo Público Mineiro* (Belo Horizonte: 1980?).

7. Biblioteca Nacional (Brasil), *Periódicos brasileiros em microformas, catálogo coletivo: periódicos editados no Estado de Minas Gerais (separata)* (Rio de Janeiro: 1985).

8. Ibid., *Periódicos brasileiros em microformas, catálogo coletivo: periódicos editados no Estado do Rio de Janeiro* (Rio de Janeiro: 1985).

9. Arquivo Público do Espírito Santo, *Jornais e relatórios de Presidentes de Província ES em microformas: catálogo* (Vitória: SEAR [Secretaria de Estado da Administração e dos Recursos Humanos], 1986).

10. *Jornais cearenses em microformas: catálogo geral* (Fortaleza: Secretaria de Cultura do Estado do Ceará, 1988).

11. *Jornais sobralenses em microformas* (Sobral: n.d.).

12. *Histórias da imprensa em Caxias do Sul* (Caxias do Sul: Museu Municipal; Arquivo Histórico Municipal, n.d.).

13. *Guide to Microforms in Print: Author, Title* (Westport, CT: Microform Review, 1978).

14. *The Micropublisher's Trade List Annual* (Weston, CT: 1975—).

15. *Newspapers Received Currently in the Library of Congress*, 7th ed. (Washington, DC: Library of Congress, Serials and Government Publications Division, 1980—).

24. Instituto Nacional da Fotografia e Programa Nacional de Preservação e Pesquisa da Fotografia

Cássia Maria Mello da Silva e Sérgio Burgi

Breve histórico

O Instituto Nacional da Fotografia (INFoto) da Fundação Nacional de Arte (FUNARTE), criado pela portaria nº 207 de 18 de maio de 1984 do Ministério da Educação e Cultura, nasceu da proposta por uma política nacional para área da fotografia, definida pelo então Núcleo de Fotografia e respaldada pela própria trajetória ascendente da linguagem fotográfica desde sua introdução no Brasil em 1840—imediatamente após o anúncio público do invento em 1839, na França—até nossos dias.

Em 1983, o Núcleo de Fotografia elaborou um diagnóstico que apontava as carências da área fotográfica e a ausência de projetos de atuação.

Foi constatado nesse levantamento, entre outros pontos, o péssimo estado de conservação em que se encontravam os acervos fotográficos brasileiros, bem como a alarmante situação das fotografias produzidas recentemente, cujas imagens têm desaparecido com grande rapidez.

A preocupação com esta realidade levou o INFoto a conceber uma política de preservação fotográfica, cuja abordagem coloca essa questão sob o seu sentido mais amplo e dinâmico, englobando tanto os acervos já existentes quanto a produção fotográfica contemporânea. O processo de preservação da imagem fotográfica deve começar no instante de sua revelação e não somente quando é anexada a algum acervo, onde costuma chegar com o seu estado de conservação já comprometido.

A execução dessa proposta foi realizada através do Projeto Preservação e Pesquisa da Fotografia, a partir de 1982. Inicialmente, o Projeto identificou grupos e instituições que realizavam trabalhos em torno do documento fotográfico e que tivessem interesse em um empreendimento mais profundo, voltado para a prospecção,

---

Nota: Cássia Maria Mello da Silva é responsável pelo texto e Sérgio Burgi pelo anexo.

organização, reflexão e divulgação desse objeto, bem como a formação de pessoal especializada na área de preservação.

Em conseqüência da atuação do Projeto de Preservação e Pesquisa da Fotografia, no nível nacional, surgiram solicitações de apoio, incentivo e assessoramento a projetos de todo o país.

O desenvolvimento da proposta fez com que em 1984 fosse criado o Programa Nacional de Preservação e Pesquisa da Fotografia (PROPRESERV), abrindo-se um espaço institucional inédito na América Latina.

Programa Nacional de Preservação e Pesquisa da Fotografia (PROPRESERV)

O PROPRESERV, criado pela portaria nº 13/84 e assinada pelo então Secretário da Cultura do Ministério de Educação e Cultura, tem investido na implantação de uma política de preservação em prol da integridade física e da divulgação de imagens históricas e contemporâneas, sendo suas principais linhas de atuação:

Preservar a memória fotográfica brasileira

Fomentar a criação de núcleos regionais de preservação fotográfica

Formar pessoal técnico especializado na área de preservação fotográfica

Localizar, identificar e referenciar o acervo brasileiro existente

Pesquisar a história da fotografia no Brasil

Pesquisar técnicas de preservação e restauração

Difundir informações técnicas através de publicações especializadas

Aperfeiçoar a tecnologia do material fotográfico existente

Os mecanismos de ação do PROPRESERV são baseados nos princípios de descentralização, democratização e exemplaridade, expressos na atuação multiplicadora local, possibilitando o fortalecimento de estruturas regionais ao mesmo tempo em que vão sendo alcançados objetivos nacionais.

Para viabilizar a execução de suas finalidades, foram criados o Centro de Conservação e Preservação Fotográfica e o Núcleo de Documentação.

O PROPRESERV apoia técnica e/ou financeiramente cerca de sessenta projetos de instituições públicas e privadas em vários pontos do país, participando das mais importantes iniciativas na área da preservação fotográfica.

Entre outras, podem ser citadas as seguintes:

Biblioteca Nacional—o mais importante acervo fotográfico do país (Rio de Janeiro)
Arquivo Público do Distrito Federal
Secretaria Estadual de Cultura de Santa Catarina
Instituto do Patrimônio Artístico e Cultural da Bahia
Fundação Niteroiense de Arte (Rio de Janeiro)
Fundação Casa das Artes de Bento Gonçalves (Rio Grande do Sul)
Fundação Cultural Alfredo Ferreira Lage (Minas Gerais)
Secretaria Municipal de Cultura de Uberlândia (Minas Gerais)
Fundação Universidade Federal de Mato Grosso do Sul
Fundação Universidade de Caxias do Sul (Rio Grande do Sul)
Prefeitura Municipal de São João Del Rei (Minas Gerais)
União dos Fotógrafos do Estado de São Paulo
Fundação Gilberto Freire (Pernambuco)
Fundação Joaquim Nabuco (Pernambuco)
Arquivo Nacional (Rio de Janeiro)
Fundação Casa de Rui Barbosa (Rio de Janeiro)
Museu Histórico Nacional (Rio de Janeiro)
Museu da Imagem e do Som (Rio de Janeiro)
Centro de Pesquisa e Documentação de História Contemporânea do Brasil (CPDOC) da Fundação Getúlio Vargas (Rio de Janeiro)

No campo da formação de pessoal técnico especializado na área de preservação, o PROPRESERV tem realizado, através do Centro de Conservação e Preservação Fotográfica, treinamentos, cursos, seminários e encontros.

Em 1985, promoveu o I Seminário sobre Preservação e Conservação de Fotografias, com apoio cultural do Serviço de Divulgação e Relações Culturais dos EUA (USIS), da Comissão Fulbright e do Instituto Brasil-Estados Unidos (IBEU), no Rio de Janeiro.

Em novembro de 1989, foi realizado no Rio de Janeiro, o Encontro "Preservação de Documentos Fotográficos," que ofereceu palestras e oficinas ministradas pelos técnicos norte-americanos Nora Kennedy (Museu de Arte Moderna de Nova York) e Peter Mustardo (Arquivo Público de Nova York). O evento foi um desdobramento do treinamento que esses técnicos realizaram no Centro para a equipe e profissionais de instituições convidadas e patrocinado pela UNESCO.

Embora as atividades de assessoramento e formação de pessoal constituam a espinha dorsal do PROPRESERV, outro atividade, estreitamente ligada a preservação, é da pesquisa sobre a história da fotografia no Brasil. Trata-se de uma linha editorial que tem por finalidade divulgar o resultado de pesquisas realizadas pelos projetos regionais, bem como trabalhos inéditos e/ou reedições de obras esgotadas. O primeiro volume que se encontra editado é *A fotografia no Brasil* de Gilberto Ferrez.*

Centro de Conservação e Preservação Fotográfica

Parte fundamental de PROPRESERV, o Centro foi criado através de um termo de cooperação ténica, firmado em 13 de março de 1985, entre a FUNARTE e a Fundação Nacional Pró-Memória (FNPM), com a intervenção da Secretaria do Patrimônio Histórico e Artístico Nacional (SPHAN). Suas atividades foram iniciadas em 1987. Contando com o apoio de agentes financiadores nacionais (Financiadora de Estudos e Projetos [FINEP], Conselho Nacional de Pesquisas [CNPq], VITAE Apoio a Cultura, Educação e Promoção Social) e internacionais (Organização de Estados Americanos [OEA] e UNESCO), o Centro recebeu investimentos equivalentes a US$ 500.000,00 (quinhentos mil dólares) desde o início de sua implantação.

Suas ações visam atender, prioritariamente, as linhas de atuação do PROPRESERV e as necessidades de pesquisa sobre a instabilidade e preservação dos documentos fotográficos, desenvolvendo técnicas apropriadas de conservação, preservação e sistemas de arquivamento. Um panorama mais detalhado dessas atividades encontra-se no Anexo I deste documento.

No campo de treinamento de pessoal especializado, o Centro tem executado diversas iniciativas, valendo ressaltar as seguintes:

a. 1º Curso de Preservação Fotográfica, para técnicos de instituições do Rio de Janeiro, São Paulo, Rio Grande do Sul, Pernambuco e Distrito Federal, apoiado pela VITAE—1988.
b. 1º Curso de Reprodução Fotográfica—1989.
c. Treinamento do técnicos para a Biblioteca Nacional, Arquivo Nacional, Fundação Casa de Rui Barbosa e Museu de Arte Moderna do Rio de Janeiro.

O Centro está, ainda, capacitado para a prestação de serviços técnicos especializados, de modo a suprir as necessidades de tratamento em laboratório de originais fotográficos, podendo definir soluções para o financiamento de suas próprias atividades.

---

*Gilberto Ferrez, *A fotografia no Brasil, 1840–1900*, 2ª ed. (Rio de Janeiro: Fundação Nacional de Arte; Fundação Nacional Pró-Memória, 1985).

Núcleo de Documentação

O Núcleo de Documentação, criado com o objetivo de apoiar técnicamente o PROPRESERV na área de organização e administração de acervos fotográficos, atua em conjunto com o Centro de Conservação e Preservação Fotográfica nas assessorias a projetos de conservação e organização de acervos fotográficos, responsabilizando-se ainda pela divulgação de informações técnicas através de publicações, cursos, oficinas e seminários.

Apesar de contar com só um técnico, o Núcleo desenvolve, no momento, dois projetos: o Manual de Catalogação de Documentos Fotográficos e o Guia dos Acervos Fotográficos Brasileiros.

O primeiro, elaborado por uma comissão inter-institucional composta por técnicos da FUNARTE, Biblioteca Nacional, Museu Histórico Nacional, Fundação do Cinema Brasileiro, Museu Imperial e do Centro de Pesquisa e Documentação de História Contemporânea do Brasil (CPDOC) da Fundação Getúlio Vargas, não possui similar no Brasil e encontra-se em fase de finalização.

O segundo, embrião do Cadastro Nacional de Acervos Fotográfico, pretende localizar, identificar e referenciar os acervos fotográficos pertencentes a instituições públicas e privadas, empresas e colecionadores. No momento, já estão referenciados os acervos dos órgãos públicos federais subordinados à Secretaria de Cultura.

Esse projeto vem suprir uma lacuna na divulgação e sistematização das informações culturais no país, podendo servir ainda de subsídio para pesquisadores e estudiosos da área fotográfica.

Sua execução só tem sido possível com a contratação de três pesquisadores em regime de prestação de serviço.

Propostas para continuidade

Acompanhamento dos projetos em andamento nas diversas regiões brasileiras:

- Implantação dos primeiros núcleos regionais de preservação fotográfica;
- Continuidade do projeto "Guia dos Acervos Fotográficos Brasileiros," com vistas a publicação do primeiro volume no 1º semestre de 1991.

Edição das seguintes publicações técnicas:

- Manual de catalogação de documentos fotográficos
- Cadernos técnicos do Centro de Conservação e Preservação Fotográfica—os dois primeiros números já estão prontos

Técnicas de acondicionamento em preservação fotográfica (título provisório)
Manual de preservação fotográfica

Realização de quatro cursos, um por semestre (do 2º semestre de 1990 ao 1º semestre de 1992), para dez técnicos cada, com o seguinte temário:

Preservação e organização de acervos fotográficos
Reprodução e duplicação de fotografias
Conservação e restauração de originais
Pesquisas sobre materiais e processos fotográficos

Realização de oito oficinas, duas por semestre (do 2º semestre de 1990 ao 1º semestre de 1992), para quinze técnicos cada, com o seguinte temário:

Técnicas de higienização de documentos fotográficos
Fabricação de invólucros para documentos fotográficos
Montagem de fotografias para exposição
Uso e calibração de instrumentos de monitoração ambiental
Técnicas de foto-acabamento
Reprodução de originais fotográficos em p/b
Duplicação de originais fotográficos em p/b
Realização do 2º Seminário sobre Preservação e Conservação Fotográfica no 2º semestre de 1991, com a finalidade de reunir as instituições mantenedoras de acervos fotográficos, bem como especialistas brasileiros e estrangeiros, para uma ampla discussão sobre a questão da preservação fotográfica no Brasil.

Conclusão

Numa rápida avaliação da trajetória do PROPRESERV ao longo de seis anos, pode-se afirmar que o trabalho desenvolvido tem encontrado ressonância nacional e internacional.

Por se tratar de uma experiência inédita na América Latina e, sobretudo, por ter reunido um grupo de profissionais de reconhecida competência técnica, o INFoto, através do PROPRESERV, consolidou sua posição de liderança absoluta no campo de preservação fotográfica. Atualmente, o PROPRESERV tem sido solicitado não só por grupos e instituições brasileiras, mas também de outros países da América Latina.

Com a extinção de FUNARTE e a possível demissão dos funcionários com menos de cinco anos de trabalho no serviço público, o PROPRESERV será fatalmente atingido, já que sete de seus oito funcionários não são estáveis.

Caso as demissões aconteçam, a paralisação das atividades do PROPRESERV é inevitável. Não há como substituir a equipe do Centro de Conservação e Preservação Fotográfica, pois não existe no Brasil pessoas com a mesma qualificação técnica uma vez que quase todos esses profissionais foram treinados no exterior, com dinheiro do Estado, para desenvolver trabalhos específicos nas áreas de conservação e preservação fotográfica.

Finalmente, cabe ressaltar a importância do trabalho de preservação dessa valorosa parte da memória nacional que é a fotografia, tanto no que tange aos acervos já constituidos quanto à imensa produção contemporânea.

ANEXO I

O Centro de Conservação e Preservação Fotográfica—PROPRESERV/FUNARTE/INFoto

Implantado através de um Termo de Cooperação Técnica, firmado em 13 de março de 1985 entre a Fundação Nacional de Arte (FUNARTE) e a Fundação Nacional Pró-Memória (FNPM), com intervenção da Secretaria do Patrimônio Histórico e Artístico Nacional (SPHAN), o Centro de Conservação e Preservação Fotográfica desenvolve—dentro do Programa Nacional de Preservação e Pesquisa da Fotografia (PROPRESERV)—um grande elenco de atividades técnicas e de pesquisa nas seguintes áreas principais:

1. Estudo de sistemas e materiais acessórios adequados ao arquivamento e guarda permanente de materiais fotográficos processados, visando a preservação destes acervos em perfeitas condições de estabilidade e permanência (pesquisa integrada sobre invólucros, mobiliário e soluções de climatização e controle ambiental).
2. Desenvolvimento de técnicas e tratamentos de conservação-restauração de originais fotográficos de valor histórico e artístico.
3. Estudo de técnicas, rotinas, e controle de qualidade necessários ao processamento fotográfico para máxima permanência, e desenvolvimento e optimização de procedimentos fotográficos para duplicação e reprodução de originais fotográficos.
4. Testes de materiais e produtos de fabricação nacional utilizados em preservação e conservação fotográfica (papéis, polímeros e adesivos para fabricação de invólucros, por exemplo), testes de envelhecimento acelerado e pesquisas sobre processos fotográficos históricos.

5. Divulgação de informações técnicas através de manuais e publicações especializadas.

6. Treinamento de pessoal em preservação e conservação fotográfica (cursos, estágios e seminários).

7. Assessoria técnica a instituições conveniadas.

Em funcionamento desde setembro de 1987, em menos de três anos de intensa atuação em todo o país, o Centro, com apenas seis funcionários técnicos e um funcionário administrativo desenvolveu diversas linhas de pesquisa com apoio de órgãos financiadores como a FINEP, CNPq, Organização dos Estados Americanos, UNESCO e VITAE, e prestou serviços e assessoria em suas áreas de competência a mais de sessenta instituições públicas e privadas.

Estas atividades só foram viabilizadas na medida em que ao longo deste período de atuação, diversos projetos realizados permitiram a contratação de pessoal técnico auxiliar e incorporação de estagiários para desenvolvimento dos serviços contratados, ampliando-se assim em muito o potencial de produção do Centro. Somente em 1989, quinze estagiários foram treinados nos diversos setores do Centro.

Assim, com uma estrutura reduzida e em um curto espaço de tempo, o Centro de Conservação e Preservação Fotográfica firmou-se como uma referência importante neste campo no país, sendo ainda o único Centro com este perfil na América Latina.

Através de intenso trabalho de intercâmbio internacional, com a formação de técnicos no exterior, apresentação de trabalhos em congressos internacionais e visitas de técnicos estrangeiros a nossas instalações, o Centro de Conservação e Preservação Fotográfica coloca-se hoje também entre os poucos centros técnicos plenamente capacitados nesta área a nível mundial.

Os investimentos realizados ao longo dos últimos cinco anos, na ordem de US$ 500.000,00, não são em hipótese nenhuma exagerados se comparados com os resultados obtidos.

Em 1990, com todos os investimentos de infra-estrutura já realizados, o Centro de Conservação e Preservação Fotográfica encontra-se perante o desafio de consolidar plenamente suas atividades técnicas e de pesquisa, bem como de formação de pessoal técnico especializado, ou pela descontinuidade de suas atividades, regredir a um estágio anterior de total falta de suporte técnico especializado nesta área tão significativa para a memória e cultura de um país, que é a da preservação de sua documentação fotográfica de valor histórico e artística existente em nossas instituições culturais, públicas e privadas.

Periodicals in the Southern Cone and Brazil

25. Index Coverage of Latin American Periodicals Published in the Southern Cone: The Humanities

Nelly S. González

Despite considerable advancement in the bibliographic control of Latin American materials, serials are still a frontier in need of attention. Periodicals are an important medium for rapid communication; it is true in the sciences and very much so in the humanities and social sciences as well. In Latin America serials play a particularly crucial role, since they are the medium through which a clear picture of the region's cultural life and social and political problems emerges.

In this paper I concentrate on the coverage of Latin American serials in the humanities which are published in the Southern Cone countries—Argentina, Chile, Paraguay, and Uruguay—and which are indexed in the standard American indexes. The Southern Cone is an ideal region for study in the humanities because of its diversity and wealth of literary figures of great stature.

The definition of a serial used for this study is stated in the *Anglo-american Cataloguing Rules* (AACR2): "A publication in any medium issued in successive parts bearing numerical or chronological designations and intended to be continued indefinitely."[1] There are several forms of serials, for example, annuals, journals, magazines, newspapers, periodicals, proceedings. All of these forms except newspapers are included as serials for this study.

The period covered is the ten-year period 1979–1989. This decade has witnessed flourishing publication activity among scholarly institutions such as universities (both private and public), research centers (some of them affiliated with academic institutions), and nonacademic institutions engaged in research (e.g., corporations, foundations, banks). Scholarly research is published as monographic series, bulletins, newsletters, memoirs, and so on.

In the humanities there exist fewer research groups than in the social sciences. Nevertheless, the most important publications in the humanities come from such organizations as literary academies, research centers affiliated with universities (both private and public), and a few research centers and foundations (e.g., Instituto de Literatura

"Ricardo Rojas" in Buenos Aires). The academies, however, survive on paupers' budgets; their membership fees are not enough to sponsor the cultural activities of their groups or their publications. In Latin America these organizations often do not have a strong tradition of serving as professional networks. Instead, they function as social organizations for well-to-do members of the community, providing social status regardless of one's scholarly achievements. Thus, social status is an attraction for membership in them.[2]

The reigning political instability in the Southern Cone nations is a factor directly related to the intellectual activity and production. The exodus of intellectuals attributable to political persecution and severe censorship has crippled their intellectual life.[3]

There is, however, a rebirth and promising cultural activity with the return to "democracy," and the decline of government terrorism, which at its peak controlled research and literary production.[4] This impeded publication of controversial or original scholarship in the humanities and social sciences.

Economic conditions of high inflation and poor availability of raw materials caused publishers to curb their activities. Argentina and Chile, once the leading publishing countries of Latin America, have been surpassed by other publishing centers, such as Brazil and Mexico.[5]

Finally, the instability of the postal services in terms of delays, theft, and high costs also contributes to the inaccessibility of publications from this region.[6]

In spite of all these problems, the number of worthy scholarly works that continue to be published is encouraging. Some institutions have established long records and traditions of serious research. Others are emerging with a variety of approaches, uncovering forgotten men and women of letters, revising history, and introducing new interpretations of day-to-day life in the region. For example, local histories have proliferated during the decade.[7]

Methodology

The list of Southern Cone periodicals in the humanities was compiled from three main indexes on Latin America published in the United States:

Handbook of Latin American Studies: Humanities (HLAS)[8]
Hispanic American Periodicals Index (HAPI)[9]
Indexed Journals: A Guide to Latin American Serials (GLAS)[10]

These three indexes were selected because they are the most authoritative, important, and unique in Latin American studies; and *HLAS* and the *HAPI* together are thought of as bibliographic "Bibles" by Latin Americanists in the United States.

Three other important general indexes which are extensive and excellent and which include Latin American serial publications were also chosen:

MLA International Bibliography of Books and Articles on the Modern Languages and Literatures (MLA) [11]
Historical Abstracts (HistAb) [12]
Readers' Guide to Periodical Literature (RG) [13]

In the process of using these two sets of indexes, it was possible to identify a number of serials published according to country and discipline and also to determine which indexes are most inclusive in their coverage of the Southern Cone. It also made it possible to identify overlapping indexing efforts and/or lack of indexing coverage of the area. Finally, it made it possible to identify those journals in the humanities which are indexed in both geographic area-specific and general indexes.

The criteria for inclusion of serials in the humanities follow the disciplines outlined in *HLAS*:

Bibliography and General Works
Art
Folklore
History
Language
Literature
Music
Philosophy

The journals covering the above disciplines published in the four countries totaled 240 (Argentina, 150; Chile, 64; Paraguay, 10; Uruguay, 16) (table C).

Analysis and Interpretation

The value of a particular index depends on both the country and subject that are being studied, since each index has strengths and weaknesses. For example, *Historical Abstracts* focuses on history and related interdisciplinary studies but does not possess balanced geographical coverage of indexed journals to complement its strong emphasis on history. A majority of cited journals in *Historical Abstracts* are from Argentina; entries from Chile, Paraguay, and Uruguay appear in much smaller numbers (table B).

Hispanic American Periodicals Index (HAPI) covers all of the subject areas addressed in this paper. It does, however, emphasize journals published in the United States. From the information presented in table A, it appears that *HAPI* and the other indexes cover journals either from Argentina or from the United States extremely well. It is rare, however, that an index covers journals published both in Argentina and in the United States (table B).

Indexed Journals: A Guide to Latin American Serials (GLAS) is a different tool. It is an index of indexes rather than an index of serials (table B). It is not surprising, therefore, that both its geographical and subject coverage is rather comprehensive. Of the indexes examined in this paper, *GLAS* has the most entries for Argentina, Chile, Paraguay, and Uruguay (table A). Only among entries relating to the United States does *GLAS* display some weakness. *GLAS* does relatively well overall in the different subject areas, but its subject coverage is strongest in geographical coverage. Unfortunately, this was a one-time publication and it has not been updated since 1983.

In contrast with *GLAS*, *Handbook of Latin American Studies (HLAS)* (table B) is a straightforward and sophisticated index of books, journal articles, and government publications. It has almost as much overall coverage in serial publications by country as *GLAS*. It ranks second in the number of entries for Argentina and Chile, ties with *GLAS* for the most entries for Paraguay, ranks third for Uruguay, and fourth for U.S.-published journals.

In terms of subject coverage, *HLAS* exhibits a few key pockets of strength. In folklore, for example, it has more entries than any of the others. It also ranks second for both history and philosophy.

The *International Bibliography of Books and Articles on the Modern Languages and Literatures (MLA)* (table B) differs from the others in that it is more geographically focused. It contains the most entries for journals published in the United States but is comparatively weak in entries for Argentina, Chile, Paraguay, and Uruguay. In the different subject areas, *MLA* has the most entries for bibliography and general works, art, language, and literature. It ranks second in the number of entries for folklore and fourth for both music and philosophy. In history it ranks fifth.

Historical Abstracts (HistAb) (table B) has the most entries in history. By far the most entries are from journals published in the United States, then come Argentina, and far behind Paraguay, Chile, and Uruguay.

Readers' Guide to Periodical Literature (RG) is the weakest of the indexes. It covers more than 180 general interest popular American periodicals. Some of the same titles are also in *Magazine Index*, which also includes some U.S. journals that focus on Latin America. Only ten serials focused on Latin America are in *RG*. Nevertheless, it is useful, since it indexes current popular journals which often cover topics that deal with Latin American current affairs and issues.

In terms of combinations of indexes, it appears that the best overall coverage would be achieved by using either *GLAS* or *HLAS* combined with *MLA*. Both *GLAS* and *HLAS* have a strong Argentine, Chilean, Paraguayan, and Uruguayan focus and the *MLA* has a strong U.S. publication focus. The weakness of the geographical focus of one index would be offset by the strengths of the others. As noted in table C, either combination would include at least one index with the largest or second largest number of subject entries.

The indexes discussed cover more Argentine serials than serials from other Southern Cone countries, as evidenced by the number of overlapping index citations for Argentina. Paraguay has the fewest overlapping entries, so it appears to be the country with the least emphasis placed on it by these six indexes. One might speculate that this is attributable to the fact that Paraguay is a small country, not a powerful force among nations. Smallness, however, cannot be automatically equated with unimportance, as witness the Central American countries Nicaragua and El Salvador, which have been in the world's eye throughout this decade.

Using these same overlapping citations criteria on subject areas, history is the subject area that is most heavily covered. Music is indisputably the least heavily covered subject area; it did not have one overlapping listing.

Subject coverage among U.S. serial publications produces an encouraging number of entries (table E). The leading discipline is literature which, combined with language, accounts for 104 entries. Bibliography and general works, history, and art follow, while again folklore, music, and philosophy have the least coverage.

Finally, comparing these serials to the latest edition of *Ulrich's Plus*, the serials not included in any of the major indexes of this study add up to an impressive 245 publications. A list of them is appended (table B).

Period Covered

During the decade 1979–1989 serial publications faced common problems in all Latin American countries. This ten-year period was marked by continuous economic and political crises owing to constant political unrest, censorship, persecution, *concientización* (consciousness-raising) of the conditions of oppressed classes, and human rights violations, making the region a challenging laboratory for research and new studies. This period was also marked by a series of commemorations of important historical events which sparked research, such as the War of the Pacific (1879–1883); the bicentennial of Andrés Bello (1781–1981); the 175th celebration of the birth of Domingo Faustino (1811—1986); the bicentennial of Simón Bolivar's birth (1783–1983); and the "Cien años de 'Azul': the 1888–1988" celebration of Rubén Dario's most acclaimed work. The year 1982 was also one of celebration for Latin American literature, with the Nobel Prize for Literature being awarded to a Latin American writer, Gabriel García Márquez.

Conclusion

In evaluating the strength of serials covered in the four Southern Cone countries in six important indexes by country and by subject area, the indexes were found to have widely differing strengths and weaknesses. Therefore, a combination of indexes would possess synergistic advantages. In the humanities, either an *MLA–GLAS* combination or an *MLA–HLAS* combination would seem to be the most desirable approach for a successful general bibliographic search for this period. Specialized, narrow searches would, of course, require a different combination of indexes. For example, one would use *HAPI* for a social sciences search and *MLA* for a literature search.

Analysis showed a lack of coverage of certain subject areas and countries, implying that more effort is required to increase coverage of these neglected subject areas and countries. "In 1983, it was encouraging that the number of Latin American publications covered by indexing services increased, yet comparatively few Latin American serials of scholarly interest were indexed."[16]

I found that there has been no significant advance in the coverage of Latin American serials publications in these six major indexes for this period. Further study is needed. A cooperative venture among index and abstract publishers could be explored in order to improve the coverage of the journals in both subject scope and geographic coverage. As indicated in Table B7 (Ulrich's) there are 245 journals published in the United States and in the Southern Cone which focus on Latin

America and the humanities but which are not indexed by any of the six major indexes.

Thus, the necessity to design a project to compare serial usage among university libraries is evident. Owing to the considerable overlap existing in the major indexes (table C), "core" lists could be generated which could assist in the acquisition of serials as well as in the decision for inclusion in indexes and abstracting services.

Table A. Index Coverage by Country

Subject	*HAPI*	*GLAS*	*HLAS*	*MLA*	*HistAb*	*RG*	Unindexed
				ARGENTINA			
Bibliography and General Works	2	8	0	12	0	0	60
Art	0	4	4	0	1	0	11
Folklore	1	1	6	1	0	0	3
History	9	25	21	1	20	0	26
Language	1	16	1	6	1	0	4
Literature	2	16	5	5	1	0	54
Music	0	4	0	0	0	0	8
Philosophy	3	34	13	2	2	0	12
Total journals indexed [a]	16	96	34	24	23	0	167
				CHILE			
Bibliography and General Works	1	5	0	22	0	0	10
Art	1	3	1	2	0	0	2
Folklore	0	1	5	0	0	0	1
History	3	11	8	2	7	0	6
Language	1	7	2	7	0	0	0
Literature	2	7	4	10	0	0	6
Music	1	1	4	0	0	0	2
Philosophy	4	13	5	1	0	0	2
Total journals indexed [a]	14	38	14	13	7	0	28
				PARAGUAY			
Bibliography and General Works	1	1	1	1	0	0	3
Art	0	1	0	0	0	0	0
Folklore	0	0	1	0	0	0	1
History	0	1	4	0	4	0	4
Language	0	1	2	0	0	0	0
Literature	0	1	2	0	0	0	3
Music	0	0	0	0	0	0	0
Philosophy	0	1	2	0	0	0	1
Total journals indexed [a]	2	5	4	1	5	0	11

[a] Total includes journals covering multiple subject areas.

Table A (continued)

Subject	*HAPI*	*GLAS*	*HLAS*	*MLA*	*HistAb*	*RG*	Unindexed
				URUGUAY			
Bibliography and General Works	0	0	2	2	0	0	11
Art	0	0	0	1	0	0	2
Folklore	0	0	0	0	0	0	0
History	1	3	4	0	1	0	10
Language	1	2	1	1	0	0	2
Literature	2	2	2	3	0	0	15
Music	0	0	0	0	0	0	1
Philosophy	0	3	3	0	0	0	3
Total journals indexed [a]	4	8	5	5	1	0	39
				UNITED STATES			
Bibliography and General Works	8	0	13	17	17	9	
Art	7	0	9	8	5	0	
Folklore	2	0	16	7	10	0	
History	13	0	56	9	61	1	
Language	8	1	13	20	1	0	
Literature	28	1	33	48	6	2	
Music	4	0	8	1	3	0	
Philosophy	1	0	9	2	1	0	
Total journals indexed [a]	76	1	109	79	61	10	

[a] Total includes journals covering multiple subject areas.

Table B. Country Coverage of Journals Covered by Index

Subject	Argentina	Chile	Paraguay	Uruguay	United States
		Handbook of Latin American Studies (HLAS)			
Bibliography and General Works	0	0	1	2	13
Art	4	1	0	0	9
Folklore	6	5	1	0	16
History	21	8	4	4	56
Language	1	2	2	1	13
Literature	5	4	2	2	33
Music	0	4	0	0	8
Philosophy	13	5	2	3	9
Total journals indexed [a]	34	14	4	5	109
		Hispanic American Periodicals Index (HAPI)			
Bibliography and General Works	2	1	1	0	8
Art	0	1	0	0	7
Folklore	1	0	0	0	2
History	9	3	0	1	13
Language	1	1	0	1	8
Literature	2	2	0	2	28
Music	0	1	0	0	4
Philosophy	3	4	0	0	1
Total journals indexed [a]	16	14	2	4	76
		A Guide to Latin American Serials (GLAS)			
Bibliography and General Works	8	5	1	0	0
Art	4	3	1	0	0
Folklore	1	1	0	0	0
History	25	11	1	3	0
Language	16	7	1	2	1
Literature	16	7	1	2	1
Music	4	1	0	0	0
Philosophy	34	13	1	3	0
Total journals indexed [a]	96	38	5	8	1

[a] Total includes journals covering multiple subject areas.

Table B (continued)

Subject	Argentina	Chile	Paraguay	Uruguay	United States
MLA International Bibliography of Books and Articles on the Modern Languages and Literatures (MLA)					
Bibliography and General Works	12	2	1	2	17
Art	0	2	0	1	8
Folklore	1	0	0	0	7
History	1	2	0	0	9
Language	6	7	0	1	20
Literature	5	10	0	3	48
Music	0	0	0	0	1
Philosophy	2	1	0	0	2
Total journals indexed [a]	24	13	1	5	79
Historical Abstracts (HistAb)					
Bibliography and General Works	0	0	0	0	17
Art	1	0	0	0	5
Folklore	0	0	0	0	10
History	20	7	4	1	61
Language	1	0	0	0	1
Literature	1	0	0	0	6
Music	0	0	0	0	3
Philosophy	2	0	0	0	1
Total journals indexed [a]	23	7	5	1	61

[a] Total includes journals covering multiple subject areas.

Table C. Journals and Their Indexing Sources by Country

Publication	*HAPI*	*GLAS*	*HLAS*	*MLA*	*HistAb*	*RG*
ARGENTINA						
Actualidad Pastoral		X				
Administración Militar y Logística		X				
Anales				X		
Anales de Arqueología y Etnología			X			
Anales de la Sociedad Rural Argentina			X			
Anales del Instituto de Arte Americano e Investigaciones Estéticas		X			X	
Anuario del Departamento de Historia		X			X	
Anuario del Instituto de Investigaciones Históricas		X			X	
Anuario Interamericano de Archivos	X				X	
Archivum		X		X	X	
Argentina Austral		X				
Argentores		X				
Argos		X				
Atenea					X	
Ateneo		X				
Atlantida		X		X		
Boletín de la Academia Argentina de Letras		X		X	X	
Boletín de la Academia Nacional de la Historia	X		X		X	
Boletín de Ciencias Políticas y Sociales			X			
Boletín de Estudios Germánicos				X		
Boletín del Archivo General de la Provincia de Santa Fe		X			X	
Boletín del Instituto Americano de Estudios Vascos		X				
Boletín del Instituto de Historia Argentina y Americana					X	
Boletín del Instituto de Historia Argentina "Doctor Emilio Ravignani"			X		X	

Publication	*HAPI*	*GLAS*	*HLAS*	*MLA*	*HistAb*	*RG*
ARGENTINA (cont.)						
Boletín Interamericano de Archivos— SEE Anuario Interamericano de Archivos						
Brasil/Cultura	X					
Buenos Aires Musical		X				
Certeza		X				
Ciencia y Fe		X				
Comentario		X				
Cristianismo y Sociedad		X				
Criterio			X	X		
Cuadernos de Cristianismo y Sociedad		X				
Cuadernos de Extensión Universitaria				X		
Cuadernos de Filosofía			X			
Cuadernos de Historia de España		X			X	
Cuadernos de la Universidad Católica de Cuyo		X				
Cuadernos de Teología		X				
Cuadernos del Idioma		X		X		
Cuadernos del Instituto Nacional de Antropología			X			
Cuadernos del Sur			X		X	
Cuadernos Monásticos		X				
Cuadrante			X			
Cursos y Conferencias		X				
Cuyo		X	X		X	
Davar		X	X			
Desarrollo Económico	X		X			
Documentos de Actualización		X				
Encuentro		X				
Ensayos y Estudios		X				
Escritos de Filosofía		X				
Estrategia—SEE Revista Argentina de Estudios Estratégicos						
Estudios Buenos Aires: Academia Literaria del Plata, 1911–				X		
Estudios Buenos Aires: Instituto de Investigaciones Históricas [beginning date unknown]		X				

Publication	*HAPI*	*GLAS*	*HLAS*	*MLA*	*HistAb*	*RG*
ARGENTINA (cont.)						
Estudios de Filosofía y Religión Orientales		X				
Estudios Históricos		X				
Estudios Teológicos y Filosóficos				X		
Etnia				X		
FEPA Estudios e Investigaciones			X			
Fichero Bibliográfico Hispanoamericano		X				
Filología		X		X		
Filosofía		X				
Genealogía		X				
Hispamérica		X				
Hispania		X				
Histonium en su Nueva Dimensión		X				
Historia		X			X	
Historia Argentina		X				
Humanitas		X		X		
Imago Mundi		X				
Incipit				X		
Información Ecuménica		X				
Integración Latinoamericana	X					
Investigación y Docencia					X	
Investigaciones y Ensayos	X		X		X	
Iris				X		
Latinoamericana		X				
Los Libros		X				
Libros Argentinos				X		
Liturgia		X				
Maj'shavot		X				
Megafon	X	X				
Mikael		X				
Norte		X				
Nuestra Arquitectura		X				
Nuestra Historia	X		X		X	
Pensamiento Cristiano		X				
Philosophia		X				
Polifonía		X				
Psallite		X				
Quaderni Italiani di Buenos Aires				X		

Publication	*HAPI*	*GLAS*	*HLAS*	*MLA*	*HistAb*	*RG*
ARGENTINA (cont.)						
Realidad Económica	X					
Relaciones de la Sociedad Argentina de Antropología			X			
Repertorio Latinoamericano	X	X				
Revista Argentina de Estudios Estratégicos	X	X	X			
Revista Argentina de Lingüística				X		
La Revista Católica		X				
Revista de Ciencias Jurídicas y Sociales				X		
Revista de Economía y Estadística			X			
Revista de Estudios Clásicos		X				
Revista de Estudios Hispánicos		X				
Revista de Filología Hispánica				X		
Revista de Filosofía			X			
Revista de Filosofía Latinoamericana			X			
Revista de Historia		X				
Revista de Historia Americana y Argentina			X		X	
Revista de la Biblioteca Nacional		X				
Revista de la Escuela Superior de Guerra		X				
Revista de la Facultad de Filosofía y Humanidades		X				
Revista de la Junta de Estudios Históricos de Mendoza		X	X		X	
Revista de la Junta Provincial de Historia de Córdoba			X			
Revista de la Lengua Inglesa		X				
Revista de la Universidad de Buenos Aires		X				
Revista de la Universidad de Córdoba			X			
Revista de la Universidad Nacional de La Plata			X			
Revista de Literaturas Modernas		X				
Revista del Archivo General de la Nación					X	

Publication	*HAPI*	*GLAS*	*HLAS*	*MLA*	*HistAb*	*RG*
			ARGENTINA (cont.)			
Revista del Instituto de Historia Antigua Oriental		X				
Revista del Instituto de Historia del Derecho			X			
Revista del Instituto del Antropología			X			
Revista del Instituto del Derecho Ricardo Levene		X			X	
Revista Genealógica Americana		X				
Revista Latinoamericana de Filosofía		X	X			
Revista Litúrgica Argentina		X				
Revista Teológica		X				
Revista Universidad Nacional				X		
Revista Universitaria de Letras				X		
Runa	X	X				
San Martín		X				
Sapientia	X		X			
Sedoi Documentación		X				
Sedoi Información		X				
Selecciones de Servicio Social		X				
La Sirviente				X		
Sociedad Argentina de Profesores de Sagrada Escritura		X				
Stromata	X	X				
Studio Croática		X				
Summa		X				
Sumarios		X				
Sur	X		X	X		
Teología		X				
Testimonio Cristiano		X				
Todo Es Historia	X					
Trabajos y Comunicaciones		X	X		X	
Tribuna Musical		X				
Universidad		X	X			
Universidades			X			
Universitas		X				
Vicus Cuadernos :Lingüística				X		
Vida Pastoral		X				

Publication	*HAPI*	*GLAS*	*HLAS*	*MLA*	*HistAb*	*RG*
CHILE						
Acta Literaria				X		
Aisthesis	X	X				
Anales de la Universidad de Chile		X		X		
Anales de la Facultad de Teología		X				
Anales del Instituto de la Patagonia		X				
Archivos del Folklore Chileno		X				
Atenea	X		X	X	X	
Auca		X				
Bizantion–Nea Hellas				X		
Boletín de Filología			X	X		
Boletín de la Academia Chilena Correspondiente de la Real Española		X				
Boletín de la Academia Chilena de la Historia	X		X		X	
Boletín de la Universidad de Chile		X				
Ca		X				
Cendoc		X				
Chungara			X			
Cuadernos de Economía	X					
Cuadernos de Historia	X		X			
Cuadernos Franciscanos de Renovación		X				
Dial		X				
EURE	X					
Ercilla		X				
Estudios		X				
Estudios Filológicos		X		X		
Estudios Filosóficos		X				
Estudios de Historia de los Instituciones Políticas y Sociales		X				
Estudios Internacionales	X					
Estudios Públicos	X					
Estudios Sociales	X		X			
Finis Terrae		X			X	
Historia	X		X			
Hoy		X				

Publication	*HAPI*	*GLAS*	*HLAS*	*MLA*	*HistAb*	*RG*
			CHILE (cont.)			
Iglesia de Santiago		X				
Lenguas Modernas		X		X		
Mapocho	X		X	X		
Mensaje		X				
El Mercurio		X				
Monografías Anexas a los Anales de la Universidad de Chile					X	
Norte Grande			X			
Nueva Atenea–SEE Atenea						
Nueva Revista del Pacifico				X		
Política y Espíritu			X			
RLA				X		
La Revista Católica		X				
Revista Chilena de Historia del Derecho		X			X	
Revista Chilena de Historia y Geografía	X		X		X	
Revista Chilena de Literatura	X			X		
Revista de Estudios Atacamenos		X				
Revista de Estudios Históricos–Jurídicos		X			X	
Revista de Filosofía		X				
Revista de Historia		X				
Revista de Lingüística Teórica y Aplicada		X				
Revista de Marina		X				
Revista del Pacifico				X		
Revista Musical Chilena	X		X			
Revista Signos				X		
Revista Universitaria		X				
Seladoc		X				
Signos		X	X			
Stylo		X				
Taller de Letras			X			
Teología y Vida		X				
Teoría		X				
Testimonio		X				

Publication	*HAPI*	*GLAS*	*HLAS*	*MLA*	*HistAb*	*RG*
PARAGUAY						
Acción		X				
Alcor		X				
Diálogo				X		
Estudios Paraguayos	X		X		X	
Historia del Paraguay		X			X	
Historia Paraguaya			X		X	
Journal of the Association of English Teachers		X				
Revista Paraguaya de Sociología	X		X		X	
Sendero		X				
Suplemento Antropológico			X		X	
URUGUAY						
Adelphos		X				
Administrative Science Quarterly			X			
Boletín de la Academia Nacional de Letras				X		
Boletín de Filología		X		X		
Boletín del Instituto Nacional		X				
Boletín Histórico		X				
Centro Latinoamericano de Economía Humana			X			
Comentarios Bibliográficos Americanos		X		X		
Cuadernos del Itu		X				
Estudios de Ciencias y Letras			X			
Foro Literario	X	X		X		
Libro Anual–Instituto Teológico del Uruguay		X				
Maldoror	X					
Revista de la Biblioteca Nacional	X		X			
Revista Histórica	X		X		X	
Revista Nacional				X		

Publication	*HAPI*	*GLAS*	*HLAS*	*MLA*	*HistAb*	*RG*
UNITED STATES						
Abstracts of Dissertations for the Degree of Doctor of Philosophy, with the Title...				X		
Administrative Science Quarterly			X			
Afro-Hispanic Review				X		
Agenda	X					
Agricultural History			X		X	
Alcance				X		
América Indígena					X	
American Anthropologist			X	X	X	
American Antiquity	X		X		X	
American Archeology					X	
American Archivist					X	
American Ethnologist			X			
American Hispanist				X		
American Historical Review			X		X	
American Jewish Archives			X			
American Neptune			X			
American Speech			X			
American University Studies II				X		
Americas	X		X	X	X	X
Americas	X		X	X	X	
The Americas Review	X			X		
Annals (OAS)			X			
Anthropological Linguistics			X			
Areito	X		X			
Arizona and the West			X			
Atisbos	X					
Aztlan	X					
The Bilingual Review	X			X		
Boletín: Handbook of Latin American Art			X			
Boletín de la Academía Norte-americana de la Lengua Española			X	X		
The Borderlands Journal	X					
Brigham Young University Studies			X			
Bulletin of Latin American Research	X					

Publication	*HAPI*	*GLAS*	*HLAS*	*MLA*	*HistAb*	*RG*
UNITED STATES (cont.)						
CEPAL Review	X					
Canto Libre	X					
Caracol	X					
Caribbean Review	X		X		X	
Catholic Historical Review			X			
The Centennial Review of Arts and Sciences			X			
Chasqui	X			X		
Chiricu				X		
Chisme–Arte	X					
Church History			X			
Círculo				X		
Comparative Literature Symposium (Proceedings)				X		
Comparative Political Studies			X			
Comparative Urban Research			X			
Confluencia	X			X		
Consenso				X		
Crítica				X		
Crítica Hispánica				X		
Cuban Studies	X		X			
Current Anthropology			X			
Current History			X			X
De Colores	X					
Diacritics			X			
Dieciocho				X		
Discurso Literario				X		
Dispositio	X					
Dissertation Abstracts International				X		
ECA	X					
Economic Development and Cultural Change	X					
La Educación	X					
Los Ensayistas				X		
Escandalar	X					
Escribano					X	
Estreno				X		
Estudios Andinos			X			
Estudios Cubanos–SEE Cuban Studies						

Publication	*HAPI*	*GLAS*	*HLAS*	*MLA*	*HistAb*	*RG*
			UNITED STATES (cont.)			
Estudios Mexicanos–SEE Mexican Studies						
Ethnohistory			X		X	
Ethnology			X		X	
Ethnomusicology			X			
Explicación de Textos Literarios	X					
Explorations in Ethnic History					X	
Feminaria	X					
Fletcher Forum: A Journal of Studies in International Affairs					X	
Fletcher Forum of World Affairs					X	
The Florida Historical Quarterly			X		X	
Folklore Americas				X		
Foreign Affairs					X	
Foreign Policy					X	
Geographical Review			X			
Georgetown University Round Table on Languages and Linguistics				X		
Gestos				X		
Grassroots Development	X					
Grito del Sol	X					
Hispamérica	X	X	X	X		
Hispania			X	X		
Hispanic American Historical Review	X		X	X	X	
Hispanic Journal	X		X	X		
Hispanic Review	X		X	X	X	
Hispanofila			X	X		
The Historian			X			
Human Rights Quarterly					X	
IMR	X					
Ideologies and Literature	X		X	X		
Interciencia	X					
Inter-American Economic Affairs	X		X			
Inter-American Music Review	X		X			

Publication	*HAPI*	*GLAS*	*HLAS*	*MLA*	*HistAb*	*RG*
UNITED STATES (cont.)						
Interamerican Review of Bibliography					X	
International Journal of American Linguistics	X		X			
International Journal of Politics, Culture and Society					X	
International Studies Notes					X	
Inti	X		X	X		
Journal of American Folklore			X			
Journal of Anthropological Research			X		X	
Journal of Borderlands Studies	X					
Journal of Caribbean Studies	X			X		
A Journal of Church and State			X			
Journal of Developing Areas	X		X			
Journal of Family History			X			
Journal of the Folklore Institute			X			
Journal of Folklore Research					X	
Journal of the History of Ideas			X		X	
Journal of Interamerican Studies			X		X	
Journal of Inter-American Studies and World Affairs	X		X		X	
Journal of Interdisciplinary History			X			
Journal of International Affairs					X	
Journal of Latin American Lore	X		X		X	
Journal of Latin American Studies	X				X	
Journal of Mayan Linguistics				X		
Journal of Mississippi History			X		X	
Journal of Modern History					X	
Journal of Politics			X			
Journal of Popular Culture					X	

Publication	*HAPI*	*GLAS*	*HLAS*	*MLA*	*HistAb*	*RG*
UNITED STATES (cont.)						
Journal of Social History			X		X	
Journal of Spanish Studies	X		X			
Journal of the West			X			
Journal of Third World Studies					X	
Kentucky Foreign Language Quarterly				X		
Kentucky Romance Quarterly			X			
Language			X			
Latin American Digest			X			
Latin American Indian Literatures Journal	X		X	X		
Latin American Literary Review	X		X	X		
Latin American Music Review	X		X	X		
Latin American Perspectives	X		X			
Latin American Research Review	X		X		X	
Latin American Review			X			
Latin American Theatre Review	X		X	X		
Letras Femeninas				X		
Linden Lane Magazine			X			
The Literary Review				X		
Literature and Contemporary Revolutionary Culture				X		
Luso-Brazilian Review	X		X	X	X	
Maize				X		
Marxist Perspectives			X			
Mesoamerica	X				X	
Mester	X		X	X		
Mexican Studies	X					
Modern Language Journal			X			
Modern Language Notes			X			
Modern Language Quarterly				X		
Monographic Review				X		
NACLA Report on the Americas	X					
Nawpa Pacha	X		X			
New Literary History					X	

Publication	*HAPI*	*GLAS*	*HLAS*	*MLA*	*HistAb*	*RG*
UNITED STATES (cont.)						
New Mexico Historical Review			X		X	
New Republic			X			
New Scholar	X		X			
New World					X	
The New York Times Book Review				X		X
The New York Times Magazine				X		X
Newsweek						X
Notes of Translation				X		
La Nueva Democracia				X		
Nueva Revista de Filología Hispánica			X			
Nuevo Texto Crítico	X					
Orbis			X			
PCCLAS Proceedings	X		X			
Pacific Historical Review			X		X	
La Palabra				X		
El Palacio					X	
Peasant Studies Newsletter			X		X	
Phylon			X			
Plantation Society in the Americas					X	
Plaza				X		
Prismal/Cabral				X		
Proceedings of the American Philosophical Society			X			
Publications in Folklore Contact Studies				X		
Publications in Modern Philology				X		
Punto de Contacto/Point of Contact	X					
RCA Review–SEE RCAH Review						
RCAH Review	X					
Review	X		X	X		
Review of Latin American Studies	X					
Revista Bilingüe–SEE The Bilingual Review						
Revista Chicano-Riqueña	X					

Publication	*HAPI*	*GLAS*	*HLAS*	*MLA*	*HistAb*	*RG*
UNITED STATES (cont.)						
Revista de Estudios Colombianos	X					
Revista de Estudios Hispánicos			X	X		
Revista Hispánica Moderna			X	X		
Revista Iberoamericana	X		X			
Revista Interamericana de Bibliografía	X		X	X	X	
Revista Monografía–SEE Monographic Review						
Rocky Mountain Review of Language and Literature				X		
SAIS Review					X	
SALALM Papers	X					
SECOLAS Annals			X	X	X	
Science and Society			X			
Series Towards a Social History of Hispanic and Luso-Brazilian Literature				X		
Signs			X			
Society for Historians of American Foreign Relations Newsletter					X	
South Eastern Latin Americanist			X			
Southern California Quarterly			X			
Southern Folklore Quarterly			X		X	
Southwestern Historical Quarterly			X		X	
Southwestern Journal of Anthropology					X	
Studies in Comparative International Development	X		X		X	
Studies in History and Politics					X	
Studies in Latin American Popular Culture	X		X	X	X	
Studies in Short Fiction	X					
Symposium				X		
Teachers of English to Speakers of Other Languages				X		
Time						X
Tinta				X		
Translation				X		

Publication	*HAPI*	*GLAS*	*HLAS*	*MLA*	*HistAb*	*RG*
UNITED STATES (cont.)						
Twayne's Critical History of the Short Story				X		
UFSI Reports			X			
ULULA				X		
UN Chronicle						X
UNESCO Courier						X
U.S. News & World Report						X
Universal Human Rights					X	
Via			X			
Vórtice	X		X	X		
Western Folklore			X			
The Western Historical Quarterly			X			
Women's Studies				X		
World Affairs					X	
World Literature Today	X		X	X		
World Politics					X	
World Press Review						X
Xavier University Studies				X		
Yearbook of Comparative and General Literature				X		

The following titles, listed in the latest edition of *Ulrich's Plus*, are not indexed in any of the sources reviewed.

ARGENTINA

ALA
Academia Nacional de Bellas Artes. Anuario
Academia Nacional de la Historia. Investigaciones y Ensayos
Academia Porteña del Lunfardo. Boletín
Academia Provincial de la Historia. Boletín
Aconcagua
Ahijuna
Alejandria
Aletheia
Amaru
Análisis-Confirmado
Anfora
Antología
Antología Poética del Partido de Esteban
Anuario de Poetas Contemporáneos
Aquario

ARGENTINA (cont.)
Aquas Vivas
Argentina
Argentina (Year) Ante el Mundo
Argentina. Biblioteca del Congreso de la Nación. Boletín
Argentina. Centro Nacional de Documentación e Información Colectiva. Boletín Bibliográfico
Argentina. Departamento de Estudios Históricos Navales. Serie E: Documentos
Argentina. Instituto de Guerra. Dirección
Argentina en Positivo
Argentina Futuro
Ars, Revista de Arte
Arte Informa
Asociación Archivística Argentina. Boletín
Autores
Bibliografía Argentina de Artes y Letras
Bibliografía Argentina Universitaria
Bibliografía Temática sobre Judaísmo Argentino
Bibliografía Teológica Comentada del Área I
Biblioteca
Biblioteca Cultura Popular
Biblioteca de Cultura Vasca
Biblioteca de Poesía
Boletín Bibliográfico Lajouane
Boletín de Historia de Arte y Estética
Boletín de Información Bibliográfica
Boletín de Literatura Argentina e Iberoamericana
Buenos Aires (Province). Archivo Histórico
Buenos Aires Musical
Capital de la Poesía
Centro de Investigaciones en Ciencias de la . . .
Clarín Internacional
Colección Conocimiento de la Argentina
Colección Estudios Latinoamericanos
Colección Pensamiento Argentino
Colección Poesía del Nuevo Tiempo
Comportamiento Humano
Cormorán y Delfín
Cuadernos de Historia del Arte
Cuadernos de la Boca del Riachuelo
Cuadernos de la Brújula
Cuadernos de Numismática y Ciencias Históricas
Cuadernos del Maipú

ARGENTINA (cont.)

Cuadrante N.O.A.
Cultura de la Argentina Contemporánea
De la Mano con el Arte
Despertador
Devenir Histórico
Dinamis
Discurso y Realidad
Documentos de Geohistoria Regional
Ecos de Portugal
Efluvios
English Language Journal
Equiu
Espacios de Crítica y Producción
Estudios Argentinos
Ethos
Ficta-Difusora de Música Antigua
Filosofar Cristiano
Fin de Siglo
Folia Histórica del Nordeste
Fondo Nacional de las Artes. Informativo
Fulturable
Futuro
Generación 70
Gente y la Actualidad
Goetheana Periódico Literario
Golpe
Guía de la Música Argentina
Hacia la Luz
Histonium en Su Nueva Dimensión
Hojas de Poesía
Hojas del Caminador, Colección de Poesía
Hojas Literarias Ilustradas
Hontanar
Ideas
Ideas en Arte y Tecnología
Igitur Revista Literaria
Imparcial
Instituto de Numismática e Historia de San . . .
Instituto Nacional de Investigaciones Folclóricas
Janus
Jazzband
Lagrimal Trifurca

ARGENTINA (cont.)
Lealtad
Lecciones de Historia Jurídica
Lenguajes
Letras de Buenos Aires
Línea
Lucanor
Magyar Tortenelmi Szemle
Microcrítica
Nuestro Anhelo
Obertura
Ornitorrinco
Páginas y Tapas
Paisano
Panorama
Patria
Patristica et Mediaevalia
Pie de Página
Pleamar
Poesía en la Calle
Poesía-Poesía
Poesía y Poetas
Por Alquimia
Porteño
Premisa
Prensa Confidencial
Primera Plana
Protagonismo
Provincia
Pueblo
Puente: Lectura para Todos
Punto de Vista
Punto Omega
Quadrivium
Referente
Relatos Inéditos Argentinos
Reportero
Retorno del Pueblo
Revista Acento
Revista Argentina
Revista de Estética
Revista de Historia de Rosario
Revista Histórica

ARGENTINA (cont.)

Revista la Nación
Río Negro, Argentina. Dirección Provincial de Cultura. Monografías
Savia Argentina
Sembrador
Señales
Siete Días Ilustrados
Sociedad Argentina de Escritores. Boletín
Somos
T & C
Tabla Redonda
Talita
Teósofo
Testigo
Torre de Papel
Ultimo Reino
Umbral 2000
Universidad de Buenos Aires. Facultad de Filosofía y Letras. Gaceta
Universidad de Buenos Aires. Instituto de Historia Antigua. Colección Estudios
Universidad Nacional de Córdoba. Biblioteca
Universidad Nacional de Cuyo. Biblioteca Ce . . .
Universo
Venga Que le Cuento
Vida Silvestre
Voz del Pueblo

Total: 166

CHILE

Andrés Bello Biblioteca. Colección
Antología del Folklore Musical Chileno
Bicicleta
Boletín Antártico Chileno
Boletín Bibliográfica de Revista "Signos"
Chile. Dirección de Bibliotecas Archivos y . . .
Chile. Ejército. Anexo Histórico. Memorial
Cormorán
Cuadernos de Filosofía
Dimensión Histórica de Chile
Época
Instituto Antártico Chileno. Contribución
Libros Chilenos en Venta
Nueva Línea
Opciones

CHILE (cont.)

Orfeo
Que Pasa
Quinta Rueda
Revista Chilena en Venta
Revista de Santiago
Revista Philosóphica
Revista Signos de Valparaíso
Selecciones del Reader's Digest
Trapananda
Trilce de Poesía
Universidad Católica de Valparaíso. Resumen
Universidad de Chile. Facultad de Artes. Revista
Vea
Total: 28

PARAGUAY

A B C Revista
Biblioteca de Estudios Paraguayos
Colección Histórica
Colección Literatura
Época
Estudios Folklóricos Paraguayos
Historia Militar del Paraguay
Instituto Femenino de Investigaciones Históricas
Nuestra Tiempo
Poetas
Síntesis
Total: 11

URUGUAY

América Meridional
Anuario Bibliográfico Uruguayo
Aquí
Archivos de la Biblioteca Nacional
Aves del Arca
Biblioteca "José Artigas". Boletín
Boletín Histórico del Ejército
Bolsilibros
Catálogo de Publicaciones Latinoamericanas
Claridad
Crítica
Cuadernos de Literatura

URUGUAY (cont.)

Cuadernos de Semiótica
Cuadernos Uruguayos de Filosofía
Eco d'Italia
Ensayo y Testimonio
Estudios Críticos
Gacetilla Austral
Garcín: Libro de Cultura
Grandes Todos
Historia Uruguaya. Segunda Serie: los Hombres
Hoy Es Historia
Imagenes
Luz del Cosmos
Narradores de Arca
Narrativa Latinoamericana
Nueva República
Numen
Ovum
Poesía
Programa
Propuesta
Pueblo Oriental
Pupila: Libros de Nuestro Tiempo
Salón Nacional de Artes Plásticas y Visuales
Torre de los Panoramas
Universidad de la República. Facultad de Humanidades y Ciencias. Revista Lingüística
Universidad de la República. Facultad de Humanidades y Ciencias. Revista Musicología
Universidad de Uruguay. Departamento de Literatura. Revista

Total: 39

Table D. Total Indexing Coverage

Subject	*HAPI*	*GLAS*	*HLAS*	*MLA*	*HistAb*	*RG*	Indexed in *Ulrich's Plus*
Bibliography and General Works	20	14	3	34	0	1	84
Art	8	8	5	11	1	0	15
Folklore	3	2	12	8	0	0	5
History	24	40	37	12	31	1	46
Language	11	27	6	34	1	0	6
Literature	32	27	13	66	1	2	78
Music	5	5	4	1	0	0	11
Philosophy	8	51	23	5	2	1	18
Total journals indexed [a]	86	147	60	121	36	10	234

[a] Total includes journals covering multiple subject areas.

Table E. Number of Journals Indexed by Country and by Subject

Subject	Argentina	Chile	Paraguay	Uruguay	United States
Bibliography and General Works	19	7	4	3	24
Art	7	4	1	1	15
Folklore	9	6	1	0	9
History	51	27	4	8	20
Language	23	14	3	4	29
Literature	26	19	3	8	75
Music	4	6	0	0	5
Philosophy	50	22	3	6	3
Total journals indexed[a]	158	68	12	18	267

[a] Total includes journals covering multiple subject areas.

NOTES

1. *Anglo-American Cataloguing Rules*, 2d ed. (Chicago, IL: American Library Association, 1978), p. 570.

2. Celso Rodríguez, "The Growing Professionalism of Latin American Journals," in *Philosophy and Literature in Latin America: A Critical Assessment of the Current Situation*, Jorge J. E. Gracia and Mireya Camurati, eds. (Albany: State University of New York Press, 1989), p. 190.

3. Gregorio Weinberg, "Aspectos del vaciamiento de la Universidad Argentina durante los recientes regímenes militares," *Cuadernos Americanos*, nueva época, 6 (Nov.-Dec. 1987), 210.

4. Andrew Graham-Yooll, "The Wild Oats They Sowed: Latin American Exiles in Europe and Some of Their Publications," in *Intellectual Migrations: Transcultural Contributions of European and Latin American Emigres: SALALM XXXI* ([Madison, WI]: SALALM Secretariat, Memorial Library, University of Wisconsin–Madison, 1987), pp. 46-53.

5. Laurence Hallewell, "Multinational Participation in Brazilian Book Publishing," in *Latin American Economic Issues: Information Needs and Sources: SALALM XXVI* ([Madison, WI]: SALALM Secretariat, University of Wisconsin–Madison; [Los Angeles]: UCLA Latin American Center Publications, University of California at Los Angeles, 1984), pp. 235-252.

6. Rodríguez, "The Growing Professionalism," p. 191.

7. "Crítica y utopía," Buenos Aires: Editorial Latinoamericana de Ciencias Sociales, in *Handbook of Latin American Studies: No. 46 Humanities*, Dolores Moyano Martin, ed., No. 5, 1982–; nos. 10/11, 1983–1984 (Austin: University of Texas, 1984), p. 298.

8. *Handbook of Latin American Studies: Humanities*, Dolores Moyano Martin, ed. (Austin (etc.): University of Texas (etc.), 1935–).

9. *HAPI: Hispanic American Periodicals Index, 1975–*, Barbara G. Valk, ed. (Los Angeles: UCLA Latin American Center Publications, University of California, 1977–).

10. Paula Hattox Covington, *Indexed Journals: A Guide to Latin American Serials* (Madison, WI: Secretariat, Seminar on the Acquisition of Latin American Library Materials, [1983]).

11. *MLA International Bibliography of Books and Articles on the Modern Languages and Literatures* (New York, NY: Modern Languages Association of America, 1979–).

12. *Historical Abstracts*, Part A, *Modern History Abstracts, 1450–1914*, Vol. 25– (Santa Barbara, CA: American Bibliographical Center of ABC-CLIO, 1971–).

Historical Abstracts, Part B, *Twentieth Century Abstracts, 1914–1988*, Vol. 25– (Santa Barbara, CA: American Bibliographical Center of ABC-CLIO, 1971–).

13. *Readers' Guide to Periodical Literature: An Author and Subject Index* (New York, NY: H. W. Wilson, 1979–).

14. Jorge J. E. Gracia, "Introduction," in *Philosophy and Literature in Latin America: A Critical Assessment of the Current Situation*, Jorge J. E. Gracia and Mireya Camurati, eds. (Albany: State University of New York Press, 1989), p. 3.

15. *Ulrich's Plus* (New York, NY: R. R. Bowker, 1986–).

16. Covington, *Indexed Journals: A Guide to Latin American Serials*, pp. iii-iv.

BIBLIOGRAPHY

Ardissone, Elena. *Bibliografía de índices de publicaciones periódicas Argentinas*. Buenos Aires, Argentina: Universidad de Buenos Aires, Instituto Bibliotecológico, 1984.

Bibliografía Chilena 1982–1984. Santiago, Chile: Biblioteca Nacional, 1989. Microfiche.

Covington, Paula Hattox. *Indexed Journals: A Guide to Latin American Serials*. Madison, WI: Secretariat, Seminar on the Acquisition of Latin American Library Materials, 1983.

Handbook of Latin American Studies, no. 1–, 1935–. Austin (etc.): University of Texas Press (etc.). Beginning with vol. 26, 1964, volumes alternate coverage between social sciences and humanities.

Hispanic American Periodicals Index, 1975–. Barbara G. Valk, ed. Los Angeles: UCLA Latin American Center Publications, University of California, 1977–.

Historical Abstracts. Part A. *Modern History Abstracts, 1450–1914*. Santa Barbara, CA: American Bibliographical Center of ABC-CLIO, 1971–.

Historical Abstracts. Part B. *Twentieth Century Abstracts, 1914–1988*. Santa Barbara, CA: American Bibliographical Center of ABC-CLIO, 1971–.

MLA Directory of Periodicals: A Guide to Journals and Series in Languages and Literatures. 1988/89 ed. New York, NY: Modern Language Association of America, 1988.

MLA International Bibliography of Books and Articles on the Modern Languages and Literatures. New York, NY: Modern Language Association of America, 1979–.

The Modern Language Association International Bibliography Acronyms List and Corresponding Call Number of Titles at the University of Illinois Library at Urbana-Champaign. Sara de Mundo Lo, comp. Urbana: University of Illinois, 1990.

Readers' Guide to Periodical Literature: An Author and Subject Index. 1900–. New York, NY: H. W. Wilson.

Ulrich's Plus. New York, NY: R. R. Bowker, 1986–.

26. Index Coverage of Latin American Journals Published in the Southern Cone: The Social Sciences

Patricia Cárdenas

Introduction

Index coverage of journals published in the Southern Cone, that is, Argentina, Chile, Paraguay and Uruguay, varies with regard to subject area covered and to place of publication. The focus of this paper is on index coverage of social science journals published in the Southern Cone.

Methodology

The subject areas examined follow categories outlined in the *Handbook of Latin American Studies*, social sciences volume: anthropology, including linguistics, economics, education, geography, government and politics, international relations, and sociology.

Two specialized sources on Latin America, *Hispanic American Periodicals Index* (*HAPI*) and the *Handbook of Latin American Studies* (*HLAS*), and various specialized subject indexes, all published in the United States and indexing foreign language journals, including *PAIS Foreign Language Index*, *LLBA-Linguistics and Language Behavior Abstracts*, and *ABC Pol Sci*, were examined, covering a ten-year period from 1979 to 1989. *Indexed Journals: A Guide to Latin American Serials* (*GLAS*) was also consulted for journal titles. The *Bibliographic Guide to Latin American Studies* was omitted as a source because of its emphasis on monographs and also because of the exclusion of serials from the OCLC tapes, which are the core source for materials included in this work.

Analysis and Interpretation

HAPI indexes approximately 250 journals "published throughout the world which regularly contain information on Latin America" and also ". . . leading journals treating Hispanics in the United States."[1] Social science articles are indexed in 32 Southern Cone journals. This was determined by scanning relevant subject headings and noting journal titles. Of these journals, 15 are published in Chile, 12 in Argentina, 3 in Paraguay, and 2 in Uruguay.

The majority of journals (21) is indexed under more than one subject. The area most covered is economics (17 journals), followed by politics (16), international relations (15), anthropology and linguistics (14), education (13), sociology (12), and geography (7).

Coverage by country for each of the subjects examined varies. Chile averages 7 titles in each area, minus geography, with 3. Argentina is strongest in international relations, economics, and politics, also averaging 7 titles; the remaining subjects average 3 journals each. Paraguay's coverage, albeit scant, averages 2 titles in each area while Uruguay has 1 journal each in only international relations and politics.

Published in separate humanities and social sciences volumes in alternate years, *HLAS* is an "extensive, annotated bibliography of material relating to Latin America" prepared by the Hispanic Division of the Library of Congress.[2] Because of the quantity of material received by the Library of Congress, the *HLAS* includes many more journals than *HAPI*. Approximately 61 are social science journals published in the Southern Cone. Of these, 33 are published in Argentina, 21 in Chile, 4 in Uruguay and 3 in Paraguay. The "Journal Abbreviations" section at the end of each subject chapter was consulted for titles and also for designating subject categories, as there are titles indexed in more than one area. Coverage is best for anthropology and linguistics (32 journals), followed by economics (24), education (18), geography (17), politics and sociology (15 each), and international relations (10).

Argentina has strong coverage in economics and anthropology (13 journals each), followed by education and geography (9 each), politics (7), international relations (6), and sociology (4). For Chile, anthropology was covered most (13 journals), followed by economics (9), education (8), politics and geography (6 each), and international relations (4). Paraguay had an average of 2 to 3 journals in each subject area, while Uruguay averaged 1 to 2 journals in anthropology, sociology, economics, and geography.

The *PAIS Foreign Language Index* is a special subject index to literature in the areas of public affairs and public policy, covering economic and social conditions and related fields. It is the foreign language counterpart of *PAIS Bulletin*, which covers English-language materials. Of approximately 1,400 journals selectively scanned, and about 400 indexed in a given year, 53 are published in the Southern Cone. Of these, 22 are from Argentina, 18 from Chile, 10 from Uruguay, and 3 from Paraguay. Economics has the most extensive coverage (50 journals), followed by politics (14), sociology (12), geography (7), education (6), and international relations (3). Argentina is the only country with coverage in each area. All four countries have the most coverage in economics, followed by politics and sociology.

LLBA-Linguistics and Language Behavior Abstracts, formerly *Language and Language Behavior Abstracts*, indexes journals in the fields of anthropology, education, linguistics, and sociology, among others. Of these, 16 are published in the Southern Cone: 8 in Chile, 6 in Argentina, and 1 each in Paraguay and Uruguay.

ABC Pol Sci indexes about 300 titles in the fields of politics, government and international relations. Of these, 121 are foreign journals. Only 1 journal is published in the Southern Cone, *Estudios Internacionales*, from Chile, which is also indexed in *HAPI*.

An examination of these sources indicates more journals indexed from Argentina and Chile, 73 and 62, respectively, and substantially fewer from Uruguay and Paraguay, 17 and 10, respectively.

Economics is the subject most extensively covered (91 journals), followed by anthropology and linguistics (62), sociology (55), education (52), politics (45), geography (31), and international relations (28).

Argentina and Chile have the most coverage in all areas. Paraguay has from 3 to 4 journals in each subject, while Uruguay ranges from 1 journal in education, international relations and geography, to 10 covering economics; the other subjects average 2 to 3 titles each.

Of 219 journal titles cited, 60 overlap among indexes. *PAIS* and the *HLAS* have 13 common titles, *PAIS* and *HAPI* have 10, *HAPI* and the *HLAS* have 13. *LLBA* has 2 common titles with both *PAIS* and *HAPI* and 3 with the *HLAS*. *HAPI* and *ABC* overlap 1 title. The titles most cited number 5: *Cepal Review* (Chile), *Cuadernos de Economía* (Chile), *Desarrollo Económico* (Argentina), *Revista Argentina de Estudios Estratégicos*, and *Revista Paraguaya de Sociología*.

Although *GLAS*, does not index journal articles, it gives a "description and evaluation, by discipline, of the principal indexes and abstracts which cover journals published in or relating to Latin America."[3] The "List of Serials by Subject" indicates place of publication and also where journals are indexed.

In the social science fields, 138 journals published in the Southern Cone are listed: 41 in economics and business, 34 in linguistics, 19 in anthropology and archeology, 18 in politics, 4 in both sociology and education, 2 in geography, and 16 under general social sciences. Of these, 53 titles are included in at least one of the indexes examined: 28 in the *HLAS*, 24 in *PAIS*, 15 in *HAPI*, 10 in *LLBA*, and 1 in *ABC*.

Conclusion

There does not appear to be any subject not covered by at least one of the indexes. Where one index does not give adequate coverage, for example, *PAIS* in international relations, *HAPI* and the *HLAS* can be consulted. In fact, these two indexes, used separately or together, cover all the subject areas examined. For economics, however, *PAIS* gives the best coverage, and for anthropology the *HLAS* is best. Where additional indexes or abstracts in a particular subject need to be consulted, *GLAS* lists and evaluates them by subject.

It should be noted that the coverage given, for example, to Argentine journals does not begin to approximate the total number published. There are 118 Argentine journals listed in the sources discussed. Only 21 are included in the publication *Catálogo de publicaciones seriadas argentinas* (number 1, October 1988), which lists 667 titles. Additionally, in the *Bibliografía Antropológica Argentina, 1980–1985*, there are 79 Argentine anthropology journals listed, of which 14 are included in this survey. For Uruguay, there are 51 journals listed in the 1987 *Anuario Bibliográfico Uruguayo* covering education, geography, anthropology, and politics; this survey cites only 22 titles, covering all the examined disciplines.

This selective survey of index coverage of journals published in the Southern Cone suggests room for expansion and improvement. This is especially true for Paraguay and Uruguay, which have only 7 and 22 titles listed, respectively, in the sources discussed. Argentina and Chile fare better, with 117 and 73 titles, respectively.

One consideration for the lack of journal coverage in certain fields, and by certain countries, is expressed by César Caviedes, professor of geography at the University of Florida, in his introduction to the Southern Cone geography section in *HLAS*, v. 49. He remarks on the "notable imbalance between the quantity and quality of publications on the geography of Argentina and Chile and the paucity of such materials in the cases of Paraguay and Uruguay—a reflection of the decline of geography as a discipline in these two countries."[4]

Political and economic conditions also reflect the state of scholarship and publishing in the Southern Cone. The reemergence of democracy in Argentina, following the fall of the military dictatorship in 1982, saw a profusion of writing on the Malvinas/Falkland War, and in the literature on economics and sociology, the latter once considered a "suspect" discipline.[5]

In the mid-1980s Uruguay also saw the reestablishment of democracy, as did Chile and Paraguay in 1989. Chile, however, even under the Pinochet dictatorship, was able to continue a strong tradition of research and scholarship, as evidenced in the quantity and quality of its publications. Unfortunately, the same cannot be said of Paraguay, as reflected by the too few journals included in this survey.

The changing political climate in Latin America will hopefully signal increased research and publication, and also greater availability of these journals for indexing purposes and eventual dissemination to a wider audience.

Table 1. Subject Coverage by Index of Articles about Argentina

Subject	*ABC Pol Sci*	*GLAS*	*HAPI*	*HLAS*	*LLBA*	*PAIS*
Anthropology-Linguistics	-	35	3	13	6	1
Economics	-	34	7	13	-	21
Education	-	11	4	9	6	-
Geography	-	7	3	9	-	3
International Relations	-	7	8	6	-	3
Political Science	-	25	6	7	-	6
Sociology	-	13	3	4	6	5
Total[a]	-	132	34	61	18	39

[a] Total includes journals covering multiple subject areas.

Table 2. Subject Coverage by Index of Articles about Chile

Subject	*ABC Pol Sci*	*GLAS*	*HAPI*	*HLAS*	*LLBA*	*PAIS*
Anthropology-Linguistics	-	23	6	13	8	3
Economics	-	20	9	14	-	17
Education	-	10	7	8	8	-
Geography	-	3	3	6	-	2
International Relations	1	2	5	4	-	-
Political Science	1	10	7	6	-	6
Sociology	-	16	7	6	8	5
Total[a]	2	84	44	57	24	33

[a] Total includes journals covering multiple subject areas.

Table 3. Subject Coverage by Index of Articles about Paraguay

Subject	*ABC Pol Sci*	*GLAS*	*HAPI*	*HLAS*	*LLBA*	*PAIS*
Anthropology-Linguistics	-	3	3	3	1	1
Economics	-	1	2	2	-	3
Education	-	1	3	2	1	-
Geography	-	1	2	2	-	1
International Relations	-	-	1	1	-	-
Political Science	-	2	2	3	-	1
Sociology	-	2	2	3	1	1
Total[a]	-	10	15	16	3	7

[a] Total includes journals covering multiple subject areas.

Table 4. Subject Coverage by Index of Articles about Uruguay

Subject	*ABC Pol Sci*	*GLAS*	*HAPI*	*HLAS*	*LLBA*	*PAIS*
Anthropology-Linguistics	-	6	-	2	1	-
Economics	-	6	-	1	-	10
Education	-	1	-	-	1	-
Geography	-	1	-	1	-	1
International Relations	-	-	1	-	-	-
Political Science	-	1	1	-	-	1
Sociology	-	2	-	2	1	1
Total[a]	-	17	2	6	3	13

[a] Total includes journals covering multiple subject areas.

Table 5. Journals Surveyed and Sources Where Indexed

ABC PolSci	Advanced Bibliography of Contents: Political Science and Government
GLAS	Indexed Journals: A Guide to Latin American Serials
HAPI	Hispanic American Periodicals Index
HLAS	Handbook of Latin American Studies
LLBA	Linguistics and Language Behavior Abstracts
PAIS	Foreign Language Index

Journal	Country	Index
Actualidad Antropológica	Argentina	GLAS
Aisthesis	Chile	HAPI
Alpha	Chile	GLAS
Ambiente y Recursos Naturales	Argentina	PAIS
Amerinda	Uruguay	GLAS/HLAS
Anales de Arqueología y Etnología	Argentina	HLAS
Anales de Ciencias Políticas y Sociales	Argentina	GLAS/HLAS/PAIS
Anales de Economía	Argentina	GLAS
Anales de la Academia Nacional de Ciencias Económicas	Argentina	HLAS
Antiquitás	Argentina	GLAS
Antropología	Chile	HLAS
Anuario. Universidad de La Plata	Argentina	GLAS
Araucaria de Chile	Chile	HAPI
Atenea	Chile	GLAS/HAPI/HLAS
Ateneo	Argentina	GLAS
Boletín. Publicaciones del Museo y de la Sociedad Arqueológica de la Serena	Chile	HLAS
Boletín de Educación Paraguaya	Paraguay	HAPI
Boletín de Estudios Geográficos	Argentina	HLAS
Boletín de Filología	Uruguay	GLAS
Boletín de la Academia Argentina de Letras	Argentina	GLAS
Boletín de la Academia Chilena de la Historia	Chile	HAPI
Boletín de la Academia Nacional de Ciencias	Argentina	HLAS
Boletín de la Academia Nacional de la Historia	Argentina	HAPI
Boletín de la Sociedad de Antropología del Uruguay	Uruguay	GLAS
Boletín de Planificación	Chile	GLAS/PAIS
Boletín de Prehistoria de Chile	Chile	HLAS

Journal	Country	Index
Boletín del Colegio de Graduados en Antropología	Argentina	GLAS
Boletín del Instituto Interamericano del Niño	Uruguay	GLAS/PAIS
Boletín del Museo Social Argentino	Argentina	GLAS
Boletín Demográfico	Chile	GLAS/PAIS
Boletín Estadístico. Banco Central	Argentina	PAIS
Boletín Estadístico. Banco Central	Paraguay	PAIS
Boletín Estadístico. Banco Central	Uruguay	PAIS
Boletín Estadístico Trimestral	Argentina	GLAS/PAIS
Boletín Informativo Technit	Argentina	GLAS/PAIS
Boletín Mensual	Uruguay	PAIS
Boletín Mensual. Banco Central	Chile	GLAS/PAIS
Boletín Uruguayo de Sociología	Uruguay	GLAS/LLBA
Business Trends	Argentina	GLAS
CEPAL Review	Chile	GLAS/HAPI/ HLAS/PAIS
Chile Gram	Chile	GLAS
Chungara	Chile	HAPI/HLAS
Ciencias Administrativas	Argentina	GLAS/HLAS
Colección Estudios CIEPLAN	Chile	PAIS
Comentario	Argentina	GLAS
Comentarios Bibliográficos Americanos	Uruguay	GLAS
Comunicación y Cultura	Argentina/ Chile	HLAS
Comunicaciones Antropológicas del Museo de Historia Natural de Montevideo	Uruguay	HLAS
Contribuciones. Konrad Adenaur-Siftung	Argentina	HLAS
Coyuntura y Desarrollo	Argentina	HLAS/PAIS
Cristianismo y Sociedad	Uruguay	HLAS
Criterio	Argentina	GLAS/HLAS
Crítica y Utopia Latinoamericana de Ciencias Sociales	Argentina	PAIS
Cuadernos de Economía	Chile	GLAS/HAPI/ HLAS/PAIS
Cuadernos de Historia	Chile	HLAS
Cuadernos de Moneda y Finanzas del Cono Sur	Argentina	PAIS
Cuadernos de la Facultad de Ciencias Sociales y Económicas	Argentina	PAIS
Cuadernos de Planeamiento	Argentina	GLAS
Cuadernos del CENAP	Argentina	GLAS
Cuadernos del CLAEH	Uruguay	GLAS/HLAS/ PAIS
Cuadernos del Idioma	Argentina	GLAS

Journal	Country	Index
Cuadernos del Instituto de Ciencia Política	Chile	GLAS
Cuadernos del Instituto Nacional de Antropología	Argentina	GLAS
Cuadernos Médico-Sociales	Chile	GLAS
Cursos y Conferencias	Argentina	GLAS
Davar	Chile	GLAS
Demografía	Chile	GLAS
Derecho de la Integración	Argentina	PAIS
Desarrollo Económico	Argentina	GLAS/HAPI/HLAS/ LLBA/PAIS
Desarrollo Rural	Chile	LLBA
Docpal	Chile	PAIS
Documento. Centro de Estudios de Planificación	Chile	GLAS
Documentos de Trabajo	Chile	GLAS/HLAS
Economía	Chile	GLAS
Economía de América Latina	Argentina	PAIS
Economía y Administración	Chile	GLAS
Economic Information of Argentina	Argentina	GLAS
Economic Survey of Latin America and the Caribbean	Chile	HAPI/HLAS
Económica	Argentina	GLAS/HLAS/ PAIS
Encuesta Industrial Trimestral	Uruguay	PAIS
English Language Journal	Argentina	GLAS/LLBA
Ensayos Económicos	Argentina	GLAS/HLAS/ PAIS
EST/ESP Chile Newsletter	Chile	LLBA
Estudios	Argentina	GLAS
Estudios. Instituto de Estudios Económicos Sobre la Realidad Argentina y Latinoamericana	Argentina	HLAS/PAIS
Estudios Arqueológicos	Argentina	GLAS
Estudios Arqueológicos	Chile	GLAS
Estudios Atacameños	Chile	GLAS
Estudios de Economía	Chile	GLAS/HLAS/ PAIS
Estudios e Investigaciones	Argentina	HLAS
Estudios Filológicos	Chile	GLAS/LLBA
Estudios Filológicos. Anejos	Chile	GLAS
Estudios Internacionales	Argentina	GLAS
Estudios Internacionales	Chile	ABC PolSci/ GLAS/HAPI
Estudios Paraguayos	Paraguay	HAPI/HLAS

Journal	Country	Index
Estudios Públicos	Chile	HAPI
Estudios Sobre la Economía Argentina	Argentina	GLAS
Estudios Sociales	Chile	GLAS/HAPI/ HLAS
Estudios y Monografías	Uruguay	GLAS
Ethos	Argentina	GLAS/HLAS
Etnia	Argentina	GLAS/HLAS
EURE (Revista Latinoamericana de Estudios Urbanos Regionales	Chile	GLAS/HAPI/ PAIS
Fichero Bibliográfico Hispanoamericano	Argentina	GLAS
Filología	Argentina	GLAS
Foro Literario	Uruguay	GLAS
GAEA	Argentina	GLAS
Hispanoamérica	Argentina	GLAS
Historia	Chile	HAPI
Hoy	Chile	GLAS
Humanitás	Argentina	GLAS/HLAS
Impuestos	Argentina	GLAS
Indicadores de Comercio Exterior	Chile	PAIS
Indicadores de Coyuntura	Argentina	PAIS
Información Económica de la Argentina	Argentina	PAIS
Información Financiera	Chile	PAIS
Informaciones Geográficas	Chile	HLAS
Informativo Estadístico	Chile	PAIS
Informe Económico. Banco Central	Chile	GLAS
Integración Latinoamericana	Argentina	GLAS/HAPI/ HLAS
Investigaciones y Ensayos	Argentina	HAPI
Journal of the Association of English Teachers	Paraguay	GLAS
Latinoamericana	Argentina	GLAS
Lectura y Vida	Argentina	LLBA
Lenguas Modernas	Chile	GLAS
Limen	Argentina	GLAS
Mapocho	Chile	HLAS
Megafón	Argentina	GLAS/HAPI
Mensaje	Chile	HAPI
La Nación	Argentina	GLAS
Newsletter Argentina	Argentina	GLAS
Notas de Población	Chile	GLAS/PAIS
Noticiario Mensual del Museo Nacional de Historia Natural	Chile	GLAS
Nuestra Historia	Argentina	HAPI

Journal	Country	Index
Nueva Política	Argentina	GLAS
Nuevo Mundo	Argentina	GLAS
Opciones	Chile	PAIS
Paleoetnología	Argentina	HLAS
Pensamiento Económico	Argentina	GLAS
Pensamiento y Acción	Chile	GLAS/PAIS
Perspectiva Universitaria	Argentina	GLAS
Política	Chile	HLAS/PAIS
Política, Economía y Sociedad	Argentina	PAIS
Política Internacional	Argentina	GLAS
Política y Espíritu	Chile	GLAS
La Prensa	Argentina	GLAS
Prensa Económica	Argentina	PAIS
Problemas Laborales	Chile	PAIS
Proyecto de Liberación	Argentina	GLAS
Publicaciones Sobre Estadística	Uruguay	GLAS
Realidad Económica	Argentina	GLAS/HAPI/ PAIS
Relaciones de la Sociedad Argentina de Antropología	Argentina	GLAS/HLAS
Repertorio Latinoamericano	Argentina	GLAS/HAPI
Resumen Mensual de Coyuntura Económica	Paraguay	PAIS
Review of the River Plate	Argentina	GLAS
Revista Argentina de Estudios Estratégicos	Argentina	GLAS/HAPI/ HLAS/PAIS
Revista Argentina de Lingüística	Argentina	LLBA
Revista Argentina de Política Económica y Social	Argentina	PAIS
Revista Argentina de Relaciones Internacionales	Argentina	GLAS
Revista Chilena de Antropología	Chile	GLAS
Revista Chilena de Historia y Geografía	Chile	HAPI/HLAS
Revista Chilena de Literatura	Chile	GLAS
Revista de Administración Pública	Argentina	GLAS
Revista de Administración Pública	Uruguay	GLAS/PAIS
Revista de Ciencias Económicas	Argentina	GLAS/PAIS
Revista de Ciencias Políticas	Chile	GLAS/PAIS
Revista de Ciencias Sociales	Chile	GLAS
Revista de Economía	Argentina	GLAS/HLAS
Revista de Economía	Uruguay	PAIS
Revista de Economía Política	Argentina	GLAS
Revista de Economía y Estadística	Argentina	HLAS
Revista de Educación	Argentina	GLAS

Journal	Country	Index
Revista de Estudios del Pacífico	Chile	HLAS
Revista de Geografía Norte Grande	Chile	HLAS
Revista de la Biblioteca Nacional	Uruguay	HAPI
Revista de la Cooperación	Argentina	GLAS
Revista de la Escuela de Defensa Nacional	Argentina	GLAS
Revista de la Facultad de Ciencias Económicas de la Universidad de Cuyo	Argentina	GLAS
Revista de la Integración	Argentina	GLAS
Revista de la Junta de Estudios Históricos de Mendoza	Argentina	HLAS
Revista de la Junta Provincial de Historia de Córdoba	Argentina	HLAS
Revista de la Universidad de Buenos Aires	Argentina	GLAS
Revista de la Universidad Nacional de Córdoba	Argentina	GLAS
Revista de la Universidad Nacional de La Plata	Argentina	HLAS
Revista de Lingüística Teórica y Aplicada	Chile	GLAS/LLBA
Revista de Literaturas Modernas	Argentina	GLAS
Revista del Centro de Investigación y Acción Social	Argentina	GLAS
Revista del Instituto de Antropología (Córdoba)	Argentina	GLAS/HLAS
Revista del Instituto de Antropología (Tucumán)	Argentina	GLAS/HLAS
Revista del Instituto de Investigaciones Educativas	Argentina	GLAS
Revista del Museo de La Plata	Argentina	GLAS/HLAS
Revista Geográfica Americana	Argentina	GLAS
Revista Histórica	Uruguay	HAPI
Revista Latinoamericana de Ciencias Políticas	Chile	GLAS/HLAS/LLBA
Revista Latinoamericana de Ciencias Sociales	Chile	GLAS/LLBA
Revista Latinoamericana de Sociología	Argentina	GLAS/LLBA
Revista Médica de Chile	Chile	HLAS
Revista Paraguaya de Sociología	Paraguay	GLAS/HAPI/HLAS/LLBA/PAIS
Revista Universitaria	Chile	HLAS
Revista Universitaria de Letras	Argentina	LLBA
RUNA (Archivo Para las Ciencias del Hombre)	Argentina	GLAS/HAPI/HLAS
Scripta Etnológica	Argentina	GLAS
Serie Investigaciones Demográficas	Argentina	GLAS
Signos	Chile	GLAS

Journal	Country	Index
Síntesis	Uruguay	GLAS/PAIS
Síntesis Informativa	Argentina	GLAS
Sociedad y Desarrollo	Chile	LLBA
Suma	Uruguay	PAIS
Suplemento Antropológico	Paraguay	GLAS/HLAS
Sur	Argentina	GLAS/HAPI
Taller de Letras	Chile	GLAS
Temática Dos Mil	Argentina	GLAS
Todo Es Historia	Argentina	HAPI
Trabajo Social	Chile	GLAS
Universidad	Argentina	HLAS
Universidades	Argentina	HLAS
Veritás Argentina	Argentina	GLAS

NOTES

1. *HAPI: Hispanic American Periodicals Index*, Barbara G. Valk, ed. (Los Angeles: UCLA Latin American Center Publications, University of California, 1977–).

2. *Guide to Reference Books*, Eugene P. Sheehy, ed. (Chicago, IL: ALA, 1986), p. 1015.

3. *Indexed Journals: A Guide to Latin American Serials*, Paula Hattox Covington, ed. (Madison, WI: SALALM Secretariat, Memorial Library, University of Wisconsin, 1983), p. iii.

4. César Caviedes, "Southern Cone (Argentina, Chile, Paraguay, and Uruguay)," *Handbook of Latin American Studies*, Vol. 49 (Austin: University of Texas Press, 1935–), pp. 439-440.

5. Carlos H. Waisman, "The Southern Cone: Argentina, Chile, and Uruguay," *Handbook of Latin American Studies*, Vol. 47 (Austin: University of Texas Press, 1935–), p. 679.

BIBLIOGRAPHY

ABC Pol Sci; Advance Bibliography of Contents: Political Science and Government Santa Barbara: CA: ABC-CLIO, 1969–.

Anuario Bibliográfico Uruguayo. Montevideo: Biblioteca Nacional, 1946–.

Catálogo de publicaciones seriadas argentinas. Buenos Aires: República Argentina, Presidencia de la Nación, Secretaría de Planificación, Instituto Nacional de Estadística y Censos, 1988.

Covington, Paula Hattox. *Indexed Journals: A Guide to Latin American Serials*. Madison, WI: Secretariat, Seminar on the Acquisition of Latin American Library Materials, Memorial Library, University of Wisconsin, 1983.

Foreign Language Index. New York, NY: Public Affairs Information Service, 1972.

Handbook of Latin American Studies. Gainesville: University of Florida Press; Austin: University of Texas Press, 1935–.

HAPI: Hispanic American Periodicals Index. Los Angeles: UCLA Latin American Center Publications, University of California, 1977–.

LLBA: Linguistics and Language Behavior Abstracts. La Jolla, CA: Sociological Abstracts, Inc., 1978–.

Saugy de Kliauga, Catalina. *Bibliografía antropológica argentina, 1980–1985/Argentine Anthropological Bibliography, 1980–1985*. Buenos Aires: Colegio de Graduados en Antropología, 1986.

27. A Latin American Periodicals Price Index

Scott Van Jacob

Introduction

One of the more challenging and frustrating tasks that librarians face is the creation of a budget that correctly predicts expenditures for the next fiscal year. In particular, those responsible for library periodicals budgets are in the difficult position of presenting budgets that will maintain their present periodical collections and allow for the purchase of the never-ending publication of worthy titles. All in all, we have not been very successful at either of these tasks. Academic journal publishing continues to grow. These journals, now totaling more than 40,000 titles worldwide, publish more than 1,000,000 articles each year.[1] Moreover, libraries are purchasing only a quarter of this total periodical universe, whereas they once purchased one third.[2] The reason for this decrease is attributable not so much to budget cuts, as one may expect, but to budget freezes. Robin Devin and Martha Kellogg have shown that academic library budgets have remained constant in a time of rapid journal and page inflation.[3] Since library periodical budgets have not kept pace with the dramatic growth in the number and cost of serial publications in the last decade, how are we to maintain and improve our collections?

The lamentable situation has prompted librarians to find ways to maximize their periodicals budgets. One approach has been to develop budget prediction models such as price indexes. The Consumer Price Index has been used for many years as a general indicator of library materials price inflation. In the 1970s, librarians and periodical vendors began to develop indexes for the purpose of charting the relative change in selected periodical prices over a period of time, thereby plotting significant subscription price variations. This information has proved to be very useful in predicting price inflation and identifying the practice of price differentiation, that is, the result of a publisher or vendor charging unfairly high prices to selected subscribers.

A leader in periodical price indexing is the Library Materials Price Index Committee (LMPIC) formed by the American Library Association's Resources and Technical Services Division. The committee sponsors the compilation and publication of price data for both domestic and international materials. Of interest to those purchasing Latin American materials is the "Latin American Books Price Index" published in the *Bowker Annual*, which is overseen by David Block.[4]

The large U.S. domestic serials vendor FAXON has worked closely with the LMPIC in periodicals price indexing. Beginning in 1975, the company formulated a periodical price index by utilizing its large database of titles. The goal of the FAXON index is to "provide generalized price data of interest to the library, publishing, and research committees."[5] Currently these data are used in such annual periodicals price surveys as *The Serials Librarian*,[6] the *Library Journal*,[7] and the *Bowker Annual*. FAXON should be commended for its efforts in providing timely pricing data on which librarians are coming to depend heavily for budget forecasting purposes.

As for Latin American periodicals, FAXON first included an analysis of periodical subscription rates from selected countries in the 1987 *Serials Librarian*'s annual survey of periodical prices.[8] This index includes the average price per periodical, the annual percent changes in price, and the number of titles used in the index for each country. The Latin American countries covered in this analysis are Argentina, Brazil, Chile, Colombia, Costa Rica, Jamaica, Mexico, Peru, and Venezuela. These countries were chosen owing to the large number of titles that FAXON carries from each of these countries. For example, FAXON carries more than 400 Brazilian titles but only seventy-nine Uruguayan titles. The large sample of Brazilian titles enables FAXON to determine the country's periodical price fluctuations much more accurately than do the few Uruguayan titles.

What is the value of providing information about Latin American periodical prices to librarians and administrators? Owing to the historical strong value of the U.S. dollar against all Latin American currencies, Latin American journals have been and largely remain affordable, resulting in little concern for the cost of these journals to U.S. buyers. Also the extensive exchange programs implemented by research libraries have limited the number of Latin American titles actually purchased. But considering the current fluctuations in most Latin American economies, the increasing postal rates, the possibility of price differentiation practices by both Latin American publishers and vendors, and the continuing budget constraints placed on academic collections, the FAXON price index may provide hard, factual information that is very useful in monitoring trends in Latin American periodical prices. Figure 1 is an example of the average prices reported by FAXON for Argentina, Brazil, and Chile from 1985 to 1989,

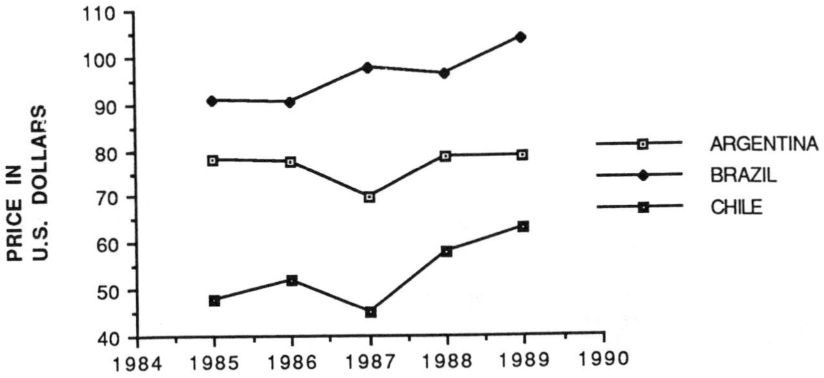

Fig. 1. FAXON annual periodical price update

countries chosen for their strong publishing industries. Note that the average subscription price, given in U.S. dollars, varies greatly over the five-year period covered. The lowest annual average price is $45.08 for 62 Chilean journals in 1987 and the highest is $103.72 for 157 Brazilian journals in 1989. These figures seem quite high and raise the question of the type of titles held in the FAXON database. Certainly, the inclusion of monographic series, annuals, proceedings, and daily newspapers raises the average journal price. For example, a subscription for the surface mail delivery of the Argentine newspaper *La Prensa* costs $360 a year. Also, postal rates increase the cost of each journal. Further, this sample provided by FAXON is client driven rather than driven by any collection development policy, thus weighting the list heavily toward a particular discipline due to client demands. If that discipline is science (which historically has higher subscription prices), the average price may be much higher than if the humanities or social sciences make up the greater part of the database.

One way to determine the mix of titles in the FAXON database is to analyze the subject makeup of the titles. Figure 2 provides a random sampling (approximately 33 percent of the titles) from the FAXON subscription lists of the countries in figure 1. The subject content was identified through the Library of Congress classification given on the MARC record in OCLC. Each title was placed into one of six broad

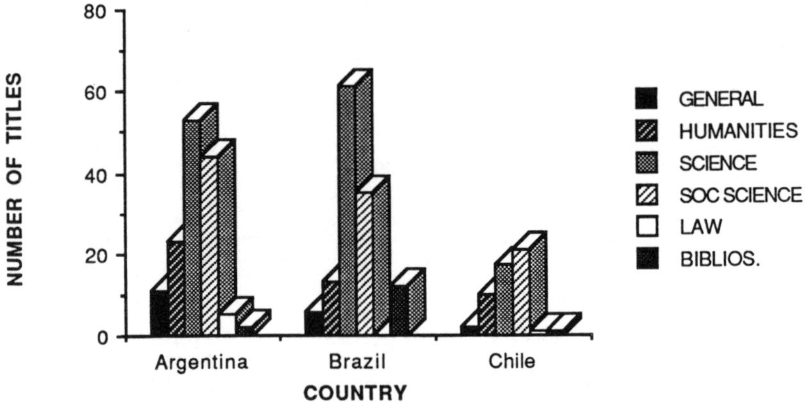

Fig. 2. Subject analysis of FAXON titles

subject categories: general, humanities, sciences, social sciences, law, and bibliography. To insure that only current periodicals were included, all titles that had ceased publication and monographic series were eliminated from the sample population. This analysis would not have been possible without the FAXON Company's consent to provide the information from its database of titles. The results show that the science titles for the three countries make up 40 percent (Argentina 38 percent, Brazil 48 percent, and Chile 33 percent), or a significant portion of the total titles in the FAXON index. Without access to the actual subscription prices of all titles, the probability of the average price per periodical being higher owing to science subscription prices is significant.

These data bring into question the value of the FAXON index as an indicator of the periodical prices that libraries actually are paying for Latin American titles. Since most Latin American collections focus on the humanities and social sciences rather than on the sciences, the FAXON index does not reflect the actual holdings of Latin American collections, thus limiting the usefulness of this index as a tool for budget analysis.

Latin American Periodicals Price Index

With these results in mind, a Latin American Periodicals Price Index must reflect the holdings of the collections it attempts to measure. These collections consist of libraries that are members of the Seminar on the Acquisition of Latin American Library Materials (SALALM). The purpose of this index is to report subscription price changes for budget purposes in order to build a historical archive of Latin American periodical pricing information for each Latin American country. By tracking price changes SALALM libraries will be alerted to dramatic or unusual price variations. The historical archive will provide over time a pattern of the behavior of Latin American periodical prices.

Since periodical indexes are not new, there are standard guidelines for developing such an instrument. This index would be designed according to the standards set in the International Standard Organization (ISO) Draft International Standard 9230: Determination of Price Indexes for Books and Serials Purchased by Libraries. The standard proposes a three-step process in developing an index: select the titles, compile the subscription prices, and present the data.

Selecting periodical titles that reflect current Latin American collection holdings is the most time-consuming and, ultimately, the most important task of this project. The criteria for selecting periodical titles are as follows: all titles must meet the ISO definition of a periodical, all titles must currently be published in Latin America, and all titles must be held by SALALM libraries. The high cost of Latin American newspapers prohibits including them in this sample.

One possible source of Latin American periodical titles is FAXON. Since the FAXON database is so large (554 Argentine titles, 490 Brazilian titles, and 324 Chilean titles), a sample can be selected from its catalog by choosing titles that are actually held by SALALM libraries. This can be accomplished by searching the library-holdings information provided by OCLC or RLIN for each FAXON title. There are two caveats to this approach. As noted, FAXON's coverage of some Latin American countries is too limited to provide a large enough sample, although in most cases the FAXON sample should be sufficient. The second is that without actually searching the union listing for each library, it can only be assumed that these libraries are still receiving these titles.

A FAXON sample's accuracy in representing SALALM library holdings can be improved in one of two ways. First, eliminate all science and law titles from the sample. What would remain are only general, humanities, and social sciences titles, a group of titles that would better match SALALM library periodical holdings. The average subscription price would therefore more accurately match what these libraries are now paying per title. Second, since there are science titles held by SALALM libraries, they need to be included in the sample. Many of these science titles may be held by only a small number of SALALM libraries. By selecting only those titles held by several SALALM libraries, a smaller but more representative sample is available. Setting the number of libraries holding each title is somewhat troublesome. Figure 3 shows where that cutoff might be. The titles from the sample above were searched on OCLC to identify the number of SALALM libraries that have them. The titles have been broken down by subject and divided further into groups by number of holding libraries. These groupings have been arbitrarily set at 1-5, 6-10, and 11-20 (see fig. 3).

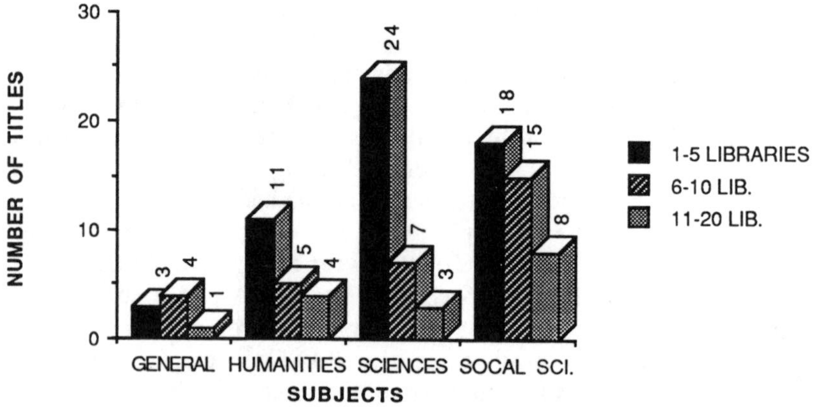

Fig. 3. Holding libraries for Argentine periodical titles

Of interest is the large number of science titles held by five or fewer libraries. If one ignores these titles, we see that the remaining science titles make up 26 percent (20 percent for Argentina, 31 percent for Brazil, and 29 percent for Chile) rather than the 40 percent of the FAXON index. While the graph demonstrates that the majority of the titles in this sample are held by five or fewer SALALM libraries, the remaining titles present a more accurate sample. If this sample is seen as too small, the required number of holding libraries may need to be lowered.

Available at FAXON are also the subscription prices for the selected titles. Considering the time and effort that would be required to contact each individual publisher for that information, FAXON's readily available subscription information is an attractive alternative. The domestic institutional rate would be the first choice of price information, but the large number of currencies would make it very difficult to interpret. Since FAXON provides the subscription price in U.S. dollars, the dollar price will be the currency on which the index is based. FAXON titles including discounted prices and/or service charges would be deleted from the sample.

With these data in hand, the yearly analysis will include the number of titles sampled and the average price per title. An average index price may be included if subscription price information for the original sample of titles is readily available on an annual basis. The average price would be utilized in calculating the index figure defined by the ISO. The equation is a follows:

$$\text{Average price} \times 100 \div \text{average price in the base year.}$$

The base year will consist of the first year of information. Over time the annual update of these data will offer insight into the long-term trends of these periodical prices. This is particularly important since price differentiation, postage rates, and currency exchange can cause subscription prices to fluctuate from year to year.

Finally, distribution of these data to interested parties might include the *SALALM Newsletter* and possibly the *Bowker Annual*. The collection and analysis would be completed by the SALALM serials subcommittee.

Conclusion

In an era of increasing fiscal restraint for libraries, the periodical price index is one of many instruments used for the prediction of future periodical funding needs. Such an index for Latin American periodicals will improve our understanding of the behavior of the subscription prices for these journals. With this information, we will be better able to maintain and improve our collections.

NOTES

1. H. Craig Peterson, "Variation in Journal Prices: A Statistical Analysis," *The Serials Librarian*, 17, no. 1/2 (1989): 1.

2. Jeffrey Gardner, "Association of Research Libraries' Project on Serials Prices," *Newsletter on Serials Pricing Issues*, no. 5 (May 1989): 3.

3. Robin B. Devin and Martha Kellogg, "The Serial/Monograph Ratio in Research Libraries: Budgeting in Light of Citation Studies," *College and Research Libraries*, 51, no. 1 (January 1990): 47.

4. *Bowker Annual*, 33d ed. (1988): 430-440. Compiled by David Block.

5. Peter R. Young, "Periodical Prices 1987–1989 Update," *The Serials Librarian*, 17, no. 1/2 (1989): 11.

6. Ibid., pp. 1-22.

7. Peter Young and Kathryn Carpenter, "Price Index for 1990: U.S. Periodicals," *Library Journal*, 115 no. 7 (April 15, 1990): 50-56.

8. Rebecca Lenzini, "Periodical Prices 1985–1987 Update," *Serials Librarian*, 13, no. 1 (September 1987): 54.

About the Authors

DAVID BLOCK is Latin American Librarian, Cornell University, Ithaca, New York.

RUBENS HARRY BORN is a staff member of OIKOS União dos Defensores da Terra, São Paulo.

MARGARIDA LUIZA RIBEIRO BRANDÃO is Professora, Departamento de Teologia and Integrante da Equipe Técnica do Núcleo de Estudos sobre a Mulher (NEM), Departamento de Serviço Social, Pontifícia Universidade Católica do Rio de Janeiro.

SÉRGIO BURGI is Coordenador Técnico of the Programa Nacional de Preservação e Pesquisa da Fotografia (PROPRESERV) of the Centro de Conservação e Preservação Fotográfica, which is part of the Instituto Nacional de Fotografia (INFoto), Fundação Nacional de Arte (FUNARTE).

PATRICIA CÁRDENAS is Assistant Librarian, Modern Languages and Linguistics Library, University of Illinois at Champaign-Urbana.

DONALD S. CASTRO is Professor of History, California State Polytechnic University, Pomona, California.

ADELINA MARIA ALVES NOVAES E CRUZ is Coordenadora do Núcleo de Informatização do Centro de Pesquisa e Documentação de História Contemporânea do Brasil (CPDOC) of the Fundação Getúlio Vargas, Rio de Janeiro.

CARL W. DEAL is Director of Library Collections, University Library, University of Illinois at Champaign–Urbana.

MARTA DOMÍNGUEZ is the owner of SEREC–Servicio de Extensión Cultural al Mundo, Santiago de Chile.

MARIA JOSÉ DA SILVA FERNANDES is a librarian, Plano Nacional de Microfilmagem de Periódicos Brasileiros, Biblioteca Nacional, Rio de Janeiro.

TERESA FITTIPALDI DE GIMENO is Jefe encargada de Biblioteca and Docente encargada de curso de la asignatura Formación y Desarrollo de Colecciones en la Licenciatura de Ciencias de la Información of the Escuela Universitaria de Bibliotecología y Ciencias Afines "Ingeniero Federico E. Capurro," Montevideo, Uruguay.

NELLY S. GONZÁLEZ is Director, Latin American Library Services, University Library, University of Illinois at Champaign-Urbana.

ANN HARTNESS, president of SALALM in 1989-1990, is Assistant Head Librarian at the Nettie Lee Benson Latin American Collection of the University of Texas at Austin.

PRISCILA LENI OLIVARES is a librarian at the Universidad de la Playa Ancha de Ciencias de la Educación, Valparaíso, Chile.

MAY LORENZO ALCALÁ is an Argentine writer who resides in Rio de Janeiro.

SOFÍA MARESKI is Jefe de Biblioteca Roosevelt del Centro Cultural Paraguayo-Americano, Asunción.

CAVAN MICHAEL MCCARTHY is Professor, Departamento de Biblioteconomia, Centro de Artes e Comunicação, Universidade Federal de Pernambuco, Recife, Brazil.

RACHEL MENEGUELLO is Diretora-Adjunta of the Arquivo "Edgard Leuenroth" and Professora de Ciência Política of the Instituto de Filosofia e Ciências Humanas, Universidade Estadual de Campinas (UNICAMP), Campinas, Brazil.

JOSÉ MINDLIN is a bibliophile and president of Metal Leve, São Paulo.

PATRÍCIA MONTE-MÓR is an anthropologist and social scientist, and the director of Interior Produções Ltda., Rio de Janeiro.

FELÍCIA MUSIKMAN is a librarian, Plano Nacional de Microfilmagem de Periódicos Brasileiros, Biblioteca Nacional, Rio de Janeiro.

JOSÉ ANTONIO PINI MARTÍNEZ is Profesor Titular of the Cátedra de "Organización y Administración de Empresas," and of the Cátedra de "Teoría de las Organizaciones" of the Facultad de Ciencias Económicas y de Administración of the Universidad de la República, Montevideo.

T. MIGUEL PRESSBURGER is an attorney, Coordenador, Instituto Apoio Jurídico Popular, and Diretor, Departamento de Pesquisa e Documentação of the Ordem dos Advogados do Brasil.

BARBARA J. ROBINSON is Curator, Boeckmann Center for Iberian and Latin American Studies, Doheny Library, University of Southern California, Los Angeles.

IRIS ROSSI is a librarian, Biblioteca Nacional, Buenos Aires.

ENRIQUE SARAVIA is Chefe do Departamento de Ensino, Escola Brasileira de Administração Pública, Fundação Getúlio Vargas, Rio de Janeiro.

JORGE SCHWARTZ is professor of Spanish-American literature, Universidade de São Paulo.

CÁSSIA MARIA MELLO DA SILVA is Coordenadora Geral do Programa Nacional de Preservação e Pesquisa da Fotografia.

SCOTT VAN JACOB is Serials Librarian, Boyd Lee Sphar Library, Dickinson College, Carlisle, Pennsylvania.

BERTA WALDMAN is a professor of literary theory and Brazilian literature at the Universidade Estadual de Campinas—UNICAMP, Campinas, Brazil.

Program of Substantive Panels, Round Tables, and Field Trips

Sunday, June 3

8:00-22:00 Committee Meetings

Monday, June 4

8:30-9:45 Committee Meetings

9:30-12:30 Executive Board

14:30-15:45 Opening Session

Opening: *Ann Hartness*, President, SALALM, University of Texas at Austin.

Welcome: *Luiz Simões Lopes*, President, Fundação Getúlio Vargas

Lygia Ballantyne, Assistant Chief, Overseas Operations Division, Library of Congress

Lia Temporal Malcher, Acting Director, Biblioteca Nacional

Keynote Address: *José Mindlin*, President, Metal Leve, and bibliophile

José Toríbio Medina Award: *Suzanne Hodgman*, University of Wisconsin—Madison

Presentation of Plaque Honoring Suzanne Hodgman, Retiring Executive Secretary of SALALM: *Ann Hartness*

Announcements: *Smith Richardson*, Library of Congress Office, Rio de Janeiro

Rapporteur General: *Charles S. Fineman*, Northwestern University

16:15-17:30 Theme Panel 1, sponsored by the Task Force on Standards for Developing and Maintaining Latin American Research Collections beyond the Twentieth Century:

Beyond Our Own Libraries: Standards, Trends and Data Collection for Latin American Collections

Coordinator, *David Block,* Cornell University

David Block, Cornell University: "National Trends in Support of Latin American Studies"

Barbara Robinson, University of Southern California: "The Development of Standards for Library Research Collections and SALALM's Task Force on Standards"

Carl Deal, University of Illinois: "Statistics for Latin American Collections: Preliminary Findings"

Rapporteur, *Tony Harvell,* University of Miami

18:00 Exhibition Opening and Reception: "Oswald de Andrade: o antropófago," Biblioteca Nacional

Tuesday, June 5

8:30-10:00 Theme Panel 2

Periodicals in the Southern Cone and Brazil

Coordinator, *Ceres Birkhead,* University of Utah

Eudora Loh, University of California at Los Angeles: "Tracking Down the Elusive: Acquiring and Accessing Latin American Government Serials"

Nelly S. González, University of Illinois at Champaign-Urbana: "Index Coverage of Latin American Periodicals in the Southern Cone: The Humanities"

Patricia Cárdenas, University of Illinois at Champaign-Urbana: "Index Coverage of Latin American Periodicals in the Southern Cone: The Social Sciences"

Scott Van Jacob, Dickinson College: "A Latin American Periodicals Price Index"

Andrew Makuch, University of Arizona: "Collection Development for Southern Cone Countries: Challenges and Changes"

Rapporteur, *Tamara Brunnschweiler,* Michigan State University

Theme Panel 3

Street and Study: Popular and Formal Expressions of Change

Coordinator, *Claudia Negrão Balby,* Prefeitura do Município de São Paulo

Donald Castro, California State Polytechnic University: "Entre bueyes no hay cornadas [Among Equals There Are No Disagreements]: The Argentine Popular Theater as a Source for the Historian"

Cavan M. McCarthy, Universidade Federal de Pernambuco: "Writing from the Front Line: An Overview of Brazilian Political Publications, Pamphlets, and Ephemera from the Period of the *Abertura,* 1978–1989"

Dolores M. Martin, Library of Congress: "Research Trends in the Humanities in Paraguay: Present State and Future Prospects, 1980s–2000s"

Rapporteur, *Jane Orttung,* Rutgers University

10:30-12:00 Theme Panel 4, sponsored by the Subcommittee on Marginalized Peoples and Ideas

Toward Democratic Change: The Role of Interest Groups in Brazil, 1964–1990

Coordinator, *Peter Johnson,* Princeton University

Joan Dassin, Ford Foundation: "Human and Civil Rights"

Rubens Harry Born, OIKOS União dos Defensores da Terra: "O movimento ambientalista: a democracia e o acesso às informações"

Margarida Luiza Ribeiro Brandão, Pontifícia Universidade Católica do Rio de Janeiro: "Uma reflexão ético-teológica sobre o símbolo da maternidade e suas implicações práticas"

Miguel Pressburger, Instituto Apoio Jurídico Popular: "Violência contra trabalhadores rurais e a omissão do poder judiciário"

Rapporteur, *Richard Phillips,* University of Colorado at Boulder

13:30-15:00 Theme Panel 5

Actualizaciones en bibliotecología en el Cono Sur

Coordinator, *Iliana Sonntag,* San Diego State University

Teresa Fittipaldi de Gimeno, Escuela Universitaria de Bibliotecología y Ciencias Afines "Ingeniero Federico Capurro," Montevideo: "Desarrollo de colecciones latino-americanas: monografías editadas y tesis de graduación, problemas de su acceso"

Sofía Mareski, Centro Cultural Paraguay-Americano, Asunción: "Desafíos bibliográficos sobre la educación paraguaya"

Priscila Leni, Universidad de Playa Ancha de Ciencias de la Educación, Valparaíso: "Un especialista en bibliotecología e información para los nuevos desafíos"

Iris Rossi, Biblioteca Nacional de la República Argentina, Buenos Aires: "La información bibliográfica argentina"

Rapporteur, *Cecilia Vélez,* University of California, Santa Barbara

Bookdealers' Panel

Trends and Tendencies in the Latin American Book Trade

Coordinator, *Lief Adleson*, Books from Mexico

15:30-17:00 Theme Panel 6

Economic Trends and Prospects in Brazil and the Southern Cone

Coordinator, *Enrique Saravia,* Fundação Getúlio Vargas

José A. Pini, Universidad de la República del Uruguay: "La economía del Uruguay: evolución y perspectivas"

Enrique Saravia, Fundação Getúlio Vargas: "Trends in the Brazilian Economy in the 1990s and Scenarios for the Year 2000"

Rapporteur, *Basil Malish,* Library of Congress

Wednesday, June 6

9:00-17:00 Visit to Petrópolis: Museu Imperial, Editora Vozes, points of interest in the city

9:00-18:00 Visits of Subcommittee on Marginalized Peoples and Ideas to issued-oriented documentation centers and activist organizations

Coordinator, *Peter Johnson,* Princeton University

15:00-16:00 Tour of Divisão de Música e Arquivo Sonoro, Biblioteca Nacional

Thursday, June 7

8:30-10:00 Round Table

Coleções especiais brasileiras

Coordinator, *Sonia Dias Gonçalves da Silva,* Universidade de Campinas

Rosemarie Horch, Instituto de Estudos Brasileiros, Universidade de São Paulo

Rachel Meneguello, Arquivo Edgard Leuenroth, Universidade de Campinas

Adelina Maria Alves Novaes e Cruz, Centro de Pesquisa e Documentação de Historia Contemporânea do Brasil

Rapporteur, *Heleni Marques Pedersoli,* University of Maryland

10:30-12:00 Theme Panel 7

Pesquisa e desenvolvimento em tecnologia da informação no Brasil

Coordinator, *Eugênio Decourt,* Fundação Getúlio Vargas

Julian Chacel, Fundação Getúlio Vargas: "Padrões tecnológicos e crescimento econômica"

Aldo Barreto, Universidade Federal do Rio de Janeiro: "A informação no mundo da técnica"

Heitor Quintela, IBM do Brasil: "Engenharia de qualidade em sistema de informação"

Rapporteur, *Patrick Dawson,* University of California, Irvine

13:30-15:00 Round Table

Brazilian Book Trade: Present Conditions and Prospects

Coordinator, *Laurence Hallewell,* University of Minnesota, Minneapolis

Ary Kuflik Benclowicz, Livraria Nobel and President, Câmara Brasileira do Livro

Márcio Souza, novelist and former publisher

José Tarcísio Pereira, Livraria Sete, Recife

Rapporteur, *Rachel Barreto-Edensword,* USIS—Mexico City

15:30-17:00 Theme Panel 8

Trends in Contemporary Literature of Brazil and the Southern Cone

Coordinator, *Jorge Schwartz,* Universidade de São Paulo

Berta Waldman, Universidade de Campinas: "O conto brasileiro contemporâneo"

May Lorenzo Alcalá, writer: "The Seventies Generation of Argentine Prose Writers: Identity and Decline"

Jorge Schwartz, Universidade de São Paulo: "A Coleção Arquivos"

Rapporteur, *Cecilia S. Sercan,* Cornell University

Friday, June 8

8:30-10:00 Round Table

Brazilian Non-Book Materials

Coordinator, *Esther Bertoletti,* Biblioteca Nacional

João Cândido Portinari, Associação Cultural Cândido Portinari, Pontifícia Universidade Católica do Rio de Janeiro: "Portinari: preservação e divulgação de sua obra"

Ricardo Cravo Albin, journalist and researcher: "Discografia brasileira"

Patrícia Monte-Mór, anthropologist and social scientist: "A produção independente no Brasil: dados para a sua história"

Felicia Musikman e *Maria José da Silva Fernandes,* Plano Nacional de Microfilmagem de Periódicos Brasileiros, Plano/Biblioteca Nacional/RJ: "Catálogos de microformas de periódicos brasileiros"

Rapporteur, *Jenny Fierro,* New York Public Library

10:30-12:00 Round Table

Brazilian Non-Book Materials (continued)

Maria Rita Galvão, Cinemateca Brasileira e Universidade de São Paulo/Escola de Comunicações e Artes: "Acesso a acervos cinematográficos brasileiros: uma visão geral"

Cássia Maria Melo e *Sérgio Burgi,* INFoto/Programa: "Instituto Nacional da Fotografia e Programa Nacional de Preservação e Pesquisa da Fotografia"

Film: "Light Memories of Rio (Rio de memórias)," by *José Inácio Parente* e *Patrícia Monte-Mór,* with a talk on the collections researched for the production of the film

Rapporteur: *Peter Bushnell,* University of Florida

Visit of Subcommittee on Cataloging and Bibliographic Technology to the Fundação Getúlio Vargas

Coordinators, *Richard Phillips,* University of Colorado at Boulder; *Eugênio Decourt*, Fundação Getúlio Vargas

13:30-15:00 Closing Session